PROGRAMMING
LANGUAGE
TRANSLATION

INTERNATIONAL COMPUTER SCIENCE SERIES

Consulting editors   **A D McGettrick**   University of Strathclyde
                       J van Leeuwen   University of Utrecht

OTHER TITLES IN THE SERIES

PROGRAMMING LANGUAGE TRANSLATION
A PRACTICAL APPROACH

Patrick D. Terry

Rhodes University, Grahamstown

ADDISON-WESLEY
PUBLISHING
COMPANY

Wokingham, England · Reading, Massachusetts · Menlo Park, California
Don Mills, Ontario · Amsterdam · Sydney · Singapore · Tokyo
Madrid · Bogota · Santiago ·San Juan

Cover graphic by kind permission of Dicomed (UK) Ltd
Phototypeset by Computerset (MFK) Ltd, Ely, Cambs.
Printed in Great Britain by R. J. Acford

British Library Cataloguing in Publication Data
Terry, P. D.
  Programming language translation: a
  practical approach.—(International
  computer science series)
  1. Translators (Computer programs)
  I. Title   II. Series
  005.4'5   QA76.6

  ISBN 0-201-18040-5

Library of Congress Cataloging-in-Publication Data
Terry, P. D.
  Programming language translation.

  (International computer science series)
  Bibliography: p.
  Includes index.
  1. Translators (Computer programs)   2. Compiling
(Electronic computers)   3. Assembling (Electronic
computers)   I. Title.   II. Series.
  QA76.6.T4427   1986   005.4'5   86-14157
  ISBN 0-201-18040-5

Trademark Notice
UCSD Pascal is trademark of the Regents of the University of California. CP/M is a trademark of Digital Research. MS-DOS is a trademark of MicroSoft Corporation. TurboPascal is a trademark of Borland International Corporation. ADA is a trademark of the US Department of Defense. UNIX is a trademark of AT & T Bell Laboratories. Z80 is a trademark of Zilog Corporation. Apple II is a trademark of Apple Corporation.

ABCDEF 89876

Preface

This book has been written to support a practically oriented course in programming language translation for senior undergraduates in Computer Science. More specifically, it is aimed at students who are probably quite competent in the art of programming, especially in Pascal, but whose mathematics may be a little weak; students who require only an introduction to the subject, so as to provide them with insight into areas of language design and implementation, rather than a deluge of theory which they will probably never use again; students who will enjoy fairly extensive case studies of translators for the sorts of languages with which they are most familiar. It will hopefully also appeal to a certain class of hobbyist who wishes to know more about how translators work.

There are several excellent books already extant in this field. What is intended to distinguish this one from the others is that it uses standard Pascal exclusively (something which is surprisingly uncommon), and gives a highly practical and pragmatic development of translators of quite moderate size, yet large enough to provide considerable challenge in the many exercises which are suggested. In addition, care has been taken to ensure that the case studies can be handled on microcomputers as well as on minis and mainframes, and that the languages they implement, however simple, are usable.

The book starts with a fairly simple overview of the translation process, and of the constituent parts of a compiler. This is followed by two chapters which discuss simple features of assembler language, accompanied by the development of an assembler/interpreter system which allows not only for very simple assembly, but also for conditional assembly, macro-assembly, error detection, and so on. Complete code for an assembler is presented, with deliberate scope left for extensions, ranging from the trivial to the extensive.

Two chapters follow on formal syntax theory and parsing. This is kept to a simple level, with a discussion of the necessary conditions for LL(1) parsing. The only parsing method treated in any detail is the method of recursive descent, as is found in many Pascal compilers.

The next chapter discusses the construction of a recursive descent compiler for a simple Pascal-like source language. The compiler is written in Pascal and produces pseudo-code for a hypothetical stack-based computer (for which an interpreter is presented).

The last three chapters extend the simple language (and its compiler) to allow for procedures and functions, demonstrating the usual stack-frame approach to storage management, and then go on to discuss the increasingly important areas of concurrent programming and data abstraction. At all times the student can see how these are handled by the compiler/interpreter system, which slowly grows in complexity and usefulness until the final product enables the development of quite sophisticated programs.

The text abounds with suggestions for further exploration, and references to more advanced texts where they can be followed up. Wherever it seems appropriate the opportunity is taken to make the reader more aware of the strong and weak points in Pascal-like languages in general, and in Pascal in particular. Examples are drawn from several other languages, such as Pascal-Plus, Edison and Modula-2.

It is, perhaps, worth a slight digression to point out some things which the book does *not* claim to be, and to justify some of the decisions made in the selection of material.

In the first place, while it is hoped that it will serve as a useful foundation for students who are already considerably more advanced, a primary aim has been to make the material as accessible as possible to students with a fairly limited background, to enhance this background, and to make them somewhat more critical of it. In many cases this background is Pascal-based, sometimes entirely so, and hence the book is deliberately Pascal-based, even though I have some sympathy with those who feel that Pascal may not be the best language for projects of this scale or nature.

That the languages and their translators are relative toys cannot be denied. The CLANG language of later chapters, for example, supports only integer variables and simple one-dimensional arrays of these, has data abstraction features limited to one level of nesting, and concurrent features allowing little beyond the simulation of some simple textbook examples. The text is not intended to be a comprehensive treatise on systems programming in general, just on certain selected topics in that area, and so very little is said about native machine code generation and optimization, linkers and loaders, the interaction and relationship with an operating system, and so on. These decisions were all taken deliberately, to keep the material readily understandable and as machine-independent as possible – the systems may be toys, but they are very usable toys! Of course the book is then open to the criticism that many of the more difficult topics in translation (such as code generation and optimization) are effectively not covered at all, and that the student may be deluded into thinking that these areas do not exist. This is not entirely true; the careful reader will find most of these topics covered in sufficient detail to fire his imagination. In selecting the topics to omit I have tried to remain within the lowest common denominator of what I imagine to be the reader's experience, and to build on the strengths as well as the weaknesses of that experience. For example, one may deplore the fact that readers brought up on using one-pass, load-and-go Pascal systems may have little or no feel for the linking and loading process. At the same time, it lies outside the scope of the present text completely to redress this balance, and it may even be argued that it is better not to attempt to do so at all, thereby focussing attention on topics which probably have been mentioned previously.

Nor can it be denied that the choice of methods used is sometimes quite far removed from the leading edge of development in this area. A good teacher will always want to put something of his own into a course, regardless of the quality of the prescribed textbook. I have found that a useful (though at times highly dangerous) technique is deliberately not to give the best solutions to a problem in a class discussion, with the optimistic aim that students can be persuaded to 'discover' them for themselves, and even gain a sense of achievement in so doing. When applied to a book the technique is particularly dangerous, but I have tried to exploit it on several occasions, even though it may give the impression that the author is ignorant.

For example, I am fully aware that my symbol table handling algorithms are sub-optimal (this is even admitted in the text). The better algorithms – like those involving hashing – are probably well enough known to any reasonable teacher, who can thus say at the appropriate point 'but there's a much better way – find out what you can about it and do it that way'. The choice of the rather dated method of recursive descent parsing is one which several reviewers have criticized. It has been retained for several reasons, not the least of which are that it is easy to explain, and that it is widely used in Pascal-like compilers (some of which provide readily accessible places where students can do their own research, as was suggested above). Finally, Pascal is like it is largely because it is essentially LL(1), and one of my secondary aims is to let the reader gain some insight into why Pascal is what it is, and what is involved in criticizing it or suggesting that it should be otherwise.

Another dangerous strategy is to give too much away, especially in a book like this aimed at courses where, so far as I am aware, the 'traditional' approach requires that the students make far more of the design decisions for themselves than my approach seems to allow them. Many of the books in the field do not show enough of *how* something is actually done: the bridge between what they give and what the student is required to produce is in excess of what is reasonable for a course which is only part of a general curriculum. I have tried to compensate by suggesting what I hope is a very wide range of searching exercises. The solutions to some of these are well known, and available in the literature. Again, the decision to omit explicit references was deliberate (perhaps dangerously so). Teachers often have to find some way of persuading the students to search the literature for themselves, and this is not done by simply opening the journal at the right page for them.

The material has been successfully used for the last few years in a course of about 40 hours of lectures with intensive, but strictly controlled and structured, related laboratory work, given to students in a pre-Honours year. The students form a group which is about 50% Physics/Mathematics and 50% Accounting/Economics in background. They are mostly unlikely to meet this sort of material again and their level of mathematical maturity is mostly quite low. Admittedly they find the detail a little overwhelming at first – at least when they try to come to terms with it in the practical work, for in lectures one can stress the principles and gloss over the fine detail. A common approach to laboratory work in programming language translation is based on small groups of students designing and implementing a compiler from the ground up. In our case, because of the time constraint (the lab work runs over about 9 to 10 weeks) there is not enough time for the complete design emphasis – the major design issues, for better or worse, are supplied in the text, which is, of course, quite detailed – and so the laboratory work takes the form of extensions to the system as described in the text, ranging from simple to quite large ones. The students work in small groups (typically two or three) and the group experience has proved to be quite invaluable.

At our university we also use an extended version of the CLANG compiler as developed in the text (one incorporating several of the extensions suggested as exercises) as a system for students to study concurrent programming *per se*, and although it is a little limited, it is more than adequate for the purpose. This version can also be made available to teaching institutions on request, as can solutions to many of the exercises.

Acknowledgements

I am conscious of my gratitude to many people for their help and inspiration while this book has been developed. Like many others, I am grateful to Niklaus Wirth, not only for Pascal itself, but also for developing Pascal-S, PL/0 and their compilers. It was in playing with these that the development of CLANG began. Closer to home, several generations of students have contributed in intangible ways. More recently John Cuthbert, Glen Forrester and, especially, Helen Purchase took the trouble to peruse the manuscript in great detail and pointed out many inconsistencies and possible improvements. In particular, the painstaking detail with which the reviewers approached their tasks was deeply appreciated, a source of inspiration, as well as a compliment. The assistance of my colleague Peter Clayton, whose courses have followed on from the one described here, has been invaluable. Particularly encouraging and helpful were Teresa Fuchs, Tess Gonet and Sarah Mallen of Addison-Wesley. I' am also indebted to Rhodes University and the University of Strathclyde for the use of computer facilities. But above all I am grateful to my wife, Sally, for her love and support through the many hours when she must have wondered where my priorities lay.

P.D. TERRY
Rhodes University
Grahamstown
August, 1985

Contents

Chapter 1 Introduction

1.1 Objectives

The use of computer languages is an essential link in the chain between man and computer. In this text we hope to make the reader more aware of some aspects of

(a) programming languages – their syntactic and semantic features, the ways of specifying syntax, problem areas, ambiguities, and the power and usefulness of various features of a language;

(b) translators for programming languages – the various types of translator (assemblers, compilers, interpreters), implementation of translators, and a consideration of what the user sees and needs.

The text has been written in a way which, it is hoped, will not be too theoretical, but will relate to languages (like Pascal) which the reader knows or can readily understand. Indeed, the only real prerequisites for using this book are that the reader have a good background in Pascal, access to a good implementation of that language, and some background in assembly language programming and simple machine architecture. We shall rely quite heavily on this background, especially on the understanding a reader has of the meaning of various programming constructs.

Important parts of the text concern themselves with case studies of simple translators written in Pascal, for simple languages. Other important parts of the text are to be found in the many exercises and suggestions for further reading and experiment on the part of the reader. In short, the emphasis is on 'doing' rather than just 'talking', and the reader who does not attempt the exercises will miss many, if not most, of the finer points.

1.2 Practical note

The Pascal source code for the assemblers, interpreters and compilers to be used in this course is currently available in machine-readable form for four systems: the UCSD Pascal system, the CP/M and MS-DOS TurboPascal systems, and the CDC Cyber Pascal system. In places the machine-readable form differs slightly from the text, to cater for operating system interfaces which tend to be non-standard between machines. These differences are mostly confined to the 'main' programs, and should cause no great difficulties.

Suggestions for moving the system to non-standard Pascal systems, as well as details of disk formats which can be supplied, will be found in Appendix 1.

1.3 References

Although the present text is self-contained, the reader will gain considerable insight from reading around the subjects covered. There is much published material on translators and languages, written at different levels. Among this we should like to single out the following.

Introductory material and treatment

J.D. Ullman, 1976. *Fundamental Concepts of Computer Systems*. Addison-Wesley, Reading, Mass.
  • A useful compendium of many subjects, including simple assembly and compilation.

N. Wirth, 1976. *Algorithms + Data Structures = Programs*. Prentice-Hall, Englewood Cliffs, NJ.
  • A splendid book. Chapter 5 discusses translation using a simple system rather similar to the one in the present text.

Intermediate level

There are several excellent books cited here. One drawback, however, is that they are not directly Pascal-based, and most of them go quite a way beyond the level of the present text.

R. Bornat, 1979. *Understanding and Writing Compilers*. Macmillan, London.
  • A very useful book, mainly using BCPL for descriptions.

P.J. Brown, 1979. *Writing Interactive Compilers and Interpreters*. John Wiley, New York.
  • A highly amusing and very useful book for the authors of BASIC-like compilers, with a number of pertinent points for all readers.

F.J.T. Davie and R. Morrison, 1981. *Recursive Descent Compiling*. Ellis Horwood, Chichester.
  • Also very useful, mainly using S-Algol for descriptions.

R.B. Hunter, 1981. *The Design and Construction of Compilers*. John Wiley, New York.
  • A most useful book, mainly using Algol 68 for descriptions. While the present book was in press, a new edition, using Pascal, was announced.

Case studies of actual compilers

A great deal can be learned from studying actual translator programs. For proprietary reasons this is quite difficult to do, but there are a few texts which, like the present one, make careful analysis of actual systems – usually for small compilers for toy languages.

D.W. Barron (ed.), 1981. *Pascal – the Language and its Implementation*. John Wiley, New York.
  • A useful collection of articles which have appeared in various places, in particular dealing with the Pascal compilers emanating from Zurich, and with the subset Pascal-S compiler from the same place.

R.E. Berry, 1982. *Programming Language Translation*. Ellis Horwood, Chichester.
  • Rather weaker on theory, but a very useful description of the subset Pascal-S interpretive compiler, often used for courses such as this, although perhaps a bit too complicated for our own needs.

P. Brinch Hansen, 1983. *Programming a Personal Computer*. Prentice-Hall, Englewood Cliffs, NJ.
  • Discusses the language Edison and its compiler.

P. Brinch Hansen, 1985. *On Pascal Compilers*. Prentice-Hall, Englewood Cliffs, NJ.
  • While the present book was in press, Brinch Hansen published a further book on compiler construction, using a variation on Pascal to implement a subset Pascal compiler–interpreter. This takes an approach rather similar to the present text, and is a very useful complementary reference. However, references made in the present book to Brinch Hansen's work refer to his earlier book on Edison.

A.C. Hartmann, 1977. *A Concurrent Pascal Compiler*. Springer, Berlin.
  • Discusses a multi-pass compiler for the language Concurrent Pascal.

S. Pemberton and M. Daniels, 1982. *Pascal Implementation – the P4 Compiler*. Ellis Horwood, Chichester.
  • A very detailed study and criticism of the portable Pascal compiler which helped spread Pascal worldwide very quickly. Further details on this can be found in the article by Nori *et al.* in Barron (1981).

J.P. Tremblay and P.G. Sorenson, 1982. *An Implementation Guide to Compiler Writing*. McGraw-Hill, New York.
  • Discusses a compiler for GAUSS, an Algol-like language.

J. Welsh and M. McKeag, 1980. *Structured System Programming*. Prentice-Hall, Englewood Cliffs, NJ.
  • Develops a subset Pascal compiler in a very systematic way. They use a superset of Pascal, called Pascal-Plus, as the host language, which tends to diminish the value of the text for the casual reader.

USUS: The UCSD Pascal Users Group (PO Box 1148, La Jolla, Ca 92038, California), among other software, makes available the source code of the UCSD Pascal compiler, release I.3 (the latest version is IV.2). This was based on the Zurich P4 compiler.

Assembly language programming

This tends to be highly machine specific, but the following are of more general appeal.

P. Calingaert, 1979. *Assemblers, Compilers, and Program Translation*. Computer Science Press, Rockville, Md.
- Also covers high-level languages.

L.A. Leventhal, 1978. *Introduction to Microprocessors – Software, Hardware, Programming*. Prentice-Hall, Englewood Cliffs, NJ.
- A useful reference for learning a lot about microprocessors and programming them in assembler for a variety of uses.

J.F. Wakerly, 1981. *Microcomputer Architecture and Programming*. John Wiley, New York.
- An excellent and wide ranging book, with general discussion as well as discussion of specific microprocessors.

More theoretical and advanced works

These are probably all beyond the level of the present text, but the keen reader should be aware of their existence.

A.V. Aho and J.D. Ullman, 1977. *Principles of Compiler Design*. Addison-Wesley, Reading, Mass.
- Widely referred to by many authors, and a mine of information.

R.C. Backhouse, 1979. *Syntax of Programming Languages: Theory and Practice*. Prentice-Hall, Englewood Cliffs, NJ.
- A detailed discussion of syntax and syntax analysis.

W.A. Barrett and J.D. Couch, 1979. *Compiler Construction: Theory and Practice*. Science Research Associates, Chicago.
- Rather similar in some respects to Aho and Ullman (1977), but with more practical detail.

F.L. Bauer and J. Eickel, 1976. *Compiler Construction; an Advanced Course*. Springer, Berlin.
- A useful collection of lecture notes from an advanced course.

D. Gries, 1971. *Compiler Construction for Digital Computers*. John Wiley, New York.

J.P. Tremblay and P.G. Sorenson, 1985. *Theory and Practice of Compiler Writing*. McGraw-Hill, New York.

Programming languages in general

There are several good books which look at the general subject of 'features' of high-level programming languages. These include the following.

D.W. Barron, 1977. *An Introduction to the Study of Programming Languages.* Cambridge University Press, Cambridge.

D.M. Harland, 1984. *Polymorphic Programming Languages – Design and Implementation.* Ellis Horwood, Chichester.

E. Horowitz, 1984. *Fundamentals of Programming Languages.* Springer, Berlin.

H.F. Ledgard and M. Marcotty, 1981. *The Programming Language Landscape* Science Research Associates, Chicago.

A.D. McGettrick, 1980. *The Definition of Programming Languages.* Cambridge University Press, Cambridge.

R.D. Tennent, 1981. *Principles of Programming Languages.* Prentice-Hall, Englewood Cliffs, NJ.

S.J. Young, 1982. *Real Time Languages – Design and Implementation.* Ellis Horwood, Chichester.

In many places in this text we shall refer to these books, generally just by the author's name, but frequently giving chapter or page references as well.

Journal references

A great deal of interesting material on our theme can be found within the pages of several journals devoted to Computer Science. For the purposes of backing up the material of this text, the reader should be aware of at least two which regularly carry relevant articles, and which are often quite easy to follow. These are *Software – Practice and Experience* (John Wiley, Chichester, England) and *ACM SIGPLAN Notices*, the journal of the special interest group for programming languages of the American Association for Computing Machinery.

Chapter 2 **Translators and interpreters**

The objective of this chapter is to present the reader with a broad overview of many of the areas which will be treated in more detail in subsequent chapters, as well as a specific discussion of the process known as interpretation.

2.1 Systems programs and translators

Users of modern computing systems can be divided into two broad categories: those who never develop their own programs, but simply use ones developed by others, and those who are concerned as much with the development of programs as with their subsequent use. This latter group – of whom we as computer scientists form a part – is fortunate in that program development is usually aided by the use of high-level languages for expressing algorithms, the use of interactive editors for program entry and modification, and the use of sophisticated job control languages for control of execution. Programmers armed with such tools have a very different picture of computer systems from those who are presented with the hardware alone, for the use of compilers, editors and operating systems – a class of tools known generally as **systems programs** – removes from humans the burden of developing all their systems at the machine level. That is not to claim that the use of such tools removes all burdens, or all possibilities for error, as the reader will be well aware!

Well within living memory much program development was done in machine language (indeed, some of it, of necessity, still is) and perhaps some readers have already used this themselves when experimenting with microcomputers. Even a brief exposure to programs written as almost meaningless collections of binary or hexadecimal digits is usually enough to make one grateful for the presence of higher level languages, clumsy and irritating though some of their features may be. In order for higher level languages to be of any use, one must be able to convert programs written in them into the binary or hexadecimal digits which the machine will understand. At an early stage it was realized that if constraints were put on the syntax of the high-level language the translation process became one which could be automated, and this led to the development of **translators** – programs which accept (as data) a textual representation of an algorithm expressed in a **source** language, and which produce (as primary output) a representation of the same algorithm expressed in another language, the **object** or **target** language. The translator must itself be written in a computer language, known as the **host** language; today it is rare to find translators written from scratch directly in machine language, although the first translators, clearly, had to be written in this way, and at the outset of translator development for any new system one has to come to terms with the machine language for that system.

The first major translators written may well have been the FORTRAN compilers developed by Backus and his colleagues at IBM in the 1950s, although machine code development aids were in existence by then. The first FORTRAN compiler is estimated to have taken about 18 man-years of effort. It is interesting to note that one of the primary concerns of the team was to develop a system which could produce object code whose efficiency of execution would compare favourably with that which expert human machine coders could write. Although it is not at first obvious, it has always been true that the automatic translation process can never produce code as efficient as can be written by a really skilled user of the machine language, and to this day there are important components of systems which are developed at (or very near to) machine level in the interests of saving time or space.

It is, of course, true that translator programs are never completely portable (although parts of them may be), and that they usually depend to some extent on other systems programs which form part of what the user sees. In particular, input/output and file management on modern computer systems are often best controlled by the **operating system** – a program or suite of programs whose job it is to control the execution of other programs so as best to share resources such as printers, plotters, disk files and tapes – using techniques such as parallel processing, multiprogramming and so on. Even the simplest microcomputers usually have some simple monitor program (usually in ROM) upon which the user must first rely to load his programs, and get them to start execution. Operating systems programming, perhaps, remained closer to the machine code level than did scientific or commercial programming for a long time, but in recent years there have been a number of successful higher level languages developed with the express purpose of catering for the design of operating systems and real-time control.

Other programs classified as systems software include special programs required by the operating system or computer service (for example to allocate files, change file names, delete files, copy files from one medium to another), and programs that may be required by translators (for example, linkage editors and loaders).

Exercises

2.1   Make a list of as many translators as you can think of which can be found on your mainframe computer.

2.2   Make a list of as many translators as you can think of which can be found on the microcomputers available for your use.

2.3   Make a list of as many systems programs and their functions as you can think of on your mainframe computer.

> **2.4** Make a list of as many systems programs and their functions as you can think of on your microcomputer systems.

2.2 Types of translator

A translator may be defined as a function whose domain is a source language and whose range is contained in an object or target language.

Source language   ⟶   Translator   ⟶   Target language
instructions   instructions

There are several classes of translator:

(a) The term **assembler** is usually associated with translators which map low-level language instructions into machine code that may then be executed directly. Individual source language statements usually map one-for-one to machine level instructions.

(b) The term **macro-assembler** is also associated with translators which map low-level language instructions into machine code, and is really another variation on (a). Many source language statements map one-for-one into their target language equivalents, but some *macro* statements map into a sequence of machine-level instructions – effectively providing a text replacement facility, and thereby extending the assembly language to suit the user. (This is not to be confused with the use of procedures or other subprograms to 'extend' high-level languages, because the method of implementation is usually very different.)

(c) The term **compiler** is usually associated with translators which map high-level language instructions into machine code that may then be executed directly. Individual source language statements usually map into many machine-level instructions.

(d) The term **preprocessor** is usually associated with translators which map a superset of a high-level language into the high-level language, or which map one high-level language into another high-level language. Supersets of high-level languages have been developed for many of the proven languages, such as FORTRAN, to extend them for particular applications (for example, simulation) where the intention is often to make algorithm design easier for the non-specialist programmer. Individual source language statements usually map into target language statements fairly directly. Some of these translators produce low-level assembler language as output.

(e) The terms **decompiler** and **disassembler** refer to translators which attempt to take object code at a low level and regenerate source code at a higher level. While this can be done quite successfully for the production of assembler-level code, it is much more difficult when one tries to recreate, say, Pascal.

Perusal of the above list and a little experience with translators will reveal that it is rarely considered part of the translator's function to execute an algorithm, merely to change its representation from one form to another. This metamorphosis may take place in several stages, each of which is, in a sense, a translation from one form to another. While the output of many translators is machine code which is left dumped at fixed locations in the machine ready for immediate execution (some translators, known as **load-and-go** translators, may even initiate execution of this code), a great many translators do not produce such fixed-address machine code. Rather, they produce something closely akin to it, known as **semicompiled** or **binary symbolic** or **relocatable** form. In this case the final loading of the code, which usually calls for trivial further translation, is achieved by a program known as a **linkage editor** or **loader** or **consolidator**.

Beginners often fail to distinguish between the compilation ('compile-time') and execution ('run-time') phases in developing and using programs written in high-level languages – indeed, they are often initially taught with this distinction deliberately blurred. One uses expressions like 'When the computer executes a *read* statement it reads a number from the input data into a variable'. This hides several low-level processes from the beginner. The underlying implications of file handling, character conversion and storage allocation are glibly ignored, as indeed is the necessity for the computer to be programmed to recognize the word 'read' in the first place. Anyone who has attempted to program these directly in assembler languages will know that many of them are non-trivial to implement.

As mentioned earlier, a translator is itself a program, written in some host language, and we can now see that several languages may be involved in the development of translators: the source language to be translated, the object or target language to be generated, and the host language to be used for implementing the translator – and possibly some intermediate languages. Most of these are, of course, hidden from the user of the system.

A useful notation used to denote a computer program, particularly a translator, is the T-diagram as shown in Figure 2.1.

Translation itself is represented by running the compiler on a machine, and placing the source program and object program on the left and right arms of the T (Figure 2.2). We can regard this as depicting an **abstract machine** whose aim in life is to convert FORTRAN source programs into 1900 machine code equivalents. These diagrams can be combined to show the interdependence of translators, loaders and so on (for example, Figure 2.3).

Many translators generate code for their host machines. These are called **self-resident translators**. Others, known as **cross-translators**, generate code for machines other than the host machine. These are often used in connection with microcomputers, which might themselves be too small to allow self-resident translators to operate satisfactorily. Of course, cross-translation introduces

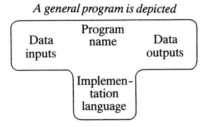

A general program is depicted

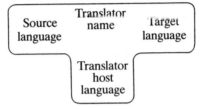

For the special case of a translator this becomes

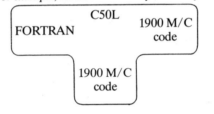

For example, on an ICL 1900 system one finds

Figure 2.1

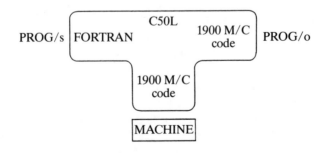

Figure 2.2

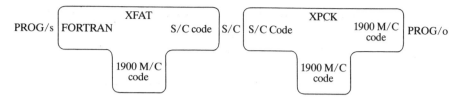

Figure 2.3

additional problems in connection with transferring the object code from the donor machine to the machine that is to execute the translated program, and this can lead to delays and frustration in program development.

Exercises

2.5 Make a list of as many assemblers as you can think of which can be found on your systems. (Some computers have several assemblers for the same object code.)

2.6 Which of the translators known to you are of the load-and-go type?

2.7 Do you know whether any of the translators you use produce relocatable code? Is this of a standard form? Do you know the names of the linkage editors or loaders used on your systems?

2.8 Are there any preprocessors on your system? What are they used for?

2.3 Interpreters

Some translators (preprocessors among them) produce (as output) intermediate code which is still a long way from the machine code of the system on which it is desired to execute the algorithm. Translation may then be continued to the level of machine code, but an important class of systems programs known as **interpreters** has evolved. These accept the output from an intermediate code translator, and produce the effect of executing the original algorithm, without mapping it down to machine level. Interpretive systems carry fairly obvious overheads in execution speed, because 'execution' of intermediate code effectively carries with it the cost of virtual translation into machine code each time an intermediate code is obeyed. Indeed, some interpretive systems (including some for BASIC) use almost no intermediate code at all, but effectively recompile each source statement each time it is obeyed. The distinction between these two approaches is summarized in Figure 2.4.

The interpretive approach has several advantages, not least of which is

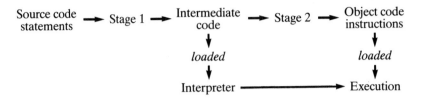

Figure 2.4

that it is easier to describe in a text like this one, where we shall make great use of it. For one thing, it can be made more user-friendly than the directly executable approach; since the interpreter works closer to the source code than does a fully translated program, error messages and other debugging aids may be readily referred to this source. It also has the advantage that new languages may be implemented in a useful form on a wide range of different machines relatively easily. This is done by producing intermediate code to a well defined standard, for which a relatively efficient interpreter is probably easily written for any machine. This method was used to spread Pascal worldwide very quickly, and partly accounts for the rapid acceptance of that language.

The interpretive approach is useful in connection with the cross-translators mentioned earlier. The code produced by such translators can sometimes be tested more effectively by simulated execution on the donor machine, rather than after transfer to the object machine. The delays inherent in the transfer from one machine to the other may be balanced by the degradation of execution time in an interpretive simulation.

Lastly, intermediate languages are often very 'compact', allowing quite large programs to be handled on quite small machines. The success of the well known UCSD Pascal and UCSD p-System stands as an example of what can be done in this respect.

Exercise

2.9 Do you know whether any of the translators which you use adopt an interpretive approach? Have you any idea how far removed from the original source code these interpreters work?

2.4 The relation between high-level languages and translators

Enough has, it is hoped, been said to make the reader aware that the design and implementation of translators is a subject with many possible angles and approaches. The same is true for the design of languages. Many a potentially attractive language has foundered through poor design, or because it proved impossible to provide a translator for the language with any degree of reliability or efficiency. This is particularly true of very large languages, and probably only a very few of these have survived – largely because of enormous financial backing.

Computer languages are generally classed as being 'high-level' (like Pascal, FORTRAN, Ada, Modula-2, Algol) or 'low-level' (like ASSEMBLER). By this stage in his or her career the reader is probably familiar with at least one high-level language and may even be quite competent in its use. High-level languages possess several fairly obvious advantages over low-level ones, as readers who have experience of both will know:

(a) *Readability*   A good high-level language will allow programs that in some ways resemble an English (or, at any rate, American) description of the underlying algorithms.

(b) *Portability*   High level languages are often 'machine independent'. To achieve this they often deny access to 'low-level' features, and are sometimes criticized by programmers who have to develop low-level machine-dependent systems.

(c) *Structure*   There is general agreement that the 'structured programming' movement of the 1960s resulted in a great improvement in the quality and reliability of code. High-level languages can be made subtly to encourage or even enforce structured programming.

(d) *Generality*   Most high-level languages allow the writing of a wide variety of programs, thus relieving the programmer of the need to become expert in many diverse languages.

(e) *Brevity*   Programs expressed in high-level languages are often considerably shorter (in terms of source lines) than their low-level equivalents.

(f) *Arithmetic*   Most computers are 'binary' in nature. Blessed with ten toes on which to check out their number-crunching programs, humans may be somewhat relieved that high-level languages usually make decimal arithmetic the rule, rather than the exception, and provide for mathematical operations in a notation consistent with standard mathematics.

(g) *Error checking*   Being human, a programmer is likely to make many mistakes in the development of a computer program. Many high-level languages – or at least their implementations – can, and often do, enforce a great deal of error checking both at compile-time and at run-time. For this they are, of course, often criticized by programmers who have to develop time-critical code, or who want their programs to abort as quickly as possible.

Many of these are rather two-edged in practice. For example, readability is usually within the confines of a rather stilted style, and some beginners are dismayed to find just how unnatural a high-level language is. Similarly, the generality of many languages is confined to relatively narrow areas, and beginners are dismayed to find areas (like string handling in Pascal) which are very poorly handled.

The development of high-level languages and of their translators are two closely related fields. Inevitably in the field of language design can be found numerous examples of compromise, dictated largely by the need to accommodate language ideas to rather uncompromising, if not unsuitable, machine architectures, and, to a lesser extent, to established operating systems on those machines.

Besides meeting the criteria mentioned above, a successful high-level language today is probably designed with the following additional criteria in mind:

(h) *Clearly defined* It must be clearly described, for the benefit of the user and of the compiler writer.

(i) *Easily translated* It should admit quick translation.

(j) *Efficient* It should permit the generation of efficient object code.

(k) *Widely available* It should be possible to develop translators for all the major machines and for all the major operating systems.

Further reading

As we proceed, we hope to make the reader more aware of some of the points raised in this section. Language design is a difficult area, and much has been and continues to be written on the topic. The reader might like to refer to Chapter 3 of Tremblay and Sorenson (1985) or Chapter 2 of Harland (1984) for recent summaries of the subject. Interesting historical background to several well known languages can be found in various articles in *ACM SIGPLAN Notices*, **13(8)** (1978).

2.5 The structure of a translator

Translators are highly complex programs, and it is unreasonable to consider the translation process as occurring in a single step. It is usual to regard it as divided into a series of **phases**, as shown in Figure 2.5. Each phase might communicate with the next by means of a suitable intermediate language, but in practice the distinction between phases often becomes a little blurred.

The **character handler** is the section that communicates with the outside world, through the operating system, to read in the characters, line by line, which make up the source text. Because character sets and file handling vary from system to system, this phase is often machine dependent.

The **lexical analyser** is the section that separates characters of the source text into groups that logically belong together to make up the **tokens** of the language – symbols like identifiers, strings, numeric constants, keywords like begin and end, operators like <=, and so on. Some of these symbols are very simply represented on the output from the lexical analyser; some need to be associated with various attributes such as their names or values.

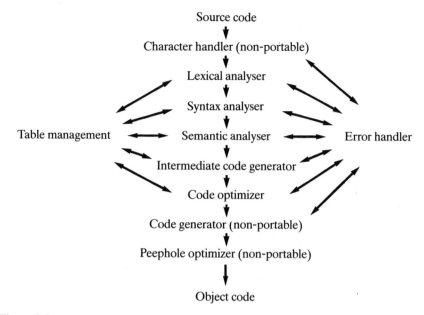

Source code

Character handler (non-portable)

Lexical analyser

Syntax analyser

Table management ⟷ Semantic analyser ⟷ Error handler

Intermediate code generator

Code optimizer

Code generator (non-portable)

Peephole optimizer (non-portable)

Object code

Figure 2.5

The **syntax analyser** groups the tokens produced by the lexical analyser into syntactic structures – which it does by **parsing** expressions and statements (This is analogous to a human analysing a sentence to find components like 'subject', 'object', 'dependent clauses' and so on.) Often the syntax analyser is combined with the **semantic analyser**, whose job it is to determine that the syntactic structures make reasonable sense. The division between syntactic and semantic analysis is often blurred. For example, in Pascal the syntax of the while statement is sometimes described as

while *expression* do *statement*

but not only must the 'expression' be syntactically correct, it must also be something which returns a Boolean value. It is possible to think of a statement in the above form with any type of 'expression' as being syntactically correct in the 'short range' (as Bornat puts it), but with semantic errors if the 'type' of the expression is not Boolean, or as syntactically incorrect in the 'long range'.

Lexical analysis is sometimes easy, and at other times not. For example, the Pascal statement

while A > 3 * B do A := A - 1

easily decodes into tokens (Table 2.1) as we read it from left to right, but the FORTRAN statement

10   DO 20 I = 1 . 30

is more deceptive. Readers familiar with FORTRAN might see it as decoding into Table 2.2, while those who enjoy perversity might like to see it as it really is (Table 2.3).

Table 2.1

while	reserved word	
A	identifier	name *A*
>	operator	comparison
3	constant	integer value 3
*	operator	multiplication
B	identifier	name *B*
do	reserved word	
A	identifier	name *A*
:=	operator	assignment
A	identifier	name *A*
-	operator	subtraction
1	constant	integer value 1

Table 2.2

10	label
DO	keyword
20	statement label
I	INTEGER identifier
=	assignment operator
1	INTEGER constant
,	separator
30	INTEGER constant

Table 2.3

10	label
DO20I	REAL identifier
=	assignment operator
1.30	REAL constant

One has to look quite hard to distinguish the period from the 'expected' comma; one would, of course, *be* perverse to use identifiers with unnecessary and highly suggestive spaces in them (spaces are irrelevant in FORTRAN). While the syntax of Pascal has been cleverly designed so that lexical analysis can be clearly separated from the rest of the analysis, the same is obviously not true of FORTRAN and other languages which, in particular, have no reserved words.

The output of the syntax analyser and semantic analyser phases is sometimes expressed in the form of an abstract **syntax tree**. This is a very useful representation, as it can be used in clever ways to optimize code generation later on. Sometimes, as for example in the case of most Pascal compilers, the tree is not explicit, but its construction is implied in the recursive calls to the procedures which perform the syntax and semantic analysis.

For example, in Pascal, the statement

```
while (1 < P) and (P < 3) do P := P + Q
```

could be depicted in tree form as shown in Figure 2.6. (The reader may have to make reference to Pascal syntax diagrams and a knowledge of Pascal precedence rules to see why the tree looks so complicated.)

The phases just discussed are all analytic in nature. The ones that follow are more synthetic. The first of these, the **intermediate code generator**, which may also in practice be integrated with earlier phases, or sometimes omitted altogether in the case of some very simple translators, may use the structure produced by the earlier phases to set up code in the form of simple code skeletons or macros. The major difference between intermediate code and actual machine code is that the intermediate code need not specify in detail

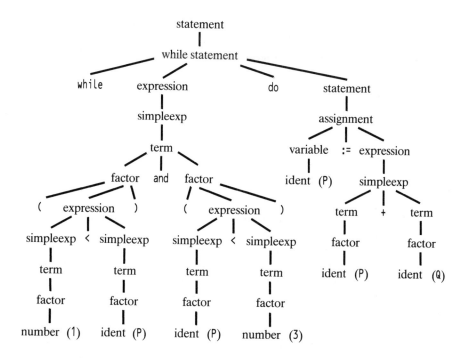

Figure 2.6

such things as the exact registers to be used, the exact addresses to be referred to, and so on.

For example, the same Pascal statement

```
while (1 < P) and (P < 3) do   P := P + Q
```

might produce intermediate code equivalent to

```
L0      if 1 < P goto L1
        goto L3
L1      if P < 3 goto L2
        goto L3
L2      P := P + Q
        goto L0
L3      continue
```

Then again, it might produce something like

```
L0      T1 := 1 < P
        T2 := P < 3
        if T1 and T2 goto L1
        goto L2
L1      P := P + Q
        goto L0
L2      continue
```

depending whether the implementors of the translator deemed it advisable to use the so-called **sequential conjunction** or **short-circuit** approach (as in the first case) or the so-called **boolean operator** approach.

Code optimization may optionally follow, in an attempt to improve the intermediate code in the interests of speed or space or both. To use the same example as before, obvious optimization would lead to code equivalent to

```
L0      if 1 >= P goto L1
        if P >= 3 goto L1
        P := P + Q
        goto L0
L1      continue
```

The penultimate phase, **code generation**, takes the output from the previous phase and produces the object code, by deciding on the memory locations for data, generating code to access such locations, selecting registers for intermediate calculations and indexing, and so on. Clearly this is a phase which calls for much skill and attention to detail, if the finished product is to be at all 'efficient'. Some translators go on to a further phase of so-called **peephole optimization** in which they attempt to reduce unnecessary operations still further by examining short sequences of generated code in closer detail.

It may be of interest to show the actual code generated by various Pascal compilers for the same example as before (see Table 2.4). The first column shows that from an ICL 1900 series compiler, the second from the 8080 Pascal

Table 2.4

LAB0	LDN	6	1	LAB0	LD	HL,1		LAB0	LD	HL,1		
	SBX	6	P		PUSH	HL			PUSH	HL		
	BPZ	6	LAB1		LD	HL,(P)			LD	HL,(P)		
	LDX	6	P		PUSH	HL			POP	DE		
	SBN	6	3		CALL	LESSTHAN			CALL	LESSTHAN		
	BPZ	6	LAB1		LD	HL,(P)			PUSH	HL		
	LDX	6	P		PUSH	HL			LD	HL,(P)		
	ADX	6	Q		LD	HL,3			PUSH	HL		
	STO	6	P		PUSH	HL			LD	HL,3		
	BRN		LAB0		CALL	LESSTHAN			POP	DE		
LAB1	. . . .				POP	HL			CALL	LESSTHAN		
					POP	DE			LD	A,L		
					LD	A,L			AND	E		
					AND	E			LD	L,A		
					RRA				BIT	0,L		
					JP	NC,LAB1			JP	Z,LAB1		
					LD	HL,(P)			LD	HL,(P)		
					EX	DE,HL			PUSH	HL		
					LD	HL,(Q)			LD	HL,(Q)		
					ADD	HL,DE			POP	DE		
					LD	(P),HL			ADD	HL,DE		
					JP	LAB0			LD	(P),HL		
				LAB1	. . .				JP	LAB0		
								LAB1	. . .			

MT+ compiler from Digital Research, the third from the Z80 Turbo Pascal compiler from Borland International. The output has been rewritten here using assembler for convenience, and for the case where P and Q were 'global' variables.

The various phases of a translator inevitably make use of a complex data structure, known as the **symbol table**, in which track is kept of the names used by the program, and associated attributes for these, such as type, and storage requirements.

As is well known, users of high-level languages are apt to make many errors in the development of even quite simple programs. Thus the various phases of the compiler, especially the earlier ones, also communicate with an **error handler** which is invoked when errors are detected. It is desirable that compilation of erroneous programs be completed, if possible, so that the user can clean several errors out of the source before recompiling, and this raises very interesting issues regarding the design of **error recovery** and **error correction** techniques. (We speak of error recovery when the translation process attempts to carry on after detecting an error, and of error correction or error repair when it attempts to correct the error from context – obviously a contentious area, as the correction may be nothing like what the programmer originally had in mind.)

Error detection at compile-time must not be confused with error detection at run-time for the object code. Many code generators are responsible for adding error checking code to the object program; for example, to check that subscripts for arrays stay in bounds. (Such code can drastically reduce the efficiency of a program, and some compilers allow it to be suppressed). This may be quite rudimentary, or it may involve adding considerable code for use with sophisticated debugging systems.

Besides being conceptually divided into phases, translators are often divided into **passes**, in each of which several phases may be combined or interleaved. A pass reads the source program, or output from a previous pass, makes some transformations, and usually writes output to an intermediate file, which may then be rescanned on a subsequent pass. The number of passes used depends on a variety of factors. Certain languages require at least two passes to generate code easily – for example, those where declaration of identifiers can occur after the first reference to the identifier, or where attributes of identifiers cannot be readily deduced from the context in which they first appear. A multi-pass compiler can often save space, an important consideration in small systems, where one wishes to translate complicated languages. It probably also allows for better provision of code optimization, error reporting and error handling. Lastly, it lends itself to team development, with different members of the team assuming responsibility for different passes. However, multi-pass compilers are usually slower than single-pass ones, and their probable need to keep track of several files makes them slightly awkward to write and to use. Compromises at the design stage often result in languages which are well suited to single-pass compilation.

As was mentioned earlier, some translators do not produce 'fixed address' machine code (which is to reside at fixed locations in memory), but rather 'relocatable' code, which requires further processing before it can be loaded and executed. A frequent use for this is in the development of libraries of special-purpose routines, possibly originating in a mixture of source languages. Routines compiled in this way are linked together by programs called linkage editors, which may be regarded almost as providing a final pass to a multi-pass system. For developing really large software projects such systems are invaluable. For the sort of 'throw away' programs on which most students cut their teeth they can be an awful nuisance, because of the overheads of managing several files, and of the time taken to link their contents together. As a result, and perhaps regrettably, students are often trained using single-pass systems, often of the load-and-go variety; in any event, standard Pascal does not provide for separately or independently compiled routines. In passing we should comment that the systems we shall be studying probably represent the limit of what should be attempted without recourse to the use of independently compiled modules. Some non-standard Pascal implementations (notably UCSD Pascal) allow for a measure of separate compilation; readers familiar with these might like to modify the case studies which follow accordingly.

Exercises

2.10 What sort of problems might a FORTRAN compiler have in analysing statements beginning

```
IF ( I(J) - I(K) ) ........
CALL IF (4 ,     ...........
IF (3 .EQ. MAX) GOTO ......
```

2.11 What sort of code would you have produced if you had been coding a statement like while (1 < P) and (P < 3) do P := P + Q in your favourite assembler language?

2.12 Write down a few other high-level constructs and try to imagine what sort of assembler-like machine code a compiler would produce for them.

2.13 What do you suppose makes it relatively easy to compile Pascal? Can you think of any aspects of Pascal that could prove really difficult?

2.14 Try to find out which of the compilers you have used are single-pass, and which are multi-pass and, for the latter, find out how many passes are involved. Which of them produce relocatable code that needs further processing by linkers or linkage editors?

2.15 We have used two undefined terms which at first seem interchangeable, namely 'separate' and 'independent' compilation. See if you can find what the differences are.

Further reading

Most books on translators have very readable introductions on the material discussed here. Look at the first chapters of those by Bornat (1979), Aho and Ullman (1977), and Tremblay and Sorenson (1985).

2.6 Bootstrapping

By now the reader may have realized that developing translators is a decidedly non-trivial exercise. If one is faced with the task of writing a translator for a fairly complex source language, one does not attempt to write it all in machine code. For example, in designing a FORTRAN compiler, one might write the compiler in ASSEMBLER, some assembly language (Figure 2.7).

Of course this is only one link in a chain, because we do not have a machine that executes assembler code directly. We still have to convert the ASSEMBLER code using an assembler program. This is conveniently repre-

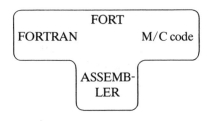

Figure 2.7

sented in terms of T-diagrams chained together (Figure 2.8).

Even this raises interesting problems. A full assembler is itself a major piece of software. It is quite common to divide languages into subsets, so that subset 1 is contained in subset 2 which in turn is contained in subset 3 and so on; that is

Subset 1		Subset 2		Subset 3
of ASSEMBLER	$\subseteq$	of ASSEMBLER	$\subseteq$	of ASSEMBLER

One then writes an assembler for subset 1 of ASSEMBLER in machine code, say on a load-and-go basis (more likely one writes in ASSEMBLER, and then hand-translates it into machine code). This subset assembler program may, perhaps, do very little other than exchange mnemonic opcodes into binary form (Figure 2.9). One can then write an assembler for subset 2 of ASSEMBLER in subset 1 of ASSEMBLER, and so on (Figure 2.10).

This process, by which a simple language is used to translate a more complicated program, which in turn may load an even more complicated program and so on, is called **bootstrapping**.

The technique is also used in constructing transportable compilers, often allowing, as part of the development, for writing the compiler in its own source language. For example, when the first ICL Pascal compiler was constructed, two Pascal compilers were already available in Zurich (where Pascal was first

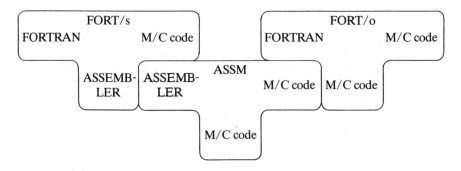

Figure 2.8

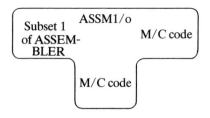

Figure 2.9

implemented). The one, produced by the above technique, could be represented as shown in Figure 2.11a, while the other could be represented as shown
in Figure 2.11b.

Now if one used PAS1 one could compile any Pascal source program into
the equivalent CDC 6000 machine code program. In particular, if it was used to
compile PAS1, one merely produced PAS1 again – this allowed a test on self-
consistency (Figure 2.12a). The first stage of the transportation process
involved changing PAS1 to generate ICL machine code – thus producing a
cross-compiler. Since this compiler was written in a high-level language, this

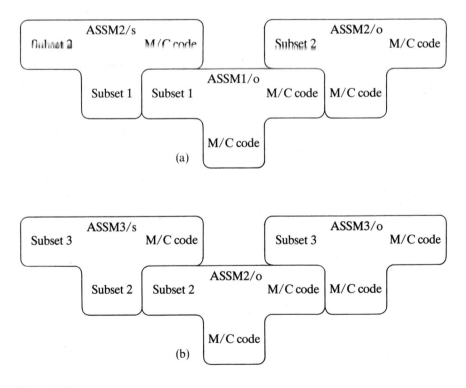

Figure 2.10

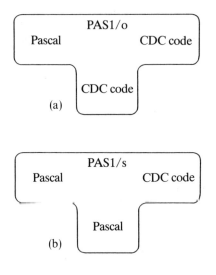

Figure 2.11

was not too difficult to do (Figure 2.12b). Of course this compiler could not yet run on any machine at all. It was first compiled using PAS1 (Figure 2.12c). This compiler could run on CDC machines, but not of course on ICL machines. One further compilation produced the final result (Figure 2.12d).

The final product could then be transported on magnetic tape to the ICL machine, and loaded quite easily. This is known as a **half bootstrap** system, because the work of transportation is essentially done entirely on the donor machine. Clearly the method is hazardous – if the PAS2/s compiler has any flaws one will end up with a totally useless product. These problems can be reduced by minimizing changes made to the original compiler, but the final product will not necessarily produce good object code, as the underlying compiler design probably incorporated features particularly suited to the donor machine. However, one can then continue development of the system in a high-level language, and refine the product accordingly. Such indeed happened when the definition of Pascal was revised. A compiler for Pascal-2 was written in Pascal-1 (a relatively easy operation) (Figure 2.13a). This was compiled with the existing Pascal-1 compiler (Figure 2.13b). The compiler for Pascal-2 was then rewritten in Pascal-2, a better language, to produce better code (Figure 2.13c) and this was compiled with the intermediate product (Figure 2.13d) to give the final product (Figure 2.13e).

Because of the inherent difficulty of the half bootstrap for porting compilers, a technique known as the **full bootstrap** is often used in the case of Pascal and other similar high-level languages. Here most of the development takes place on the target machine. It will again be helpful to illustrate with the well known example of the Pascal-P implementation kit.

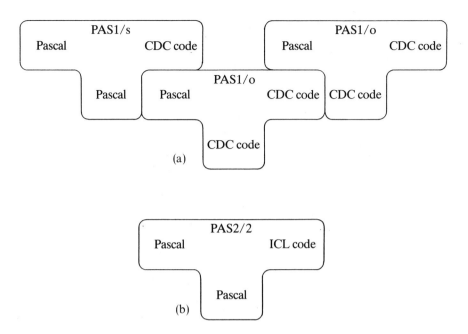

(a)

(b)

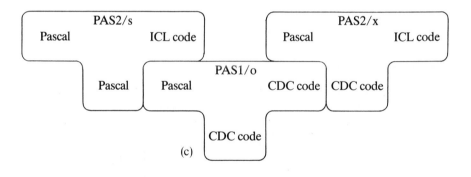

(c)

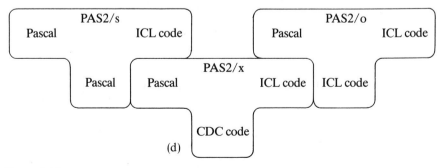

(d)

Figure 2.12

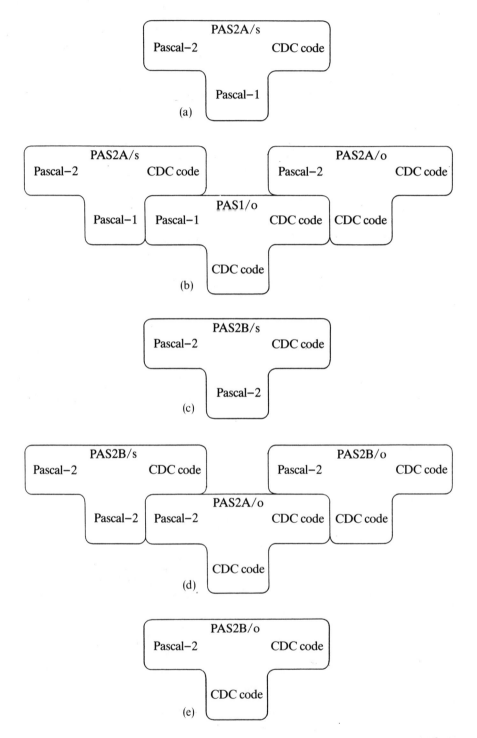

Figure 2.13

The donor group at Zurich produces a kit consisting of

(a)   the source form of a Pascal compiler, written in a very complete subset of the language, known as Pascal-P, which will translate Pascal-P source programs into a well defined and well documented intermediate language, known as P-code, which is the 'machine code' for a hypothetical stack-based computer, known as a P-machine;

(b)   the P-codes that would be produced by the Pascal-P compiler, were it to compile itself;

(c)   an interpreter for the P-code language, supplied as a Pascal algorithm.

The interpreter serves only as a model for writing a similar program for the target machine, to allow it to look like the hypothetical P-machine. If one loads this interpreter – that is to say, the version of it tailored to fit the target machine – into the target machine, one is in a position to 'execute' P-code as though it were machine code, as indicated in Figure 2.14.

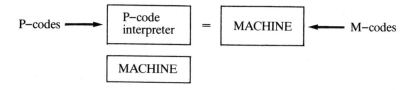

Figure 2.14

To get the machine to 'obey' a Pascal program, one must translate it into P-codes, and then feed these into the interpreter, along with the 'data' to produce the 'results' (Figure 2.15). In particular, if one feeds the interpreter with the P-codes for the Pascal-P compiler itself, one produces a program whose 'data' will be a Pascal source program, and whose 'results' will be the equivalent Pascal program, expressed in P-code. These P-codes can then be fed into the interpreter in turn, together with the data for the Pascal source program, to produce the results. Notice how one uses the interpreter twice – once primed with the P-codes for the Pascal-P compiler (to give the effect of a Pascal compiler running on a P-machine) and then a second time primed with the P-codes for the source program.

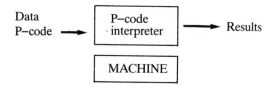

Figure 2.15

As a further special case, if one primes the interpreter with the P-codes for the Pascal-P compiler, and then gives it as data the Pascal-P compiler source written in Pascal-P, the results should be the same P-codes as were used to prime the interpreter. This test for consistency provides some measure of confidence in one's interpreter. The way to develop one's own compiler is then as follows.

One first writes a compiler to translate Pascal-P source programs to the local machine code. This compiler can be written in Pascal-P source, and can use the source of the Pascal-P to P-code compiler (part of the kit) as a guide (Figure 2.16a). This is then put through the P-machine (Figure 2.16b). Now we feed the source of our Pascal/machine code compiler through the P-machine (Figure 2.16c) to give Figure 2.16d.

Further reading

T diagrams were first introduced by Bratman (1961). They were further refined by Earley and Sturgis (1970), and are also used in the books by Hunter (1981), and by Davie and Morrison (1981).

The ICL bootstrap is further described by Welsh and Quinn (1972). Bootstrapping is also discussed by Lecarme and Peyrolle-Thomas (1973), and by Nori *et al.* (1981).

The P-machine and the original P-compiler are well described by Pemberton and Daniels (1982).

2.7 An interpreter for a stack-oriented computer

Later sections of this text look at developing a compiler for a hypothetical machine which uses its primary memory as a stack. It may help to consolidate the ideas of the last few sections by presenting the machine, its machine language and an interpreter for the language immediately. This machine is a similar but highly simplified version of the one used in the UCSD system and the Pascal-P system mentioned earlier.

The use of a stack memory will later be shown to facilitate compilation of high-level languages which allow recursion, as well as the compilation of complicated arithmetic expressions.

Compared with normal register-based machines, this one may at first seem a little strange. In common with most machines it stores code and data in memory which can be modelled as a linear array. However, it is convenient to regard the 'code' and the 'data' (stack) memory as separated, and to regard the bottom end of the stack as reserved for 'variables' and the rest of it for 'working storage', as shown in Figure 2.17. That is to say, the first instruction in any program will be to reserve space on the bottom end of memory for variables, simply by incrementing the stack pointer by the number of elements needed for the variables. The elements of the stack are simple integers.

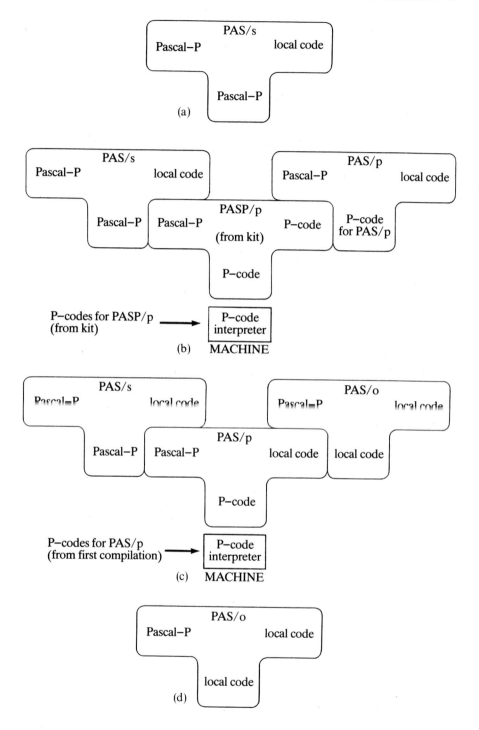

Figure 2.16

Code area	Variables	Stack (growing ➤)	Unused

Figure 2.17

The machine appears to be coded in an assembler language, which makes life rather easier for the programmer, although addresses must be stipulated in absolute form. The main opcodes for the machine are given below (later we shall add more).

NEG   Negate Top of stack
ADD   Add Next-to-top to Top-of-stack, leave result as Top-of-stack
SUB   Subtract Top-of-stack from Next-to-top, leave result as Top-of-stack
MUL   Multiply Next-to-top by Top-of-stack, leave result as Top-of-stack
DVD   Divide Next-to-top by Top-of-stack, leave result as Top-of-stack
EQL   Leave 1 as Top-of-stack if Next-to-top = Top-of-stack, 0 otherwise
NEQ   Leave 1 as Top-of-stack if Next-to-top $\neq$ Top-of-stack, 0 otherwise
GTR   Leave 1 as Top-of-stack if Next-to-top > Top-of-stack, 0 otherwise
LSS   Leave 1 as Top-of-stack if Next-to-top < Top-of-stack, 0 otherwise
LEQ   Leave 1 as Top-of-stack if Next-to-top $\leq$ Top-of-stack, 0 otherwise
GEQ   Leave 1 as Top-of-stack if Next-to-top $\geq$ Top-of-stack, 0 otherwise

(All the above actually pop two elements, form a result, and then push this back onto the stack.)

STK   Dump stack to printer (useful for debugging)
PRN   Print Top-of-stack as an integer value, pop stack
PRS   Print the Top-of-stack elements below top of stack, as ASCII characters, pop stack by Top-of-stack + 1 elements
NLN   Print carriage-return-line-feed sequence
INN   Read integer value, store on stack element whose address is currently Top-of-stack, pop stack
INT A Increment stack pointer by A (A is a constant)
LDI A Push integer value A onto stack
LDA A Push address of A onto stack (currently equivalent to LDI A)
LDV   Replace top of stack by element whose address is currently Top-of-stack (an operation we shall call *dereferencing*)
STO   Store Top-of-stack in memory at the address given as Next-to-top, pop two elements off stack
HLT   Halt
BRN A Unconditional branch to instruction A
BZE A Branch to instruction A if Top-of-stack is zero, pop stack
NOP   No operation

Note that we are using Top-of-stack and Next-to-top to denote the actual integer values which are currently stored respectively on and just below the top positions of the stack memory.

A sample program follows, for a very simple algorithm.

Algorithm 2.7.1

```
begin
 repeat
   read (A);  B ← A + B
 until A = 0
 write (B)
end
```

This would require two variables A and B. The machine code for this program might read

```
 0  INT  2    0 is for A, 1 is for B
 1  LDA  0    push address of A on stack
 2  INN       read value, store on A
 3  LDA  1    push address of B on stack
 4  LDA  0    push address of A on stack
 5  LDV       dereference — value of A now on stack
 6  LDA  1    push address of B on stack
 7  LDV       dereference — value of B now on stack
 8  ADD       add A to B
 9  STO       store result as new value of B
10  LDA  0    push address of A on stack
11  LDV       dereference — value of A now on stack
12  LDI  0    push constant 0 onto stack
13  EQL       check equality
14  BZE  1    branch if A ≠ 0
15  LDA  1    push address of B on stack
16  LDV       dereference — value of B now on stack
17  PRN       write result
18  HLT       stop
```

In developing an interpreter for this system, so far as data structures go, we require a large array S in which to represent the machine's data area, and a large array PCODE in which to store the pseudo instructions. These are conveniently represented by a record type

```
type
  INSTRUCTIONS = packed record
                   F : OPCODES (*function code*);
                   A : INTEGER (*displacement address*)
                 end (*INSTRUCTIONS*);
```

So far as algorithmic components are concerned, there are essentially two to consider. The first of these is a simple loader cum assembler, and the second is the interpreter proper.

Code is assumed to be supplied to the machine in free format, one code per line. Comments and labels may be added, as in the above example, but these are to be ignored.

The essence of the loader can be expressed as

```
begin
  NEXTCODE ← 0
  while not EOF(CODEFILE) do
      SKIPLABEL
      if not EOF(CODEFILE) then
          read(CODEFILE, MNEMONIC)
          convert MNEMONIC to OPCODE
          if OPCODE is followed by address then read(CODEFILE, ADDRESS)
          store OPCODE and ADDRESS in PCODE[NEXTCODE]
          increment NEXTCODE
          ignore comments
end
```

The interpreter itself is essentially controlled by repetitive execution of a large case statement, and follows the lines of

```
begin
  initialize program counter P and stack pointer T
  set program status PS to RUNNING
  repeat
    I ← PCODE[P]; increment P   (*fetch*)
    with I do                   (*execute*)
      case F of
        . . .
      end
  until PS ≠ RUNNING
  if PS ≠ FINISHED then POSTMORTEM
end
```

Listing 1 includes code for a Pascal program which will emulate the machine discussed above. In this, as in other case studies in this text, details of file assignments have been suppressed, as these will vary from implementation to implementation; suggestions for the modifications needed for some common Pascal implementations will be found in Appendix 1. We should remark that there is rather more error checking code in this interpreter than we should like – in the ones presented later (see Listing 12) we shall be able to cut out some of this.

Exercises

2.16 How closely does the machine code for the P-machine resemble anything you have seen before?

2.17 If you had to hand-translate P-machine code into your favourite ASSEMBLER, how difficult would it be?

2.18 Are there any opcodes that have been omitted from the set above which would be absolutely essential to define a viable 'integer' machine?

2.19 Why do you suppose interpreters might find it difficult to handle I/O errors in user programs?

2.20 Can you think of ways in which this interpreter can be improved, as regards both efficiency and user friendliness? In particular, try adding debugging aids over and above the simple stack dump already provided. Can you think of any ways in which it could be made to detect infinite loops in a user program, or to allow itself to be manually interrupted by an irate or frustrated user?

2.21 The interpreter attempts to detect corruption of the stack through over- and underflow. It does not quite succeed – improve on it. One might argue that correct code will never cause such corruption to occur, but experience has shown that beginners often 'push' without 'popping' or vice versa, and so the checks are very necessary.

2.22 Would you write code anything like that given in the example if you had to translate Algorithm 2.7.1 into a familiar ASSEMBLER language directly?

2.23 Use the stack language and its interpreter to write and test a simple program to achieve the following

```
begin
  read(A); SMALLEST ← A; LARGEST ← A
  while A ≠ 0 do
    if A > LARGEST then LARGEST ← A
    if A < SMALLEST then SMALLEST ← A
    read(A)
  write(SMALLEST, LARGEST)
end.
```

2.24 Use the stack language and its interpreter to write and test a program that will read a sequence of numbers and print out those that form an ascending sub-sequence. For example, from 1 2 12 7 4 14 6 23 we should print 1 2 12 14 23. For convenience terminate the sequence with, say, 0.

2.25 Use the stack language and its interpreter to write and test a program that will read a sequence of numbers and report on the longest repeated sub-sequence. For example, for data reading 1 2 3 3 3 3 4 5 4 4 4 4 4 4 6 5 5 it should report '4 appeared 7 times'. For convenience terminate the sequence with, say, 9999.

2.26 One of the advantages of an emulated machine is that it is usually very easy to extend it (provided the host language for the interpreter can support the features required). Try introducing two new opcodes, say INC and PRC, which will read and print single character data respectively. Then rework Exercises 2.24 and 2.25 for a sequence of characters terminated by a blank.

2.27 As a further variation on the emulated machine, develop a variation where the branch instructions are 'relative' rather than 'absolute'. This makes for rather simpler transition to relocatable code.

Further reading

The Pascal-P interpreter is well covered in the book by Pemberton and Daniels (1982). Other descriptions of pseudo-machines and of stack machines are to be found in Chapter 5 of the book by Wakerly (1981).

Listing 1 Interpreter for stack machine

```
1    program PMACHINE (INPUT, OUTPUT, CODEFILE, DATA, RESULTS);
2    (* Interpreter for simple pseudo-machine language of Section 2.6
3       P.D. Terry.      11th January 1985.   Version 1.0 *)
4    const
5       CODEMAX = 1000 (*Size of code array*);
6    type
7       SHORTSTRING = packed array [1 .. 3] of CHAR;
8       OPCODES = (*order important*)
9         (LDI, LDA, INT, BRN, BZE, NEG, ADD, SUB, MUL, DVD, OD, EQL, NEQ, LSS,
10         GEQ, GTR, LEQ, STK, STO, HLT, INN, PRN, PRS, NLN, LDV, NOP, NUL);
11      INSTRUCTIONS = packed record
12                     F : OPCODES (*function code*);
13                     A : INTEGER (*displacement address*)
14                   end (*INSTRUCTIONS*);
15   var
16      (*some implementations require INPUT, OUTPUT : TEXT; *)
17      CODEFILE,                                (*Pcodes*)
18      DATA, RESULTS   : TEXT                    (*I/O*);
19      NEXTCODE        : INTEGER                 (*code index*);
20      PCODE           : array [0 .. CODEMAX] of INSTRUCTIONS (*the code*);
21      ERRORS          : BOOLEAN                 (*check input*);
22      MNEMONIC        : array [OPCODES] of SHORTSTRING     (*for loader*);
23      HASADDRESSFIELD : set of OPCODES          (*with addresses*);
24
25      procedure LOADCODE;
```

```
26    (*Simple loader for pseudo-assembler object code*)
27      var
28        THISCODE : SHORTSTRING (*mnemonic for matching*);
29        I        : INTEGER     (*loop control*);
30        CH       : CHAR        (*general char for input*);
31
32      procedure UPPERCASE;
33        begin
34          if CH in ['a' .. 'z'] then CH := CHR(ORD(CH) - ORD('a') + ORD('A'))
35        end (*UPPERCASE*);
36
37      procedure SKIPLABEL;
38        begin
39          repeat
40            READ(CODEFILE, CH)
41          until EOF(CODEFILE) or (CH in ['A' .. 'Z', 'a' .. 'z'])
42        end (*SKIPLABEL*);
43
44      begin (*LOADCODE*)
45        NEXTCODE := 0; ERRORS := FALSE;
46        while not EOF(CODEFILE) do
47          begin
48            SKIPLABEL;
49            if not EOF(CODEFILE) then
50              begin
51                with PCODE[NEXTCODE] do
52                  begin
53                    UPPERCASE; THISCODE[1] := CH;
54                    for I := 2 to 3 do (*rest of mnemonic*)
55                      begin READ(CODEFILE, CH); UPPERCASE; THISCODE[I] := CH end;
56                    F := LDI (*prepare to search for opcode*);
57                    MNEMONIC[NUL] := THISCODE;
58                    while THISCODE <> MNEMONIC[F] do F := SUCC(F);
59                    if F = NUL then
60                      begin
61                        WRITELN(OUTPUT, 'INVALID OPCODE ', THISCODE,
62                              ' AT ', NEXTCODE);
63                        ERRORS := TRUE
64                      end;
65                    if F in HASADDRESSFIELD then
66                      if EOLN(CODEFILE)
67                        then
68                          begin
69                            WRITELN(OUTPUT, 'MISSING ADDRESS AT ', NEXTCODE);
70                            ERRORS := TRUE
71                          end
```

```
72                          else READ(CODEFILE, A);
73                       READLN(CODEFILE)
74                   end (*with*);
75                 NEXTCODE := (NEXTCODE + 1) mod CODEMAX
76            end (*if*)
77        end (*while*);
78      for I := NEXTCODE to CODEMAX do PCODE[I].F := NUL (*Invalid opcode*)
79    end (*LOADCODE*);
80
81    procedure LISTCODE;
82    (*Reflect code for checking purposes*)
83      var
84        I : INTEGER;
85      begin
86        for I := 0 to NEXTCODE - 1 do with PCODE[I] do
87          if F in HASADDRESSFIELD
88            then WRITELN(OUTPUT, I:10, MNEMONIC[F]:4, A:5)
89            else WRITELN(OUTPUT, I:10, MNEMONIC[F]:4)
90      end (*LISTCODE*);
91
92    procedure INTERPRET;
93    (*The interpreter itself*)
94      const
95        STACKMAX = 1000                      (*limit on data area*);
96      var
97        P,                                   (*program counter*)
98        T,                                   (*stack pointer*)
99        LOOP  : INTEGER                      (*for loops*);
100       I     : INSTRUCTIONS                 (*currently active*);
101       S     : array [0 .. STACKMAX] of INTEGER (*stack memory*);
102       PS    : (RUNNING, FINISHED, STKCHK, DATCHK,
103               EOFCHK, DIVCHK, FCTCHK, LOWCHK) (*program status*);
104
105     procedure DECTBY (I : INTEGER);
106     (*Decrement stack pointer, checking for underflow*)
107       begin T := T - I; if T < 0 then PS := LOWCHK end;
108
109     procedure INCTBY (I : INTEGER);
110     (*Increment stack pointer, checking for overflow*)
111       begin T := T + I; if T > STACKMAX then PS := STKCHK end;
112
113     procedure CHECKDATA;
114     (*Attempt to check 'numeric' data for validity*)
115       begin
116         while not EOF(DATA) and (DATA ↑ = ' ') do GET(DATA);
117         if EOF(DATA) then PS := EOFCHK else
```

```
118        if not (DATA↑ in ['0' .. '9', '+', '-' ]) then PS := DATCHK
119      end (*CHECKDATA*);
120
121    function STACKOKAY : BOOLEAN;
122    (*Check that stack pointer has not underflowed.  This should not
123      happen with correct code, but it is just as well to check*)
124      begin
125        if T < 0 then PS := LOWCHK; STACKOKAY := PS = RUNNING
126      end (*STACKOKAY*);
127
128    procedure STACKDUMP;
129    (*Dump data area - useful for debugging*)
130      var
131        LOOP : INTEGER;
132      begin
133        WRITELN(RESULTS);
134        WRITELN(RESULTS, 'Stack dump at ', P - 1:1, ' T = ', T:1);
135        for LOOP := 0 to T do
136          begin
137            WRITE(RESULTS, LOOP:4, ':', S[LOOP]:5);
138            if (LOOP+1) mod 8 = 0 then WRITELN(RESULTS)
139          end;
140        WRITELN(RESULTS)
141      end (*STACKDUMP*);
142
143    procedure POSTMORTEM;
144    (*Report run-time error and position*)
145      begin
146        case PS of
147          DIVCHK : WRITE(RESULTS, 'Division by zero');
148          EOFCHK : WRITE(RESULTS, 'No more data');
149          DATCHK : WRITE(RESULTS, 'Invalid data');
150          STKCHK : WRITE(RESULTS, 'Stack overflow');
151          LOWCHK : WRITE(RESULTS, 'Stack underflow');
152          FCTCHK : WRITE(RESULTS, 'Invalid opcode');
153        end;
154        WRITELN(RESULTS, ' at ', P-1:1)
155      end (*POSTMORTEM*);
156
157    begin (*INTERPRET*)
158      (*open and RESET(DATA), REWRITE(RESULTS) files as appropriate*)
159      for LOOP := 0 to STACKMAX do S[LOOP] := 0 (*clear all memory*);
160      T := -1; P := 0; PS := RUNNING;
161      repeat
162        I := PCODE[P]; P := P + 1 (*fetch*);
163        with I do                 (*execute*)
```

```
164        case F of
165          NOP: ;
166          NUL: PS := FCTCHK;
167          NEG: if STACKOKAY then S[T] := -S[T];
168          ADD:
169            begin DECTBY(1); if PS = RUNNING then S[T] := S[T] + S[T+1] end;
170          SUB:
171            begin DECTBY(1); if PS = RUNNING then S[T] := S[T] - S[T+1] end;
172          MUL:
173            begin DECTBY(1); if PS = RUNNING then S[T] := S[T] * S[T+1] end;
174          DVD:
175            begin
176              DECTBY(1);
177              if PS = RUNNING then
178                if S[T+1] = 0 then PS := DIVCHK else S[T] := S[T] div S[T+1]
179            end;
180          OD : if STACKOKAY then if ODD(S[T]) then S[T] := 1 else S[T] := 0;
181          EQL:
182            begin DECTBY(1); if PS = RUNNING then S[T] := ORD(S[T] = S[T+1]) end;
183          NEQ:
184            begin DECTBY(1); if PS = RUNNING then S[T] := ORD(S[T] <> S[T+1]) end;
185          LSS:
186            begin DECTBY(1); if PS = RUNNING then S[T] := ORD(S[T] < S[T+1]) end;
187          GEQ:
188            begin DECTBY(1); if PS = RUNNING then S[T] := ORD(S[T] >= S[T+1]) end;
189          GTR:
190            begin DECTBY(1); if PS = RUNNING then S[T] := ORD(S[T] > S[T+1]) end;
191          LEQ:
192            begin DECTBY(1); if PS = RUNNING then S[T] := ORD(S[T] <= S[T+1]) end;
193          STK: STACKDUMP;
194          PRN: begin if STACKOKAY then WRITE(RESULTS, S[T]:1); DECTBY(1) end;
195          PRS: if STACKOKAY then
196                  begin
197                    for LOOP := T - S[T] to T - 1 do WRITE(RESULTS, CHR(S[LOOP]));
198                    DECTBY(S[T] + 1)
199                  end;
200          NLN: WRITELN(RESULTS);
201          INN: begin
202                  CHECKDATA;
203                  if PS = RUNNING then if STACKOKAY then READ(DATA, S[S[T]]);
204                  DECTBY(1)
205                end;
206          LDI: begin INCTBY(1); if PS = RUNNING then S[T] := A end;
207          LDA: begin INCTBY(1); if PS = RUNNING then S[T] := A end;
208          LDV: if STACKOKAY then S[T] := S[S[T]];
209          STO: begin
```

```
210                      DECTBY(1);
211                        if PS = RUNNING then
212                          begin
213                            if S[T] >= 0 then S[S[T]] := S[T+1] else PS := LOWCHK;
214                            DECTBY(1)
215                          end
216                    end;
217              INT: INCTBY(A);
218              HLT: PS := FINISHED;
219              BRN: P := A;
220              BZE: begin if STACKOKAY then if S[T] = 0 then P := A; DECTBY(1) end
221          end
222        until PS <> RUNNING;
223        if PS <> FINISHED then POSTMORTEM;
224        (*close RESULTS file if necessary*)
225      end (*INTERPRET*);
226
227    procedure INITIALIZE;
228      begin
229        MNEMONIC[NOP] := 'NOP'; MNEMONIC[NUL] := 'NUL'; MNEMONIC[LDI] := 'LDI';
230        MNEMONIC[LDA] := 'LDA'; MNEMONIC[INT] := 'INT'; MNEMONIC[BRN] := 'BRN';
231        MNEMONIC[BZE] := 'BZE'; MNEMONIC[NEG] := 'NEG'; MNEMONIC[ADD] := 'ADD';
232        MNEMONIC[SUB] := 'SUB'; MNEMONIC[MUL] := 'MUL'; MNEMONIC[DVD] := 'DVD';
233        MNEMONIC[OD]  := 'ODD'; MNEMONIC[EQL] := 'EQL'; MNEMONIC[NEQ] := 'NEQ';
234        MNEMONIC[LSS] := 'LSS'; MNEMONIC[GEQ] := 'GEQ'; MNEMONIC[GTR] := 'GTR';
235        MNEMONIC[LEQ] := 'LEQ'; MNEMONIC[STK] := 'STK'; MNEMONIC[STO] := 'STO';
236        MNEMONIC[HLT] := 'HLT'; MNEMONIC[INN] := 'INN'; MNEMONIC[PRN] := 'PRN';
237        MNEMONIC[PRS] := 'PRS'; MNEMONIC[NLN] := 'NLN'; MNEMONIC[LDV] := 'LDV';
238        HASADDRESSFIELD := [LDI .. BZE]
239      end (*INITIALIZE*);
240
241    begin (*PMACHINE*)
242      (*open and RESET(CODEFILE), INPUT and OUTPUT files as appropriate *)
243      INITIALIZE; LOADCODE; LISTCODE;
244      if not ERRORS then INTERPRET;
245      (*close OUTPUT file if necessary*)
246    end (*PMACHINE*).
```

Chapter 3 **Simple assemblers**

This chapter is concerned with the implementation of simple assembler language translator programs. To distinguish between programs written in 'assembler code', and the 'assembler program' which translates these, we shall use the convention that ASSEMBLER means the language and 'assembler' means the translator.

The basic purpose of an assembler is to translate ASSEMBLER language mnemonics into binary or hexadecimal machine code. Some assemblers do little beyond this, but most modern assemblers offer a variety of additional features, and the boundary between assemblers and compilers has become somewhat blurred.

We shall assume that the reader has a working knowledge of simple assembler languages. Readers who do not will find adequate discussions in the excellent books by Wakerly (1981), Leventhal (1978), and Calingaert (1979).

3.1   A simple ASSEMBLER language for an 8-bit machine

Rather than discuss the construction of an assembler for a machine-specific language, we shall implement one for a rather simple ASSEMBLER language of our own, for a hypothetical machine with an 8-bit word, a single 8-bit accumulator A, an 8-bit stack pointer SP, and an 8-bit index register X. There are also two condition flags, Z (set when an operation gives a zero result) and P (set when an operation gives a non-negative result, or, more exactly, one in the range 0 through 127 in the usual two's complement convention). Some machine operations are described by a single byte, others by two bytes, having the format

> Byte 1   Opcode
> Byte 2   Address field

The set of machine code functions available is quite small. Those marked * in Tables 3.1 and 3.2 affect the condition flags.

The functions in Table 3.1 are all single-byte instructions. Those in Table 3.2 are all double-byte instructions.

The ASSEMBLER for the machine is to have instructions of the form described rather loosely by the syntax diagrams in Figure 3.1 (later these will be extended somewhat).

Any alphanumeric symbol used in the ADDRESS field must also occur somewhere in a LABEL field. A LABEL may have at most eight significant characters.

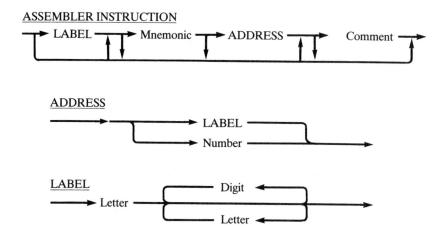

Figure 3.1

Table 3.1

Mnemonic		Opcode		Function
		Hex	Decimal	
NOP		0	0	No operation
CLA		1	1	Clear accumulator
CLX		2	2	Clear index register
INC	*	3	3	Increment accumulator by 1
DEC	*	4	4	Decrement accumulator by 1
INX	*	5	5	Increment index register by 1
DEX	*	6	6	Decrement index register by 1
TAX		7	7	Transfer accumulator to index register
INI	*	8	8	Load accumulator with integer typed at keyboard
INA	*	9	9	Load accumulator with ASCII value typed at keyboard
OTI		A	10	Print accumulator (interpreted as an integer) to screen
OTA		B	11	Print accumulator (interpreted as an ASCII value) to screen. If accumulator is greater than maximum ASCII value, force newline (on machines with reduced character sets, for example)
PSH		C	12	Push accumulator onto stack
POP	*	D	13	Pop stack into accumulator
RET		E	14	Return from subroutine (return address popped from stack)
HLT		F	15	Halt program execution

Table 3.2

Mnemonic			Hex	Decimal	Function
			Opcode		
LDA	*B*	*	10	16	Load accumulator directly with contents of location whose address is given as *B*
LDX	*B*	*	11	17	Load accumulator with contents of location whose address is given as *B*, indexed by contents of *X*-register (that is, an address computed as the value of *B* + *X*)
LDI	*B*	*	12	18	Load accumulator with the immediate value *B*
STA	*B*		13	19	Store accumulator on the location whose address is given as *B*
STX	*B*		14	20	Store accumulator on the location whose address is given as *B*, indexed by contents of *X*-register
ADD	*B*	*	15	21	Add to accumulator the contents of the location whose address is given as *B*
ADX	*B*	*	16	22	Add to accumulator the contents of the location whose address is given as *B*, indexed by contents of *X*-register
ADI	*B*	*	17	23	Add the immediate value *B* directly to accumulator
SUB	*B*	*	18	24	Subtract from accumulator the contents of the location whose address is given as *B*
SBX	*B*	*	19	25	Subtract from accumulator the contents of the location whose address is given as *B*, indexed by contents of *X*-register
SBI	*B*	*	1A	26	Subtract the immediate value *B* directly from accumulator
CMP	*B*	*	1B	27	Compare the accumulator with the contents of the location whose address is given as *B*
CPX	*B*	*	1C	28	Compare the accumulator with the contents of the location whose address is given as *B*, indexed by contents of *X*-register
CPI	*B*	*	1D	29	Compare the accumulator directly with the value *B* (All comparisons are done by virtual subtraction of operand from accumulator and setting flags)
LSP	*B*		1E	30	Load stack pointer with contents of location whose address is given as *B*
LSI	*B*		1F	31	Load stack pointer immediately with the value *B*
BRN	*B*		20	32	Branch to the address given as *B*
BZE	*B*		21	33	Branch to the address given as *B* if the Z condition flag is set
BNZ	*B*		22	34	Branch to the address given as *B* if the Z condition flag is unset

Table 3.2 (cont.)

| Mnemonic | Opcode | | Function |
	Hex	Decimal	
BPZ *B*	23	35	Branch to the address given as *B* if the P condition flag is set
BNG *B*	24	36	Branch to the address given as *B* if the P condition flag is unset
JSR *B*	25	37	Call subroutine whose address is given as *B*, pushing return address onto the stack

The directives for the assembler have the same general form, and include those shown in Table 3.3. A simple example of code in this language is shown in Table 3.4, with machine code assembled. As is conventional, hexadecimal notation is used to show assembled programs; numeric values in the source are specified in decimal, however.

Table 3.3

Label	Mnemonic	Address	Action
not used	BEG	not used	Mark the beginning of the code
not used	END	not used	Mark the end of the code
not used	ORG	address	Specify 'address' in memory where the code following is to be loaded
optional	DC	value	Set aside one (optionally labelled) byte, set initially to the 'value' chosen
optional	DS	length	Set aside 'length' bytes, with optional label associated with the first byte
identifier	EQU	value	Set 'identifier' as a synonym for the given 'value'

3.2 An emulator for the 8-bit machine

An emulator is easily built for the 8-bit machine of the last section, rather similar in many ways to that used in the earlier case study. The shell of this is given in Listing 2, with some useful routines for debugging, and the details are left as an exercise.

Table 3.4

ASSEMBLER				Address		Machine code	
	BEG						
	ORG	125	; Hex 7D				
MAX	EQU	15	; Hex 0F				
	LDA	A		7D	125	10	85
	ADD	B		7F	127	15	86
	STA	C		81	129	13	87
	BRN	LABEL		83	131	20	8C
A	DC	0		85	133	00	
B	DC	12		86	134	0C	
C	DS	5		87	135	??	
					136	??	
					137	??	
					138	??	
					139	??	
LABEL	LDI	MAX		8C	140	12	0F
	ADD	C		8E	142	15	87
	BZE	LABEL		90	144	21	8C
	HLT			92	146	0F	
	END						

Listing 2   Interpreter for simple 8-bit machine (Section 3.1)

```
1  program PMACHINE (INPUT, OUTPUT, CODEFILE, DATA, RESULTS);
2  (*Simple emulator for assembled programs in the language of Section 3.1
3    P.D. Terry    16 January 1985.    Version 1a *)
4  const
5    VERSION = '1a';
6    ADD = 21;  ADI = 23;  ADX = 22;  BNG = 36;  BNZ = 34;  BPZ = 35;
7    BRN = 32;  BZE = 33;  CLA =  1;  CLX =  2;  CMP = 27;  CPI = 29;
8    CPX = 28;  DEC =  4;  DEX =  6;  HLT = 15;  INA =  9;  INC =  3;
9    INI =  8;  INX =  5;  JSR = 37;  LDA = 16;  LDI = 18;  LDX = 17;
10   LSI = 31;  LSP = 30;  NOP =  0;  OTA = 11;  OTI = 10;  POP = 13;
11   PSH = 12;  RET = 14;  SBI = 26;  SBX = 25;  STA = 19;  STX = 20;
12   SUB = 24;  TAX =  7   (*machine ops*);
13   NUL = 39              (*undefined*);
14  type
15    BYTES = 0 .. 255;
16  var
17    (*some implementations require INPUT, OUTPUT : TEXT *)
18    DATA, RESULTS, CODEFILE : TEXT          (*data and code*);
19    CH         : CHAR                       (*last character read*);
20    MCODE      : array [BYTES] of BYTES      (*generated machine code*);
```

```
21   HEXSTRING    : packed array [1 .. 16] of CHAR (*for easy conversion*);
22   VALIDOPCODES : set of 0 .. 37                (*for checking code*);
23
24 procedure HEX (I, N : BYTES);
25 (*Write I as hex digit with N trailing blanks*)
26   begin
27     WRITE(OUTPUT, HEXSTRING[I div 16+1], HEXSTRING[I mod 16+1], ' ':N)
28   end (*HEX*);
29
30 (* +++++++++++++++++++++++++ READCODE +++++++++++++++++++++++++++++ *)
31
32 procedure READCODE;
33 (*Read MCODE from CODEFILE for interpretation*)
34   var
35     I : BYTES;
36   begin
37     for I := 0 to 255 do READ(CODEFILE, MCODE[I])
38   end (*READCODE*);
39
40 (* +++++++++++++++++++++++++ DUMPCODE +++++++++++++++++++++++++++++ *)
41
42 procedure DUMPCODE;
43 (*Dump MCODE to OUTPUT for debugging*)
44   var
45     I, J, THISBYTE : BYTES;
46   begin
47     THISBYTE := 0; WRITELN(OUTPUT);
48     for I := 1 to 16 do
49       begin
50         for J := 1 to 16 do
51           begin
52             WRITE(OUTPUT, MCODE[THISBYTE]:4);
53             THISBYTE := THISBYTE + 1
54           end;
55         WRITELN(OUTPUT)
56       end
57   end (*DUMPCODE*);
58
59 (* +++++++++++++++++++++++++ INTERPRET +++++++++++++++++++++++++ *)
60
61 procedure INTERPRET;
62   const
63     HIGHEST = 127           (*character ordinal value - system dependent*);
64   var
65     A,                      (*accumulator*)
66     SP,                     (*stack pointer*)
```

```
67     X,                    (*index register*)
68     THISCODE,             (*current instruction*)
69     PC      : BYTES       (*program count*);
70     Z, P,                 (*condition flags*)
71     TRACING : BOOLEAN     (*for debugging*);
72     ASCII   : CHAR        (*for character output*);
73     PS      : (RUNNING, FINISHED, EOFCHK, DATCHK, FCTCHK) (*status*);
74
75   procedure CHECKDATA;
76   (*Check 'numeric' data for validity ++++++++ to be supplied here ++++*)
77
78   procedure TRACE;
79   (*Produce trace of registers for debugger*)
80     begin
81       WRITE(OUTPUT, ' OPCODE= '); HEX(THISCODE, 2);
82       WRITE(OUTPUT, 'PC= '); HEX(PC, 2); WRITE(OUTPUT, 'A= ' );  HEX(A, 2);
83       WRITE(OUTPUT, 'X= ' ); HEX(X, 2);  WRITE(OUTPUT, 'SP= '); HEX(SP, 2);
84       WRITELN(OUTPUT, ' Z=', ORD(Z):4, ' P=', ORD(P):4)
85     end (*TRACE*);
86
87   procedure POSTMORTEM;
88     (*Action on execution error*)
89     begin
90       case PS of
91         FCTCHK : WRITE(OUTPUT, 'Illegal opcode');
92         EOFCHK : WRITE(OUTPUT, 'No more data');
93         DATCHK : WRITE(OUTPUT, 'Invalid data');
94       end;
95       WRITELN(OUTPUT, ' at ', PC-1:1);
96       TRACE; DUMPCODE
97     end (*POSTMORTEM*);
98
99   procedure SETFLAGS (REGISTER : BYTES);
100  (*Set P and Z flags from contents of REGISTER ++++ to be supplied here ++++*)
101        begin end;
102
103  begin (*INTERPRET*)
104    Z := FALSE; P := FALSE; A := 0; X := 0; SP := 255; PS := RUNNING;
105    WRITE('Entry point? '); READLN(PC);
106    WRITE('Trace on? '); repeat READLN(CH) until CH in ['Y', 'y', 'N', 'n'];
107    TRACING := CH in ['Y', 'y'];
108    (*Open and RESET(DATA), REWRITE(RESULTS) files as appropriate*)
109    repeat
110      THISCODE := MCODE[PC];
111      if TRACING then TRACE;
112      PC := SUCC(PC);
```

```
113        if not (THISCODE in VALIDOPCODES) then PS := FCTCHK else
114          case THISCODE of
115            NOP : ;
116            CLA : A := 0;
117            CLX : X := 0;
118
119            . . .
120
121            PSH : begin MCODE[SP] := A; SP := PRED(SP) end;
122            POP : begin SP := SUCC(SP); A := MCODE[SP]; SETFLAGS(A) end;
123
124            . . .
125
126            RET : begin SP := SUCC(SP); PC := MCODE[SP] end;
127            HLT : PS := FINISHED;
128
129            . . .
130
131            STA : begin MCODE[MCODE[PC]] := A; PC := SUCC(PC)  end;
132            STX : begin MCODE[(MCODE[PC] + X) mod 256] := A; PC := SUCC(PC) end;
133            . . .
134
135          end (*case*)
136        until PS <> RUNNING;
137        if PS <> FINISHED then POSTMORTEM;
138        (*close RESULTS file if necessary*)
139      end (*INTERPRET*);
140
141  begin (*PMACHINE*)
142    HEXSTRING := '0123456789ABCDEF'; VALIDOPCODES := [0 .. 37];
143    (*open and RESET(CODEFILE), INPUT, OUTPUT as appropriate*)
144    READCODE;
145    INTERPRET;
146    (*close OUTPUT file if necessary*)
147  end (*PMACHINE*).
```

Exercises

3.1 What addressing mode is used by each of the opcodes in our machine?

3.2 Many 8-bit microprocessors have 2-byte (16-bit) index registers, and one, two, and three-byte instructions. What peculiar or restrictive features does our machine possess compared to such processors?

3.3   Complete the emulator for a simple 8-bit machine using the instruction set described above. Bear in mind the limitations of the machine arising from your answer to Exercise 3.2.

3.4   Write programs in the simple ASSEMBLER language to:

(a)   find the largest of three numbers;

(b)   find the average of a set of non-zero numbers, the list being terminated by a zero;

(c)   compute $N!$ for small N (try using an iterative as well as a recursive approach);

(d)   read a word and then write it backwards – the word is terminated with a period. Try using an array and also the stack;

(e)   determine the prime numbers between 0 and 255;

(f)   determine the longest repeated sequence in a sequence of digits;

(g)   read an input sequence, and then write the embedded monotonically increasing sequence;

(h)   read a small array of integers or characters and sort into order.

3.5   Based on your experiences with Exercise 3.4, comment on the usefulness, redundancy and any other features of the code set for the machine.

3.6   How well does the informal description of the ASSEMBLER language serve to allow you to develop programs and an interpreter for the machine?

3.3   One- and two-pass assemblers, and symbol tables

If the reader cares to try the assembly translation process, he or she will realize that this cannot be done on one pass through the ASSEMBLER code. In the silly example given earlier, for example, the instruction

```
LDA   A
```

cannot be translated further than 10 ?? until one knows the address of A, which is only discovered later, when the directive

```
A   DC   0
```

is encountered. In general the process of assembly is always non-trivial, the complication arising, even in a language as simple as this one, from the inevitable presence of **forward references**.

An assembler may solve these problems by performing two distinct passes over the source text. The primary aim of the first pass of such a **two-pass assembler** is to draw up a table, called the **symbol table**, in which, once the pass is complete, all necessary information on each user-defined identifier has been recorded. A second pass over the source then allows full assembly to take place quite easily, referring to the symbol table where necessary to fill in addresses, and values of constants.

For the simple example program at the end of the last section a symbol table might look like Table 3.5.

Table 3.5

Name	Address or value
MAX	15 (Hex 0F)
A	133 (Hex 85)
B	134 (Hex 86)
C	135 (Hex 87)
LABEL	140 (Hex 8C)

Diagrammatically we may represent the action of a two-pass assembler as in Figure 3.2. The first pass can perform other manipulations as well, such as checking for errors. Pass 2 depends on being able to rescan the source code, and so Pass 1 usually makes a copy of this on some backing store, possibly in a slightly altered form from the original.

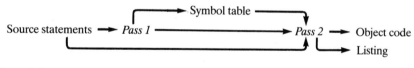

Figure 3.2

The other method of assembly is via a **one-pass assembler**. Here the source is scanned but once, and the construction of the symbol table is rather more complicated, as outstanding references must be recorded for later **fixup** or **back-patching** once their addresses or values become known.

It will rapidly become obvious that construction of a sophisticated assembler, using either method, calls for a fair amount of ingenuity. Consequently, several points will be illustrated rather simply and naïvely below, and refinements will be left to the interested reader in the form of exercises.

Assemblers all make considerable use of tables. There are always (conceptually at least) two of these:

(a) The *opcode translation table* In this will be found (at least) matching pairs of mnemonics and their numeric equivalents. This table is of fixed length in simple assemblers.

(b)   The *symbol table*   In this will be entered (at least) the user-defined identifiers, and their corresponding addresses or values. This table varies in length with the program being assembled.

Two other tables often found in assemblers are:

(c)   The *directive* or *pseudo-op table*   In this will be found (at least) the mnemonics for the directives or pseudo operations. The table is of fixed length, and may be incorporated into the opcode translation table in some cases.

(d)   The *literal table*   In this may be entered various user-defined literals (constants, strings and so on), some of which may not be able to be directly incorporated into machine instructions. For example, an 'immediate mode' instruction such as

```
LDI    250
```

may not be available on a particular machine, although it might be allowed in an ASSEMBLER language for that machine. An assembler might then handle it by replacing it by

```
        LDA    LARGE
        . . . . . . .
LARGE   DC     250
```

with due precaution being taken to store LARGE clear of the code area.

More sophisticated macro-assemblers need several other tables to be able to handle the user-defined opcodes, their parameters, and the source text which constitutes the definition of a macro. We return to this in the next chapter.

3.4   A simple two-pass assembler

The ideas behind two-pass assembly may be made clearer by slowly refining a simple assembler for the language given earlier. The system allows only for the creation of 'fixed address' as opposed to 'relocatable' code, and we assume that the assembler and the assembled code can co-reside in memory. We are confined to write a cross-assembler, not only because no such real machine exists, but also because the machine is far too rudimentary to support a resident assembler – let alone a Pascal host language.

The first pass, as has been stated, has as its primary aim the creation of a symbol table. The 'name' entries in this are easily made as the label fields of the source are read. Even though it is not responsible for code generation, to complete the 'address' entries the first pass has to keep track, as it scans the source, of the addresses at which the code and data values (which will later be assembled) will be located. These addresses are controlled by the directives ORG and DS (which affect the address explicitly), as well as by the directive DC and the opcodes which will later result in the creation of one or two machine words. The directive EQU is a special case; it simply gives a naming facility.

The opcode and symbol tables might be most simply implemented as linear arrays, for example:

```
var
   OPTABLE :  array [0 .. NUMBEROPCODES] of
                  record
                    SPELLING : packed array [1 .. 8] of CHAR;
                    OPCODE  : 0 .. 255
                  end;
   SYMBOLTABLE : array [0 .. SOMELIMIT] of
                  record
                    NAME    : packed array [1 .. 8] of CHAR;
                    ADDRESS : 0 .. 255
                  end;
   LASTSYM : 0 .. SOMELIMIT;
```

but it is not suggested that these structures are anything like the best ones to use in any but totally trivial examples. The opcode table would be initialized before execution commenced, so that all mnemonics and opcodes had their known values; the symbol table would be initialized before assembly commenced by setting LASTSYM to zero.

Pass one is responsible for source handling, lexical, syntactic and semantic analysis. In essence this might be described by an algorithm like the following, where, we hasten to add, considerable liberties have been taken with our Pascal-like syntax.

```
initialize tables and set PASSONE ← TRUE
while PASSONE do
   read line of source and unpack into constituent fields
      LABEL, MNEMONIC, ADDRESSFIELD (*which could be a NAME or NUMBER*)
   use MNEMONIC to identify OPCODE from OPTABLE
   copy line of source to backing store for later use by pass two
   case MNEMONIC of
      "BEG": NEXTBYTE ← 0
      "ORG": NEXTBYTE ← ADDRESSFIELD.NUMBER
      "DS ": if LABEL is present then add (LABEL, NEXTBYTE) to SYMBOLTABLE
            NEXTBYTE ← NEXTBYTE + ADDRESSFIELD.NUMBER
      "EQU": add (LABEL, ADDRESSFIELD.NUMBER) to SYMBOLTABLE
      "END": PASSONE ← FALSE:
      all others (*including DC*):
            if LABEL is present then add (LABEL, NEXTBYTE) to SYMBOLTABLE
            NEXTBYTE ← NEXTBYTE + number of bytes to be generated
   end (*case*)
```

Pass two is responsible mainly for code generation, but may have to redo some of the source handling and syntactic analysis.

```
rewind backing store file and set PASSTWO ← TRUE
while PASSTWO do
  read a line of source from backing store
  unpack into constituent fields LABEL, MNEMONIC, ADDRESSFIELD
  use MNEMONIC to identify OPCODE from OPTABLE
  case MNEMONIC of
    "BEG": NEXTBYTE ← 0
    "ORG": NEXTBYTE ← ADDRESSFIELD.NUMBER
    "DS ": NEXTBYTE ← NEXTBYTE + ADDRESSFIELD.NUMBER
    "EQU": no action (*EQU dealt with on pass one*)
    "END": PASSTWO ← FALSE
    "DC ": MCODE[NEXTBYTE] ← VALUEOF(ADDRESSFIELD); NEXTBYTE ← NEXTBYTE + 1
    all others:
      MCODE[NEXTBYTE] ← OPCODE;  NEXTBYTE ← NEXTBYTE + 1
      if a two-byte OPCODE then
        MCODE[NEXTBYTE] ← VALUEOF(ADDRESSFIELD); NEXTBYTE ← NEXTBYTE + 1
      end (*if*)
  end (*case*)
  produce source listing of this line
```

The simplest way of searching the OPTABLE might be to use the algorithm

```
OPTABLE[0].SPELLING ← MNEMONIC (*sentinel*)
LOOK ← NUMBEROPCODES
while MNEMONIC ≠ OPTABLE[LOOK].SPELLING do LOOK ← LOOK - 1
```

although it is easy to improve on this tremendously by ensuring that the OPTABLE is sorted into ascending order by mnemonic, and then using a binary search. Even better ways involve the use of hashing functions.

Adding an entry to a symbol table (declared as above) is easy.

```
LASTSYM ← LASTSYM + 1
SYMBOLTABLE[LASTSYM].NAME ← LABEL
SYMBOLTABLE[LASTSYM].ADDRESS ← NEXTBYTE
```

If we were to use this simple symbol table structure, then on the second pass the VALUEOF(ADDRESSFIELD) could be found as follows:

```
if ADDRESSFIELD is an INTEGER
  then VALUEOFADDRESSFIELD ← ADDRESSFIELD.NUMBER
  else (*scan symbol table for matching entry*)
    SYMBOLTABLE[0].NAME ← ADDRESSFIELD.NAME (*sentinel*)
    LOOK ← LASTSYM
    while ADDRESSFIELD.NAME ≠ SYMBOLTABLE[LOOK].NAME do LOOK ← LOOK - 1
    VALUEOFADDRESSFIELD ← SYMBOLTABLE[LOOK].ADDRESS
```

although, again, it might be worth sorting the table between passes and then using a binary search.

These structures are rather too simple, as, indeed, are our algorithms, which assume that the searches will always succeed. In refining our ideas into a working assembler we shall try to improve on them.

The source code for our first assembler will be found in Listing 3, and, in the description which follows, reference will be made to this listing by line number.

3.4.1 Source handling

In terms of Figure 2.5, the first phase will concern the source character handler, which must scan the SOURCE text, and analyse it into lines, from which the lexical analyser will be able to extract tokens or symbols. Such a phase is easily written. We introduce the declarations

```
const
  LINEMAX = 81                    (*limit on source line*);
type
  LINEINDEX = 0 .. LINEMAX;
var
  CH      : CHAR                  (*Last character read*);
  CC,                            (*Character pointer*)
  LL      : LINEINDEX             (*Line length*);
  LINE    : ARRAY [LINEINDEX] of CHAR (*Last line read*);
  ENDLINE : BOOLEAN              (*True at end of source line*);
```

and then a Pascal procedure GETCH for returning the next character in SOURCE follows quite easily (lines 118–130 of Listing 3).

Notes

(a)   Before this procedure is called for the first time it will be necessary to initialize CC = LL = 0, so that the first call will read the first line.

(b)   No provision has been made here for producing a source listing. It could be done at this point, but in the case of a two-pass assembler the listing is usually delayed until the second pass, when it can be made more complete and useful to the user. In any case, a free-format input can be converted to a fixed-format output, which will probably look considerably better.

(c)   Any client routines (those that call GETCH) should not have to worry about anything other than the values of CH, CC and ENDLINE. The main (indeed, the only) client routine is, of course, the lexical analyser.

(d)   Note that a blank character is added to the end of LINE. This is useful for ensuring that an identifier or number which ends a line is properly terminated.

3.4.2 Lexical analysis

The next phase to be tackled is that of lexical analysis. In the simple language used here we can recognize that the source characters can be assembled into either numbers, alphanumeric names (as for labels or opcodes) or comment strings. Accordingly we introduce the further constant and type definitions

```
const
  ALENG = 8                              (*length of short string*);
  SLENG = 25                             (*length of comment*);
  BLANK = '        '                     (*blank short string*);
  BLANKSTRING = '                    '   (*blank comment string*);
type
  ALFA    = packed array [1 .. ALENG] of CHAR;
  STRINGS = packed array [1 .. SLENG] of CHAR;
  SYMBOLS = (NULSYM, IDSYM, NUMSYM, COMSYM);
```

The interface between lexical and syntax analyser can then be provided by the following variables, which must be defined by the lexical analysis.

```
var
  SYM     : SYMBOLS (*Last SYMBOL read*);
  ID      : ALFA    (*Last IDENTIFIER read*);
  NUM     : INTEGER (*Last NUMBER read*);
  ASTRING : STRINGS (*Last COMMENT read*);
```

Providing a procedure GETSYM for the determination of these symbols is quite easy, being governed essentially by a case statement, as can be seen from lines 158–216 of Listing 3. The essence of this – again taking considerable liberties with syntax – may be expressed

```
procedure GETSYM;
(*Get next SYMBOL from SOURCE*)

  procedure GETWORD;
  (*Assemble identifier ID or opcode, in UPPERCASE for consistency*)

  procedure GETNUMBER;
  (*Assemble number NUM*)

  begin (*GETSYM*)
    skip leading spaces, or to end of line
    case CH of
      letters: SYM := IDSYM; GETWORD;
      digits : SYM := NUMSYM; GETNUMBER;
      ';'    : SYM := COMSYM; unpack ASTRING;
      ' '    : SYM := NULSYM (*line had no more symbols*)
  end (*GETSYM*);
```

Notes

(a) The code given assumes the existence of a Pascal implementation which recognizes a full character set, and which can support set of CHAR.

(b) In determining the value of NUM we also copy the digits into ID for the purposes of later listing. At this stage we assume that overflow will not occur in determining the value of NUM.

(c) Identifiers longer than ALENG and comments longer than SLENG are merely truncated.

(d) Identifiers are converted to upper case for consistency. Comments are left alone.

(e) A null symbol is returned if the end of a line is reached without finding another symbol.

3.4.3 Syntax analysis

Syntax analysis in the first pass requires that we unpack a source line into its constituent fields, using the GETSYM routine, and that we also write the source line to a WORK file for later use by the second pass. The procedure for unpacking is relatively straightforward, but has to allow for the various combinations of present or absent fields. The syntax analyser can be programmed fairly simply following the syntax diagram in Figure 3.1 as a flowchart. The essence of this is as follows; the complete code can be found in lines 218–251 of Listing 3.

```
procedure SYNTAXANALYSIS;
(*Unpack a LINE into SOURCELINE for further analysis and ready to
  save on WORK file for second pass*)
  procedure GETADDRESS;
  (*handle ADDRESSFIELD - later will get more complicated*)
  begin (*SYNTAXANALYSIS*)
    with SOURCELINE do
      initialize all fields to blank
      assume ALPHAMERIC address
      look at first character CH on line
      if CH is neither ';' or ' ' then deal with LAB field
      deal with optional MNEMONIC, ADDRESSFIELD, COMMENT
  end (*SYNTAXANALYSIS*);
```

Notes

(a) The procedure for GETADDRESS is simple here, but will later be modified to allow expressions as addresses.

(b) To save unpacking all over again on pass two we introduce further types

```
const
  NUMBEROPCODES = 45 (*for this simple language*);
```

```
type
  OPCODES   = 0 .. NUMBEROPCODES;
  KINDS = (NUMERIC, ALPHAMERIC);
  ADDRESSES = record (*address fields*)
                  NUMBER : INTEGER (*value if known*);
                  NAME   : ALFA    (*character representation*);
                  KIND   : KINDS
              end (*ADDRESSES*);
  UNPACKEDLINES = record (*source text, unpacked into symbols*)
                  LAB, MNEMONIC : ALFA;
                  OPENTRY       : OPCODES;
                  ADDRESSFIELD  : ADDRESSES;
                  COMMENT       : STRINGS
              end (*UNPACKEDLINES*);
```

Here OPENTRY is a field which can, and indeed must, be defined on the first pass by comparing the MNEMONIC with the entries in the opcode table. We also have associated variables:

```
var
  SOURCELINE : UNPACKEDLINES;
  WORK       : file of UNPACKEDLINES;
```

As its name suggests, WORK is an intermediate work file for communicating between the two passes. It will be discarded after assembly, and so can, in principle, remain hidden from the user. In practice some implementations may demand that it be associated with a known external file.

3.4.4 Semantic analysis

The code for the first pass can now be refined from the algorithms given earlier. Mostly this is semantic analysis dealing with the construction of the symbol table. The code is to be found on lines 256–320 of Listing 3.

Notes

(a) The opcode table is conveniently stored in an array of record type

```
var
  OPTABLE : array [OPCODES] of
              record
                SPELLING : ALFA;
                OPCODE   : OPCODES
              end (*OPTABLE*);
```

(b) We have chosen to define a function to find the correct entry in the opcode table. Rather than use the simple linear search suggested earlier, we give a simple (but faster) binary search in function FINDOPENTRY. If the mnemonic cannot be matched we return a NUL entry (in the case of a line with a blank opcode field) or an ERR entry (when an opcode is provided, but cannot be recognized and must be assumed to be in error).

(c) Clearly the fields in OPTABLE need to be initialized before the assembly commences. A way for doing this will be suggested later, when all the initialization code will be grouped together.

(d) The semantic analyser needs to keep track of the location counter NEXTBYTE, which is updated as opcodes are recognized, and which may be explicitly altered by the directives ORG, DS and DC. The arithmetic is done modulo-256 because of the limitations of the target machine. Even though no code is generated until the second pass, NEXTBYTE must be tracked on both passes.

(e) Although ADDTOSYMBOLTABLE could be defined along the simple lines suggested earlier, it would be preferable, if one were implementing the assembler in a language like Pascal which supports 'dynamic' allocation, to set the symbol table up as a stack or, better still, as a tree. Here we have shown how a stack could be used, and left the tree refinement as an exercise. We introduce further types SYMLINKS and SYMENTRIES, and one variable LASTSYM:

```
type
  BYTES = 0 .. 255;
  SYMLINKS  = ↑SYMENTRIES;
  SYMENTRIES = record (*symbol table*)
                 NAME    : ALFA     (*name*);
                 SLINK   : SYMLINKS (*to next entry*);
                 ADDRESS : BYTES    (*value when defined*)
               end (*SYMENTRIES*);
var
  LASTSYM : SYMLINKS              (*last entry in symbol table*);
```

The procedure follows the lines of those to be found in many texts on Pascal programming, and hopefully needs no further comment here.

3.4.5 Code generation

On the second pass we get the unpacked source lines from the WORK file, and proceed to generate the code, at the same time producing the source listing. The code for this can be found in lines 325–404 of Listing 3.

Notes

(a) As stated earlier, we assume that all the code can be contained in an array of length 256

```
var
  MCODE   : array [BYTES] of BYTES   (*generated machine code*);
```

A more realistic assembler might not be able to do this, but for a two-pass assembler few problems would arise, as the code could be written out to a file as fast as it was generated.

(b) We shall have to be able to determine the value of an address (either directly, or from the symbol table). The search in the latter is easily programmed as function VALUEOF (lines 329–345). We are assuming that all labels will have been explicitly declared, so that the symbol table will be complete at the end of the first pass. Errors such as arise from non-declaration will be dealt with in the next chapter.

(c) Contrary to what was suggested earlier, we do not have to repeat the lexical and syntactic analysis, if the unpacked line is written to WORK, rather than the original source. Of course, we could dispense with WORK and rescan SOURCE, but that would be wasteful.

3.4.6 User interface

An assembler program typically gives the user a listing of the source code, usually with assembled code alongside it. Occasionally extra frills are provided, like cross-reference tables for identifiers and so on. Our one is quite simple, as can be seen from the code in various places. We note that

(a) The second pass is somewhat cluttered by the code used to produce the source listing for the user. Here we have introduced calls on a simple procedure HEX to print out the value of a byte in hexadecimal notation. Given that we have declared

```
var HEXSTRING : packed array [1 .. 16] of CHAR;
```

and initialized

```
HEXSTRING := '0123456789ABCDEF';
```

the conversion follows easily in lines 110–114.

(b) It may be useful to print the symbol table, which could be done at any time after the first pass has set it up. In terms of our linked structure this is quite easily done by procedure PRINTSYMBOLTABLE (lines 132–150), which follows the standard method of scanning a linked list.

(c) Exactly how the object code is to be treated is a matter for debate. Here we have just introduced a simple procedure DUMPCODE (lines 406–422), which dumps the 256 bytes in a form suitable for input to the machine emulator program of Listing 2.

(d)   Little attempt has been made to report on errors, save in the case of an invalid opcode (the line is simply ignored).

3.4.7 Initialization

The last point to be considered is that of initialization before the assembly commences. This is quite straightforward. The opcode values can be defined as constants (lines 6–16), and initialization of the OPTABLE is dealt with in procedure INITIALIZE (lines 426–470), which also provides some other easy initialization code for the elements of CC, LL, MCODE, LASTSYM, ONEBYTEOPS, TWOBYTEOPS and HEXSTRING.

The assembler main program is now trivially easy:

```
begin (*ASSEMBLER*)
   INITIALIZE;
   FIRSTPASS;
   SECONDPASS;
   DUMPCODE
end (*ASSEMBLER*).
```

An example of the output produced by this assembler is given below. The program does not, of course, do anything useful.

```
UU                     BEG
7D                     ORG    125     ; HEX 7D
7D           MAX       EQU    15      ; HEX 0F
7D    10 85            LDA    A
7F    15 86            ADD    B
81    13 87            STA    C
83    20 8C            BRN    LABEL
85    00   A           DC     0
86    0C   B           DC     12
87         C           DS     5
8C    12 0F LABEL      LDI    MAX
8E    15 87            ADD    C
90    21 8C            BZE    LABEL
92    0F               HLT
93                     END

Symbol Table
------------

LABEL    8C   140
C        87   135
B        86   134
A        85   133
MAX      0F   15
```

Listing 3 Two-pass assembler for language of Section 3.1

```
1   program ASSEMBLER (INPUT, OUTPUT, CODEFILE, WORK);
2   (*Simple two-pass assembler for language of Section 3.1
3     P.D. Terry,  May 1986.     Version 1b*)
4   const
5     VERSION = '1b';
6     ADD = 21;  ADI = 23;  ADX = 22;  BNG = 36;  BNZ = 34;  BPZ = 35;
7     BRN = 32;  BZE = 33;  CLA =  1;  CLX =  2;  CMP = 27;  CPI = 29;
8     CPX = 28;  DEC =  4;  DEX =  6;  HLT = 15;  INA =  9;  INC =  3;
9     INI =  8;  INX =  5;  JSR = 37;  LDA = 16;  LDI = 18;  LDX = 17;
10    LSI = 31;  ISP = 30;  NOP =  0;  OTA = 11;  OTI = 10;  POP = 13;
11    PSH = 12;  RET = 14;  SBI = 26;  SBX = 25;  STA = 19;  STX = 20;
12    SUB = 24;  TAX =  7                        (*Machine ops*);
13    BEG = 40;  DC  = 41;  DS  = 42;  FIN = 43;
14    EQU = 44;  ORG = 45                        (*directives*);
15    NUL = 39                                   (*undefined*);
16    ERR = 38                                   (*error*);
17    NUMBEROPCODES = 45;
18
19    (* ++++++++ used by the lexical analyser and syntax analyser ++++++++ *)
20
21    LINEMAX = 81                          (*limit on source line*);
22    ALENG = 8                             (*length of short string*);
23    SLENG = 25                            (*length of comment*);
24    BLANK = '        '                    (*blank short string*);
25    BLANKSTRING = '                         ' (*blank comment string*);
26
27  type
28    BYTES = 0 .. 255;
29    OPCODES = 0 .. NUMBEROPCODES;
30
31    (* ++++++++ used by the lexical analyser +++++++++++++++++++++++++++++ *)
32
33    LINEINDEX = 0 .. LINEMAX;
34    ALFA      = packed array [1 .. ALENG] of CHAR;
35    STRINGS   = packed array [1 .. SLENG] of CHAR;
36    SYMBOLS   = (NULSYM, IDSYM, NUMSYM, COMSYM);
37
38    (* ++++++++ used by the syntax  analyser +++++++++++++++++++++++++++++ *)
39
40    KINDS = (NUMERIC, ALPHAMERIC);
41    ADDRESSES = record (*addressfields*)
42                  NUMBER : INTEGER (*value if known*);
43                  NAME   : ALFA    (*character representation*);
44                  KIND   : KINDS
```

```
45                  end (*ADDRESSES*);
46      UNPACKEDLINES = record (*source text, unpacked into symbols*)
47                     LAB, MNEMONIC : ALFA;
48                     OPENTRY      : OPCODES;
49                     ADDRESSFIELD : ADDRESSES;
50                     COMMENT      : STRINGS
51                  end (*UNPACKEDLINES*);
52
53      (* ++++++++ used by the semantic analyser +++++++++++++++++++++++++++ *)
54
55      SYMLINKS = ↑SYMENTRIES;
56      SYMENTRIES = record (*symbol table*)
57                     NAME    : ALFA      (*name*);
58                     SLINK   : SYMLINKS  (*to next entry*);
59                     ADDRESS : BYTES     (*value when defined*)
60                  end (*SYMENTRIES*);
61   var
62      (* ++++++++ used by the character handler +++++++++++++++++++++++++++ *)
63
64      (*some implementations require declaration of INPUT, OUTPUT : TEXT *)
65      SOURCE, CODEFILE : TEXT;
66      CH       : CHAR                     (*Last character read*);
67      CC,                                 (*Character pointer*)
68      LL       : LINEINDEX                (*Line length*);
69      LINE     : ARRAY [LINEINDEX] of CHAR (*Last line read*);
70      HEXSTRING : packed array [1 .. 16] of CHAR  (*For conversion*);
71      ENDLINE   : BOOLEAN                 (*True at end of source line*);
72
73      (* ++++++++ used by the lexical analyser +++++++++++++++++++++++++++ *)
74
75      SYM      : SYMBOLS                  (*Last SYMBOL read*);
76      ID       : ALFA                    (*Last IDENTIFIER read*);
77      NUM      : INTEGER                  (*Last NUMBER read*);
78      ASTRING  : STRINGS                  (*Last COMMENT read*);
79
80      (* ++++++++ used by the syntax analyser +++++++++++++++++++++++++++ *)
81
82      SOURCELINE : UNPACKEDLINES;
83      WORK       : file of UNPACKEDLINES;
84
85      (* ++++++++ used by the semantic analyser +++++++++++++++++++++++++++ *)
86
87      OPTABLE : array [OPCODES] of (*attributes*)
88                 record
89                    SPELLING : ALFA;
90                    OPCODE   : OPCODES
```

```
91               end (*OPTABLE*);
92    ONEBYTEOPS, TWOBYTEOPS : set of OPCODES;
93    LASTSYM : SYMLINKS                    (*last entry in symbol table*);
94
95    (* ++++++++ used by the code generator +++++++++++++++++++s++++++++++++ *)
96
97    NEXTBYTE : BYTES                       (*location counter*);
98    MCODE    : array [BYTES] of BYTES      (*generated machine code*);
99
100   procedure QUIT (N : INTEGER);
101   (* ++++++++++ implementation dependent, for handling fatal errors ++++++ *)
102     begin
103       case N of
104         1: WRITELN(OUTPUT, 'Incomplete program');
105         2: WRITELN(OUTPUT, 'Unrecognized character')
106       end;
107       (*close OUTPUT file if necessary and abort program*)
108     end (*QUIT*);
109
110   procedure HEX (I, N : BYTES);
111   (*Write I as hex number, followed by N blanks*)
112     begin
113       WRITE(OUTPUT, HEXSTRING[I div 16 + 1], HEXSTRING[I mod 16 + 1], ' ':N)
114     end (*HEX*);
115
116   (* +++++++++++++++++++++++++ Source handler +++++++++++++++++++++++++++ *)
117
118     procedure GETCH;
119     (*Get next character from SOURCE*)
120       begin
121         if CC = LL then
122           begin (*new line*)
123             if EOF(SOURCE) then QUIT(1);
124             LL := 0; CC := 0;
125             while not EOLN(SOURCE) do
126               begin LL := LL + 1; READ(SOURCE,CH); LINE[LL] := CH end;
127             LL := LL + 1; READLN(SOURCE); LINE[LL] := ' ' (*end clearly blank*)
128           end (*new line*);
129         CC := CC + 1; CH := LINE[CC]; ENDLINE := CC = LL
130       end (*GETCH*);
131
132     procedure PRINTSYMBOLTABLE;
133     (*Summarize symbol table at end of listing*)
134       var
135         SYMENTRY : SYMLINKS;
136       begin
```

```
137        WRITELN(OUTPUT);
138        WRITELN(OUTPUT, 'Symbol Table'); WRITELN(OUTPUT, '------------');
139        SYMENTRY := LASTSYM;
140        while SYMENTRY <> nil do
141          begin
142            with SYMENTRY ↑ do
143              begin
144                WRITE(OUTPUT, NAME, ' '); HEX(ADDRESS, 1);
145                WRITELN(OUTPUT, ADDRESS:5)
146              end;
147            SYMENTRY := SYMENTRY ↑.SLINK
148          end;
149        WRITELN(OUTPUT)
150      end (*PRINTSYMBOLTABLE*);
151
152 (* ++++++++++++++++++ Syntax and lexical analyser +++++++++++++++++++++++ *)
153
154 procedure SYNTAXANALYSIS;
155 (*Unpack a LINE into SOURCELINE for further analysis and ready to save on
156   WORK file for second pass*)
157
158   procedure GETSYM;
159   (*Get next SYMBOL from SOURCE*)
160     var
161       K : INTEGER;
162
163     function ALETTER : BOOLEAN;
164       begin ALETTER := CH in ['A' .. 'Z', 'a' .. 'z'] end (*ALETTER*);
165
166     function ADIGIT : BOOLEAN;
167       begin ADIGIT :=  CH in ['0' .. '9'] end (*ADIGIT*);
168
169     function DIGIT : INTEGER;
170       begin DIGIT := ORD(CH) - ORD('0') end (*DIGIT*);
171
172     procedure GETWORD;
173     (*Assemble identifier or opcode, in UPPERCASE for consistency*)
174       begin
175         while ALETTER or ADIGIT do
176           begin
177             if CH in ['a'..'z'] then CH := CHR(ORD(CH) - ORD('a') + ORD('A'));
178             if K <= ALENG then begin ID[K] := CH; K := K + 1 end;
179             GETCH
180           end
181       end (*GETWORD*);
182
```

```
183     procedure GETNUMBER;
184       begin
185         while ADIGIT do
186           begin
187             NUM := 10 * NUM + DIGIT;
188             if K <= ALENG then begin ID[K] := CH; K := K + 1 end;
189             GETCH
190           end
191       end (*GETNUMBER*);
192
193   begin (*GETSYM*)
194     NUM := 0; K := 1; ID := BLANK;
195     while (CH = ' ') and not ENDLINE do GETCH;
196     if not (ADIGIT or ALETTER or (CH in [';', ' ']) ) then QUIT(2);
197     case CH of
198       'a', 'b', 'c', 'd', 'e', 'f', 'g', 'h', 'i', 'j', 'k', 'l', 'm',
199       'n', 'o', 'p', 'q', 'r', 's', 't', 'u', 'v', 'w', 'x', 'y', 'z',
200       'A', 'B', 'C', 'D', 'E', 'F', 'G', 'H', 'I', 'J', 'K', 'L', 'M',
201       'N', 'O', 'P', 'Q', 'R', 'S', 'T', 'U', 'V', 'W', 'X', 'Y', 'Z':
202         begin SYM := IDSYM; GETWORD end;
203       '0', '1', '2', '3', '4', '5', '6', '7', '8', '9':
204         begin SYM := NUMSYM; GETNUMBER end;
205       ';':
206         begin
207           SYM := COMSYM; ASTRING := BLANKSTRING;
208           while not ENDLINE do
209             begin
210               if K <= SLENG then begin ASTRING[K] := CH; K := K + 1 end;
211               GETCH
212             end
213         end;
214       ' ': SYM := NULSYM;
215     end (*case*)
216   end (*GETSYM*);
217
218   procedure GETADDRESS;
219   (*Unpack the address field of LINE into SOURCELINE*)
220     begin
221       with SOURCELINE, ADDRESSFIELD do
222         begin
223           if SYM = NUMSYM then KIND := NUMERIC;
224           NUMBER := NUM; NAME := ID
225         end;
226       GETSYM (*comment*)
227     end (*GETADDRESS*);
228
```

```
229     begin (*SYNTAXANALYSIS*)
230       with SOURCELINE do
231         begin
232           LAB := BLANK; COMMENT := BLANKSTRING; MNEMONIC := BLANK;
233           with ADDRESSFIELD do
234             begin NUMBER := 0; KIND := ALPHAMERIC; NAME := BLANK end;
235           GETCH;
236           if not (CH in [';', ' ']) then begin GETSYM; LAB := ID end;
237           GETSYM (*probably an opcode*);
238           if SYM = COMSYM then COMMENT := ASTRING
239           else if SYM <> NULSYM then
240             begin
241               MNEMONIC := ID;
242               GETSYM (*probably an address*);
243               if SYM = COMSYM then COMMENT := ASTRING
244               else if SYM <> NULSYM then
245                 begin
246                   GETADDRESS;
247                   if SYM = COMSYM then COMMENT := ASTRING
248                 end
249             end
250         end (*with SOURCELINE*)
251     end (*SYNTAXANALYSIS*);
252
253
254   (* +++++++++++++++++++++++++++++++ FIRSTPASS +++++++++++++++++++++++++ *)
255
256   procedure FIRSTPASS;
257     var
258       PASSONE : BOOLEAN;
259
260     function FINDOPENTRY (MNEMONIC : ALFA) : OPCODES;
261     (*Search opcode table (binary search) *)
262       var
263         LOOK, L, R : INTEGER;
264       begin
265         L := 1; R := NUMBEROPCODES;
266         repeat
267           LOOK := (L + R) div 2;
268           if MNEMONIC > OPTABLE[LOOK].SPELLING
269             then L := LOOK + 1 else R := LOOK - 1
270         until (MNEMONIC = OPTABLE[LOOK].SPELLING) or (L > R);
271         if MNEMONIC = OPTABLE[LOOK].SPELLING
272           then FINDOPENTRY := LOOK else FINDOPENTRY := 0 (*ERR entry*)
273       end (*FINDOPENTRY*);
274
```

```
275    procedure ADDTOSYMBOLTABLE (LAB : ALFA; ADR : BYTES);
276    (*Add LAB to symbol table with value ADR*)
277      var
278        SYMENTRY : SYMLINKS;
279      begin
280        NEW(SYMENTRY);
281        with SYMENTRY ↑ do
282          begin NAME := LAB; SLINK := LASTSYM; ADDRESS := ADR end;
283        LASTSYM := SYMENTRY
284      end (*ADDTOSYMBOLTABLE*);
285
286    begin (*FIRSTPASS*)
287      PASSONE := TRUE; NEXTBYTE := 0;
288      while PASSONE do
289        begin
290          SYNTAXANALYSIS;
291          with SOURCELINE do
292            begin
293              OPENTRY := FINDOPENTRY(MNEMONIC);
294              with OPTABLE[OPENTRY] do
295                begin
296                  if OPCODE in [BEG, ORG, DS, EQU, FIN, NUL]
297                  then
298                    case OPCODE of
299                      BEG: NEXTBYTE := 0;
300                      ORG: NEXTBYTE := ADDRESSFIELD.NUMBER mod 256;
301                      DS, NUL:
302                        begin
303                          if LAB <> BLANK then ADDTOSYMBOLTABLE(LAB, NEXTBYTE);
304                          NEXTBYTE := (NEXTBYTE + ADDRESSFIELD.NUMBER) mod 256
305                        end;
306                      EQU: ADDTOSYMBOLTABLE(LAB, ADDRESSFIELD.NUMBER);
307                      FIN: PASSONE := FALSE;
308                    end (*case*)
309                  else (*machine ops and DC*)
310                    begin
311                      if LAB <> BLANK then ADDTOSYMBOLTABLE(LAB, NEXTBYTE);
312                      if OPCODE in TWOBYTEOPS
313                        then NEXTBYTE := (NEXTBYTE + 2) mod 256
314                        else NEXTBYTE := (NEXTBYTE + 1) mod 256
315                    end;
316                  WORK ↑ := SOURCELINE; PUT(WORK) (*save for pass two*)
317                end (*with OPTABLE[OPENTRY]*)
318            end (*with SOURCELINE*)
319        end (*while PASSONE*);
320    end (*FIRSTPASS*);
```

```
321
322
323   (* +++++++++++++++++++++++++++++++++++++ SECOND PASS +++++++++++++++++++++ *)
324
325   procedure SECONDPASS;
326     var
327       PASSTWO : BOOLEAN;
328
329     function VALUEOF (ADDRESSFIELD : ADDRESSES) : BYTES;
330     (*Determine value of ADDRESSFIELD, possibly from symbol table*)
331       var
332         SYMENTRY: SYMLINKS;
333       begin
334         case ADDRESSFIELD.KIND OF
335           NUMERIC :
336             VALUEOF := ADDRESSFIELD.NUMBER mod 256;
337           ALPHAMERIC:
338             begin
339               SYMENTRY := LASTSYM;
340               while ADDRESSFIELD.NAME <> SYMENTRY ↑.NAME do
341                 SYMENTRY := SYMENTRY ↑.SLINK;
342               VALUEOF := SYMENTRY ↑.ADDRESS
343             end (*ALPHAMERIC*)
344         end (*case*)
345       end (*VALUEOF*);
346
347     begin (*SECONDPASS*)
348       PASSTWO := TRUE; NEXTBYTE := 0;
349       RESET(WORK);
350       while PASSTWO do
351         begin
352           with WORK↑, OPTABLE[OPENTRY]  do
353             begin
354               if OPCODE in [BEG, ORG, DS, EQU, FIN, DC]
355                 then
356                   begin
357                     case OPCODE OF
358                       BEG: begin NEXTBYTE := 0; HEX(NEXTBYTE, 10) end;
359                       ORG:
360                         begin
361                           NEXTBYTE := VALUEOF(ADDRESSFIELD); HEX(NEXTBYTE, 10)
362                         end;
363                       DS:
364                         begin
365                           HEX(NEXTBYTE, 10);
366                           NEXTBYTE := (NEXTBYTE + VALUEOF(ADDRESSFIELD)) mod 256
```

```
367                        end;
368                    EQU: HEX(NEXTBYTE, 10);
369                    FIN: begin HEX(NEXTBYTE, 10); PASSTWO := FALSE end;
370                    DC:
371                      begin
372                        HEX(NEXTBYTE, 4);
373                        MCODE[NEXTBYTE] := VALUEOF(ADDRESSFIELD);
374                        HEX(MCODE[NEXTBYTE], 4);
375                        NEXTBYTE := (NEXTBYTE + 1) mod 256
376                      end (*DC*);
377                  end (*case*);
378                end (*directives*)
379              else
380                if (OPCODE <> NUL) and (OPCODE <> ERR)
381                  then
382                    begin (*Machine ops*)
383                      HEX(NEXTBYTE, 4); MCODE[NEXTBYTE] := OPCODE;
384                      HEX(MCODE[NEXTBYTE], 1);
385                      NEXTBYTE := (NEXTBYTE + 1) mod 256;
386                      if OPCODE in TWOBYTEOPS
387                        then
388                          begin
389                            MCODE[NEXTBYTE] := VALUEOF(ADDRESSFIELD);
390                            HEX(MCODE[NEXTBYTE], 1);
391                            NEXTBYTE := (NEXTBYTE + 1) mod 256
392                          end
393                        else WRITE(OUTPUT, '   ')
394                    end (*machine ops*)
395                  else
396                    if OPCODE = NUL
397                      then WRITE(OUTPUT, '           ')
398                      else WRITE(OUTPUT, 'Error      ');
399            WRITELN(OUTPUT, LAB, MNEMONIC:6, ADDRESSFIELD.NAME:10, COMMENT)
400          end (*with*);
401        GET(WORK)
402      end (*while*);
403    PRINTSYMBOLTABLE
404  end (*SECONDPASS*);
405
406  procedure DUMPCODE;
407  (*Dump MCODE to CODEFILE for later loading*)
408    var
409    I, J, THISBYTE : INTEGER;
410    begin
411      (*open and REWRITE(CODEFILE) as appropriate*)
412      THISBYTE := 0;
```

```
413       for I := 1 to 16 do
414         begin
415           for J := 1 to 16 do
416             begin
417               WRITE(CODEFILE, MCODE[THISBYTE] : 4); THISBYTE := THISBYTE + 1
418             end;
419           WRITELN(CODEFILE)
420         end;
421       (*close CODEFILE if necessary*)
422     end (*DUMPCODE*);
423
424  (* ++++++++++++++++++++++ Table initialization ++++++++++++++++++++++ *)
425
426  procedure INITIALIZE;
427  (*Initialize opcode table and various other variables*)
428     var
429       I, J : INTEGER;
430
431     procedure ENTER (ID : ALFA; THISCODE : OPCODES);
432       begin
433         with OPTABLE[I] do begin SPELLING := ID; OPCODE := THISCODE end;
434         I := I + 1
435       end (*ENTER*);
436
437     begin
438       I := 0 (*enter opcodes and mnemonics in alphabetic order*);
439       ENTER('Error ', ERR) (*bogus one for erroneous data*);
440       ENTER('      ', NUL) (*blank one for line without opcode*);
441       ENTER('ADD   ', ADD); ENTER('ADI   ', ADI);
442       ENTER('ADX   ', ADX); ENTER('BEG   ', BEG);
443       ENTER('BNG   ', BNG); ENTER('BNZ   ', BNZ);
444       ENTER('BPZ   ', BPZ); ENTER('BRN   ', BRN);
445       ENTER('BZE   ', BZE); ENTER('CLA   ', CLA);
446       ENTER('CLX   ', CLX); ENTER('CMP   ', CMP);
447       ENTER('CPI   ', CPI); ENTER('CPX   ', CPX);
448       ENTER('DC    ', DC ); ENTER('DEC   ', DEC);
449       ENTER('DEX   ', DEX); ENTER('DS    ', DS );
450       ENTER('END   ', FIN); ENTER('EQU   ', EQU);
451       ENTER('HLT   ', HLT); ENTER('INA   ', INA);
452       ENTER('INC   ', INC); ENTER('INI   ', INI);
453       ENTER('INX   ', INX); ENTER('JSR   ', JSR);
454       ENTER('LDA   ', LDA); ENTER('LDI   ', LDI);
455       ENTER('LDX   ', LDX); ENTER('LSI   ', LSI);
456       ENTER('LSP   ', LSP); ENTER('NOP   ', NOP);
457       ENTER('ORG   ', ORG); ENTER('OTA   ', OTA);
458       ENTER('OTI   ', OTI); ENTER('POP   ', POP);
```

```
459   ENTER('PSH    ', PSH); ENTER('RET    ', RET);
460   ENTER('SBI    ', SBI); ENTER('SBX    ', SBX);
461   ENTER('STA    ', STA); ENTER('STX    ', STX);
462   ENTER('SUB    ', SUB); ENTER('TAX    ', TAX);
463   HEXSTRING := '0123456789ABCDEF';
464   LASTSYM := nil;
465   CC := 0; LL := 0 (*Initialize source handler*);
466   ONEBYTEOPS := [NOP .. HLT]; TWOBYTEOPS := [LDA .. JSR];
467   for J := 0 to 255 do MCODE[J] := NUL (*fill with rubbish*);
468   WRITELN(OUTPUT, 'Two-Pass Assembler Mark ', VERSION); WRITELN(OUTPUT);
469   (*open and REWRITE(WORK) file as appropriate*)
470   end (*INITIALIZE*);
471
472   begin (*ASSEMBLER*)
473   (*open and RESET(SOURCE) and OUTPUT files as appropriate*)
474   INITIALIZE;
475   FIRSTPASS;
476   SECONDPASS;
477   DUMPCODE;
478   (*close OUTPUT file if necessary*)
479   end (*ASSEMBLER*).
```

Exercises

3.7 Extend the assembler to allow hexadecimal constants as alternatives in addresses, for example

```
LAB LDI $0A      ; 0A(hex) = 10(decimal)
```

3.8 Another convention is to allow hexadecimal constants like 0FFh or 0FFH, with a trailing H implying hexadecimal. A hex number must then start with a 'digit' in the range 0 to 9, so that it can be distinguished from an identifier. Implement this option. Why is it harder to handle than the convention suggested in Exercise 3.7?

3.9 Extend the assembler to allow a single character as an address, for example

```
LAB   LDI 'A'      ; load immediate 'A' (ASCII 041H)
```

The character must, of course, be converted into the corresponding ordinal value by the assembler. How do you allow it to use the quote character itself as an address?

3.10 Make a further extension to allow a character string to be used in the DC directive address, for example

```
GENIUS DC "TERRY"
```

is to be treated as equivalent to

```
GENIUS DC  'T'
       DC  'E'
       DC  'R'
       DC  'R'
       DC  'Y'
```

Is it desirable or necessary to place strings between different quotes to those used by single characters?

3.11 Change the assembler so that the symbol table is stored in a binary tree, for speed of access thereafter.

3.12 An even better way of handling the symbol table makes use of a so-called 'hash table'. Carry out some research into this method, and incorporate your findings in a modified assembler.

3.13 The assembler will currently accept a line containing only a non-blank LABEL field. Is there any advantage in being able to do this?

3.14 Notice the way an error is reported if the opcode cannot be identified. Could the same device be used to report other errors easily, and if so how?

3.15 What will happen if a label is not defined properly? Should this not be repaired?

3.16 What will happen if a label is defined more than once?

3.5 A simple one-pass assembler

As we have already mentioned, the main reason for having two passes is to handle the problem of **forward references**; that is, the use of labels before their locations or values have been defined. Most of the work of lexical analysis and assembly can be accomplished directly on the first pass, as can be seen from a close study of the algorithms in the last section.

In Listing 4 we present the shell of a one-pass assembler for the same language as before. The truth of the claim in the previous paragraph can be seen by a careful study of procedure FIRSTPASS (lines 148–216), which should be compared with procedure SECONDPASS of the assembler in Listing 3. The only significant difference is that SECONDPASS did not have to call on ADDTOSYMBOLTABLE, which FIRSTPASS in the one-pass assembler must do when it finds a label definition.

The outstanding difficulty in the construction of a one-pass assembler lies in the fact that on the first pass it will not always be possible to determine the value of an address field as it is first encountered. However, it is relatively easy to cope with the problem of forward references. We create an additional table, called the **branch ahead table**, which we maintain as a dynamic structure, using declarations of the form

```
BALINKS     = ↑BAREFERENCES;
BAREFERENCES = record (*forward references for undefined labels*)
                 BYTE   : BYTES    (*to be patched*);
                 BALINK : BALINKS  (*to next reference*)
               end (*BAREFERENCES*);
```

In the BYTE fields of the BAREFERENCES we record the addresses of as yet incompletely defined object code bytes. We also extend the symbol table entries to be of the form

```
SYMLINKS    = ↑SYMENTRIES;
SYMENTRIES = record (*symbol table*)
                 NAME    : ALFA    (*name*);
                 SLINK   : SYMLINKS (*to next entry*);
                 DEFINED : BOOLEAN  (*true if now defined*);
                 BLINK   : BALINKS  (*to outstanding references*);
                 ADDRESS : BYTES    (*value when defined*)
               end (*SYMENTRIES*);
```

When a label **reference** or so-called **applied occurrence** is encountered in the address field of an instruction, function VALUEOF arranges to examine the symbol table for the appropriate entry, as before. Several possibilities arise:

(a)   If the label has already been defined, it will be in the symbol table marked as DEFINED = TRUE, and the address can be obtained from the ADDRESS field.

(b)   If the label is not yet in the symbol table, an entry is made in this table, with DEFINED = FALSE, and the BLINK field is used to point to a newly created entry in the branch ahead table, in the BYTE field of which we record the location of the object byte which has still to be determined.

(c)   If the label is already in the symbol table, but still flagged DEFINED = FALSE, then a further entry is made to the branch ahead table, linked to the earlier entries for the same label.

This may be made clearer by considering the following program segment (shown fully assembled, for convenience).

```
00                 BEG
7D                 ORG    125    ; HEX 7D
7D         MAX     EQU    15     ; HEX 0F
7D    10 89        LDA    A
7F    15 8A        ADD    B
81    15 89        ADD    A
83    13 8B        STA    C
85    13 89        STA    A
87    20 90        BRN    LABEL
89    00   A       DC     0
```

When the instruction at 7Dh (LDA A) is encountered, A is entered in the symbol table, undefined, linked to an entry in the branch ahead table, which refers to

7Eh. The next instruction enters B in the symbol table, undefined, linked to a new entry in the branch ahead table, which refers to 80h. The next instruction adds an entry to the branch ahead table, which refers to 82h, itself linked to the entry that refers to 7Eh, and so on, until by the time the instruction at 89h (ADC0) is encountered, the tables look like Figure 3.3.

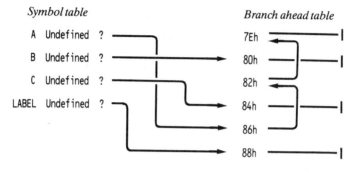

Figure 3.3

In passing we might comment that in a real system this strategy might lead to extremely large structures. These can, fairly obviously, be kept smaller if the bytes labelled by the DC and DS instructions arc all placed before the 'code' which manipulates them, and some assemblers might even insist that this be done.

Since we shall also have to examine the symbol table when a label **definition** or so-called **defining occurrence** is encountered, it turns out to be convenient to introduce a further procedure FINDENTRY to do the symbol table searching. This involves a simple algorithm to scan through the symbol table, being prepared for either finding or not finding an entry. The problem of possibly trying to access a Pascal dynamic record pointed to by a nil pointer must be solved; in fact we go further to code the routine so that it always finds the appropriate entry, if necessary creating a new node for the purpose. The variable FOUND records whether the entry refers to a previously created node or not. The code is given in procedure lines 58–74 of Listing 4.

The code for VALUEOF changes somewhat (lines 94–131 of Listing 4). The general idea is as shown below. Note that this is now a function with 'side-effects', and so might be frowned upon by the purists.

```
function VALUEOF (ADDRESSFIELD : ADDRESSES) : INTEGER;
  begin
    case ADDRESSFIELD.KIND of
      NUMERIC :
        VALUEOF ← ADDRESSFIELD.NUMBER mod 256
      ALPHAMERIC :
        VALUEOF ← 0 (*in case undefined*)
        look up NAME in symbol table
```

```
                if it was there previously
                    then
                        if DEFINED then VALUEOF ← ADDRESS in symbol table
                        else make new entry in branch ahead table
                    else
                        make first entry in branch ahead table
        end
```

As already mentioned, when a a non-blank LABEL field is encountered, the symbol table is searched as well. Two main possibilities arise:

(a) If the label was not previously there, the new entry is completed, flagged DEFINED = TRUE, the ADDRESS field is set to the now known value.

(b) If it was previously there, flagged DEFINED = FALSE, the links are followed to the entries in the branch ahead table, allowing us to complete assembly of the bytes referenced there. Afterwards this chain can be destroyed; the symbol table entry itself is then updated, with DEFINED = TRUE, and the ADDRESS field set to the now known value.

The code for this is easily written. That for processing the branch ahead entries is in procedure PROCESSCHAIN (lines 76–81), and for amending the symbol table in procedure ADDTOSYMBOLTABLE (lines 83–92).

This may be made clearer by considering the same program fragment as before (shown fully assembled, for convenience).

```
00                  BEG
7D                  ORG     125    ; HEX 7D
7D          MAX     EQU     15     ; HEX 0F
7D    10 89         LDA     A
7F    15 8A         ADD     B
81    15 89         ADD     A
83    13 8B         STA     C
85    13 89         STA     A
87    20 90         BRN     LABEL
89    00    A       DC      0
```

When the definition for A is encountered at 89h, the branch ahead table links are followed from 86h to 82h to 7Eh, and these bytes are altered to have the value 137 (89h). Thereafter the symbol table and branch ahead table effectively become as shown in Figure 3.4. The source listing can be only incompletely produced by a one-pass assembler, as some addresses will not be known at the time the listing is done. This is shown by the following example.

```
00                  BEG
7D                  ORG     125    ; HEX 7D
7D          MAX     EQU     15     ; HEX 0F
7D    10 00         LDA     A
7F    15 00         ADD     B
81    15 00         ADD     A
```

```
83    13 00          STA    C
85    13 00          STA    A
87    20 00          BRN    LABEL
89    00    A        DC     0
8A    0C    B        DC     12
8B          C        DS     5
90    12 0F LABEL    LDI    MAX
92    15 8B          ADD    C
94    21 90          BZE    LABEL
96    0F             HLT
97                   END
```

Symbol Table

```
LABEL    90    144
C        8B    139
B        8A    138
A        89    137
MAX      0F    15
```

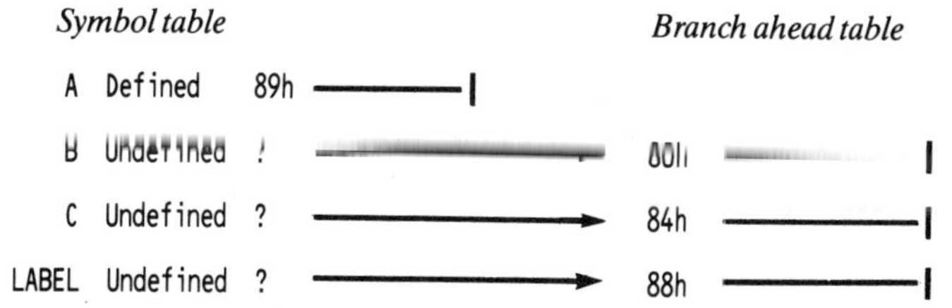

Symbol table			Branch ahead table	
A	Defined	89h ———————|		
B	Undefined	? ————————————————	80h ————————— |	
C	Undefined	? ————————————→	84h ————————|	
LABEL	Undefined	? ————————————→	88h ————————|	

Figure 3.4

Exercises

3.17 What modifications (if any) are needed to incorporate the extensions suggested as exercises at the end of the last section into the simple one-pass assembler?

3.18 We mentioned in Section 3.4 that there was no great difficulty in assembling large programs with a two-pass assembler. How do you suppose one handles programs too large to co-reside with a one-pass assembler?

3.19 Should we not make use of a *variant record* type for storing the entries in the symbol table? Review this aspect of Pascal, as you are probably unfamiliar with it, by making a suitable modification to the assembler.

3.20 What currently happens in one-pass assembly if a label is redefined? Should one be allowed to do this (that is, is there any advantage to be gained from being allowed to do so), and if not, what should be done to prevent it?

Listing 4   Shell of one-pass assembler for language of Section 3.1

```
1   program ASSEMBLER (INPUT, OUTPUT, CODEFILE);
?   (* Simple one-pass assembler for language of Section 3.1
3     P.D. Terry, January 1985.     Version 1a*)
4   const
5     (*as in two-pass assembler*)
6   type
7     (*as in two-pass assembler, except for the following additions*)
8
9     (* ++++++++ used by the semantic analyser ++++++++++++++++++++++++++++ *)
10
11    OPCODES = 0 .. NUMBEROPCODES;
12    BALINKS = ↑BAREFERENCES;
13    BAREFERENCES = record (*forward references for undefined labels*)
14                     BYTE   : BYTES      (*to be patched*);
15                     BALINK : BALINKS    (*to next reference*)
16                   end (*BAREFERENCES*);
17    SYMLINKS  = ↑SYMENTRIES;
18    SYMENTRIES = record (*symbol table*)
19                     NAME    : ALFA       (*name*);
20                     SLINK   : SYMLINKS   (*to next entry*);
21                     DEFINED : BOOLEAN    (*true if now defined*);
22                     BLINK   : BALINKS    (*to outstanding references*);
23                     ADDRESS : BYTES      (*value when defined*)
24                   end (*SYMENTRIES*);
25  var
26    (*as in the two-pass assembler, ++++++++++++++ but omitting
27    WORK      : file of UNPACKEDLINES;   *)
28
29
30  procedure QUIT (N : INTEGER);
31    (*as in two-pass assembler*)
32
33  procedure HEX (I, N : BYTES);
34    (*as in two-pass assembler*)
35
36  (* +++++++++++++++++++++++ Source handler +++++++++++++++++++++++ *)
```

```
37
38   procedure GETCH;  (*as in two-pass assembler*)
39
40   procedure PRINTSYMBOLTABLE;  (*as in two-pass assembler*)
41
42   (* ++++++++++++++++++++++++++++++ Lexical analyser +++++++++++++++++++++++ *)
43
44   procedure SYNTAXANALYSIS;  (*as in two-pass assembler*)
45
46     procedure GETSYM;  (*as in two-pass assembler*)
47
48     procedure GETADDRESS;  (*as in two-pass assembler*)
49
50   (* ++++++++++++++++++++++++++++++ First and only pass +++++++++++++++++++ *)
51
52    procedure FIRSTPASS;
53      var
54        PASSONE,
55        FOUND    : BOOLEAN (*used in symbol table searches*);
56        SYMENTRY : SYMLINKS (*location of an identifier in symbol table*);
57
58      procedure FINDENTRY (LAB : ALFA);
59      (*Search for symbol entry matching 'LAB' in symbol table*)
60        begin
61          SYMENTRY := LASTSYM; FOUND := FALSE;
62          while not FOUND and (SYMENTRY <> nil) do
63            if LAB = SYMENTRY ↑.NAME
64              then FOUND := TRUE else SYMENTRY := SYMENTRY ↑.SLINK;
65          if not FOUND then (*make new node*)
66            begin
67              NEW(SYMENTRY);
68              with SYMENTRY ↑ do
69                begin
70                  NAME := LAB; DEFINED := FALSE; BLINK := nil; SLINK := LASTSYM
71                end;
72              LASTSYM := SYMENTRY
73            end
74        end (*FINDENTRY*);
75
76      procedure PROCESSCHAIN (LINK : BALINKS; ADDRESS : BYTES);
77      (*Fill in forward references once known, starting at LINK*)
78        begin
79          while LINK <> nil do
80            begin MCODE[LINK ↑.BYTE] := ADDRESS; LINK := LINK ↑.BALINK end
81        end (*PROCESSCHAIN*);
82
```

```
83    procedure ADDTOSYMBOLTABLE (LAB : ALFA; ADR : BYTES);
84    (*New entry, or complete an incomplete entry*)
85      begin
86        FINDENTRY(LAB);
87        with SYMENTRY ↑ do
88          begin
89            if FOUND then PROCESSCHAIN(BLINK, ADR);
90            DEFINED := TRUE; ADDRESS := ADR; BLINK := nil
91          end
92      end (*ADDTOSYMBOLTABLE*);
93
94    function VALUEOF (ADDRESSFIELD : ADDRESSES) : INTEGER;
95    (*Determine value of address field if possible, and add to branch
96      ahead table if not*)
97      var
98        BAENTRY  : BALINKS;
99      begin
100       case ADDRESSFIELD.KIND of
101         NUMERIC :
102           VALUEOF := ADDRESSFIELD.NUMBER mod 256;
103         ALPHAMERIC:
104           begin
105             VALUEOF := 0 (*in case still undefined*);
106             FINDENTRY(ADDRESSFIELD.NAME);
107             if FOUND
108               then (*entry was made previously*)
109                 if SYMENTRY ↑.DEFINED
110                   then VALUEOF := SYMENTRY ↑.ADDRESS
111                   else
112                    ̄begin (*add another node to reference chain*)
113                       NEW(BAENTRY);
114                       with BAENTRY ↑ do
115                         begin
116                           BALINK := SYMENTRY ↑.BLINK;
117                           BYTE := NEXTBYTE
118                         end;
119                       SYMENTRY ↑.BLINK := BAENTRY
120                     end (*add to chain*)
121               else (*first entry in reference chain*)
122                 begin
123                   NEW(SYMENTRY ↑.BLINK);
124                   with SYMENTRY ↑.BLINK ↑ do
125                     begin
126                       BALINK := nil; BYTE := NEXTBYTE
127                     end
128                 end (*first entry in reference chain*)
```

```
129              end (*ALPHAMERIC*)
130           end (*case*)
131         end (*VALUEOF*);
132
133     function FINDOPENTRY (MNEMONIC : ALFA) : OPCODES;
134     (*Search opcode table (binary search) *)
135       var
136         LOOK, L, R : INTEGER;
137       begin
138         L := 1; R := NUMBEROPCODES;
139         repeat
140           LOOK := (L + R) div 2;
141           if MNEMONIC > OPTABLE[LOOK].SPELLING
142             then L := LOOK + 1 else R := LOOK - 1
143         until (MNEMONIC = OPTABLE[LOOK].SPELLING) or (L > R);
144         if MNEMONIC = OPTABLE[LOOK].SPELLING
145           then FINDOPENTRY := LOOK else FINDOPENTRY := 0 (*ERR entry*)
146       end (*FINDOPENTRY*);
147
148     begin (*FIRSTPASS*)
149       PASSONE := TRUE; NEXTBYTE := 0;
150       while PASSONE do
151         begin
152           SYNTAXANALYSIS;
153           with SOURCELINE do
154             begin
155             OPENTRY := FINDOPENTRY(MNEMONIC);
156             with OPTABLE[OPENTRY] do
157               begin
158                 if OPCODE <> ERR then
159                   begin
160                     if OPCODE in [NUL, BEG, ORG, DS, EQU, FIN, DC]
161                       then
162                         case OPCODE of
163                           BEG: begin NEXTBYTE := 0; HEX(NEXTBYTE, 10) end;
164                           ORG:
165                             begin
166                               NEXTBYTE := VALUEOF(ADDRESSFIELD); HEX(NEXTBYTE, 10)
167                             end;
168                           NUL:
169                             begin
170                               if LAB <> BLANK then ADDTOSYMBOLTABLE(LAB, NEXTBYTE);
171                               HEX(NEXTBYTE, 10)
172                             end;
173                           DS:
174                             begin
```

```
175                     if LAB <> BLANK then ADDTOSYMBOLTABLE(LAB, NEXTBYTE);
176                     HEX(NEXTBYTE, 10);
177                     NEXTBYTE := (NEXTBYTE+VALUEOF(ADDRESSFIELD)) mod 256
178                   end;
179                 EQU:
180                   begin
181                     HEX(NEXTBYTE, 10);
182                     ADDTOSYMBOLTABLE(LAB, ADDRESSFIELD.NUMBER)
183                   end;
184                 FIN: begin HEX(NEXTBYTE, 10); PASSONE := FALSE end;
185                 DC:
186                   begin
187                     if LAB <> BLANK then ADDTOSYMBOLTABLE(LAB, NEXTBYTE);
188                     HEX(NEXTBYTE, 4);
189                     MCODE[NEXTBYTE] := VALUEOF(ADDRESSFIELD);
190                     HEX(MCODE[NEXTBYTE], 4);
191                     NEXTBYTE := (NEXTBYTE + 1) mod 256
192                   end (*DC*)
193                 end (*case*)
194               else
195                 begin (*Machine ops*)
196                   if LAB <> BLANK then ADDTOSYMBOLTABLE(LAB, NEXTBYTE);
197                   HEX(NEXTBYTE, 4); MCODE[NEXTBYTE] := OPCODE;
198                   HEX(MCODE[NEXTBYTE], 1);
199                   NEXTBYTE := (NEXTBYTE + 1) mod 256;
200                   if OPCODE in TWOBYTEOPS
201                     then
202                       begin
203                         MCODE[NEXTBYTE] := VALUEOF(ADDRESSFIELD);
204                         HEX(MCODE[NEXTBYTE], 1);
205                         NEXTBYTE := (NEXTBYTE + 1) mod 256
206                       end
207                     else WRITE(OUTPUT, '   ')
208                 end (*machine ops*)
209             end (*OPCODE <> ERR*)
210           else WRITE(OUTPUT, 'Error      ');
211         WRITELN(OUTPUT, LAB, MNEMONIC:6, ADDRESSFIELD.NAME:10, COMMENT)
212       end (*with*)
213     end (*with*)
214   end (*while*);
215   PRINTSYMBOLTABLE
216 end (*FIRSTPASS*);
217
218 procedure DUMPCODE;  (*as in two-pass assembler*)
219
220 procedure INITIALIZE;
```

```
221    (*as in two-pass assembler except for absence of REWRITE(WORK) *)
222
223    begin (*ASSEMBLER*)
224      (*open and RESET(SOURCE) and OUTPUT files as appropriate*)
225      INITIALIZE;
226      FIRSTPASS;
227      DUMPCODE;
228      (*close OUTPUT file if necessary*)
229    end (*ASSEMBLER*).
```

Chapter 4 **Advanced assembler features**

It cannot be claimed that the assemblers of the last chapter were anything other than toys (but by now the student will be familiar with the drawbacks of 'academic courses'!). In this chapter we discuss some extensions to the ideas put forward previously, and then leave the reader with a number of suggestions for exercises which will help turn the assembler into something more closely resembling the real thing.

The code for a complete one-pass assembler using the extensions to be discussed here is to be found in Listing 5. The program is rather large, although in essence rather similar to the simple one-pass assembler of Listing 4. As before, references will be given by line number to sections of this code.

4.1 Undefined variables

Some assemblers do not place the restriction on the user that all labels must be defined in the source code. For example, with our present scheme, a program for reading and adding two numbers would have to be written:

```
        BEG
        INI     ; first number
        STA A   ; store temporary
        INI     ; second number
        ADD A
        OTI     ; print result
        HLT
A       DS 1    ; allocate temporary
        END
```

An assembler might perform the allocation of single byte variables (such as A) for itself, after the code has been completely specified. In the case of our one-pass assembler, for example, there will still be entries in the symbol table flagged DEFINED = FALSE by the time the END directive is reached. The last part of the assembly process can be to scan this table, and allocate single bytes in sequence to each of these entries, followed by the usual processing of the branch ahead table links. This is easily achieved with code like that in procedure UNDEFINEDVARIABLES in lines 534–552.

This raises some interesting issues, and it is not suggested that the practice is particularly widespread. With a more realistic system, which allowed 'byte' and 'word' objccts, it would be unreasonable to expect the assembler to know how much storage should be reserved.

4.2 Simple expressions as addresses

Many assemblers allow the programmer the facility of including expressions in the address field of instructions. For example, we might have the following (shown fully assembled).

```
00                   BEG
00    09             INA            ; FIRST CHARACTER
01    13 19          STA    A
03    09             INA            ; SECOND CHARACTER
04    13 1A          STA    A+1
06    09             INA            ; THIRD CHARACTER
07    1D 2E          CPI    PERIOD   ; CHECK FULL STOP
09    21 06          BZE    *-4
0B    1D 2C          CPI    PERIOD-2 ; CHECK COMMA
0D    22 06          BNZ    *-8
0F    10 19          LDA    A
11    0B             OTA            ; PRINT FIRST CHARACTER
12    10 1A          LDA    A+1
14    0B             OTA            ; PRINT SECOND CHARACTER
15    12 13          LDI    65-PERIOD
17    0B             OTA
18           PERIOD  EQU    46       ; ASCII '.'
18    0F             HI T
19    00      A      DS     4
1D                   END

Symbol Table
------------
PERIOD   2E   46
A        19   25
```

(Once again, this does not really do anything useful.)

Here we have used addresses like A+1 (meaning one location after that assigned to A), PERIOD-2 (meaning, in this case, an obvious 44), and *-4 and *-8 (a rather dangerous notation, meaning '4 bytes before the present one' and '8 bytes before the present one', respectively). These are all very common extensions to the allowed instruction formats. Quite how complicated the expressions can become in a real assembler is not a matter for discussion here, but it is of interest to see how much more complicated our one-pass assembler will become if we restrict ourselves to addresses of a form described by the syntax diagrams in Figure 4.1, where * stands for 'address of this byte'. Note that we can, in principle, have as many terms as we like, although the previous example used only one or two.

ADDRESS

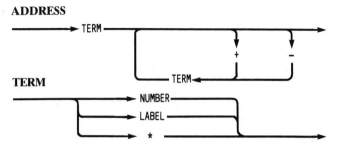

Figure 4.1

In a one-pass assembler, address fields of this kind can be handled fairly easily, even allowing for the problem of forward references such as we have in the above example. We compute the value of the address as fully as we can – in some cases (as in *-4) this will be completely – and in the branch ahead table entries we record not only the address of the bytes to be altered when the labels are finally defined, but also whether the defined values are to be added to or subtracted from the value already residing in that byte. There is a slight complication in that all expressions must be computed modulo-256 (thus suggesting a two's complement representation).

Perhaps this will be made clearer by considering how a one-pass assembler would handle the above code, where we have deliberately delayed the definition of A and PERIOD until the end. For the A+1 address in the instruction STA A+1 we assemble as though the instruction were STA 1, and for the PERIOD-2 address in the instruction CPI PERIOD-2 we assemble as though the instruction were CPI -2, or, since addresses are computed modulo-256, as though the instruction were CPI 254. At the point just before PERIOD is defined, the assembled code would look as follows

```
00              BEG
00    09        INA                ; FIRST CHARACTER
01    13 00     STA    A
03    09        INA                ; SECOND CHARACTER
04    13 01     STA    A+1
06    09        INA                ; THIRD CHARACTER
07    1D 00     CPI    PERIOD      ; CHECK FULL STOP
09    21 06     BZE    *-4
0B    1D FE     CPI    PERIOD-2    ; CHECK COMMA
0D    22 06     BNZ    *-8
0F    10 00     LDA    A
11    0B        OTA                ; PRINT FIRST CHARACTER
12    10 01     LDA    A+1
14    0B        OTA                ; PRINT SECOND CHARACTER
15    12 41     LDI    65-PERIOD
17    0B        OTA
```

with the entries in the symbol and branch ahead tables looking like Figure 4.2.

To incorporate these changes will require modifications to the lexical analyser (which now has to be able to recognize the characters +, - and * as corresponding to lexical tokens or symbols), to the syntax analyser (which will now have more work to do in decoding the address field of an instruction – what was previously the complete address is now possibly just one term of a complex address), and to the semantic analyser (which will now have to keep track of how far each address has been computed, as well as maintaining the symbol table).

4.2.1 Character handling

The problem of making a source listing may conveniently be deferred to a procedure (and removed from PASSONE itself). This is provided by procedure PRINTLINE in lines 174–191 of Listing 5.

4.2.2 Lexical analysis

Changing the lexical analyser is quite easy. We extend the SYMBOLS type

```
type
    SYMBOLS = (NULSYM, IDSYM, NUMSYM, COMSYM, PLUS, MINUS, ASTERISK);
```

and add another character pointer

```
var
    CS : LINEINDEX (*Character pointer*);
```

whose job it will be to record the start of a symbol read in (so that we can later make a neat listing of the address field, which is now a collection of symbols)
The changes to the lexical analyser can be found in a revised GETSYM in lines 263–331 of Listing 5.

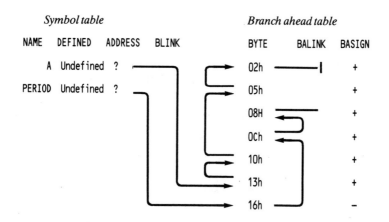

Figure 4.2

4.2.3 Syntax analysis

In performing syntactic analysis of an address it is useful to extend the types introduced earlier as follows:

```
TOKENS = record (*elements of address fields*)
            TNAME    : ALFA               (*name*);
            TNUMBER  : INTEGER            (*numeric value*);
            TSTRING  : STRINGS            (*characters in it*);
            TLENGTH  : INTEGER            (*width*);
            TSYM     : SYMBOLS            (*kind*)
        end (*TOKENS*);
ADDRESSES = record (*address fields*)
            NUMBER   : INTEGER            (*value so far*);
            KIND     : KINDS;
            ENTRY    : array [1 .. 15] of TOKENS  (*elements*);
            ENTRIES  : 0 .. 15            (*number of elements*)
        end (*ADDRESSES*);
BALINKS      = ↑BAREFERENCES;
BAREFERENCES = record (*forward references for undefined labels*)
            BYTE    : BYTES       (*to be patched*);
            BASIGN  : -1 .. 1     (*treatment*);
            BALINK  : BALINKS     (*to next reference*)
        end (*BAREFERENCES*);
```

The code for procedure SYNTAXANALYSIS itself remains essentially unchanged, but there is a lot of change associated with GETADDRESS, which must now record the various tokens which form the terms and signs in the address, for later listing, and for processing when it is desired to compute the value to be stored in the address byte.

Notes

(a) We enter the routine with SYM set to the first symbol in the address. This SYM was, earlier, representative of the complete address field. The code for GETADDRESS can be found in lines 333–359 of Listing 5.

(b) We should, perhaps, comment on the choice of an **array** to record the entries in an address field. Since each of these will have a varying number of terms, it might be thought better (especially with all the practice we are having) to use a dynamic structure. This has not been done here because, although dynamic structures are easy to create, they are less easy to destroy on some Pascal systems. We would be creating a structure for each source line; rather than do this we opt instead to re-use the same array repeatedly, as it is not needed once the line has been dealt with.

(c) There is some slightly clumsy code associated with the mechanics of producing a source listing. Ideally we should like the syntax analyser not to have to deal with the character handler variables like LINE and CC, but there seems no easy alternative in this case (as we are allowing free format input).

(d)   There is additional code associated with error checking, which we shall discuss in Section 4.5.

4.2.4 Semantic analysis

In coding the function for finding the value of an ADDRESSFIELD we note that the syntax diagrams for ADDRESSFIELD given earlier act as flow diagrams for the function, and for the local function TERMVALUE which is used to deal with individual terms. The code for VALUEOF is to be found in lines 444–517 of Listing 5, and needs close study.

Notes

(a)   The nested function TERMVALUE is just a slight modification of the function given as VALUEOF in the simple one-pass assembler, using the fields of a single TOKEN rather than of the complete ADDRESSFIELD. Minor changes include the need to store BASIGN in the branch ahead table entries, and to deal with the asterisk (which is, after all, just a numeric equivalent).

(b)   VALUEOF itself has a relatively simple algorithm. We begin by assuming that it will consist of only one term; only if there is more than one do we record the KIND as an EXPRESSION.

(c)   There is need to work modulo 256 as before, because of the limitations of the target machine, but note that we store the individual terms in their full integer glory.

(d)   As a side-effect, the value of the address field is computed in the NUMBER field so far as is known.

(e)   Unknown labels are given a value of zero, as references to them will later be patched up.

(f)   ADDTOSYMBOLTABLE remains the same; the changes to PROCESSCHAIN are quite simple, and can be found in lines 422–431 of Listing 5.

4.3 An introduction to macro-processing facilities

Programming in ASSEMBLER is a tedious business at the best of times, because assembler languages are essentially very simple, and lack the powerful constructs possible in high-level languages. One way in which life can be made easier for the programmer is to permit him to use **macros**, which are devices to allow the assembler language to be extended at the whim of the user. These effectively allow the definition of new mnemonics, which can be used repeatedly within the program thereafter. To define a macro-instruction we shall adopt a convention on the lines of

```
LABEL   MAC     P1,P2,P3 . . .      ; P1,P2,P3 ... are formal parameters
                lines of code as usual,
                which may use P1,P2,P3 . . . in various fields
                END                 ; show end of definition
```

where LABEL is the name of the new instruction, and MAC is a new directive. For example, we might have

```
SUM     MAC     A,B,C   ; Macro to add A to B and store in C
        LDA     A
        ADD     B
        STA     C
        END             ; of macro SUM
```

It must be emphasized that the macro definition gives a template or model, and does not of itself immediately generate executable code. The program will, in all probability, not have labels or variables with the same names as those given to the formal parameters.

If a program contains one or more of such macro definitions, we may use them subsequently to generate executable code by a **macro invocation**, which takes a form exemplified by

```
SUM     X,Y,Z
```

where SUM, the name of the macro, appears in the opcode field, and X,Y,Z are the actual parameters. Thus, code of the apparent form

```
        SUM     X,Y,Z
L1      SUM     P,Q,R
```

is said to be *expanded* to generate actual code equivalent to

```
        LDA     X
        ADD     Y
        STA     Z
L1      LDA     P
        ADD     Q
        STA     R
```

A **macro** facility should not be confused with a **subroutine** facility. The definition of a macro causes no code to be assembled, nor is there any obligation on the programmer ever to invoke any particular macro. On the other hand, defining a subroutine does cause code to be generated immediately. Whenever a macro is expanded the assembler generates code equivalent to the macro body, but with the actual parameters textually substituted for the formal parameters. For the call of a subroutine the assembler simply generates a special form of jump to the subroutine.

In the example above the parameters appear only in the address fields of the lines constituting the macro definition, but they are not restricted to this use. For example, the macro

```
CHK     MAC     A,B,OPCODE,LAB
LAB     LDA     A
        CPI     B
        OPCODE  LAB
        END             ; of macro CHK
```

if invoked by code of the form

```
CHK     X,Y,BNZ,L1
```

would produce code equivalent to

```
L1      LDA     X
        CPI     Y
        BNZ     L1
```

If we require that each macro must be fully defined before it is ever invoked (this is no real limitation if one thinks about it), we may add a macro facility to the one-pass assembler quite easily.

The first problem to be solved is that of macro definition. This is easily recognized as imminent by the FIRSTPASS procedure, which we shall recast in the form

```
begin (*FIRSTPASS*)
  PASSONE := TRUE; NEXTBYTE := 0;
  while PASSONE do
    begin
      SYNTAXANALYSIS;
      if SOURCELINE.MNEMONIC = 'MAC    '
        then DEFINEMACRO else ASSEMBLELINE
    end;
  UNDEFINEDVARIABLES;
  PRINTSYMBOLTABLE; PRINTMACROS
end (*FIRSTPASS*);
```

The definition of a macro is handled in two phases. Firstly, we must make an entry into a macro table giving the name of the macro, details of how many parameters there are, and their formal names. Secondly, we must make provision to store the source text of the macro so that it may be rescanned every time a macro expansion is called for. These tables afford us another opportunity for using dynamic structures, and we introduce

```
type
  MACLINKS   = ↑MACENTRIES;
  MACENTRIES = record (*macro table entries*)
                 MNAME   : ALFA      (*macro identifier*);
```

```
          PARAMS    : 0 .. 15     (*number of parameters*);
          PNAME     : array [1 .. 15] of TOKENS (*parameters*);
          MLINK     : MACLINKS    (*to next macro definition*);
          FIRSTLINE : MACLINES    (*to first line in definition*)
        end (*MACENTRIES*);
  var
    LASTMAC : MACLINKS                (*last entry in macro table*);
```

Here MLINK affords the way of linking the entries in the macro table (which we shall store as a stack here for simplicity), and FIRSTLINE is a pointer to the actual body of the macro code definition, which we store as a queue in a further dynamic structure, supported by definitions of the form

```
  type
    MACLINES = ↑LINES;
    LINES    = record (*source text of macro definition*)
                 TEXT : UNPACKEDLINES   (*one source line*);
                 LINK : MACLINES        (*to next line in definition*)
               end (*LINES*);
```

We observe that we have again chosen to store the parameter names in an array – it might be better to store them in a dynamic structure too.

4.3.1 Initialization

We must add the mnemonic for a MAC opcode to the opcode table, which implies trivially easy changes to INITIALIZE and the introduction of another constant.

4.3.2 Lexical analysis

The changes needed to the lexical analyser are also trivial. Essentially we must extend the SYMBOLS type again

```
  type
    SYMBOLS = (NULSYM, IDSYM, NUMSYM, COMSYM, PLUS, MINUS, ASTERISK, COMMA);
```

and allow the GETSYM procedure to recognize the comma in a similar way to that in which it handles asterisks, pluses and minuses. The changes can be seen in the code in lines 263–331 of Listing 5.

4.3.3 Syntax analysis

The SYNTAXANALYSIS procedure is already equipped to handle unpacking a macro definition line, and no further changes are needed.

4.3.4 Semantic analysis – macro definition

Adding to the macro table is easy, and is handled by procedure ADDTOMACROTABLE in lines 559–583 of Listing 5. Note that we do not bother to store the separating commas in the PNAME array.

Procedure DEFINEMACRO (lines 585–601), which calls on ADDTOMACROTABLE, is fairly simple. Care must be taken to construct the structure of lines as a queue, the first entry in which has to be a special case.

Notes

(a)   This procedure is called with SOURCELINE already unpacked, from the line which contains the MAC opcode and an 'address field' containing a list of parameters. After calling on ADDTOMACROTABLE to store the names of the macro and its parameters, it must proceed to call SYNTAXANALYSIS to unpack further lines in the macro definition, and queue these, until the END directive signals the end of the definition.

(b)   It might be thought that the code could be developed more directly on the lines of

```
procedure DEFINEMACRO;
  var
    LAST, LINEENTRY : MACLINES;
  begin
    ADDTOMACROTABLE;
    SYNTAXANALYSIS (*unpack first line of definition code template*);
    while SOURCELINE.MNEMONIC <> 'END     ' do
      begin (*store source text of macro in a queue*)
        NEW(LINEENTRY);
        if LASTMAC↑.FIRSTLINE = nil (*first line of macro text*)
          then LASTMAC↑.FIRSTLINE := LINEENTRY
          else LAST↑.LINK := LINEENTRY;
        with LINEENTRY↑ do (*store the line itself*)
          begin TEXT := SOURCELINE; LINK := nil end;
        LAST := LINEENTRY; SYNTAXANALYSIS
      end
  end (*DEFINEMACRO*);
```

but with a little thought we can improve on this by writing the procedure as given in the listing. This will allow us to define one macro within another – notice how easily this is handled by the use of recursion. As we shall see, recursion is a most desirable technique to have in translator host languages.

(c)   The code as given allows us to define one macro from within another. If this is done, the two definitions are both entered into the macro table immediately. This should be clearly distinguished from an alternative, and possibly better, strategy, which would be to allow one macro only to define another macro when it was itself expanded.

4.3.5   Semantic analysis – macro expansion

We may now turn our attention to the procedure for assembling a line. This is, essentially, the same as before. The difference is that, before assembly, we check the MNEMONIC field to see whether it is a user-defined macro name rather than a standard machine opcode. If it is, we expand the macro, essentially by assembling from the text stored in the macro body, rather than from the incoming source. The code for this is given in procedure ASSEMBLELINE, in lines 691–777 of Listing 5.

Notes

(a)   ASSEMBLELINE is a rather altered version of what was previously called FIRSTPASS (see Listing 4). The important section of this for the present discussion appears at the start:

```
      procedure ASSEMBLELINE;
**        var
**            MACENTRY : MACLINKS;
          begin
            with SOURCELINE do
**               if MACRO(MNEMONIC) then EXPAND(MACENTRY) else
                 begin
                   OPENTRY := FINDOPENTRY(MNEMONIC);
                   with OPTABLE[OPENTRY] do
                     begin
                       if OPCODE <> ERR then
      (*as before*)
```

(b)   This routine has called on a Boolean function to determine whether we are to expand a macro or not. This is easily written and is given as MACRO in lines 609–619 of Listing 5. Notice that it has the side-effect of determining the entry in the macro table, if it exists, which would not please the purists.

The procedure for expanding a macro is quite easy too, and is given as procedure EXPAND in lines 621–670 of Listing 5.

Notes

(a)   Note that EXPAND must take into account the possibility that a macro invocation may be labelled.

(b)   EXPAND in its simplest form is merely a scan through the linked list of source text in the macro definition, copying each line in turn into the global variable SOURCELINE.

(c)   EXPAND calls on ASSEMBLELINE to assemble each line of the macro after it has been placed into SOURCELINE from the macro text structure. Once again we can make use of recursion to allow one macro to call on another (or, for that matter, one macro to be passed the name of another macro as an actual parameter).

(d)   The process of getting the actual parameters and substituting them for the formal parameters is straightforward, if tedious, and is handled in procedures GETACTUALPARAMETERS and SUBSTITUTEACTUALPARAMETERS. We 'get' the actual parameters, once only, from the SOURCELINE which contains the macro name as a MNEMONIC field. For each line in the expansion process we must first check each field to see whether its spelling matches an actual parameter name, and, if so, make the substitution before passing the SOURCELINE across to ASSEMBLELINE.

4.4   Conditional assembly

To realize the full power of an assembler (even one with no macro facilities), it may be desirable to add the facility for what is called **conditional assembly**, whereby the assembler can determine at assembly time whether to include certain instructions or not. A simple form of this is obtained by introducing an extra directive IF, used in code of the form

```
        IF      EXPRESSION
```

which signals to the assembler that the *following* line is to be assembled only if the *assembly-time* value of EXPRESSION is non-zero. Frequently this line will be a macro invocation, but it does not have to be. Thus, for example, we might have

```
SUM     MAC     A,B,C
        LDA     A
        ADD     B
        STA     C
        END             ; macro
        . . .
FLAG    EQU     1
        . . .
        IF      FLAG
        SUM     X,Y,RESULT
```

which (in this case) would generate code equivalent to

```
        LDA     X
        ADD     Y
        STA     RESULT
```

but if we had set FLAG EQU 0 the macro expansion for SUM would not have taken place.

This may seem a little silly, and another example may be more to the point. Suppose we have defined the macro

```
SUM     MAC     A,B,C,FLAG
        LDA     A
        IF      FLAG
        ADI     B
        IF      FLAG-1
        ADX     B
        STA     C
        END             ; macro
```

Then if we ask for the expansion

```
        SUM     X,45,RESULT,1
```

we get the assembled code equivalent to

```
        LDA     X
        ADI     45
        STA     RESULT
```

but if we ask for the expansion

```
        SUM     X,45,RESULT,0
```

we get the assembled code equivalent to

```
        LDA     X
        ADX     45
        STA     RESULT
```

This facility is almost trivially easily added to our one-pass assembler – we note that the value of EXPRESSION must be completely defined by the time the IF directive is encountered, which may be a little more restrictive than we could allow with a two-pass assembler.

4.4.1 Initialization

We introduce the directive by making a trivial addition to INITIALIZE, and the addition of another constant for IFF.

4.4.2 Syntax and lexical analysis

No changes are needed here.

4.4.3 Semantic analysis

The FIRSTPASS procedure changes very little – we introduce a Boolean variable INCLUDE, and set this TRUE initially.
    The procedure ASSEMBLELINE has a few small changes.

```
        begin (*ASSEMBLELINE*)
**      if not INCLUDE then INCLUDE := TRUE else
```

```
           with SOURCELINE do
             if MACRO(MNEMONIC) then EXPAND(MACENTRY) else
               begin
                 OPENTRY := FINDOPENTRY(MNEMONIC);
                 with OPTABLE[OPENTRY] do
                   begin
                     if OPCODE <> ERR then
                       begin
**                       if OPCODE in [NUL, BEG, ORG, DS, EQU, FIN, DC, IFF] then
                         case OPCODE of
                         (*mostly as before, with the addition*)
**                       IFF:
                           begin
                             INCLUDE := VALUEOF(ADDRESSFIELD) <> 0;
                             WRITE(OUTPUT, ' ':12)
                           end
                           . . .
```

(We are assuming that nobody will place an IF directive immediately preceding a macro definition, although it may frequently be the case that one is placed before a macro expansion.)

4.5 Error detection

Our assembler is still very much a toy, in that no attempt has been made to detect errors made during the assembly process – a facility that all users are likely to require.

As the reader will soon come to appreciate, error detection adds considerably to the complexity of the assembly process. Errors can be divided up on the basis of where they can be detected; among others, some important potential errors are as follows:

(a) *Errors that can be detected by the character handler*
  • premature end of source file – this might be a rather fatal error, or it could be used to supply an effective END line, as is done by some assemblers (such as the one supplied with CP/M systems);

(b) *Errors that can be detected by the lexical analyser*
  • use of totally unrecognizable characters;
  • use of symbols whose names are too long;
  • comment fields that are too wide;
  • overflow in forming numeric constants;
  • use of non-digit characters in numbers.

(c) *Errors that can be detected by the syntax analyser*
  • use of symbols in the label or mnemonic field which do not start with a letter;

- use of totally unrecognizable symbols, or misplaced symbols, such as numbers where the comment field should appear;
- failure to form address fields correctly, by misplacing operators, omitting commas in parameter lists and so on.

(d) *Errors that can be detected by the semantic analyser*   These are rather more subtle, for the semantics of ASSEMBLER programming are often deliberately vague. Some 'obvious' errors are

- use of undefined mnemonics;
- supplying address fields to one-byte instructions, or to directives like BEG, END;
- omitting the address for a two-byte instruction or directive;
- labelling any of the BEG, ORG, IF or END directives;
- supplying a non-numeric address field to ORG or EQU (this may be allowable in some circumstances);
- attempting to reference an address outside the available memory: a simple recovery action here is to treat all addresses modulo the available memory size, but this almost certainly needs reporting;
- use of the address of 'data' as the address in a 'branch' instruction: this is sometimes used in 'trick' programming, and so is often not regarded as an error, but except in the hands of experts it can cause chaos;
- undefined labels: this can only be detected on the second pass of a two-pass assembler, and may, as we have seen, not be an error at all, if the assembler is capable of assigning 'variables' itself (of course, branches to undefined labels might cause havoc);
- duplicate definition, either of macro names, of formal parameter names, or of label names (again, this may be allowed);
- failure to supply the correct number of actual parameters in a macro expansion;
- attempting to use address fields for directives like ORG, DS, IF and EQU which cannot be fully evaluated at the time these directives take effect. This is a particularly nasty one in a one-pass system, for branch ahead references will be made to bytes that do not exist!

The above list is not complete, and the reader is urged to reflect on what other errors might be made by the user of the assembler.

How best to report errors is a matter of taste. Many assemblers are fairly cryptic in this regard, reporting each error only by giving a code number or letter alongside the line in the listing where the error was detected. A moment's thought will reveal that many errors can be detected on the first pass of a two-pass assembler, and it might be thought reasonable not to attempt the second pass if errors are detected on the first one. However, if a complete listing is to be produced, showing object code alongside source code, then this will have to wait for the second pass if forward references are to be filled in.

In the assembler in Listing 5 we have contented ourselves with demonstrating how the easier errors may be detected and reported, a problem which is neatly handled by the use of the set type in Pascal. We introduce

```
type
  ERRSET = set of (NONALFA, UNKNOWN, TOOLONG, LABELLED, UNLABELLED,
                   NONNUMERIC, NOADDRESS, HASADDRESS, BADADR, NOTDEFINED);
var
  ERRORS : ERRSET;
```

As we start to assemble each line we set ERRORS to the empty set; as errors are detected, the set can be augmented, and at an appropriate time error reporting can take place using a procedure along the lines of

```
procedure REPORTERRORS;
  begin
    if ERRORS <> [] then
      begin
        WRITELN(OUTPUT,'The following line contains errors and has been abandoned');
        if NONALFA in ERRORS then WRITELN(OUTPUT,'Alphanumeric symbol expected');
        if UNKNOWN in ERRORS then WRITELN(OUTPUT,'Unknown symbol encountered');
        . . . .
```

(The full procedure is found in lines 193–212 of Listing 5.)

Some errors can best be detected at the lexical analysis phase. For example, in GETWORD we might write

```
procedure GETWORD;
  begin
    while ALETTER or ADIGIT do
      begin
        if K <= ALENG
          then begin ID[K] := CH; K := K + 1 end
          else ERRORS := ERRORS + [TOOLONG];
        GETCH
      end
  end (*GETWORD*);
```

An interesting application is found in GETADDRESS, where we make use of a set ALLOWED, which changes as we scan from element to element:

```
      procedure GETADDRESS;
        var
          C1, C2                 : LINEINDEX (*character pointers*);
          ADDRESSSYMS, ALLOWED : set of SYMBOLS;
        begin
**        ALLOWED := [IDSYM, NUMSYM, ASTERISK];
**        ADDRESSSYMS := ALLOWED + [PLUS, MINUS, COMMA];
```

```
          C1 := CS (*start of literal field for listing*);
          with SOURCELINE, ADDRESSFIELD do
            begin
**            while SYM in ADDRESSSYMS do
                begin (*construct list of tokens forming address*)
**                if not (SYM in ALLOWED) then ERRORS := ERRORS + [BADADR];
                  ENTRIES := ENTRIES + 1;
                  with ENTRY[ENTRIES] do
                    begin
                      TNAME := ID; TNUMBER := NUM; TSYM := SYM;
                      TLENGTH := (CC - C1) mod SLENG (*force into range*);
                      for C2 := 1 to TLENGTH do (*copy token for later listing*)
                        begin TSTRING[C2] := LINE[C1]; C1 := C1 + 1 end
                    end;
**                ALLOWED := ADDRESSSYMS - ALLOWED;
                  GETSYM; C1 := CS
                end
            end (*with*)
          end (*GETADDRESS*);
```

Another useful example is in ASSEMBLELINE, which now incorporates a call to a procedure CHECKSEMANTICS to check on various combinations of extraneous or missing fields (lines 698 and 672–689).

To handle the awkward problem mentioned earlier of attempting to use address fields for EQU, DS, ORG and IF which are not known at assembly time, function VALUEOF uses the Boolean variables TERMDEFINED and FULLYEVALUATED to monitor the state of the computation (lines 472, 505 and 512).

4.6 Relocatable code

The assemblers we have considered so far have been load-and-go type assemblers, producing the machine instructions for the absolute locations where they will reside when the code is finally executed. However, when developing a large program it is convenient to be able to assemble it in sections and store each separately, finally linking the sections together before execution. To some extent this can be done with our present system, by placing an extra load on the programmer to ensure that all the sections of code and data are assembled for different areas in core, and letting him keep track of where they all start and stop. A small amount of modification is needed to procedure DUMPCODE, which presently dumps all 256 bytes to the CODEFILE (lines 791–808 of Listing 5) to allow it to dump fewer bytes, with a leading count, and an indication of where the first of these is subsequently to be loaded.

This is so trivial that it need be discussed no further here. In any case, such a scheme, while in keeping with the highly simplified view of actual code generation used in this book, is highly unsatisfactory. More sophisticated systems provide the facility for generating relocatable code, where the decision as to where it will finally reside is delayed until loading time.

At first sight even this seems easy to implement. Associated with each byte that is generated we associate a flag, saying whether the byte will finally be loaded unchanged, or whether it must be modified at load time by adding an offset to it. For example, the section of code

```
00                  BEG
00    10 06         LDA    A
02    17 37         ADI    55
04    13 07         STA    B
06    0C    A       DC     12
07    00    B       DC     0
08                  END
```

contains two bytes (assembled as at 01h and 05h) which refer to addresses which would alter if the code was relocated. The assembler could easily produce output for the loader on the lines of (bytes given in hex)

10 0	06 1	17 0	37 0	13 0	07 1	0C 0	00 0

where the first of each pair gives the byte; the second is a flag denoting whether the byte needs to be offset at load time. A 'relocatable code' file of this sort of information could, again, be preceded by a count of the number of bytes to be loaded. The loader could read a set of such files, effectively concatenating the code into memory from some specified overall starting address, and keeping track as it did so of the offset to be used.

Unfortunately, the full ramifications of this soon reach far beyond the scope of a naïve discussion. The main point of concern is how to decide which bytes must be regarded as 'relocatable'. Those defined by 'constants', such as the opcodes themselves, or entries in the symbol table generated by EQU directives are clearly 'absolute'. Entries in the symbol table defined by 'labels' in the label field of instructions may be thought of as 'relocatable', but bytes defined by expressions which involve the use of such labels are harder to analyse. This may be illustrated by a simple example.

Suppose we had the instruction

```
LDA    A - B
```

If A and B are absolute, or are both relocatable, and both defined in the section of code being assembled, the difference is absolute. If B is absolute and A is relocatable, the difference is still relocatable. If A is absolute and B is relocatable, the difference should probably be ruled inadmissible. Similarly, if we have an instruction like

```
LDA    A + B
```

the sum is absolute if both A and B are absolute, is relocatable if A is relocatable and B is absolute, and probably inadmissible otherwise. Similar arguments may be extended to handle an expression with more than two operands (but notice that expressions with multiplication and division become still harder to analyse).

The problem is exacerbated still further if – as will inevitably happen when such facilities are properly exploited – the programmer wishes to make reference to labels which are *not* defined in the code itself, but which may, perhaps, be defined in a separately assembled routine. It is not unreasonable to expect the programmer explicitly to declare the names of all labels to be used in this way, perhaps along the lines of

```
BEG
DEF     A,B,C     ; these are available for external use
USE     X,Y,Z     ; these are not defined, but required
. . .
```

In this case it is not hard to see that the information presented to the loader will have to be quite considerably more complex, effectively including those parts of the symbol table relating to the elements of the DEF list, and those parts of the branch ahead tables which relate to the USE list. Rather cowardly, we shall refrain from attempting to discuss these issues in further detail here, but leave them as interesting topics for the more adventurous reader to pursue on his or her own.

Exercises

The following exercises range from being almost trivial to rather long and involved, but the reader who successfully completes them will have learned a lot about the assembly translation process, and possibly even something about assembly language programming.

4.1 Ensure that the extensions to the simple assembler suggested at the end of Chapter 3 work correctly for the enlarged assembler.

4.2 We have chosen to extend the one-pass assembler, rather than the two-pass assembler. Attempt to extend the two-pass assembler in the same way.

4.3 How could you prevent programmers from branching to 'data', or from treating 'instruction' locations as data – assuming that you thought it desirable to do so? (As we have mentioned, assembler languages usually allow the programmer complete freedom in respect of the treatment of identifiers, something which is expressly forbidden in Pascal, but which many programmers regard as a most desirable feature of a language.)

4.4 What features could you include in, and what restrictions could you remove from the assembly process if you used a two-pass rather than a one-pass assembler? Try to include these extra features in your two-pass assembler.

4.5   Would it not be a good idea to warn the programmer of the action taken with regard to undefined labels? How and where might this be done?

4.6   Conditional assembly may be enhanced by allowing constructions of the form

```
IF      EXPRESSION
line 1
line 2

. . .
ENDIF
```

with the implication that the code up to the directive ENDIF is only assembled if EXPRESSION evaluates to a non-zero result at assembly time. Is this really a necessary or a desirable variation? How could it be implemented?

Other extensions might allow

```
IF      EXPRESSION
line 1
line 2

. . .
ELSE
line m
line n

. . .
ENDIF
```

with obvious meanings.

4.7   Conditional assembly might be made easier if one could use Boolean expressions rather than numerical ones, for example

```
IF      A > 0
```

or

```
IF      A <> 0 AND B = 1
```

How difficult would this be to implement?

4.8   In some systems one may not really have machine operations equivalent to the 'immediate' opcodes like LDI, ADI and so on, but it makes for ease of programming if we can assume that they exist. An assembler would then have to translate

```
LDI     34
```

as

```
LDA     CONST
```

with

```
CONST    DC      34
```

added implicitly (but, of course, clear of the executable code). How could you introduce this 'literal' facility? Be careful to let it deal with more complicated address fields, such as

```
LDI     A+7-*
```

4.9 Is it possible to allow a one-pass assembler to handle address fields which contain more general forms of expression, including multiplication and division? Attempt to do so, restricting your effort to the case where the expression is evaluated strictly from left to right. Do you suppose such a feature is of any real use?

4.10 We have already commented that a drawback of using Pascal dynamic structures for storing the elements of a composite address field is that it may be difficult to recover the storage when the structures are destroyed or are no longer needed. Would this drawback detract from their use in constructing the symbol table or branch ahead table?

4.11 We have carefully chosen our opcode mnemonics for the language so that they are lexically unique. However, some assemblers do not do this. For example, the 6502 assembler as used in the Apple microcomputer has instructions like

```
    LDA    2        equivalent to our    LDA     2
```

and

```
    LDA    #2       equivalent to our    LDI     2
```

that is, an extra character in the address field denotes whether the addressing mode is 'direct' or 'immediate'. In fact it may be even worse than that; for example, the LDA mnemonic in the 6502 assembler may be converted into one of eight machine instructions, depending on the exact form of the address field. What differences would it make to the assembly process if you had to cater for such conventions? To make it realistic, study the 6502 assembler mnemonics in detail.

4.12 Another variation on address field notation is provided by the Intel 8080 assembler, which uses mnemonics like

```
    MOV A,B    and    MOV B,A
```

to generate single byte instructions (78 hex and 47 hex respectively). How would this affect the assembly process?

4.13 How would one add a directive

```
    RAD  EXPRESSION
```

to allow a programmer to change the default base for numbers to that determined by the assembly-time value of EXPRESSION?

4.14   Some assemblers allow the programmer the facility to use 'local' labels, which are not really part of a global symbol list. For example, that provided on the UCSD p-System allows code like

```
LAB     MVI   A,4
        JMP   $2
        MVI   B,C
$2      NOP
        LHLD  1234
LAB2    XCHG
        POP   H
$2      POP   B
        POP   D
        JMP   $2
LAB3    NOP
```

Here the $2 label between the LAB1 and LAB2 labels and the $2 label between the LAB2 and LAB3 labels are local to those demarcated sections of code. How difficult is it to add this sort of facility to an assembler, and what would be the advantages in having it?

4.15   Some assemblers allow the programmer to use the opcode mnemonics as known constants in forming expressions, for example

```
        LDA   BRN
        STA   INST
INST    BZE   EXIT
```

which has the effect of modifying the BZE EXIT to a BRN EXIT. How would the assembler have to be changed to accommodate this feature?

The following exercises are all concerned with macro processing.

4.16   The following gives one way of solving a very simple problem

```
        BEG
NEWLINE EQU   130     ; carriage return line feed
WRITE   MAC   A,B     ; write integer A and character B
        LDA   A
        OTI           ; write integer
        LDI   B
        OTA           ; write character
        END           ; of WRITE macro
READ    MAC   A
        INI
```

```
              STA     A
              WRITE   A,NEWLINE ; reflect on output
              END               ; of READ macro
     LARGE    MAC     A,B,C     ; store larger of A,B in C
              LDA     A
              CMP     B
              BPZ     *+3
              LDA     B
              STA     C
              END               ; of LARGE macro

              READ    X
              READ    Y
              READ    Z
              LARGE   X,Y,LARGE
              LARGE   LARGE,Z,LARGE
     EXIT     WRITE   LARGE,NEWLINE
              HLT
              END               ; of program
```

If this were assembled by our macro assembler, what would the symbol, branch ahead and macro tables look like just before the line labelled EXIT was assembled? Is it permissible to use the identifier LARGE as the name both of a macro and of a label?

4.17 The LARGE macro is a little dangerous, perhaps. Addresses like *+3 are apt to cause trouble when modifications are made, because people forget to change absolute addresses or offsets. Discuss the implications of coding the body of this macro as

```
              LDA     A
              CMP     B
              BPZ     LAB
              LDA     B
     LAB      STA     C
              END               ; of LARGE macro
```

4.18 Should a macro be allowed to contain a reference to itself? This will allow recursion, in a sense, in assembly language programming, but how does one prevent the system from getting into an indefinite expansion? Can it be done with the facilities so far developed? If not, what must be added to the language to allow the full power of recursive macro calls?

4.19 $N!$ can be defined recursively as

if $N = 1$ then $N! = 1$ else $N! := N(N-1)!$

In the light of your answer to Exercise 4.18, can you make use of this idea to let the macro assembler developed so far generate code for computing 4! by using recursive macro calls?

4.20 Can you develop macros using the language suggested here which will allow you to simulate the if ... then ... else, while ... do, repeat ... until, and for loop constructions allowed in Pascal-like languages?

4.21 In our system, a macro may be defined *within* another macro. Is there any advantage in allowing this, especially as macros are all entered in a globally accessible macro table? Would it be possible to make nested macros obey scope rules similar to those found in Pascal systems?

4.22 Suppose a macro may contain another macro definition, but that this is only entered into the macro table when the first macro is expanded, and not when it is defined. Are there any advantages in being able to do this, and how would our system need to be altered to implement it?

4.23 Suppose two macros use the same formal parameter names. Does this cause problems when attempting macro expansion? Pay particular attention to the problems that might arise in the various ways in which nesting of macro expansions might be required.

4.24 Should one be able to redefine macro names? What does our system do if this is attempted, and how should it be changed to support your idea?

4.25 Should the number of formal and actual parameters be allowed to disagree? What does our system do if the numbers do not agree? Suggest ways of checking that the number of formal and actual parameters agree.

4.26 Would it be possible to use expressions, rather than single identifiers or numbers, as actual parameters in macro expansion? For example, could we define

```
JOLLY   MAC     FEE,FI,FO,FUM
        LDA     FEE
        ADD     FI
        STA     FO
        BRN     FUM
        END
```

and then expand along the lines of

```
JOLLY   GOOD+1,SHOW+6,WHAT,NEXT
```

giving

```
        LDA     GOOD+1
        ADD     SHOW+6
```

```
STA    WHAT
BRN    NEXT
```

(It would probably be more easily implemented on the lines of

```
JOLLY    (GOOD+1),(SHOW+6),WHAT,NEXT
```

but you should spend some time considering both ways.)

4.27 How difficult is it to add a facility to macros of partial substitution, for example, declaring

```
THIS MAC    %IS,VERY,%SILLY
        LD%IS    VERY%SILLY 1
        STA      RESULT
        END
```

which, if expanded as

```
THIS    I,SHORT,+
```

would result in

```
LDI    SHORT+1
STA    RESULT
```

and if expanded as

```
THIS    A,SHORT,-
```

would result in

```
LDA    SHORT-1
STA    RESULT
```

Larger projects

4.28 To what extent can a macro assembler be used to accept code in one assembly language and translate it into opcodes for another one? The Z80 and 8080 languages are very similar in many ways. Examine the prospects for defining macros so that an 8080 assembler can accept Z80 mnemonics. Some Z80 instructions have no 8080 equivalents. Can we use a macro facility to bypass this problem?

4.29 Develop a one-pass or two-pass assembler for the stack-oriented language discussed in Chapter 2.

4.30 What would be the implications of writing an assembler on a computer where the generated code and the assembler could not co-reside?

4.31 Modify your assembler to provide for the generation of relocatable code, and possibly for code which might be handled by a linkage editor, and modify the interpreter which you (should have) developed in Chapter 3 to include a more sophisticated linkage editor and loader.

4.32 A little thought shows that the ability merely to load code anywhere is not sufficient to allow the full power provided by developing programs in pieces. One section of code may (and probably will) make reference to addresses and labels in other sections, addresses which cannot possibly be known when the sections are developed in isolation. How do you cater for this problem?

4.33 As an even more realistic project, examine the 6502 assembler language, or the 8080 assembler language, or the Z80 assembler language, and write a good macro assembler for it.

Further reading

The book by Calingaert (1979) provides a good discussion of the macro processing problem. Another book in this area is by Brown (1974). As far as actual 8080 and Z80 coding is concerned, you might like to refer to Miller (1981) for some ideas. The book by Wakerly (1981)has excellent explanations of assembly level programming, the assembly, linking and loading process, and architectures of several modern machines.

Listing 5   Macro assembler for language of Chapters 3 and 4

```
1 program ASSEMBLER (INPUT, OUTPUT, CODEFILE, SOURCE);
2 (* One-pass macro assembler for language of Chapter 4
3    Mark 3a      P.D.Terry    July 1985     Version 3a *)
4 const               °
5    VERSION = '3a';
6    ADD = 21;  ADI = 23;  ADX = 22;  BNG = 36;  BNZ = 34;  BPZ = 35;
7    BRN = 32;  BZE = 33;  CLA =  1;  CLX =  2;  CMP = 27;  CPI = 29;
8    CPX = 28;  DEC =  4;  DEX =  6;  HLT = 15;  INA =  9;  INC =  3;
9    INI =  8;  INX =  5;  JSR = 37;  LDA = 16;  LDI = 18;  LDX = 17;
10   LSI = 31;  LSP = 30;  NOP =  0;  OTA = 11;  OTI = 10;  POP = 13;
11   PSH = 12;  RET = 14;  SBI = 26;  SBX = 25;  STA = 19;  STX = 20;
12   SUB = 24;  TAX =  7                        (*Machine ops*);
13   IFF = 46                                   (*conditional*);
14   MAC = 47                                   (*introduce macro*);
15   BEG = 40;  DC  = 41;  DS  = 42;  FIN = 43;
16   EQU = 44;  ORG = 45                        (*directives*);
17   NUL = 39                                   (*undefined*);
18   ERR = 38                                   (*error*);
```

```
19   NUMBEROPCODES = 47;
20
21   (* ++++++++ used by the lexical analyser and syntax analyser ++++++++ *)
22
23   LINEMAX = 81;
24   ALENG = 8                          (*length of short string*);
25   SLENG = 25                         (*length of comment*);
26   BLANK = '        '                 (*blank short string*);
27   BLANKSTRING = '                   ' (*blank comment string*);
28
29 type
30   BYTES = 0 .. 255;
31
32   (* ++++++++ used by the lexical analyser ++++++++++++++++++++++++++++ *)
33
34   LINEINDEX = 0 .. LINEMAX;
35   ALFA      = packed array [1 .. ALENG] of CHAR;
36   STRINGS   = packed array [1 .. SLENG] of CHAR;
37   SYMBOLS   = (NULSYM, IDSYM, NUMSYM, COMSYM, PLUS, MINUS, COMMA, ASTERISK);
38
39   (* ++++++++ used by the syntax  analyser ++++++++++++++++++++++++++++ *)
40
41   OPCODES = 0 .. NUMBEROPCODES;
42   KINDS = (NUMERIC, ALPHAMERIC, EXPRESSION);
43   ERRSET = set of (NONALFA, UNKNOWN, TOOLONG, LABELLED, UNLABELLED,
44                    NONNUMERIC, NOADDRESS, HASADDRESS, BADADR, NOTDEFINED);
45   TOKENS = record (*elements of address fields*)
46                 TNAME    : ALFA            (*name*);
47                 TNUMBER  : INTEGER         (*numeric value*);
48                 TSTRING  : STRINGS         (*if a string*);
49                 TLENGTH  : INTEGER         (*width*);
50                 TSYM     : SYMBOLS         (*kind*)
51             end (*TOKENS*);
52   ADDRESSES = record (*address field*)
53                 NUMBER  : INTEGER          (*value so far*);
54                 KIND    : KINDS;
55                 ENTRY   : array [1 .. 15] of TOKENS (*elements*);
56                 ENTRIES : 0 .. 15          (*number of elements*);
57                 FULLYEVALUATED : BOOLEAN   (*true if evaluated*)
58             end (*ADDRESSES*);
59   UNPACKEDLINES = record (*source text, unpacked into symbols*)
60                 LAB, MNEMONIC  : ALFA;
61                 OPENTRY        : OPCODES;
62                 ADDRESSFIELD   : ADDRESSES;
63                 COMMENT        : STRINGS
64             end (*UNPACKEDLINES*);
```

```
 65
 66   (* ++++++++ used by the semantic analyser ++++++++++++++++++++++++++ *)
 67
 68   BALINKS = ↑BAREFERENCES;
 69   BAREFERENCES = record (*forward references for undefined labels*)
 70                    BYTE   : BYTES      (*to be patched*);
 71                    BASIGN : -1 .. 1    (*treatment*);
 72                    BALINK : BALINKS    (*to next reference*)
 73                 end (*BAREFERENCES*);
 74   SYMLINKS = ↑SYMENTRIES;
 75   SYMENTRIES = record (*symbol table*)
 76                    NAME    : ALFA       (*name*);
 77                    SLINK   : SYMLINKS   (*to next entry*);
 78                    DEFINED : BOOLEAN    (*true if now defined*);
 79                    BLINK   : BALINKS    (*to outstanding references*);
 80                    ADDRESS : BYTES      (*value when defined*)
 81                 end (*SYMENTRIES*);
 82
 83   (* ++++++++ used for macro assembly ++++++++++++++++++++++++++++++++ *)
 84
 85   MACLINES = ↑LINES;
 86   LINES = record (*source text of macro definitions*)
 87            TEXT : UNPACKEDLINES    (*one source line*);
 88            LINK : MACLINES         (*to next line in definition*)
 89          end (*LINES*);
 90   MACLINKS = ↑MACENTRIES;
 91   MACENTRIES = record (*macro table*)
 92                    MNAME     : ALFA        (*macro identifier*);
 93                    PARAMS    : 0 .. 15     (*number of parameters*);
 94                    PNAME     : array [1 .. 15] of TOKENS (*parameters*);
 95                    MLINK     : MACLINKS    (*to next macro definition*);
 96                    FIRSTLINE : MACLINES    (*to first line in definition*)
 97                 end (*MACENTRIES*);
 98
 99 var
100   (* ++++++++ used by the character handler +++++++++++++++++++++++++ *)
101
102   (*some implementations require INPUT, OUTPUT : TEXT*)
103   SOURCE, CODEFILE : TEXT;
104   CH       : CHAR                            (*Last character read*);
105   CC, CS,                                     (*Character pointers*)
106   LL       : LINEINDEX                        (*Line length*);
107   LINE     : ARRAY [LINEINDEX] of CHAR        (*Last line read*);
108   HEXSTRING : packed array [1 .. 16] of CHAR  (*For conversion*);
109   ENDLINE  : BOOLEAN                          (*True at end of source line*);
110
```

```
111  (* ++++++++ used by the lexical analyser ++++++++++++++++++++++++++++ *)
112
113  SYM      : SYMBOLS                    (*Last SYMBOL read*);
114  ID       : ALFA                       (*Last IDENTIFIER read*);
115  NUM      : INTEGER                    (*Last NUMBER read*);
116  ASTRING  : STRINGS                    (*Last COMMENT read*);
117
118  (* ++++++++ used by the syntax analyser +++++++++++++++++++++++++++++ *)
119
120  SOURCELINE : UNPACKEDLINES;
121
122  (* ++++++++ used by the semantic analyser ++++++++++++++++++++++++++++ *)
123
124  OPTABLE : array [OPCODES] of   (*attributes*)
125              record
126                SPELLING : ALFA;
127                OPCODE   : OPCODES;
128              end (*OPTABLE*);
129  ONEBYTEOPS, TWOBYTEOPS : set of OPCODES   (*to distinguish attributes*);
130  LASTSYM : SYMLINKS                    (*last entry in symbol table*);
131  LASTMAC : MACLINKS                    (*last entry in macro table*);
132
133  (* ++++++++ used by the code generator +++++++++++++++++++++++++++++++ *)
134
135  NEXTBYTE : BYTES                      (*location counter*);
136  MCODE    : array [BYTES] of BYTES     (*generated machine code*);
137
138  (* ++++++++ used by the error handler ++++++++++++++++++++++++++++++++ *)
139
140  ERRORS   : ERRSET                     (*errors so far*);
141
142 procedure QUIT (N : INTEGER);
143 (* ++++++++++ implementation dependent, for handling fatal errors ++++++ *)
144   begin
145     case N of
146       1: WRITELN(OUTPUT, 'Incomplete program');
147       2: WRITELN(OUTPUT, 'Unrecognized character')
148     end;
149     (*close OUTPUT if necessary and abort program*)
150   end (*QUIT*);
151
152 (* +++++++++++++++++++++++++ Source handler +++++++++++++++++++++++++++ *)
153
154 procedure HEX (I, N : BYTES);
155 (*Write I as hex pair with N trailing spaces*)
156   begin
```

```
157      WRITE(OUTPUT, HEXSTRING[I div 16+1], HEXSTRING[I mod 16+1], ' ':N)
158   end (*HEX*);
159
160 procedure GETCH;
161 (*Get next character from SOURCE*)
162   begin
163     if CC = LL then
164       begin (*new line*)
165         if EOF(SOURCE) then QUIT(1);
166         LL := 0; CC := 0;
167         while not EOLN(SOURCE) do
168           begin LL := LL + 1; READ(SOURCE, CH); LINE[LL] := CH end;
169         LL := LL + 1; READLN(SOURCE); LINE[LL] := ' ' (*end clearly blank*)
170       end (*new line*);
171     CC := CC + 1; CH := LINE[CC]; ENDLINE := CC = LL
172   end (*GETCH*);
173
174 procedure PRINTLINE (BLANKS : INTEGER);
175 (*Source listing*)
176   var
177     I, J, L : INTEGER;
178   begin
179     L := 0;
180     with SOURCELINE, ADDRESSFIELD do
181       begin
182         WRITE(OUTPUT, ' ':BLANKS, LAB, MNEMONIC:6);
183         for I := 1 to ENTRIES do with ENTRY[I] do
184           begin
185             for J := 1 to TLENGTH do WRITE(OUTPUT, TSTRING[J]);
186             L := L + TLENGTH
187           end;
188         if L < 25 then WRITE(OUTPUT, ' ':25-L);
189         WRITELN(OUTPUT, COMMENT)
190       end
191   end (*PRINTLINE*);
192
193 procedure REPORTERRORS;
194   begin
195     if ERRORS <> [] then
196       begin
197         WRITELN(OUTPUT);
198         WRITELN(OUTPUT,'The following line contains errors'); PRINTLINE(13);
199         if NONALFA in ERRORS then WRITELN(OUTPUT,'Alphanumeric symbol expected');
200         if UNKNOWN in ERRORS then WRITELN(OUTPUT,'Unknown symbol encountered');
201         if TOOLONG in ERRORS then WRITELN(OUTPUT,'Alphameric symbol too long');
202         if LABELLED in ERRORS then WRITELN(OUTPUT,'Statement may not be labelled');
```

```
203        if UNLABELLED in ERRORS then WRITELN(OUTPUT,'Statement must be labelled');
204        if NONNUMERIC in ERRORS then WRITELN(OUTPUT,'Address field must be numeric');
205        if NOADDRESS in ERRORS then WRITELN(OUTPUT,'Address field must be present');
206        if HASADDRESS in ERRORS then WRITELN(OUTPUT,'Address field must be absent');
207        if NOTDEFINED in ERRORS then WRITELN(OUTPUT,'Address field undefined');
208        if BADADR in ERRORS then WRITELN(OUTPUT,'Bad address format');
209        WRITELN(OUTPUT);
210        ERRORS := [] (*clear again*)
211      end
212   end (*REPORTERRORS*);
213
214 procedure PRINTSYMBOLTABLE;
215 (*Summarize symbol table at end of listing*)
216   var
217     SYMENTRY : SYMLINKS;
218   begin
219     WRITELN(OUTPUT);
220     WRITELN(OUTPUT, 'Symbol Table'); WRITELN(OUTPUT, '------------');
221     SYMENTRY := LASTSYM;
222     while SYMENTRY <> nil do
223       begin
224         with SYMENTRY ↑ do
225           begin
226             WRITE(OUTPUT, NAME, ' '); HEX(ADDRESS, 1);
227             WRITELN(OUTPUT, ADDRESS:5)
228           end;
229         SYMENTRY := SYMENTRY ↑.SLINK
230       end;
231     WRITELN(OUTPUT)
232   end (*PRINTSYMBOLTABLE*);
233
234 procedure PRINTMACROS;
235 (*Summarize macro table at end of listing*)
236   var
237     MACENTRY : MACLINKS;
238     I : INTEGER;
239     M : MACLINES;
240   begin
241     MACENTRY := LASTMAC;
242     WRITELN(OUTPUT);
243     WRITELN(OUTPUT, 'Macro Table'); WRITELN(OUTPUT, '-----------');
244     while MACENTRY <> nil do
245       begin
246         WRITELN(OUTPUT); WRITELN(OUTPUT);
247         with MACENTRY ↑ do
248           begin
```

```
249              WRITE(OUTPUT, MNAME, ': ');
250               for I := 1 to PARAMS do WRITE(OUTPUT, PNAME[I].TNAME:10);
251               WRITELN(OUTPUT); M := FIRSTLINE
252            end;
253          while M <> nil do
254            begin SOURCELINE := M↑.TEXT; PRINTLINE(1); M := M↑.LINK end;
255          MACENTRY := MACENTRY↑.MLINK
256        end (*MACENTRY<>nil*)
257   end (*PRINTMACROS*);
258
259 (* +++++++++++++++++++++++++++++++ Lexical analyser +++++++++++++++++++++++++*)
260
261 procedure SYNTAXANALYSIS;
262
263   procedure GETSYM;
264   (* Get next SYMBOL from SOURCE*)
265     var
266       K : INTEGER;
267
268     function ALETTER : BOOLEAN;
269       begin ALETTER := CH in ['A' .. 'Z', 'a' .. 'z']  end (*ALETTER*);
270
271     function ADIGIT : BOOLEAN;
272       begin ADIGIT := CH in ['0' .. '9'] end (*ADIGIT*);
273
274     function DIGIT : INTEGER;
275       begin DIGIT := ORD(CH) - ORD('0') end (*DIGIT*);
276
277     procedure GETWORD;
278     (*Assemble identifier or opcode, in UPPERCASE for consistency*)
279       begin
280         while ALETTER or ADIGIT do
281           begin
282             if CH in ['a'..'z'] then CH := CHR(ORD(CH) - ORD('a') + ORD('A'));
283             if K <= ALENG
284               then begin ID[K] := CH; K := K + 1 end
285               else ERRORS := ERRORS + [TOOLONG];
286             GETCH
287           end
288       end (*GETWORD*);
289
290     procedure GETNUMBER;
291     (*Assemble decimal number*)
292       begin
293         while ADIGIT do
294           begin
```

```
295            NUM := 10 * NUM + DIGIT;
296            if K <= ALENG
297              then begin ID[K] := CH; K := K + 1 end
298              else ERRORS := ERRORS + [TOOLONG];
299            GETCH
300          end
301      end (*GETNUMBER*);
302
303    begin (*GETSYM*)
304      NUM := 0; K := 1; ID := BLANK;
305      while (CH = ' ') and not ENDLINE do GETCH; CS := CC (*first non-blank*);
306      if not (ADIGIT or ALETTER or (CH in [',', '*', '+', '-', ';', ' ']) )
307        then QUIT(2);
308      case CH of
309        'a', 'b', 'c', 'd', 'e', 'f', 'g', 'h', 'i', 'j', 'k', 'l', 'm',
310        'n', 'o', 'p', 'q', 'r', 's', 't', 'u', 'v', 'w', 'x', 'y', 'z',
311        'A', 'B', 'C', 'D', 'E', 'F', 'G', 'H', 'I', 'J', 'K', 'L', 'M',
312        'N', 'O', 'P', 'Q', 'R', 'S', 'T', 'U', 'V', 'W', 'X', 'Y', 'Z':
313          begin SYM := IDSYM; GETWORD end;
314        '0', '1', '2', '3', '4', '5', '6', '7', '8', '9':
315          begin SYM := NUMSYM; GETNUMBER end;
316        ';':
317          begin
318            SYM := COMSYM; ASTRING := BLANKSTRING;
319            while not ENDLINE do
320              begin
321                if K <= SLENG then begin ASTRING[K] := CH; K := K + 1 end;
322                GETCH
323              end
324          end;
325        '+': begin SYM := PLUS; GETCH end;
326        '-': begin SYM := MINUS; GETCH end;
327        '*': begin SYM := ASTERISK; GETCH end;
328        ',': begin SYM := COMMA; GETCH end;
329        ' ': SYM := NULSYM
330      end (*case*)
331    end (*GETSYM*);
332
333    procedure GETADDRESS;
334      var
335        C1, C2 : LINEINDEX (*character pointers*);
336        ADDRESSSYMS, ALLOWED : set of SYMBOLS;
337      begin
338        ALLOWED := [IDSYM, NUMSYM, ASTERISK];
339        ADDRESSSYMS := ALLOWED + [PLUS, MINUS, COMMA];
340        C1 := CS (*start of literal field for listing*);
```

```
341        with SOURCELINE, ADDRESSFIELD do
342          begin
343            while SYM in ADDRESSSYMS do
344              begin (*construct list of tokens forming address*)
345                if not (SYM in ALLOWED) then ERRORS := ERRORS + [BADADR];
346                ENTRIES := ENTRIES + 1;
347                with ENTRY[ENTRIES] do
348                  begin
349                    TNAME := ID; TNUMBER := NUM; TSYM := SYM;
350                    TLENGTH := CC - C1;
351                    if TLENGTH > SLENG then TLENGTH := SLENG (*truncate*);
352                    for C2 := 1 to TLENGTH do (*copy token for later listing*)
353                      begin TSTRING[C2] := LINE[C1]; C1 := C1 + 1 end
354                  end;
355                ALLOWED := ADDRESSSYMS - ALLOWED;
356                GETSYM; C1 := CS
357              end
358          end (*with*)
359    end (*GETADDRESS*);
360
361  begin (*SYNTAXANALYSIS*)
362    ERRORS := [] (*start each line clean*);
363    with SOURCELINE do
364      begin
365        LAB := BLANK; COMMENT := BLANKSTRING; MNEMONIC := BLANK;
366        with ADDRESSFIELD do
367          begin NUMBER := 0; KIND := ALPHAMERIC, ENTRIES := 0 end;
368        GETCH;
369        if not (CH in [' ', ';']) then
370          begin
371            GETSYM;
372            if SYM <> IDSYM then ERRORS := ERRORS + [NONALFA] else LAB := ID
373          end;
374        GETSYM (*opcode? *);
375        if SYM = COMSYM then COMMENT := ASTRING else
376        if SYM <> NULSYM then
377          begin
378            if SYM <> IDSYM
379              then ERRORS := ERRORS + [NONALFA] else MNEMONIC := ID;
380            GETSYM (*address? *);
381            if SYM = COMSYM then COMMENT := ASTRING else
382            if SYM <> NULSYM then
383              begin
384                GETADDRESS;
385                if SYM = COMSYM then COMMENT := ASTRING
386                else if SYM <> NULSYM then ERRORS := ERRORS + [UNKNOWN]
```

```
387                end
388             end
389          end (*with SOURCELINE*);
390      if ERRORS <> [] then begin REPORTERRORS; SYNTAXANALYSIS (*next line*) end
391     end (*SYNTAXANALYSIS*);
392
393
394   (* +++++++++++++++++++++++++++++++ First and only pass +++++++++++++++++++ *)
395
396    procedure FIRSTPASS;
397      var
398        I       : INTEGER  (*for loop*);
399        PASSONE,
400        FOUND,              (*used in symbol table searches*)
401        INCLUDE : BOOLEAN  (*conditional assembly*);
402        SYMENTRY : SYMLINKS (*location of an identifier in symbol table*);
403
404      procedure FINDENTRY (LAB : ALFA);
405      (*Search for symbol entry matching 'LAB' in symbol table*)
406        begin
407          SYMENTRY := LASTSYM; FOUND := FALSE;
408          while not FOUND and (SYMENTRY <> nil) do
409            if LAB = SYMENTRY ↑.NAME
410              then FOUND := TRUE else SYMENTRY := SYMENTRY ↑.SLINK;
411          if not FOUND then (*make new node*)
412            begin
413              NEW(SYMENTRY);
414              with SYMENTRY ↑ do
415                begin
416                  NAME := LAB; DEFINED := FALSE; BLINK := nil; SLINK := LASTSYM
417                end;
418              LASTSYM := SYMENTRY
419            end
420        end (*FINDENTRY*);
421
422      procedure PROCESSCHAIN (LINK : BALINKS; ADDRESS : BYTES);
423      (*Fill in forward references once known*)
424        begin
425          while LINK <> nil do
426            begin
427              with LINK ↑ do
428                MCODE[BYTE] := (MCODE[BYTE] + BASIGN * ADDRESS + 256) mod 256;
429                LINK := LINK ↑.BALINK
430            end
431        end (*PROCESSCHAIN*);
432
```

```
433    procedure ADDTOSYMBOLTABLE (LAB : ALFA; ADR : BYTES);
434    (*New entry, or complete an incomplete entry*)
435      begin
436        FINDENTRY(LAB);
437        with SYMENTRY ↑ do
438          begin
439            if FOUND then PROCESSCHAIN(BLINK, ADR);
440            DEFINED := TRUE; ADDRESS := ADR; BLINK := nil
441          end
442      end (*ADDTOSYMBOLTABLE*);
443
444    function VALUEOF (var ADDRESSFIELD : ADDRESSES) : INTEGER;
445    (*Determine value of address field as far as possible*)
446      var
447        I          : INTEGER;
448        TERMKIND   : KINDS;
449        TERMDEFINED : BOOLEAN (*true if a term is known completely*);
450        SIGNNOW    : -1 .. 1 (*sign of current term*);
451
452      function TERMVALUE (TOKEN : TOKENS) : INTEGER;
453      (*Determine value of a term in address if possible, and add to branch
454       ahead table if not*)
455        var
456          BAENTRY  : BALINKS   (*for new entry in branch ahead table*);
457        begin
458          with TOKEN do
459            begin
460              case TSYM of
461                NUMSYM   : TERMKIND := NUMERIC;
462                IDSYM    : TERMKIND := ALPHAMERIC;
463                ASTERISK : begin TERMKIND := NUMERIC; TNUMBER := NEXTBYTE end
464              end (*case*);
465              case TERMKIND of
466                NUMERIC:
467                  begin TERMDEFINED := TRUE; TERMVALUE := TNUMBER mod 256 end;
468                ALPHAMERIC:
469                  begin
470                    TERMVALUE := 0 (*in case undefined *);
471                    FINDENTRY(TNAME);
472                    TERMDEFINED := SYMENTRY ↑.DEFINED;
473                    if FOUND
474                      then (*entry was made previously*)
475                        if SYMENTRY ↑.DEFINED
476                          then TERMVALUE := SYMENTRY ↑.ADDRESS
477                          else
478                            begin (*add to reference chain*)
```

```
479                            NEW(BAENTRY);
480                            with BAENTRY ↑ do
481                              begin
482                                BALINK := SYMENTRY ↑.BLINK;
483                                BASIGN := SIGNNOW; BYTE := NEXTBYTE
484                              end;
485                            SYMENTRY ↑.BLINK := BAENTRY
486                          end (*add to chain*)
487                        else (*first entry in reference chain*)
488                          begin
489                            NEW(SYMENTRY ↑.BLINK);
490                            with SYMENTRY ↑.BLINK ↑ do
491                              begin
492                                BALINK := nil; BYTE := NEXTBYTE;
493                                BASIGN := SIGNNOW
494                              end
495                          end (*first entry in reference chain*)
496                    end (*ALPHAMERIC*)
497                end (*case TERMKIND*)
498            end (*with TOKEN*)
499          end (*TERMVALUE*);
500
501    begin (*VALUEOF*)
502      with ADDRESSFIELD do
503        begin
504          SIGNNOW := 1; NUMBER := TERMVALUE(ENTRY[1]);
505          FULLYEVALUATED := TERMDEFINED;
506          KIND := TERMKIND; I := 2;
507          while I < ENTRIES do
508            begin
509              KIND := EXPRESSION; SIGNNOW := 1;
510              if ENTRY[I].TSYM = MINUS then SIGNNOW := -1; I := I + 1;
511              NUMBER := (NUMBER + TERMVALUE(ENTRY[I])*SIGNNOW + 256) mod 256;
512              FULLYEVALUATED := FULLYEVALUATED and TERMDEFINED;
513              I := I + 1
514            end;
515          VALUEOF := NUMBER
516        end (*with ADDRESSFIELD*)
517    end (*VALUEOF*);
518
519    function FINDOPENTRY (MNEMONIC : ALFA) : OPCODES;
520    (*Search opcode table (binary search) *)
521      var
522        LOOK, L, R : INTEGER;
523      begin
524        L := 1; R := NUMBEROPCODES;
```

```
525        repeat
526          LOOK := (L + R) div 2;
527          if MNEMONIC > OPTABLE[LOOK].SPELLING
528            then L := LOOK + 1 else R := LOOK - 1
529        until (MNEMONIC = OPTABLE[LOOK].SPELLING) or (L > R);
530        if MNEMONIC = OPTABLE[LOOK].SPELLING
531          then FINDOPENTRY := LOOK else FINDOPENTRY := 0 (*ERR entry*)
532      end (*FINDOPENTRY*);
533
534    procedure UNDEFINEDVARIABLES;
535    (*Allocate storage space for undefined variables assuming that all these
536      refer to storage locations *)
537      var
538        SYMENTRY : SYMLINKS;
539      begin
540        SYMENTRY := LASTSYM;
541        while SYMENTRY <> nil do
542          begin
543            with SYMENTRY↑ do
544              if not DEFINED then
545                begin
546                  MCODE[NEXTBYTE] := 0; ADDRESS := NEXTBYTE;
547                  PROCESSCHAIN(BLINK, NEXTBYTE);
548                  DEFINED := TRUE; NEXTBYTE := (NEXTBYTE + 1) mod 256
549                end;
550            SYMENTRY := SYMENTRY↑.SLINK
551          end (*SYMENTRY <> nil*)
552      end (*UNDEFINEDVARIABLES*);
553
554    procedure DEFINEMACRO;
555    (*Accept source code for a macro definition*)
556      var
557        LAST, LINEENTRY : MACLINES;
558
559      procedure ADDTOMACROTABLE;
560      (*Add to table of macro identifiers *)
561        var
562          MACENTRY : MACLINKS;
563          I        : INTEGER;
564        begin
565          NEW(MACENTRY);
566          with MACENTRY↑, SOURCELINE, ADDRESSFIELD do
567            begin
568              FIRSTLINE := nil; MNAME := LAB; MLINK := LASTMAC;
569              PARAMS := 0; I := 1;
570              while I <= ENTRIES do (*deal with parameters*)
```

```
571                    begin
572                      if ODD(I) then
573                        begin
574                          PARAMS := PARAMS + 1; PNAME[PARAMS] := ENTRY[I]
575                        end
576                      else
577                        if ENTRY[I].TSYM <> COMMA
578                          then ERRORS := ERRORS + [UNKNOWN];
579                      I := I + 1
580                    end
581                end (*with*);
582              LASTMAC := MACENTRY; REPORTERRORS
583          end (*ADDTOMACROTABLE*);
584
585      begin (*DEFINEMACRO*)
586        PRINTLINE(13); ADDTOMACROTABLE;
587        SYNTAXANALYSIS;
588        while SOURCELINE.MNEMONIC <> 'END     ' do
589          if SOURCELINE.MNEMONIC = 'MAC     '
590            then begin DEFINEMACRO; SYNTAXANALYSIS end
591            else
592              begin (*store source text of macro in a queue*)
593                PRINTLINE(13); NEW(LINEENTRY);
594                if LASTMAC↑.FIRSTLINE = nil (*first line of macro text*)
595                  then LASTMAC↑.FIRSTLINE := LINEENTRY
596                  else LAST↑.LINK := LINEENTRY;
597                with LINEENTRY↑ do begin TEXT := SOURCELINE; LINK := nil end;
598                LAST := LINEENTRY; SYNTAXANALYSIS
599              end;
600          PRINTLINE(13)
601        end (*DEFINEMACRO*);
602
603      procedure ASSEMBLELINE;
604      (*Assemble single line of source code*)
605        var
606          MACENTRY : MACLINKS;
607          I        : INTEGER;
608
609        function MACRO (MNEMONIC : ALFA) : BOOLEAN;
610        (*Search macro table for match to opcode field*)
611          var
612            SEARCHING : BOOLEAN;
613          begin
614            MACENTRY := LASTMAC; SEARCHING := TRUE;
615            while SEARCHING and (MACENTRY <> nil) do
616              if MNEMONIC = MACENTRY↑.MNAME
```

```
617               then SEARCHING := FALSE else MACENTRY := MACENTRY ↑.MLINK;
618          MACRO := not SEARCHING
619        end (*MACRO*);
620
621      procedure EXPAND (MACRO : MACLINKS);
622      (*Expand macro by assembling from stored text of macro, rather than
623        from source input *)
624        var
625          ACTUAL : array [1 .. 15] of TOKENS;
626          M     : MACLINES;
627
628        procedure GETACTUALPARAMETERS;
629          var
630            I, P : INTEGER;
631          begin
632            I := 1; P := 0;
633            with SOURCELINE.ADDRESSFIELD do
634              while I <= ENTRIES do
635                begin
636                  if ODD(I)
637                    then begin P := P + 1; ACTUAL[P] := ENTRY[I] end
638                    else
639                      if ENTRY[I].TSYM <> COMMA then ERRORS := ERRORS + [UNKNOWN];
640                  I := I + 1
641                end;
642            REPORTERRORS
643          end (*GETACTUALPARAMETERS*);
644
645        procedure SUBSTITUTEACTUALPARAMETERS;
646          var
647            I, J : INTEGER;
648          begin
649            with SOURCELINE, ADDRESSFIELD, MACRO ↑ do
650              for I := 1 to PARAMS do
651                begin
652                  if LAB = PNAME[I].TNAME then LAB := ACTUAL[I].TNAME;
653                  if MNEMONIC = PNAME[I].TNAME
654                    then MNEMONIC := ACTUAL[I].TNAME;
655                  for J := 1 to ENTRIES do
656                    if ENTRY[J].TNAME = PNAME[I].TNAME
657                      then ENTRY[J] := ACTUAL[I]
658                end (*for, with*)
659          end (*SUBSTITUTEACTUALPARAMETERS*);
660
661      begin (*EXPAND*)
662        if SOURCELINE.LAB <> BLANK
```

```
663              then ADDTOSYMBOLTABLE(SOURCELINE.LAB, NEXTBYTE);
664           PRINTLINE(13); GETACTUALPARAMETERS; M := MACRO↑.FIRSTLINE;
665          while M <> nil do
666            begin
667              SOURCELINE := M↑.TEXT; M := M↑.LINK;
668              SUBSTITUTEACTUALPARAMETERS; ASSEMBLELINE
669            end
670         end (*EXPAND*);
671
672      procedure CHECKSEMANTICS;
673      (*Elementary semantic checks by class of opcode*)
674        begin
675          with SOURCELINE, ADDRESSFIELD, OPTABLE[OPENTRY] do
676            begin
677              if (OPCODE in [BEG, FIN, ORG, IFF]) and (LAB <> BLANK)
678                then ERRORS := ERRORS + [LABELLED];
679              if (OPCODE = EQU) and (LAB = BLANK)
680                then ERRORS := ERRORS + [UNLABELLED];
681              if (OPCODE in TWOBYTEOPS + [EQU, DS, DC, IFF, ORG])
682                  and (ENTRIES = 0)
683                then ERRORS := ERRORS + [NOADDRESS];
684              if (OPCODE in [BEG, FIN] + ONEBYTEOPS) and (ENTRIES > 0)
685                then ERRORS := ERRORS + [HASADDRESS];
686              if (OPCODE = ERR)
687                then ERRORS := ERRORS + [UNKNOWN];
688            end (*with*)
689        end (*CHECKSEMANTICS*);
690
691      begin (*ASSEMBLELINE*)
692        ERRORS := [] (*start clean for semantic checking*);
693        if not INCLUDE then INCLUDE := TRUE else
694        with SOURCELINE do
695          if MACRO(MNEMONIC) then EXPAND(MACENTRY) else
696            begin
697              OPENTRY := FINDOPENTRY(MNEMONIC);
698              CHECKSEMANTICS;
699              with OPTABLE[OPENTRY] do
700                begin
701                  if OPCODE <> ERR then
702                    begin
703                      if OPCODE in [NUL, BEG, ORG, DS, EQU, FIN, DC, IFF] then
704                        case OPCODE of
705                          BEG:
706                            begin NEXTBYTE := 0; HEX(NEXTBYTE, 10) end;
707                          ORG:
708                            begin
```

```
709                          NEXTBYTE := VALUEOF(ADDRESSFIELD);
710                          if not ADDRESSFIELD.FULLYEVALUATED
711                            then ERRORS := ERRORS + [NOTDEFINED];
712                          HEX(NEXTBYTE, 10)
713                       end;
714                    NUL:
715                      begin
716                        if LAB <> BLANK
717                          then ADDTOSYMBOLTABLE(LAB, NEXTBYTE);
718                        HEX(NEXTBYTE, 10)
719                      end;
720                    DS:
721                      begin
722                        if LAB <> BLANK
723                          then ADDTOSYMBOLTABLE(LAB, NEXTBYTE);
724                        HEX(NEXTBYTE, 10);
725                        NEXTBYTE := (NEXTBYTE+VALUEOF(ADDRESSFIELD) + 256) mod 256;
726                        if not ADDRESSFIELD.FULLYEVALUATED
727                          then ERRORS := ERRORS + [NOTDEFINED]
728                      end;
729                    EQU:
730                      begin
731                        HEX(NEXTBYTE, 10);
732                        ADDTOSYMBOLTABLE(LAB, VALUEOF(ADDRESSFIELD));
733                        if not ADDRESSFIELD.FULLYEVALUATED
734                          then ERRORS := ERRORS + [NOTDEFINED]
735                      end;
736                    FIN:
737                      begin HEX(NEXTBYTE, 10); PASSONE := FALSE end;
738                    DC:
739                      begin
740                        if LAB <> BLANK
741                          then ADDTOSYMBOLTABLE(LAB, NEXTBYTE);
742                        HEX(NEXTBYTE, 4);
743                        MCODE[NEXTBYTE] := VALUEOF(ADDRESSFIELD);
744                        HEX(MCODE[NEXTBYTE], 4);
745                        NEXTBYTE := (NEXTBYTE + 1) mod 256
746                      end (*DC*);
747                    IFF:
748                      begin
749                        INCLUDE := VALUEOF(ADDRESSFIELD) <> 0;
750                        if not ADDRESSFIELD.FULLYEVALUATED
751                          then ERRORS := ERRORS + [NOTDEFINED];
752                        WRITE(OUTPUT, ' ':12)
753                      end (*IFF*);
754                  end (*case*)
```

```
755                  else
756                    begin (*Machine ops*)
757                      if LAB <> BLANK
758                        then ADDTOSYMBOLTABLE(LAB, NEXTBYTE);
759                      HEX(NEXTBYTE, 4); MCODE[NEXTBYTE] := OPCODE;
760                      HEX(MCODE[NEXTBYTE], 1);
761                      NEXTBYTE := (NEXTBYTE + 1) mod 256;
762                      if OPCODE in TWOBYTEOPS
763                        then
764                          begin
765                            MCODE[NEXTBYTE] := VALUEOF(ADDRESSFIELD);
766                            HEX(MCODE[NEXTBYTE], 1);
767                            NEXTBYTE := (NEXTBYTE + 1) mod 256
768                          end
769                        else WRITE(OUTPUT, '   ')
770                    end (*machine ops*)
771                  end (*OPCODE<>ERR*)
772                else WRITE(OUTPUT, '??            ')
773              end (*with OPTABLE*);
774            PRINTLINE(1);
775            REPORTERRORS
776          end (*with SOURCELINE*);
777      end (*ASSEMBLELINE*);
778
779    begin (*FIRSTPASS*)
780      INCLUDE := TRUE; PASSONE := TRUE; NEXTBYTE := 0;
781      while PASSONE do
782        begin
783          SYNTAXANALYSIS;
784          if SOURCELINE.MNEMONIC = 'MAC   '
785            then DEFINEMACRO else ASSEMBLELINE
786        end;
787      UNDEFINEDVARIABLES;
788      PRINTSYMBOLTABLE; PRINTMACROS
789    end (*FIRSTPASS*);
790
791    procedure DUMPCODE;
792    (*Dump MCODE to CODEFILE for later loading*)
793      var
794        I, J, NEXTBYTE : INTEGER;
795      begin
796        (*open and REWRITE(CODEFILE) as appropriate*)
797        NEXTBYTE := 0;
798        for I := 1 to 16 do
799          begin
800            for J := 1 to 16 do
```

```
801            begin
802              WRITE(CODEFILE, MCODE[NEXTBYTE]:4);
803              NEXTBYTE := NEXTBYTE + 1
804            end;
805          WRITELN(CODEFILE)
806        end;
807      (*close CODEFILE if necessary*)
808    end (*DUMPCODE*);
809
810  (* ++++++++++++++++++++++++ Table initialization ++++++++++++++++++++++++ *)
811
812  procedure INITIALIZE;
813  (*Initialize opcode table, pointers, and code array*)
814    var
815    I, J : INTEGER;
816
817    procedure ENTER (ID : ALFA; THISCODE : OPCODES);
818      begin
819        with OPTABLE[I] do begin SPELLING := ID; OPCODE := THISCODE end;
820        I := I + 1
821      end (*ENTER*);
822
823    begin
824    I := 0 (*enter opcodes and mnemonics in alphabetic order*);
825    ENTER('Error   ', ERR) (*bogus one for erroneous data*);
826    ENTER('        ', NUL) (*for lines with no opcode*);
827    ENTER('ADD     ', ADD); ENTER('ADI     ', ADI);
828    ENTER('ADX     ', ADX); ENTER('BEG     ', BEG);
829    ENTER('BNG     ', BNG); ENTER('BNZ     ', BNZ);
830    ENTER('BPZ     ', BPZ); ENTER('BRN     ', BRN);
831    ENTER('BZE     ', BZE); ENTER('CLA     ', CLA);
832    ENTER('CLX     ', CLX); ENTER('CMP     ', CMP);
833    ENTER('CPI     ', CPI); ENTER('CPX     ', CPX);
834    ENTER('DC      ', DC ); ENTER('DEC     ', DEC);
835    ENTER('DEX     ', DEX); ENTER('DS      ', DS );
836    ENTER('END     ', FIN); ENTER('EQU     ', EQU);
837    ENTER('HLT     ', HLT); ENTER('IF      ', IFF);
838    ENTER('INA     ', INA); ENTER('INC     ', INC);
839    ENTER('INI     ', INI); ENTER('INX     ', INX);
840    ENTER('JSR     ', JSR); ENTER('LDA     ', LDA);
841    ENTER('LDI     ', LDI); ENTER('LDX     ', LDX);
842    ENTER('LSI     ', LSI); ENTER('LSP     ', LSP);
843    ENTER('MAC     ', MAC); ENTER('NOP     ', NOP);
844    ENTER('ORG     ', ORG); ENTER('OTA     ', OTA);
845    ENTER('OTI     ', OTI); ENTER('POP     ', POP);
846    ENTER('PSH     ', PSH); ENTER('RET     ', RET);
```

```
847      ENTER('SBI    ', SBI); ENTER('SBX    ', SBX);
848      ENTER('STA    ', STA); ENTER('STX    ', STX);
849      ENTER('SUB    ', SUB); ENTER('TAX    ', TAX);
850      LASTSYM := nil; LASTMAC := nil; HEXSTRING := '0123456789ABCDEF';
851      CC := 0; LL := 0 (*Initialize source handler*);
852      ONEBYTEOPS := [NOP .. HLT]; TWOBYTEOPS := [LDA .. JSR];
853      for J := 0 to 255 do MCODE[J] := NUL (*fill with rubbish*);
854      WRITELN(OUTPUT, 'One-Pass Macro Assembler ', VERSION); WRITELN(OUTPUT);
855    end (*INITIALIZE*);
856
857  begin (*ASSEMBLER*)
858    (*open and RESET(SOURCE), REWRITE(OUTPUT) as appropriate*)
859    INITIALIZE;
860    FIRSTPASS;
861    DUMPCODE;
862    (*close OUTPUT file if necessary*)
863  end (*ASSEMBLER*).
```

Chapter 5 **Languages and grammars**

We have covered quite a lot of ground in the previous chapters, but we must stress again that the translators we have developed are by no means of production quality. Nor have we really discussed the very real problems that might arise if we were to attempt assembly suitable for an environment other than a simple load-and-go one.

However, it is to be hoped that the reader may have some idea of how the translation process might be carried out for a language in which the syntax and semantics are very simply or loosely defined. In ASSEMBLER level programming, frequently, almost anything seems to be allowed – little or no distinction is drawn between code and data, few checks are carried out that instructions will have a sensible outcome, and so on. The same is not true of higher level languages, to which we shall now turn. In using such languages the user has to be far more aware of the details of syntax than when using ASSEMBLER, as, indeed, does the potential implementor of translators for them.

A study of the syntax and semantics of programming languages may be made at many levels, and is an important part of modern Computer Science. One can approach it from a very mathematical viewpoint, or from a very informal one. In what follows we shall adopt a fairly informal attitude, and touch only briefly on certain aspects of the subject, aspects which we hope will be of interest, and which will be comprehensible to readers familiar with a block-structured language such as Pascal. These include the specification of language syntax, the practical design of languages, and the implementation of simple compilers.

5.1   Syntax, semantics and pragmatics

In order to communicate, people require languages. In ordinary speech they use natural languages like English or French; for more specialized applications they use technical languages like that of Mathematics, for example

$$\forall x \, \exists \varepsilon :: |x - \xi| < \varepsilon$$

We are mainly concerned with programming languages, which are notations for describing computations. A useful programming language must be suited both to *describing* and to *implementing* the solution to a problem, and it is difficult to find languages that satisfy both requirements – efficient implementation seems to require the use of low-level languages, and easy description seems to require the use of high-level languages.

Most people are taught their first programming language by example. This is admirable in many respects, and probably unavoidable, since 'learning the language' is invariably carried out in parallel with a more fundamental process of 'learning to develop algorithms'. But the technique suffers from the drawback that the tuition is incomplete. One can only be shown a certain number of examples, and inevitably will be left with questions of the 'can I do this?' or 'how do I do this?' variety. In recent years a great deal of effort has been spent on formalizing programming (and other) languages, and in finding ways to describe them and to define them. Of course, a formal programming language has to be described by using another language. This language of description is called the **metalanguage**. Early programming languages were described using English as the metalanguage. It is a requirement of the word 'definition' that the metalanguage be completely unambiguous (which is not a strong feature of English, used loosely as we all tend to do), and some people still find that the best way to answer the questions posed above is to ask them of the compilers which implement the languages. This is highly unsatisfactory, as compilers are known to be error-prone, and (even within the products from one manufacturer) to differ in the way they handle the same source language.

Natural languages, technical languages and programming languages are alike in several respects. In each case the **sentences** of a language are composed of sets of **strings** of **symbols** or **words**, and the construction of these sentences is governed by the application of two sets of rules.

(a) **Syntax rules** describe the **form** of the sentences in the language. For example, in English, the sentence 'The wise man avoids computers' is syntactically correct, while the sentence 'The avoids wise man computers' is incorrect. To take another example, the language of binary numerals uses the symbols 0 and 1, arranged in strings formed by concatenation, so that the sentence 101 is syntactically correct for this language, but the sentence 1110211 is syntactically incorrect.

(b) **Semantic rules**, on the other hand, define the meaning of syntactically correct sentences in a language. By itself the 'sentence' 101 has no meaning without the addition of semantic rules to the effect that it is to be interpreted as the representation of the number 'five' using a positional convention.

Besides being aware of syntax and semantics, the user of a programming language cannot avoid coming to terms with some of the pragmatic issues involved with implementation techniques, programming methodology, and so on. These factors invariably govern subtle aspects of the design of almost every practical language, often in a most irritating way. For example, in FORTRAN the length of an identifier is restricted to only six characters – a legacy of the word size on the IBM computer for which the first FORTRAN compiler was written.

It probably will not have dawned on the reader that the design of Pascal (and of several of its successors and contemporaries) was governed largely by a desire to make it easy to compile. It is a tribute to its designer that, in spite of limitations which this desire naturally introduced, Pascal has become so popular, and the model for so many other languages and extensions.

Of all the aspects of programming, the design of a language requires the greatest skill and judgement. There is evidence to show that one's language is not only useful for expressing one's ideas, but, because language is used so often in formulating and developing ideas, one's knowledge of language largely determines *how* and, indeed, *what* one can think. In the case of programming languages, there has been much controversy over this. For example, in languages like FORTRAN – for long the *lingua franca* of the scientific computing community – recursive algorithms are 'difficult' to implement (not impossible, just difficult!), with the result that many programmers who have been brought up on FORTRAN find recursion strange and difficult, even something to be avoided at all costs. It is true that recursive algorithms are sometimes 'inefficient', and that compilers for languages that 'allow' recursion may exacerbate this; it is also true that some algorithms are more simply explained in a recursive way than in one that depends on explicit repetition (the best examples probably being those associated with tree manipulation).

The design of a programming language must thus strive to allow 'useful' concepts, and yet strive also not to become so large that it becomes impossible to learn, or to implement. We urge the reader, as he or she works through the following sections, to try to develop a critical approach to the language we shall use as a model of one to be implemented, and also to the one which we shall use to implement its compiler.

The formal study of syntax as applied to programming languages took a great step forward in about 1960, with the publication of the *Algol 60 Report*, which used an elegant, yet simple, notation known as **Backus–Naur Form** (sometimes called **Backus Normal Form**) which we shall study shortly. Simply understood notations for describing semantics have not been so forthcoming, and many semantic features of languages are still described informally, or by example.

Exercises

5.1 Are there any features of Pascal (or FORTRAN) whose presence you cannot understand, perhaps because you have never had cause to use them?

5.2 Are there any features or deficiencies in Pascal (or in FORTRAN) which you have found to hinder your ability to solve programming problems?

5.3 Are there any features of Pascal (or of FORTRAN) that you feel are unnecessary, perhaps because their presence makes it possible to do the same thing in too many different ways?

5.4 Why exactly do you think COBOL is so popular as a 'commercial' language, and why is FORTRAN so popular as a 'scientific' language?

5.2 Formal languages

In trying to specify programming languages rigorously we must be aware of some features of **formal language theory**. This is a subject that can become highly mathematical; although we shall strive to avoid extremes, some knowledge of the terminology and notation used is unavoidable. Consequently, we shall start with a few abstract definitions.

(a) A **symbol** is an atomic entity, represented by a character, or sometimes by a reserved word or keyword, for example $+$, ; **end**.

(b) An **alphabet** or **vocabulary** A is a non-empty finite set of symbols. For example, the alphabet of Pascal includes the symbols

$$- \quad / \quad * \quad a \quad b \quad c \quad A \quad B \quad C \quad \textbf{begin} \quad \textbf{case} \quad \textbf{end}$$

(c) A **word** or **string** 'over' an alphabet A is a sequence $\sigma = a_1 a_2 \ldots a_n$ of symbols from the alphabet.

(d) It is often useful to hypothesize the existence of a string of length zero, called the **null string** or **empty word** and denoted by ε (some authors use λ instead). This has the property that if it is concatenated to the left or right of any word, that word remains unaltered.

(e) The set of all strings over an alphabet A is denoted by $A*$.

(f) A **language** L over an alphabet A is a subset of $A*$. Note that this involves no concept of meaning. A language is simply a set of strings. A language consisting of a finite number of strings can be defined simply by listing all those strings, or giving a rule for their derivation. For example, we might have

$$L = \{([a+)^n(b])^n \mid n > 0\}$$

(the vertical stroke can be read 'such that') which defines exciting mathematical expressions like

$$[a + b]$$
$$[a + [a + b]b]$$
$$[a + [a + [a + b]b]b]$$

Most practical languages are, of course, rather more complicated than can be defined in this way, and so we introduce the concept of

(g) A **grammar**, which is essentially a set of rules for choosing the subsets of $A*$ in which we are interested. A grammar has four components

- N – a set of **non-terminal** symbols,
- T – a set of **terminal** symbols,
- S – a special **goal** or **start** or **distinguished** symbol,
- P – a set of **productions**.

(h) The set N is often spoken of as denoting the **syntactic classes** of the grammar. The union of the sets N and T denotes the **vocabulary** V of the grammar.

(i)   A **sentence** is a string composed entirely of terminal symbols.

This probably all sounds very abstract, so let us try to enlarge a little, by considering English as a written language. The set T here would be one containing the 26 letters of the common alphabet and punctuation marks. The set N would be the set containing syntactic descriptors – simpler ones like 'noun', 'adjective', 'verb', as well as more complex ones like 'noun phrase', 'adverbial clause' and 'complete sentence'. The set P would be one containing syntactic rules, such as a description of a 'noun phrase' as a sequence of 'adjective' followed by 'noun'. Clearly this set can become very large indeed – much larger than T or even N. The productions, in effect, tell us how we can *derive* sentences in the language, starting from the distinguished symbol S (which is always a non-terminal such as 'complete sentence') and, by making successive substitutions, working through a sequence of so-called **sentential forms** towards the final string which contains terminals only.

Note that when we talk of 'sets' we can, and often shall, use the word in the mathematical sense. Thus, for example, we demand that the sets N and T above are disjoint, or that $N \cap T = \phi$, where ϕ is the empty set. Further, when referring to the types of strings generated by productions, a common notation is as follows. If a is a symbol, then

a^+ is used to denote a sequence of one or more a's;
$a*$ is used to denote a sequence of zero or more a's.

A similar notation applies to sets of symbols. If A is a set of symbols then

A^+ denotes the set of sequences of one or more symbols from A;
$A*$ denotes the set of sequences of zero or more symbols from A.

Thus, if a string α consists of zero or more terminals (and no non-terminals) we should write

$\alpha \in T*$

while if α consists of one or more non-terminals (but no terminals), then

$\alpha \in N^+$

and if α consists of zero or more terminals and/or non-terminals

$\alpha \in (N \cup T)*$

A convention often used when describing strings and sets in the abstract is to use small Greek letters $(\alpha, \beta, \gamma, \ldots)$ to represent strings of terminals and/or non-terminals, capital Roman letters $(A, B, C, \ldots)$ to represent single non-terminals, and small Roman letters $(a, b, c, \ldots)$ to represent single terminals. Each author seems to have his own set of conventions, so the reader should be on guard when consulting the literature.

Whole 'English' words, like 'sentence' or 'noun' are often non-terminals, but when describing programming languages with 'reserved' words, these latter (like 'end', 'begin' and 'case') are inevitably terminals – the distinction may sometimes be made with the use of alternative typeface.

There are various ways of specifying productions. Essentially a production is a rule relating to a pair of strings, say γ and δ, specifying how one may be transformed into the other. This is often written

$$\gamma \rightarrow \delta$$

To introduce our last abstract definitions, let us suppose that σ and τ are two strings each consisting of zero or more non-terminals and/or terminals (that is, $\sigma, \tau \in (N \cup T)^*$).

(j)   If we can obtain the string τ from the string σ by employing *one* of the productions of the grammar G, then we say that σ *directly produces* τ (or that τ *is directly derived from* σ), written

$$\sigma \Rightarrow \tau$$

(that is, if $\sigma = \alpha\delta\beta$ and $\tau = \alpha\gamma\beta$, and $\delta \rightarrow \gamma$ is a production in G, then $\sigma \Rightarrow \tau$).

(k)   If we can obtain the string τ from the string σ by applying N productions of G, with $N \geqslant 1$, then we say that σ *produces* τ *in a non-trivial way* (or that τ is *derived from* σ *in a non-trivial way*), written

$$\sigma \Rightarrow^+ \tau$$

(That is, if there exists a sequence $\alpha_0, \alpha_1, \alpha_2, \ldots, \alpha_k$ $(k \geqslant 1)$, such that

$$\sigma = \alpha_0$$
$$\alpha_{j-1} \Rightarrow \alpha_j \text{ (for } 1 \leqslant j \leqslant k)$$

and

$$\alpha_k = \tau$$

then $\sigma \Rightarrow^+ \tau$.)

(l)   If we can produce the string τ from the string σ by applying N productions of G, with $N \geqslant 0$ (this includes the above and, in addition, the trivial case where $\sigma = \tau$), then we say that σ *produces* τ (or that τ *is derived from* σ), written

$$\sigma \Rightarrow^* \tau$$

(m)   In terms of this notation, a **sentential form** is the goal or start symbol, or *any* string which can be derived from it; that is, any string σ such that $S \Rightarrow^* \sigma$.

(n)   Formally we can now define a language $L(G)$ produced by a grammar G by the relation

$$L(G) = \{\sigma \in T^* \mid S \Rightarrow^* \sigma\}$$

5.3   BNF notation for productions

As we have remarked, a production is a rule relating to a pair of strings, say γ and δ, specifying how one may be transformed into the other. This may be denoted $\gamma \rightarrow \delta$, and for simple theoretical grammars use is often made of this notation, using the conventions about the use of upper case letters for non-terminals and lower case ones for terminals. For more realistic grammars, such as those used to specify programming languages, an alternative notation known as BNF is, perhaps, the most common way of specifying productions. The notation was invented by Backus, and was first called Backus Normal Form. Later it was realized that it was not, strictly speaking, a 'normal form', and was renamed Backus–Naur Form. Backus and Naur were two of the authors of the *Algol 60 Report*, which was the first major attempt formally to specify the syntax of a programming language using such a notation.

In BNF notation a non-terminal is usually given a descriptive name, and is written in angle brackets to distinguish it from a terminal symbol. (We remember that non-terminals are used in the construction of sentences, although they do not actually appear in the final sentence.) In BNF, productions have the form

$\qquad$ *leftside* ::= *definition*

where '::=' can be interpreted as 'is defined as' or 'produces', and both *leftside* and *definition* consist of a string concatenated from one or more terminals and non-terminals. In fact, in terms of our earlier notation

$\qquad$ *leftside* $\in (N \cup T)^+$

and

$\qquad$ *definition* $\in (N \cup T)^*$

although we must be even more restrictive than that, for 'leftside' must contain at least one non-terminal, so that we should rather write

$\qquad$ *leftside* $\in (N^+ \cup T^*)$

Frequently we find several productions with the same 'leftside', and these are often abbreviated by listing the 'definitions' as a set of one or more alternatives, separated by a vertical bar symbol '|'.

For example, the set of productions

⟨sentence⟩	::= the ⟨qualified noun⟩ ⟨verb⟩	
	| ⟨pronoun⟩ ⟨verb⟩	(1,2)
⟨qualified noun⟩ ::=	⟨adjective⟩ ⟨noun⟩	(3)
⟨noun⟩	::= man | girl | boy | lecturer	(4,5,6,7)
⟨pronoun⟩	::= he | she	(8,9)
⟨verb⟩	::= drinks | sleeps | mystifies	(10,11,12)
⟨adjective⟩	::= tall | thin | thirsty	(13,14,15)

defines a non-terminal ⟨sentence⟩ as consisting of either the terminal 'the' followed by a ⟨qualified noun⟩ followed by a ⟨verb⟩ or as a ⟨pronoun⟩ followed by a ⟨verb⟩. A ⟨qualified noun⟩ is an ⟨adjective⟩ followed by a ⟨noun⟩, and a ⟨noun⟩ is one of the terminal symbols 'man' or 'girl' or 'boy' or 'lecturer'. A ⟨pronoun⟩ is either of the terminals 'he' or 'she', while a ⟨verb⟩ is either 'drinks' or 'sleeps' or 'mystifies'. Here ⟨sentence⟩, ⟨noun⟩, ⟨qualified noun⟩, ⟨pronoun⟩, ⟨adjective⟩ and ⟨verb⟩ are non-terminals. These do not appear in sentences of the language, which include such majestic prose as

$\qquad$ he drinks
$\qquad$ the thirsty boy drinks
$\qquad$ the thin lecturer mystifies

In a set of productions one non-terminal (usually the first) is usually singled out as the so-called **goal** or **start symbol**. If we want to *generate* an arbitrary sentence we start with the goal symbol and successively replace each non-terminal on the right of the production defining that non-terminal, until all non-terminals have been removed. In the above example the symbol ⟨sentence⟩ is, obviously, the goal symbol.

Thus, for example, we could start with ⟨sentence⟩ and from this derive the sentential form

the ⟨qualified noun⟩ ⟨verb⟩

In terms of definition (j) of the last section we should say that ⟨sentence⟩ *directly produces* 'the ⟨qualified noun⟩ ⟨verb⟩'.

If we now apply production 3 (⟨qualified noun⟩ ::= ⟨adjective⟩ ⟨noun⟩) we get the sentential form

the ⟨adjective⟩ ⟨noun⟩ ⟨verb⟩

In terms of the definitions of the last section, 'the ⟨qualified noun⟩ ⟨verb⟩' directly produces 'the ⟨adjective⟩ ⟨noun⟩ ⟨verb⟩', while ⟨sentence⟩ has produced this sentential form in a non-trivial way. If we now follow this by applying production 14 (⟨adjective⟩ ::= thin) we get the form

the thin ⟨noun⟩ ⟨verb⟩

Application of production 10 (⟨verb⟩ ::= drinks) gets to the form

the thin ⟨noun⟩ drinks

Finally, applying production 6 (⟨noun⟩ ::= boy) we get the sentence

the thin boy drinks

The end result of all this is often represented in a tree-like way, as shown in Figure 5.1. In the tree representation, the order in which the productions were used is not so apparent: a **parse tree** is a representation in which as many productions as possible are applied at each level.

A moment's thought should reveal that there are many possible paths from the start to the final sentence, depending on the order in which the productions are substituted. It is convenient to be able to single out a particular derivation as being *the* derivation. This is generally called the **canonical derivation**, and although the choice is essentially arbitrary, the usual one is that where at each stage in the derivation the leftmost non-terminal is the one that is replaced – this is called a **left canonical derivation**. (Similarly we could define a **right canonical derivation**.)

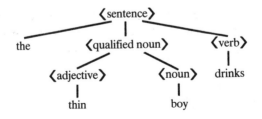

Figure 5.1

Not only is it important to use grammars generatively in this way, it is also important – perhaps more so – to be able to take a given sentence and determine whether it is a valid member of the language – that is, to see whether it could have been obtained from the goal symbol by a suitable choice of derivations. This is the problem of **parsing**, and there are several ways in which we can attempt to solve it. A fairly natural way is to start with the goal symbol and the sentence, and by reading the sentence from left to right try to deduce which series of productions must have been applied.

Let us try this on the sentence

the thin boy drinks

If we start with the goal ⟨sentence⟩ we can derive a wide variety of sentences. Some of these will arise if we choose to continue by using production 1, some if we choose 2. By reading no further than 'the' in the given sentence we can be fairly confident that we should try production 1.

⟨sentence⟩ ::= the ⟨qualified noun⟩ ⟨verb⟩.

In a sense we now have a residual input string 'thin boy drinks' which somehow must match ⟨qualified noun⟩ ⟨verb⟩. We could now choose to substitute for ⟨verb⟩ or for ⟨qualified noun⟩. Again limiting ourselves to working from left to right, our residual sentential form ⟨qualified noun⟩ ⟨verb⟩ must next be transformed into ⟨adjective⟩ ⟨noun⟩ ⟨verb⟩ by applying production 3.

In a sense we now have to match 'thin boy drinks' with a residual sentential form ⟨adjective⟩ ⟨noun⟩ ⟨verb⟩. We could choose to substitute for any of ⟨adjective⟩, ⟨noun⟩ or ⟨verb⟩; if we read the input string from the left we see that by using production 14 we can reduce the problem of matching a residual input string 'boy drinks' to the residual sentential form ⟨noun⟩ ⟨verb⟩. And so it goes; we need not labour a very simple point here.

The parsing problem is not always as easily solved as we have done, and we shall have more to say about this in the next chapter. From a practical viewpoint, we should probably predict that the algorithms used for parsing a sentence to see whether it can be derived from the goal symbol will be very different from algorithms which might be used to generate sentences (almost at random) starting from the start symbol.

In BNF, a production may define a non-terminal recursively, so that the same non-terminal may occur both on the left and right sides of the ::= sign. For example, if the production for ⟨qualified noun⟩ were changed to

⟨qualified noun⟩ ::= ⟨noun⟩ | ⟨adjective⟩ ⟨qualified noun⟩   (3a,3b)

this would define a ⟨qualified noun⟩ as either a ⟨noun⟩, or an ⟨adjective⟩ followed by a ⟨qualified noun⟩ (which in turn may be a ⟨noun⟩ or an ⟨adjective⟩ followed by a ⟨qualified noun⟩ and so on). In the final analysis a ⟨qualified noun⟩ would give rise to zero or more ⟨adjective⟩s followed by a ⟨noun⟩. Of course, a recursive definition can only be used provided that there is some way of terminating it. The single production

⟨qualified noun⟩ ::= ⟨adjective⟩ ⟨qualified noun⟩   (3b)

is effectively quite useless on its own, and it is the alternative production

⟨qualified noun⟩ ::= ⟨noun⟩   (3a)

which provides the means for terminating the recursion.

5.4   Null (lambda) productions

The alternatives for the right-hand side of a production usually consist of a string
of one or more terminal and/or non-terminal symbols. We recall that we may
have a string, usually denoted by ε, but consisting of no symbols, and this may
also be found in productions. For example, the set of productions

⟨integer⟩   ::= ⟨digit⟩ ⟨rest of integer⟩
⟨rest of integer⟩ ::= ⟨digit⟩ ⟨rest of integer⟩ | ε
⟨digit⟩   ::= 0 | 1 | 2 | 3 | 4 | 5 | 6 | 7 | 8 | 9

defines ⟨rest of integer⟩ as a sequence of zero or more ⟨digit⟩s, and hence
⟨integer⟩ would be defined as a sentence of one or more ⟨digit⟩s. In terms of our
earlier notation we should have

⟨rest of integer⟩ $\in$ ⟨digit⟩*

while

⟨integer⟩ $\in$ ⟨digit⟩ $^+$

The production

⟨rest of integer⟩ ::= ε

is called a **null production**, or an ε**-production**, or sometimes a **lambda production**
(from an alternative convention of using λ instead of ε for the null string).

Exercises

Develop grammars to describe each of the following

5.5   A person's name, with optional title and qualifications (if any), for
example

    P.D. Terry, Ph.D.
    Master Kenneth David Terry

5.6   A railway goods train, with one (or more) locomotives, several
varieties of trucks and a guard's van at the rear.

5.7   A mixed passenger and goods train, with one (or more) locomotives,
then one or more goods trucks, followed either by a guard's van, or by
one or more passenger coaches, the last of which should be a

passenger brake van. In the interests of safety, try to build in a regulation to the effect that fuel trucks may not be marshalled immediately behind the locomotive, or immediately in front of a passenger coach.

5.8   A book, with covers, contents, chapters and an index.

5.9   A shopping list, with one or more items, for example

> 6 Sage microcomputers
> 124 bottles Castle Lager
> 750 ml bottle whisky
> 12 cases Rhine Wine
> large box aspirins

5.5   Ambiguous grammars

An important property which one looks for in programming languages is that every sentence which can be generated by the language should have a unique parse tree, or, equivalently, a unique left (or right) canonical parse. If a sentence produced by a grammar has two or more parse trees then the grammar is said to be ambiguous. An easy example of this is provided by the following grammar for simple ⟨expressions⟩ in algebra.

$$
\begin{array}{lll}
\langle goal\rangle & ::= \langle expression\rangle & (1) \\
\langle expression\rangle & ::= \langle expression\rangle \mid \langle expression\rangle & (2) \\
& \mid \langle expression\rangle * \langle expression\rangle & (3) \\
& \mid \langle identifier\rangle & (4) \\
\langle identifier\rangle & ::= X \mid Y \mid Z & (5,6,7)
\end{array}
$$

In this grammar the sentence $X + Y * Z$ has two distinct parse trees and two canonical derivations. We refer to the numbers to show the derivation steps.

The parse tree in Figure 5.2 corresponds to the derivation

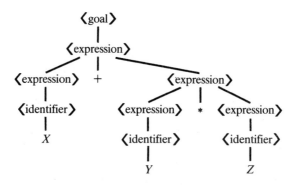

Figure 5.2

$$
\begin{array}{lr}
\langle\text{goal}\rangle ::= \langle\text{expression}\rangle & (1)\\
::= \langle\text{expression}\rangle + \langle\text{expression}\rangle & (2)\\
::= \langle\text{identifier}\rangle + \langle\text{expression}\rangle & (4)\\
::= X + \langle\text{expression}\rangle & (5)\\
::= X + \langle\text{expression}\rangle * \langle\text{expression}\rangle & (3)\\
::= X + \langle\text{identifier}\rangle * \langle\text{expression}\rangle & (4)\\
::= X + Y * \langle\text{expression}\rangle & (6)\\
::= X + Y * \langle\text{identifier}\rangle & (4)\\
::= X + Y * Z & (7)
\end{array}
$$

while the second derivation

$$
\begin{array}{lr}
\langle\text{goal}\rangle ::= \langle\text{expression}\rangle & (1)\\
::= \langle\text{expression}\rangle * \langle\text{expression}\rangle & (3)\\
::= \langle\text{expression}\rangle + \langle\text{expression}\rangle * \langle\text{expression}\rangle & (2)\\
::= \langle\text{identifier}\rangle + \langle\text{expression}\rangle * \langle\text{expression}\rangle & (4)\\
::= X + \langle\text{expression}\rangle * \langle\text{expression}\rangle & (5)\\
::= X + \langle\text{identifier}\rangle * \langle\text{expression}\rangle & (4)\\
::= X + Y * \langle\text{expression}\rangle & (6)\\
::= X + Y * \langle\text{identifier}\rangle & (4)\\
::= X + Y * Z & (7)
\end{array}
$$

has a corresponding parse tree shown in Figure 5.3.

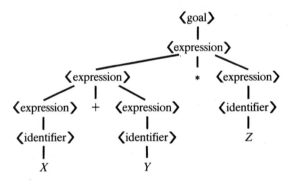

Figure 5.3

If the only use for grammars was to determine whether a string belonged to the language, ambiguity would be of little consequence. However, for programming languages, part of the meaning of a program is sometimes specified in terms of the corresponding syntactic structure, and then ambiguity must obviously be avoided. In the example above, the two trees correspond to two different evaluation sequences for the operators '*' and '+'. In the first case the 'meaning' would be the usual mathematical one, namely $X + (Y * Z)$, but in the second case the meaning would effectively be $(X + Y) * Z$.

If we are to avoid such ambiguities we must be careful to structure the grammar and productions correctly. The following grammar would suffice:

$$G = \{N, T, S, P\}$$
$$N = \{\langle\text{goal}\rangle, \langle\text{expression}\rangle, \langle\text{term}\rangle, \langle\text{factor}\rangle\}$$
$$T = \{X, Y, Z, +, *\}$$
$$S = \langle\text{goal}\rangle$$
$$P =$$

$\langle\text{goal}\rangle$	$::= \langle\text{expression}\rangle$	(1)
$\langle\text{expression}\rangle$	$::= \langle\text{term}\rangle \mid \langle\text{expression}\rangle + \langle\text{term}\rangle$	(2,3)
$\langle\text{term}\rangle$	$::= \langle\text{factor}\rangle \mid \langle\text{term}\rangle * \langle\text{factor}\rangle$	(4,5)
$\langle\text{factor}\rangle$	$::= X \mid Y \mid Z$	(6,7,8)

Unfortunately no algorithm exists (or can exist) which can take an arbitrary grammar and determine with certainty and in a finite amount of time whether it is ambiguous or not. All that one can do is to develop fairly simple but non-trivial conditions which, if satisfied by a grammar, assure one that it is unambiguous. Fortunately all practical programming languages can be defined by languages which satisfy these conditions.

The most famous example of an ambiguous grammar probably concerns the **if** ... **then** ... **else** statement in Algol-like languages. Let us demonstrate this by defining a simple grammar for such a language.

$$G = \{N, T, S, P\}$$
$$N = \{\langle\text{program}\rangle, \langle\text{statement}\rangle, \langle\text{assignment}\rangle, \langle\text{expression}\rangle, \langle\text{variable}\rangle,$$
$$\langle\text{condition}\rangle, \langle\text{ifstatement}\rangle\}$$
$$T = \{:=, I, J, K, X, Y, Z, \textbf{if}, \textbf{then}, \textbf{else}, =, \neq\}$$
$$S = \langle\text{program}\rangle$$
$$P =$$

$\langle\text{program}\rangle$	$::= \langle\text{statement}\rangle$
$\langle\text{statement}\rangle$	$::= \langle\text{assignment}\rangle \mid \langle\text{ifstatement}\rangle$
$\langle\text{assignment}\rangle$	$::= \langle\text{variable}\rangle := \langle\text{expression}\rangle$
$\langle\text{expression}\rangle$	$::= \langle\text{variable}\rangle$
$\langle\text{variable}\rangle$	$::= I \mid J \mid K \mid X \mid Y \mid Z$
$\langle\text{ifstatement}\rangle$	$::= \textbf{if } \langle\text{condition}\rangle \textbf{ then } \langle\text{statement}\rangle$
	$\mid \textbf{if } \langle\text{condition}\rangle \textbf{ then } \langle\text{statement}\rangle \textbf{ else } \langle\text{statement}\rangle$
$\langle\text{condition}\rangle$	$::= \langle\text{expression}\rangle = \langle\text{expression}\rangle$
	$\mid \langle\text{expression}\rangle \neq \langle\text{expression}\rangle$

In this grammar the string

if $I = J$ **then if** $I = K$ **then** $X := Y$ **else** $X := Z$

has two possible parse trees. The reader is invited to drawn these out as an exercise, but the essential point is that we can parse the string to 'mean'

if $I = J$ **then** (**if** $I = K$ **then** $X := Y$ **else** $X := Z$)
            else (nothing)

or

> **if** $I = J$ **then** (**if** $I = K$ **then** $X := Y$ **else** nothing)
>   **else** $(X := Z)$

Any language which includes a sentence such as this may be inherently ambiguous unless certain restrictions are placed on, say, the part following the **then** of an **if** statement. In Algol 60, rules were imposed of the form

> $\langle$conditional statement$\rangle ::= \langle$ifstatement$\rangle$
> $| \langle$ifstatement$\rangle$ **else** $\langle$statement$\rangle$

where

> $\langle$ifstatement$\rangle ::= \langle$ifclause$\rangle$ $\langle$unconditional statement$\rangle$
> $\langle$ifclause$\rangle \qquad ::= $ **if** $\langle$condition$\rangle$ **then**

One was allowed to write **if ... then ... else**, but not **if ... then if ...**.
Even here we have to be careful. Consider a grammar with productions

> $\langle$statement$\rangle ::= $ **if** $\langle B \rangle$ **then** $\langle U \rangle$ | **if** $\langle B \rangle$ **then** $\langle U \rangle$ **else** $\langle$statement$\rangle$
> $| \langle A \rangle$
> $\langle U \rangle \qquad ::= $ **for** $\langle C \rangle$ **do** $\langle$statement$\rangle$ $| \langle A \rangle$
> $\langle B \rangle \qquad ::= \langle$condition$\rangle$
> $\langle C \rangle \qquad ::= \langle$for loop control sequence$\rangle$
> $\langle A \rangle \qquad ::= \langle$other statement types$\rangle$

Here we avoid the ambiguity of **if ... then if** as in Algol 60, but now

> **if** $\langle B \rangle$ **then for** $\langle C \rangle$ **do if** $\langle B \rangle$ **then** $\langle A \rangle$ **else** $\langle A \rangle$

permits interpretation either as

> **if** $\langle B \rangle$ **then for** $\langle C \rangle$ **do** (**if** $\langle B \rangle$ **then** $\langle A \rangle$ **else** $\langle A \rangle$)

or

> **if** $\langle B \rangle$ **then** (**for** $\langle C \rangle$ **do if** $\langle B \rangle$ **then** $\langle A \rangle$ **else** (nothing))
>   **else** $\langle A \rangle$

In the *Revised Report on Algol* this dilemma was avoided by restricting the form of an $\langle$unconditional statement$\rangle$ so as not to include a $\langle$for statement$\rangle$.

In Pascal, as is probably well known, an **else** is deemed to be attached to the most recent unmatched **then**, and the problem is avoided that way. In other languages it is avoided by introducing words like **endif** and **elseif**, but it is possible to arrive at a set of productions which are unambiguous, namely

> $\langle$statement$\rangle \qquad ::= \langle$matched stmt$\rangle$ | $\langle$unmatched stmt$\rangle$
> $\langle$matched stmt$\rangle \quad ::= $ **if** $\langle$condition$\rangle$ **then** $\langle$matched stmt$\rangle$
>   **else** $\langle$matched stmt$\rangle$
> $| \langle$other statement$\rangle$
> $\langle$unmatched stmt$\rangle ::= $ **if** $\langle$condition$\rangle$ **then** $\langle$statement$\rangle$
> $|$ **if** $\langle$condition$\rangle$ **then** $\langle$matched stmt$\rangle$
>   **else** $\langle$unmatched stmt$\rangle$

Exercise

5.10 Convince yourself that the last set of productions for **if** ... **then** ... **else** statements is unambiguous.

5.6 Equivalent grammars

It has probably dawned on the reader that, as with the extermination of the feline species, so it is in the development of grammars.

Two grammars are **equivalent** if they describe the same language; that is, they can generate exactly the same set of sentences (not necessarily the same set of sentential forms or parse trees). As an example, the left-recursive productions describing simple expressions in the last section could be replaced with a syntactically equivalent equivalent right-recursive set

$P =$

$\langle$goal$\rangle$	::= $\langle$expression$\rangle$	(1)
$\langle$expression$\rangle$	::= $\langle$term$\rangle \mid \langle$term$\rangle + \langle$expression$\rangle$	(2,3)
$\langle$term$\rangle$	::= $\langle$factor$\rangle \mid \langle$factor$\rangle * \langle$term$\rangle$	(4,5)
$\langle$factor$\rangle$	::= $X \mid Y \mid Z$	(6,7,8)

As we shall see, not all grammars are suitable as the starting point for developing practical parsing algorithms, and an important part of compiler theory is thus to be able to find equivalent grammars. This in itself is not quite as easy as it might first appear. We have already commented that it is frequently the case that the semantic structure of a sentence is reflected in its syntactic structure (this is a very useful property for programming language specification). Thus, while the above two sets of productions lead to the same sentences, the terminals + and * fairly obviously have the 'meaning' of addition and multiplication. The first set of productions has implied semantics of 'left to right' evaluation of the operators + and *, while the second set has implied semantics of 'right to left' evaluation.

Exercises

5.11 Examine the claims made for the two sets of productions for $\langle$expression$\rangle$ and find examples to demonstrate their respective associativity.

5.12 Develop sets of productions which allow the operations of subtraction and division as well as addition and multiplication.

5.13 Develop sets of productions which allow expressions of the form

$$-X + (Y + Z) * ((Y - X))$$

that is to say, fairly general mathematical expressions, with bracketing, leading unary signs, the operations of addition, subtraction, division and multiplication, with the conventional precedence rules implied by the productions.

5.14 Extend Exercise 5.13 to allow for exponentiation as well.

5.7 Context sensitivity

Some potential ambiguities belong to a class usually termed **context-sensitive**. English is full of such examples, which the average person parses with ease. For example, the sentences

Time flies like an arrow

and

Fruit flies like a banana

in one sense have identical construction,

⟨noun⟩ ⟨verb⟩ ⟨adverbial phrase⟩

but, unless we were preoccupied with aerodynamics, in listening to them we would probably subconsciously parse the second along the lines of

⟨adjective⟩ ⟨noun⟩ ⟨verb⟩ ⟨noun phrase⟩

Other examples are harder to distinguish. What is the meaning of

Move one foot forward

to an Imperial Infantryman, or

Charge at a point

to a Physicist serving with the Cavalry? (The male reader should note that a course in formal language theory is no excuse for disobeying orders; the female reader should be thankful, for once, for discrimination.)

Examples like this can be found in programming languages too. In FORTRAN a statement of the form

$A = B(J)$

could either be a reference to the Jth element of array B, or a reference to an evaluation of a function B with integer argument J. Mathematically there is little difference – an array can be thought of as a mapping, just as a function can, but FORTRAN programmers probably rarely think that way.

5.8   Classes of grammars

Based on pioneering work by a linguist, Noam Chomsky, computer scientists now distinguish four classes of grammar. The classification depends on the format of the productions, and may be summarized as follows.

5.8.1   Type 0 grammars (unrestricted)

An unrestricted grammar is one in which there are no restrictions on the form of any of the productions, which thus have the form

$$\alpha \to \beta \qquad \alpha, \beta \in (N \cup T)^*$$

An unrestricted grammar must contain at least one production $\alpha \to \beta$ with $|\alpha| > |\beta|$, where $|\alpha|$ denotes the length of α. Such a production can be used to 'erase' symbols: for example, $aAB \to aB$ erases A from the context aAB. This type is so rare in computer applications that we shall consider it no further here. Practical grammars, from the point of view of developing translators based on them, need to be far more restricted.

5.8.2   Type 1 grammars (context-sensitive)

Until now all our practical examples of productions have had a single non-terminal on the left side. A grammar in which productions may have more than one symbol on the left side is termed context-sensitive. The exact definition of a context-sensitive grammar seems to differ from author to author. One definition is that

(a)   The number of symbols in the string on the left is less than or equal to the number of symbols on the right side of any production.

(b)   A grammar must contain at least one production with a left side longer than one symbol for the grammar to be context-sensitive.

(c)   Arising from (a) it follows that the null string is strictly not allowed as the right side of any production. However, this is often overlooked, as ε-productions are often needed to terminate recursive definitions.

Productions are thus of the form

$$\alpha \to \beta \qquad \text{with } |\alpha| \leqslant |\beta| \qquad \alpha, \beta \in (N \cup T)^*$$

In another definition, productions are said to be limited to the forms

$$\alpha A \beta \to \alpha \gamma \beta \qquad \text{with } \alpha, \beta \in (N \cup T)^*,\ A \in N^+,\ \gamma \in (N \cup T)^+$$

However, examples are often given where productions are of a more general form, namely

$$\alpha A \beta \to \zeta \gamma \xi \qquad \text{with } \alpha,\ \beta,\ \zeta,\ \xi \in (N \cup T)^*,\ A \in N^+,\ \gamma \in (N \cup T)^+$$

Here we can see the meaning of 'context-sensitive' more clearly – the non-terminal A may be replaced by γ if A is found in the context of α and β.

A much quoted simple example of such a grammar is as follows

$$G = \{N, T, S, P\}$$
$$N = \{\langle A\rangle, \langle B\rangle, \langle C\rangle\}$$
$$T = \{a, b, c\}$$
$$S = \langle A\rangle$$
$$P =$$

$$\langle A\rangle ::= a\langle A\rangle\langle B\rangle\langle C\rangle \mid ab\langle C\rangle \tag{1,2}$$
$$\langle C\rangle\langle B\rangle ::= \langle B\rangle\langle C\rangle \tag{3}$$
$$b\langle B\rangle ::= bb \tag{4}$$
$$b\langle C\rangle ::= bc \tag{5}$$
$$c\langle C\rangle ::= cc \tag{6}$$

Let us derive a sentence in this grammar. $\langle A\rangle$ is the start string: let us choose to apply production (1)

$$\langle A\rangle ::= a\langle A\rangle\langle B\rangle\langle C\rangle$$

and then in this new string choose another $\langle A\rangle$ production, namely (2) to get

$$\langle A\rangle ::= a\ ab\langle C\rangle\ \langle B\rangle\langle C\rangle$$

and follow this by the use of (3). (We could also choose (5) at this point.)

$$\langle A\rangle ::= aab\ \langle B\rangle\langle C\rangle\ \langle C\rangle$$

We follow this by (4) to get

$$\langle A\rangle ::= aa\ bb\ \langle C\rangle\langle C\rangle$$

followed by (5) to get

$$\langle A\rangle ::= aab\ bc\ \langle C\rangle$$

followed finally by (6) to give

$$\langle A\rangle ::= aabbcc$$

With this grammar we could reach a string to which no production can be applied. For example, after reaching the sentential form

$$aab\langle C\rangle\langle B\rangle\langle C\rangle$$

if we choose (5) instead of (3) we obtain

$$aabc\langle B\rangle\langle C\rangle$$

and no further production can be applied to this string. The consequence of such a failure to obtain a terminal string is simply that we must try other possibilities until we find those that yield terminal strings. The consequences for the reverse problem, namely parsing, are that we may have to resort to considerable backtracking to decide whether a string is a sentence in the language.

Exercises

5.15 Derive (or show how to parse) the strings

    abc   and   *aaabbbccc*

in the above grammar.

5.16 Show informally that the strings

    abbc, aabc and *abcc*

cannot be derived in this grammar.

5.17 Derive a context-sensitive grammar for strings of 0s and 1s so that the number of 0s and 1s is the same.

5.18 Attempt to write context-sensitive productions from which the English examples in Section 5.7 could be derived.

5.19 An attempt to use context sensitive productions in an actual computer language was made by Lee (*Computer Journal*, **15**, 37–41 (1972)), who gave such productions for the **PRINT** statement in BASIC. Such a statement may be described informally as having the keyword **PRINT** followed by an arbitrary number of expressions and strings. Between each pair of expressions one must have a separator, but between any other pair (string–expression, string–string or expression–string) the separator is optional. Study Lee's work, criticize it, and attempt to write the productions for the BASIC **PRINT** statement using a context-free grammar.

5.8.3 Type 2 grammars (context-free)

A more restricted subset of context-sensitive grammars yields the context-free grammars. A grammar is context-free if the left side of every production consists of a single non-terminal, and the right side consists of any non-empty sequence of terminals and non-terminals, so that productions have the form

    $A \rightarrow \alpha$ with $A \in N$, $\alpha \in (N \cup T)^+$

Again, strictly no ε-productions are allowed, but in practice this is usually relaxed to allow $\alpha \in (N \cup T)^*$.

The earlier examples were of this form and we shall consider a larger example shortly, for a toy programming language.

Grammars for programming languages are usually largely context-free, with occasional lapses which are often patched up with a few extra rules. Two of these are commonly found in languages like Pascal, and are neatly discussed by Aho and Ullman (1977), page 140.

(a)   Using a context-free grammar it is not possible to specify that the declaration of a variable must precede its use.

(b)   Using a context-free grammar it is not possible to specify that the number of formal and actual parameters in a procedure call must be the same.

5.8.4   Type 3 grammars (regular, right-linear or left-linear)

Imposing still further constraints on productions leads us to the concept of a regular grammar. This can take one or other (but not both at once) of two forms. It is **right-linear** if the right side of every production consists of one terminal symbol optionally followed by a single non-terminal, and if the left side is a single non-terminal, so that productions have the form

$$A \rightarrow a \text{ or } A \rightarrow aB \qquad \text{with } a \in T, \ A,B \in N$$

It is **left-linear** if the right side of every production consists of one terminal optionally preceded by a single non-terminal, so that productions have the form

$$A \rightarrow a \text{ or } A \rightarrow Ba \qquad \text{with } a \in T, \ A,B \in N$$

A simple example of such a grammar is one for describing binary integers

$$\langle \text{binary integer} \rangle ::= 0 \ \langle \text{binary integer} \rangle \mid 1 \ \langle \text{binary integer} \rangle \mid 0 \mid 1$$

Regular grammars are rather restrictive; local features of programming languages like the definitions of integer numbers and identifiers can be described by them, but not much more.

A language L(G) is said to be of type k if it can be generated by a type k grammar. It should be clear from the above that type 3 languages are a subset of type 2 languages which are a subset of type 1 languages which are a subset of type 0 languages.

The fact that a language can be described by a context-free grammar does not necessarily preclude our being able to find an equivalent regular grammar. For example, the following two grammars are equivalent

```
G1 = (N, T, S, P)
N  = {⟨integer⟩, ⟨digit⟩}
T  = {0 1 2 3 4 5 6 7 8 9}
S  = ⟨integer⟩
P  = ⟨integer⟩ ::= ⟨digit⟩
                 | ⟨digit⟩ ⟨integer⟩
       ⟨digit⟩ ::= 0 | 1 | 2 ...

G2 = (N, T, S, P)
N  = {⟨integer⟩}
T  = {0 1 2 3 4 5 6 7 8 9}
S  = ⟨integer⟩
P  = ⟨integer⟩ ::= 0 | 1 | 2 ...
                 | 0 ⟨integer⟩
                 | 1 ⟨integer⟩
                   ...
```

The other productions in each case are obvious, and need not be given in full.

Exercise

5.20 Can you describe signed integers and FORTRAN identifiers in terms of regular grammars as well as in terms of context-free grammars?

5.9 Extensions to BNF

Various simple extensions are often employed with BNF notation for the sake of increased readability and for the elimination of unnecessary recursion (which has a strange habit of confusing people brought up on iteration). Recursion in BNF is often employed as a means of specifying simple repetition, as for example

⟨unsigned integer⟩ ::= ⟨digit⟩ | ⟨digit⟩ ⟨unsigned integer⟩

(which uses right recursion) or

⟨unsigned integer⟩ ::= ⟨digit⟩ | ⟨unsigned integer⟩ ⟨digit⟩

(which uses left recursion).

Then we often find several productions used to denote alternatives which are very similar, for example

⟨integer⟩   ::= ⟨unsigned integer⟩ | ⟨sign⟩ ⟨unsigned integer⟩
⟨unsigned integer⟩ ::= ⟨digit⟩ | ⟨digit⟩ ⟨unsigned integer⟩
⟨sign⟩   ::= + | −

using six productions (besides the omitted obvious ones for ⟨digit⟩) to specify the form of an ⟨integer⟩.

The extensions introduced to simplify these constructions are

(a) The use of curly brackets or braces { } to denote repetition of a string zero or more times.

(b) The use of square brackets [ ] to denote an optional item (occurs zero or one time).

(c) The use of round brackets or parentheses ( ) to group items together.

Using these ideas we might define an integer by

⟨integer⟩   ::= [⟨sign⟩] ⟨unsigned integer⟩
⟨unsigned integer⟩ ::= ⟨digit⟩ {⟨digit⟩}
⟨sign⟩   ::= + | −

or even by

⟨integer⟩ ::= [(+ | −)] ⟨digit⟩ {⟨digit⟩}

In passing, we note that the use of these brackets can cause confusion when describing languages where the brackets themselves can denote terminal symbols. The usual device then is to print terminals in another typeface, to underline them, or to place them between quotation marks, for example

$\langle$digit$\rangle ::= "1" \mid "2" \mid "3" \mid "4" \mid "5" \mid "6" \mid "7" \mid "8" \mid "9" \mid "0"$
$\langle$relop$\rangle ::= ">" \mid "<" \mid "<=" \mid ">=" \mid "=" \mid "<>"$

A variation on the use of braces allows the (otherwise impossible) specification of a limit on the number of times a symbol may be repeated – for example to express that an identifier in FORTRAN may have a maximum of six characters. This is done by writing the lower and upper limits as sub- and super-scripts to the right of the curly brackets, as for example

$\langle$FORTRAN identifier$\rangle ::= \langle$letter$\rangle \; \{(\langle$letter$\rangle \mid \langle$digit$\rangle)\}_0^5$

It should not have escaped attention that the names chosen for non-terminals usually convey some semantic implication to the reader, and we have stressed that the way in which productions are expressed often serves to emphasize this still further. Sometimes the semantic overtones are made more explicit by the use of italic typeface, as for example

$\langle$*integer* assignment$\rangle ::= \langle$*integer* variable$\rangle := \langle$*integer* expression$\rangle$

which is syntactically equivalent to the simpler

$\langle$assignment$\rangle ::= \langle$variable$\rangle := \langle$expression$\rangle$

Finally, we should note a convention employed by some authors whereby terminals are written in lower case, and non-terminals are written in UPPER CASE. After a little experience with grammars it is usually easy to discern the terminals from the non-terminals, and the angle brackets are just a nuisance to write down.

5.10   Syntax diagrams

An entirely different method of syntax definition is the graphic representation known as syntax diagrams, syntax charts, or sometimes 'railroad diagrams'. These have been used to define the syntax of Pascal and FORTRAN 77. The rules take the form of flow diagrams, the possible paths representing the possible sequences of symbols. One starts at the left of a diagram, and traces a path which may transfer to another diagram if an UPPER CASE word or rectangle box is reached (corresponding to a non-terminal), or may include a terminal in lower case, or contained in a circle or box with rounded ends. For example, an identifier may be defined as in Figure 5.4, with a similar diagram applying to LETTER , which we can probably assume readers to be intelligent enough to draw for themselves.

IDENTIFIER

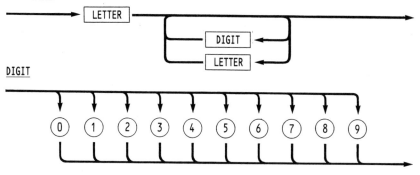

DIGIT

Figure 5.4

Exercises

5.21 Write the definition of the assembler language developed in the earlier chapters of this text in BNF, EBNF, and syntax diagram form.

5.22 Draw syntax diagrams, and then develop a context-free grammar that specifies the set of decimal literals that may be written in FORTRAN. Examples of these literals are

$$-21.5 \quad 0.25 \quad 3.7E-6 \quad .5E7 \quad 6E6 \quad 100.0E+3$$

5.23 Draw syntax diagrams, and then develop a grammar for describing FORTRAN FORMAT statements. Can this be done in a context-free way, or do you need to introduce context-sensitivity?

5.11 A complete simple language

We give here the complete specification of a simple programming language, which will be used as the basis for discussion and enlargement at several points in the future. The language, called CLANG (an acronym for Concurrent **Lang**uage, also chosen because it has a fine ring to it), is Pascal-like, and should be immediately comprehensible to Pascal programmers. At this level it closely resembles one called PL/0, discussed by Wirth (1976), Chapter 5.

The semantics of CLANG, and especially the concurrent aspects which give it its name, will be discussed in later chapters. It will suffice to comment that the only data type (for the moment) is the scalar INTEGER — a constraint which we shall not try to specify syntactically here.

For purposes of comparison we give the syntax in BNF, in extended BNF, and using syntax diagrams. The grammars are 'equivalent', though there is not necessarily a one-to-one correspondence between productions and diagrams.

There is some possible confusion in the use of the characters (and) for meta-symbols and as terminals, but the reader should be able to recognize the difference quite easily.

⟨program⟩   ::= **program** ⟨identifier⟩ ; ⟨block⟩ .

⟨block⟩   ::= ⟨constdeclarations⟩ ⟨vardeclarations⟩ ⟨statementpart⟩

⟨constdeclarations⟩   ::= **const** ⟨restconstdec⟩ | ε

⟨restconstdec⟩   ::= ⟨constsequence⟩
       | ⟨restconstdec⟩ ⟨constsequence⟩

⟨constsequence⟩   ::= ⟨identifier⟩ = ⟨number⟩ ;

or, for ⟨constdeclarations⟩ in EBNF

⟨constdeclarations⟩   ::= **const** ⟨identifier⟩ = ⟨number⟩ ;
       { ⟨identifier⟩ = ⟨number⟩ ; }
       | ε

⟨vardeclarations⟩   ::= **var** ⟨identsequence⟩ ; | ε

⟨identsequence⟩   ::= ⟨identifier⟩
       | ⟨identsequence⟩ , ⟨identifier⟩

or, for ⟨vardeclarations⟩, in EBNF

⟨vardeclarations⟩   ::= **var** ⟨identifier⟩ { , ⟨identifier⟩ } ; | ε

⟨statementpart⟩   ::= ⟨compoundstatement⟩

⟨compoundstatement⟩   ::= **begin** ⟨statementsequence⟩ **end**

⟨statementsequence⟩   ::= ⟨statement⟩
       | ⟨statementsequence⟩ ; ⟨statement⟩

or, for ⟨statementsequence⟩, in EBNF

⟨statementsequence⟩   ::= ⟨statement⟩ { ; ⟨statement⟩ }

⟨statement⟩   ::= ⟨compoundstatement⟩ | ⟨assignment⟩
       | ⟨ifstatement⟩ | ⟨whilestatement⟩
       | ⟨writestatement⟩ | ⟨readstatement⟩
       | ε

⟨assignment⟩   ::= ⟨identifier⟩ := ⟨expression⟩

⟨ifstatement⟩   ::= **if** ⟨condition⟩ **then** ⟨statement⟩

⟨whilestatement⟩   ::= **while** ⟨condition⟩ **do** ⟨statement⟩

⟨writestatement⟩   ::= **write** (⟨writelist⟩) | **write**

⟨readstatement⟩   ::= **read** (⟨identsequence⟩)

⟨condition⟩   ::= **odd** (⟨expression⟩
       | ⟨expression⟩ ⟨relop⟩ ⟨expression⟩

⟨writelist⟩   ::= ⟨expression⟩ | ⟨string⟩
       | ⟨writelist⟩ , ⟨expression⟩
       | ⟨writelist⟩ , ⟨string⟩

or, for ⟨writelist⟩, in EBNF

| ⟨writelist⟩ | ::= (⟨expression⟩ \| ⟨string⟩) |
| | { , (⟨expression⟩ \| ⟨string⟩) } |

⟨expression⟩	::= ⟨term⟩ | ⟨sign⟩ ⟨term⟩
	| ⟨expression⟩ ⟨addop⟩ ⟨term⟩
⟨term⟩	::= ⟨factor⟩ | ⟨term⟩ ⟨mulop⟩ ⟨factor⟩

or, for ⟨expression⟩ and ⟨term⟩, in EBNF

| ⟨expression⟩ | ::= [⟨sign⟩] ⟨term⟩ { ⟨addop⟩ ⟨term⟩ } |
| ⟨term⟩ | ::= ⟨factor⟩ { ⟨mulop⟩ ⟨factor⟩ } |

⟨factor⟩	::= ⟨identifier⟩ | ⟨number⟩ | (⟨expression⟩)
⟨identifier⟩	::= ⟨letter⟩ | ⟨identifier⟩ ⟨letter⟩
	| ⟨identifier⟩ ⟨digit⟩

or, for ⟨identifier⟩, in EBNF

| ⟨identifier⟩ | ::= ⟨letter⟩ { (⟨letter⟩ \| ⟨digit⟩) } |

| ⟨number⟩ | ::= ⟨digit⟩ \| ⟨number⟩ ⟨digit⟩ |

or, in EBNF

| ⟨number⟩ | ::= ⟨digit⟩ { ⟨digit⟩ } |

| ⟨string⟩ | ::= ' ⟨charsequence⟩ ' |
| ⟨charsequence⟩ | ::= ⟨character⟩ \| ⟨charsequence⟩ ⟨character⟩ |

or, for ⟨charsequence⟩, in EBNF

| ⟨charsequence⟩ | ::= ⟨character⟩ { ⟨character⟩ } |

⟨character⟩	::= ⟨letter⟩ | ⟨digit⟩
	| ⟨otherprintablecharacter⟩
⟨letter⟩	::= a | b | c | d | e | f | g | h | i | j | k | l | m |
	n | o | p | q | r | s | t | u | v | w | x | y | z |
	A | B | C | D | E | F | G | H | I | J | K | L | M |
	N | O | P | Q | R | S | T | U | V | W | X | Y | Z
⟨digit⟩	::= 0 | 1 | 2 | 3 | 4 | 5 | 6 | 7 | 8 | 9
⟨relop⟩	::= = | < > | < | > | <= | > =
	(*obviously* < *and* > *here are not*
	demarcating non-terminals)
⟨sign⟩	::= ⟨addop⟩
⟨addop⟩	::= + | −
⟨mulop⟩	::= * | /
⟨otherprintablecharacter⟩	::= IMPLEMENTATION DEFINED

In the syntax diagrams (in Figure 5.5) we have, in the interests of saving space, combined several productions into one diagram in places. Strictly we have given alternative grammars, and not alternative representations for the same grammar, and the reader is invited to spot where the differences lie.

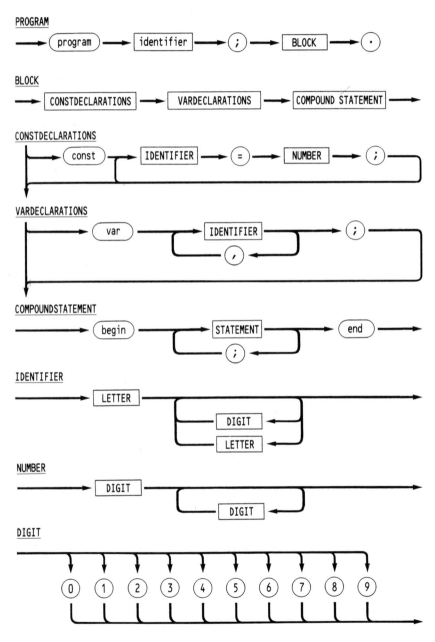

Figure 5.5

LETTER

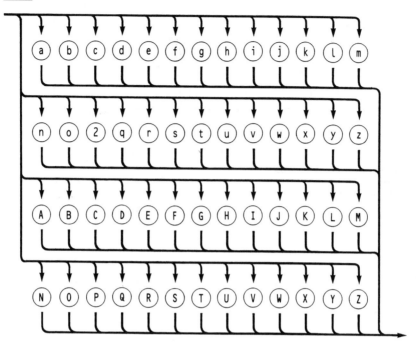

STATEMENT

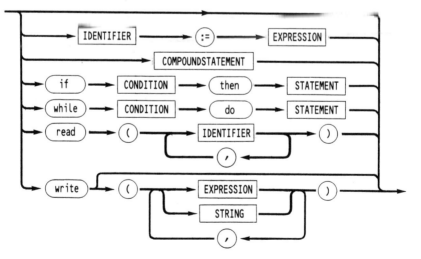

Figure 5.5

CONDITION

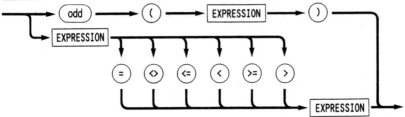

EXPRESSION

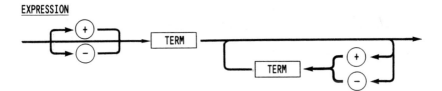

TERM

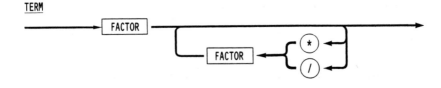

FACTOR

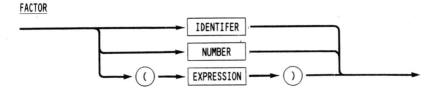

STRING

Figure 5.5

Exercises

5.24 What would you have to add to the language definition to incorporate
(a) A Pascal-like **repeat ... until** statement?
(b) the **if ... then ... else** statement?

(c) the **case** statement?

(d) the **for** loop?

(e) the **mod** operator?

Make the additions to the BNF, to the EBNF, and to the syntax diagrams.

5.25 We have made no attempt to describe the semantics of programs written in CLANG, but to a reader familiar with Pascal they should be self-evident. Write simple programs in the language to

(a) find the sum of the numbers between two input data, which can be supplied in either order;

(b) use Euclid's algorithm to find the HCF of two integers;

(c) determine which of a set of year dates correspond to leap years;

(d) read a sequence of numbers and print out the embedded monotonic increasing sequence.

In the light of your experience in preparing these solutions, and from the intuition which you have from your background in Pascal, can you foresee any gross deficiencies in CLANG as a language for handling problems in integer arithmetic (apart from its lack of procedural facilities, which we shall deal with in a later chapter)?

5.26 Close scrutiny of the language definition shows that even the most rudimentary aspects of semantics, familiar to all Pascal programmers, have been omitted. No attempt has been made to distinguish between the various classes of ⟨identifier⟩. Modify the language definition to try to reflect these distinctions.

5.27 Further study should show a problem associated with ⟨string⟩ familiar to Pascal programmers. If a ⟨string⟩ is demarcated by single quotes, how do we define a ⟨string⟩ which itself contains the quote character? We can avoid the issue by defining ⟨otherprintable-character⟩ as 'implementation defined' – we simply exclude the single quote from this set. How should we modify the syntax to allow strings to contain quotes? Study how it is done in Pascal and in Modula-2, and write productions which reflect each of the schemes used in those languages.

5.28 How might one add productions to the language to specify that an arbitrary number of blanks may occur between (but not within) the symbols of the program? Extend this to include rules for the formation and insertion of Pascal-like comments.

5.29 Do the productions use right or left recursion? Write an equivalent grammar which uses the opposite form of recursion.

5.30 How closely do the BNF productions and the EBNF productions match the syntax diagrams? Can you get an even closer correspondence?

Further reading

The material in this chapter is very standard, and good treatments of it can be found in many books. The keen reader might do well to look at the alternative presentation in the books by Hunter (1981), pages 18–34; Bornat (1979), pages 253–271; Davie and Morrison (1981), pages 34–45, or Tremblay and Sorenson (1985), Chapter 2. This last reference is considerably more rigorous than the others, drawing several fine points which we have glossed over, but it is still quite readable. The pioneering paper by Chomsky (1959) is also worth reading.

5.12 Formal treatment of semantics

As yet we have made no attempt to describe the semantics of programs written in CLANG, or, indeed, in any of our other 'languages', and have just assumed that these would be self-evident to a reader who has already come to terms with a language like Pascal. In one sense this is satisfactory for our purposes, but in principle it is highly unsatisfactory not to have a simple, yet rigidly formal means of specifying the semantics of a language, and in this section we wish to touch very briefly on ways in which this might be overcome.

We have already commented that the division between syntax and semantics is not always clear-cut, something which may be exacerbated by the tendency to specify productions using names with clearly semantic overtones, and whose sentential forms already reflect meanings to be attached to operator precedence and so on. When specifying semantics a distinction is often attempted between what is termed **static semantics** – features which, in effect, mean something that can be checked at compile time, such as the requirement that one may not branch into the middle of a procedure, or that assignment may only be attempted if type checking has been satisfied – and **dynamic semantics** – features which really only have meaning at run-time, such as the effect of a branch statement on the flow of control, or the effect of an assignment statement on elements of storage.

Historically, attempts formally to specify semantics have not met with the same success as those which culminated in the development of BNF notation for specifying syntax, and we find that the semantics of many, if not most, common programming languages have been explained in terms of an American document, often regrettably imprecise, invariably loaded with jargon, and difficult to follow (even when one has learned the jargon). It will suffice to give two examples:

(a) In a draft description of Pascal, the syntax of the **with** statement was defined by

⟨with-statement⟩   ::= **with** ⟨record-variable-list⟩
                        do ⟨statement⟩

⟨record-variable-list⟩ ::= ⟨record-variable⟩ { , ⟨record-variable⟩ }
⟨variable-identifier⟩ ::= ⟨field-identifier⟩

with the commentary that 'The occurrence of a ⟨record-variable⟩ in the ⟨record-variable-list⟩ is a defining occurrence of its ⟨field-identifier⟩s as ⟨variable-identifier⟩s for the ⟨with-statement⟩ in which the ⟨record-variable-list⟩ occurs.'

The reader might be forgiven for finding this awkward, especially in the way it indicates that within the ⟨statement⟩ the ⟨field-identifier⟩s may be used as though they were ⟨variable-identifier⟩s.

(b)　In the same description we find the **while** statement described by

⟨while-statement⟩ ::= **while** ⟨Boolean-expression⟩ **do** ⟨statement⟩

with the commentary that 'The ⟨statement⟩ is repeatedly executed while the ⟨Boolean-expression⟩ yields the value TRUE. If its value is FALSE at the beginning, the ⟨statement⟩ is not executed at all. The ⟨while-statement⟩

while b **do** body

is equivalent to

if b **then repeat** body **until not** b.'

If one is to be very critical, one might be forgiven for wondering what exactly is meant by 'beginning' (does it mean the beginning of the program, or of execution of this one part of the program?), and one might wonder at the need to introduce 'b' and 'body', especially without any explanation. One might also conclude, especially from all the emphasis given to the effect when the ⟨Boolean-expression⟩ is initially FALSE, that in that case the ⟨while-statement⟩ is completely equivalent to an empty statement. This is not necessarily true, for evaluation of the ⟨Boolean-expression⟩ might require calls to a function which has side-effects; nowhere (at least in the vicinity of this description) is this point mentioned.

The net effect of such imprecision and obfuscation is that users of a language often resort to writing simple test programs to help them understand language features, that is to say, they use the operation of a machine itself to explain the language. This is a technique that can be disastrous on at least two scores. In the first place, the test examples may be incomplete, or too special, and only a half-truth will be gleaned. Secondly, and perhaps more fundamentally, one is then confusing an abstract language with one concrete implementation of that language. Since implementations may be error prone, incomplete, or, as often happens, may have 'extensions' that do not form part of the language at all, the possibilities for misconception are enormous.

However, one approach to formal specification, known as **operational semantics**, essentially refines this *ad hoc* arrangement. To avoid the problems mentioned above, the (written) specification usually describes the action of a program construction in terms of the changes in state of an abstract machine which is supposed to be executing the construction. Of course, to understand this, the reader has to understand the definition of the abstract machine, and not only might this be confusingly theoretical, it might also be quite unlike the actual machines so far encountered. As in all semantic descriptions, one is simply shifting the problem of 'meaning' from one area to another! Another drawback of this approach is that it tends to obscure the 'meaning' with a great detail of what is essentially useful knowledge for the implementor of the language, but almost irrelevant for the user of the same.

Other approaches taken to specifying semantics tend to rely rather more heavily on mathematical logic and mathematical notation, and for this reason may be almost impossible to understand if the programmer is one of the many thousands whose mathematical background is comparatively weak. One of these, which has been used by Hoare and Wirth (1973) to specify the semantics of most of Pascal, uses so-called **axiomatic semantics**, and it is worth a slight digression to examine the notation used. It is particularly apposite when taken in conjunction with the subject of **program proving**, but, as will become apparent, rather limited in the way in which it specifies what a program actually seems to be doing.

In the notation, S is used to represent a statement or statement sequence, and letters like P, Q and R are used to represent **predicates**, that is, the logical values of Boolean variables or expressions. A notation like

$$\{P\}S\{Q\}$$

denotes a so-called **inductive expression**, and is intended to convey that if P is TRUE before S is executed, then Q will be TRUE after S terminates (assuming that it does terminate, which may not always happen). P is often called the **precondition** and Q the **postcondition** of S. Such inductive expressions may be concatenated with logical operations like $\wedge$ (*and*) and $\ulcorner$ (*not*) and $\Rightarrow$ (*implies*) to give expressions like

$$\{P\}S_1\{Q\} \wedge \{Q\}S_2\{R\}$$

from which one can infer that

$$\{P\}S_1; S_2\{R\}$$

which is written even more succinctly as a **rule of inference**

$$\frac{\{P\}S_1\{Q\} \wedge \{Q\}S_2\{R\}}{\{P\}S_1; S_2\{R\}}$$

Expressions like

$$P \Rightarrow Q \text{ and } \{Q\}S\{R\}$$

and

$$\{P\}S\{Q\} \text{ and } Q \Rightarrow R$$

lead to the **consequence rules**

$$\frac{P \Rightarrow Q \text{ and } \{Q\}S\{R\}}{\{P\}S\{R\}}$$

and

$$\frac{\{P\}S\{Q\} \text{ and } Q \Rightarrow R}{\{P\}S\{R\}}$$

In these rules, the top line is called the **antecedent** and the bottom one is called the **consequent**; so far as program proving is concerned, to prove the truth of the consequent it is necessary only to prove the truth of the antecedent.

In terms of this notation one can write down rules for nearly all of Pascal remarkably tersely. For example, the **while** statement can be 'described' by

$$\frac{\{P \wedge B\}S\{P\}}{\{P\} \text{ **while** } B \text{ **do** } S \{P \wedge \neg B\}}$$

and the **if** statements by

$$\frac{\{P \wedge B\}S\{Q\} \text{ and } P \wedge \neg B \Rightarrow Q}{\{P\} \text{ **if** } B \text{ **then** } S\{Q\}}$$

$$\frac{\{P \wedge B\}S_1\{Q\} \text{ and } \{P \wedge \neg B\}S_2\{Q\}}{\{P\} \text{ **if** } B \text{ **then** } S_1 \text{ **else** } S_2\{Q\}}$$

With a little reflection one can understand this notation quite easily, but it has its drawbacks. Firstly, the rules given are valid only if the evaluation of B proceeds without side-effects (compare the discussion earlier). Secondly, there seems to be no explicit description of what the machine implementing the program actually does to alter its state – the idea of 'repetition' in the rule for the **while** statement probably does not exactly strike the reader as obvious!

Further reading

In what follows we shall, perhaps cowardly, rely on the reader's intuitive grasp of semantics. However, the keen reader might like to follow up the ideas germinated here. Useful places to start are the very readable book by McGettrick (1980) and the books by Tennant (1981) and Harland (1984). The axiomatic semantic definition of Pascal is to be found in the paper by Hoare and Wirth (1973). The draft description of Pascal is to be found in the article by Addyman *et al.* (1979). This was later modified to become the ISO Pascal Standard, known variously as ISO 7185 and BS 6192, published by the British Standards Institute, London (a copy is given as an appendix to the book by Wilson and Addyman (1982)). A similar standard appeared in America, published by the IEEE, New York. In his book, Brinch Hansen (1983) has a very interesting chapter on the problems he encountered in trying to specify Edison completely and concisely.

Chapter 6 **Top-down parsing**

In this chapter we build on the ideas developed in the last one and discuss the relationship between the formal definition of the syntax of a programming language and the methods which can be used to parse programs written in that language. As with so much else in this text, we shall restrict ourselves rather severely in the methods considered. Hopefully we still cover enough to make the reader aware of certain crucial issues.

6.1 Factorization of a grammar

Designing an unambiguous grammar for the syntax of a programming language is not merely an interesting academic exercise. The effort is, in practice, usually made so as to be able to aid the development of a translator for the language (and, of course, so that programmers who use the language may have a reference to consult when All Else Fails and they have to Read The Instructions).

As we have commented, we may be able to find several equivalent grammars for a language. One problem with the grammars found in textbooks is that, like complete programs found in textbooks, the final presentation often hides the thought which has gone into their derivation. To try to redress the balance, let us look at a rough description of a typical language construct, and think of several grammars which seem to define it.

Suppose we had a language in which all variables were 'declared', where the declarations came before 'statements', and where semicolons were apparently separators. This should be familiar, but we shall impose the constraint that at least one variable must be declared. From this informal description we would probably infer that programs might take the form

var
      x : type;
      y : type;
      . . .;
begin
      statement;
      . . .
end.

and we might try to write productions for this in several ways, each of which amounts to a *factorization* of the grammar. For example, we might start with

⟨program⟩ ::= **var** ⟨varlist⟩ ; **begin** ⟨statementlist⟩ **end** .

but if we have learned anything about top-down programming and stepwise refinement we might prefer to divide this in an obvious way

⟨program⟩   ::= ⟨declarationpart⟩ ; ⟨statementpart⟩
⟨declarationpart⟩ ::= **var** ⟨varlist⟩
⟨statementpart⟩   ::= **begin** ⟨statementlist⟩ **end** .

Next we might try our hand at writing productions for ⟨varlist⟩. The simplest case would have only one variable declared; clearly optional repetition should handle other cases. Flush with our knowledge of recursive BNF we might try writing

⟨varlist⟩ ::= ⟨onevar⟩ | ⟨varlist⟩ ; ⟨onevar⟩
⟨onevar⟩ ::= ⟨identifier⟩ : ⟨type⟩ $\qquad$ (G1)

or, using 'right' rather than 'left' recursion

⟨varlist⟩ ::= ⟨onevar⟩ | ⟨onevar⟩ ; ⟨varlist⟩ $\qquad$ (G2)

Then again, we might like to emphasize the fact that we must have one variable, followed, perhaps, by a few more, and come up with something like

⟨varlist⟩   ::= ⟨onevar⟩ ⟨restoflist⟩
⟨restoflist⟩ ::= ε | ; ⟨varlist⟩ $\qquad$ (G3)

Here the recursion is not quite so direct, but it is there, nevertheless. Some of us have a fear of recursion, and might prefer to write the whole thing using EBNF as

⟨varlist⟩ ::= ⟨onevar⟩ { ; ⟨onevar⟩ } $\qquad$ (G4)

For future reference we shall denote the variations arising from these alternatives for ⟨varlist⟩ by G1, G2, G3 and G4 respectively.

If we had started our programming careers with PL/I, and survived, we might think of a semicolon as a terminator rather than as a separator. Faced with an informal description of the language, we should probably come up with

⟨program⟩   ::= ⟨declarationpart⟩ ⟨statementpart⟩
⟨declarationpart⟩ ::= **var** ⟨varlist⟩
⟨statementpart⟩   ::= **begin** ⟨statementlist⟩ **end** .

The simplest case for ⟨varlist⟩ would need to declare but one variable (with a trailing semicolon); both this and the more complex cases could be defined using recursive BNF as

⟨varlist⟩ ::= ⟨onevar⟩ ; | ⟨varlist⟩ ⟨onevar⟩ ;
⟨onevar⟩ ::= ⟨identifier⟩ : ⟨type⟩ $\qquad$ (G5)

As before, we might try to stress the fact that at least one variable must be declared by writing productions like

⟨varlist⟩   ::= ⟨onevar⟩ ; ⟨restoflist⟩
⟨restoflist⟩ ::= ε | ⟨varlist⟩ $\qquad$ (G6)

or, using EBNF, like

⟨varlist⟩ ::= ⟨onevar⟩ ; { ⟨onevar⟩ ; } $\qquad$ (G7)

For future reference we shall denote the variations that arise from these alternatives for ⟨varlist⟩ by G5, G6 and G7 respectively.

What we have been demonstrating here is the process of **factorization**. We can, of course, go the other way, a process called, not surprisingly, **substitution**. We might elide productions suggested by G7 to give

⟨program⟩ ::= **var** ⟨identifier⟩ : ⟨type⟩ ; { ⟨identifier⟩ : ⟨type⟩ ; }
        begin ⟨statementlist⟩ **end** .

Exercise

6.1 Draw syntax diagrams which reflect the different approaches taken to factorizing this grammar.

6.2 Some simple restrictions on grammars

Had he looked at our grammars, Mr Orwell might have been tempted to declare that, while they might be equal, some are more equal than others. Even with only limited experience we might foresee that some grammars will have features that make their use as the basis of parsing algorithms difficult, if not impossible. There are several standard restrictions called for by different parsing techniques, among which are some fairly obvious ones.

6.2.1 Useless productions and reduced grammars

For a grammar to be of practical value, especially in the automatic construction of parsers and compilers, it should not contain superfluous rules that cannot be used in parsing a sentence. Detection of useless productions may seem a waste of time, but it may also point to a clerical error (perhaps an omission) in writing the productions. An example of a grammar with useless productions is

$$G = \{N , T , S , P\}$$
$$N = \{W , X , Y , Z\}$$
$$T = \{a\}$$
$$S = W$$
$$P =$$

$W \rightarrow aW$	(1)
$W \rightarrow Z$	(2)
$W \rightarrow X$	(3)
$Z \rightarrow aZ$	(4)
$X \rightarrow a$	(5)
$Y \rightarrow aa$	(6)

The useful productions are (1), (3) and (5). Production (6) ($Y \rightarrow aa$) is useless, because there is no way of introducing Y into a sentential form (that is, $S \not\Rightarrow^* \alpha Y \beta$

for any α, β). Productions (2) and (4) are useless, because Z cannot be used to generate a terminal string (that is, $Z \not\Rightarrow^* \alpha$ for any $\alpha \in T^*$).

In fact, non-terminals which cannot be reached in any derivation from the start symbol are sometimes added so as to assist in describing the language – an example might be to write, for Pascal

$\langle$comment$\rangle$ ::= (* $\langle$commentstring$\rangle$ *)
$\langle$commentstring$\rangle$ ::= $\langle$character$\rangle$ | $\langle$commentstring$\rangle$ $\langle$character$\rangle$

A **reduced grammar** is one which does not contain superfluous rules of these two types (non-terminals which can never be reached from the start symbol, and non-terminals which cannot produce terminal strings).

More formally, a context-free grammar is said to be reduced if, for each non-terminal B, we can write

$$S \Rightarrow^* \alpha B \beta$$

for some strings α and β where

$$B \Rightarrow^* \gamma$$

for some $\gamma \in T^+$.

6.2.2 ε-free grammars

Intuitively we might expect that detecting the presence of 'nothing' would be a little awkward, and for this reason certain compiling techniques require that a grammar should contain no ε-productions (those involving the null string). Such a grammar is referred to as an ε-free grammar.

ε-productions are often used in BNF as a way of terminating recursion, and are often easily removed. For example, the productions

$\langle$integer$\rangle$ ::= $\langle$digit$\rangle$ $\langle$rest of integer$\rangle$
$\langle$rest of integer$\rangle$ ::= $\langle$digit$\rangle$ $\langle$rest of integer$\rangle$ | ε
$\langle$digit$\rangle$ ::= 0 | 1 | 2 | 3 | 4 | 5 | 6 | 7 | 8 | 9

are easily replaced by the ε-free equivalent

$\langle$integer$\rangle$ ::= $\langle$digit$\rangle$ | $\langle$integer$\rangle$ $\langle$digit$\rangle$
$\langle$digit$\rangle$ ::= 0 | 1 | 2 | 3 | 4 | 5 | 6 | 7 | 8 | 9

Such replacement may not always be so easy: the reader might like to look at the language of Section 5.11, which uses ε-productions as alternatives in $\langle$constdeclarations$\rangle$, $\langle$vardeclarations$\rangle$ and $\langle$statement$\rangle$, and attempt to eliminate them.

6.2.3   Cycle-free grammars

A production in which the right side consists of a single non-terminal

$$A \rightarrow B \quad \{A, B \in N\}$$

is termed a **single production**. Fairly obviously, a single production of the form

$$A \rightarrow A$$

serves no useful purpose, and should never be present. It could be argued that it causes no harm, as, presumably, it would be an alternative which was never used (so being useless in a sense not quite that discussed above). A less obvious example is provided by the set of productions

$$A \rightarrow B$$
$$B \rightarrow C$$
$$C \rightarrow A$$

Not only is this useless in this new sense, it is highly undesirable from the point of obtaining a unique parse, and so all parsing techniques require a grammar to be **cycle free** – it must not contain a derivation of the form

$$A \Rightarrow^+ A$$

6.3   Deterministic top-down parsing

The task of translators is, of course, not the generation of sentences of a language, but the recognition of them. This implies that the generating steps which led to the construction of a sentence must be deduced from the finished sentence. How difficult this is to do depends on the complexity of the production rules of the grammar. For Pascal-like languages it is, in fact, not too bad, but in the case of languages like FORTRAN it becomes quite complicated, for reasons which, perhaps, are not at first apparent.

Many different methods for parsing sentences have been developed. We shall concentrate on a rather simple, and yet quite effective one, known as **top-down parsing** by **recursive descent**, which can be applied to Pascal, and many other modern Pascal-like languages, including the toy one of Section 5.11.

The reason for the phrase 'by recursive descent' will become apparent later. For the moment we note that top-down methods start from the goal symbol and try to regenerate the sentence by substituting the correct choice of production at each step. In doing this they are guided by looking at the 'next' terminal in the string they have been given to parse.

To illustrate top-down parsing, consider the toy grammar

$$G = \{N, T, S, P\}$$
$$N = \{A, B\}$$
$$T = \{x, y, z\}$$
$$S = A$$
$$P =$$

$$
\begin{array}{ll}
A \rightarrow xB & (1) \\
B \rightarrow z & (2) \\
B \rightarrow yB & (3)
\end{array}
$$

Let us try to parse the sentence $xyyz$, which clearly is formed from the terminals of this grammar. We start with the goal symbol and the input string

Sentential form $S = A$ Input string $xyyz$

To the sentential form A we can apply the production (1) – in fact we can only apply this one – and we get

Sentential form xB Input string $xyyz$

So far we are obviously doing all right. The leading terminals in both the sentential form and the input string match, and we can effectively discard them from both; what we have now implies that from the non-terminal B we must be able to derive yyz.

Sentential form B Input string yyz

We could choose either of productions (2) or (3) in handling the non-terminal B; simply looking at the input string indicates that (3) is the obvious choice. If we apply this production we get

Sentential form yB Input string yyz

which implies that from the non-terminal B we must be able to derive yz.

Sentential form B Input string yz

Again we are led to use production (3) and we get

Sentential form yB Input string yz

which implies that from the non-terminal B we must be able to derive the terminal z directly   which of course we can do by applying (2).

The reader can easily verify that a sentence composed only of the terminal x, such that $xxxx$, could not be derived from the goal symbol, nor could one with y as the rightmost symbol, such as $xyyyy$.

The method we are using is a special case of so-called **LL(k) parsing**. The terminology comes from the notion that we are scanning the input string from Left to right (the first L), applying productions to the Leftmost non-terminal in the sentential form we are manipulating (the second L), and looking only as far ahead as the next k terminals in the input string to help decide which production to apply at any stage. In our example, obviously, $k = 1$; LL(1) parsing is the most common form of LL(k) parsing in practice.

Parsing in this way is not always possible, as is evident from the following silly example

$$G = \{N, T, S, P\}$$
$$N = \{A, B\}$$
$$T = \{x, y, z\}$$
$$S = A$$
$$P =$$

$$A \rightarrow xB \qquad (1)$$
$$A \rightarrow xC \qquad (2)$$
$$B \rightarrow xB \qquad (3)$$
$$B \rightarrow y \qquad (4)$$
$$C \rightarrow xC \qquad (5)$$
$$C \rightarrow z \qquad (6)$$

If we try to parse the sentence $xxxz$ we might proceed as follows

Sentential form $S = A$ Input string $xxxz$

In manipulating the sentential form A we must make a choice between production (1) and (2). We do not get any real help from looking at the first terminal in the input string, so let us try production (1). This leads us to

Sentential form xB Input string $xxxz$

which implies that we must be able to derive xxz from B. We now have a much clearer choice; of the productions for B it is (3) which will yield an initial x, so we try it and get to

Sentential form xB Input string xxz

which implies that we must be able to derive xz from B. If we apply (1) again we get

Sentential form xB Input string xz

which implies that we must be able to derive z directly from B, which we cannot do. If we reflect on this we see that either we cannot derive the string, or we made a wrong decision somewhere along the line. (Fairly obviously here we went wrong right at the beginning: had we used production (2) and not (1) we should have matched the string quite easily.)

When faced with this sort of dilemma a parser might adopt the strategy of simply proceeding according to one of the possible options, being prepared to retreat along the chosen path if no further progress is possible. Any **backtracking** action is clearly inefficient, and even with a grammar as simple as this there is almost no limit to the amount of backtracking one might have to be prepared to do. One approach to language design would clearly demand that syntactic structures that can only be described by productions which run the risk of requiring backtracking algorithms should be identified, and avoided.

This may not be possible after the event of releasing the language, of course – FORTRAN is full of examples where it seems backtracking might be needed. The usual famous example is found in the pair of statements

```
DO 10 I = 1 , 2
```

and

```
DO 10 I = 1 . 2
```

These are distinguishable as two totally different statement types (**DO** statement and **REAL** assignment) only by the period/comma. This kind of problem has been avoided in many languages now in use by the introduction of reserved words, and by an insistence on the significance of spaces (neither of which are features of FORTRAN, but neither of which seem to cause difficulties for programmers who have never known otherwise).

The consequences of backtracking for full-blooded translators are far more severe than our toy example might suggest. Typically these do not simply read single characters (even 'unreading' characters is awkward enough for a computer), but also construct explicit or implicit trees, generate code, create symbol tables and so on – all of which may have to be undone, perhaps just to be redone in a very slightly different way. In addition, backtracking makes the detection of malformed sentences more complicated. All in all, it is best avoided.

Put in another way, we should like to be able to confine ourselves to the use of **deterministic** parsing methods, that is, ones where at each stage we can be sure of which production to apply next – or, if we cannot find a production to use, where we can be sure that the input string is malformed.

It might occur to the reader that some of these problems (including some real ones too, like the FORTRAN example just given) could be resolved by looking ahead more than one symbol in the input string. Perhaps in our toy problem we should have been prepared to scan four symbols ahead? A little more reflection shows that even this is quite futile here. The language this grammar generates could be described by

$$L(G) = \{x^n p \mid n > 0,\ p \in \{y, z\}\}$$

or, since the reader may not like mathematics, in English, by

at least one, but otherwise as many x's in a row as you like, followed by a single y or z

We should remark that being prepared to look more than one terminal ahead is a strategy that can work well in some situations, although, like backtracking, it will clearly be more difficult to implement.

6.4 Restrictions on grammars so as to allow LL(1) parsing

The top-down approach to parsing looks so promising that we should consider what restrictions have to be placed on a grammar in order to allow us to use the LL(1) approach (and, in particular, the method of recursive descent). Once these have been established we should pause to consider the effects they might have on the design or specification of 'real' languages.

A little reflection on the examples above will show that the problems arise when we have alternative productions for the same non-terminal, and should lead to the insight that the *initial* symbols which can be derived from alternative right sides of the production for a given non-terminal must be distinct.

We may express this formally by the following rule:

Rule 1

Given a production

$$A \to \xi_1 \mid \xi_2 \mid \ldots \xi_n$$

the sets of initial terminal symbols of all sentences that can be generated from each of the ξ_k's must be disjoint, that is

$$\text{FIRST}(\xi_j) \cap \text{FIRST}(\xi_k) = \phi \quad \text{for all } j \neq k$$

where the set $\text{FIRST}(\xi_k)$ is the set of all terminal symbols that can appear in the first position of sentences derived from ξ_k. That is

$$a \in \text{FIRST}(\xi_k) \qquad \text{if } \xi_k \Rightarrow a\zeta$$

Now if all the alternatives for a non-terminal A are simply of the form

$$\xi_k = a_k \zeta_k \qquad (a_k \in T^+, \zeta_k \in (N \cup T)^*)$$

it is quite easy to check the grammar very quickly. All productions have right-hand sides starting with a terminal, and obviously $\text{FIRST}(a_k \zeta_k) = \{a_k\}$.

It is a little restrictive to expect that we can write or rewrite all productions with alternatives in this form. More likely we shall have several alternatives of the form

$$\xi_k = B_k \zeta_k$$

where B_k is another non-terminal. In this case to find $\text{FIRST}(B_k \zeta_k)$ we shall have to consider the production rules for B_k, and look at the first terminals which can arise from those (and so it goes on, because there may be alternatives all down the line). All of these must be added to the set $\text{FIRST}(\xi_k)$. The whole process of finding the required sets may be summarized as follows:

(a)   if the first symbol of the right-hand string ξ_k is a terminal then $\text{FIRST}(\xi_k)$ is of the form $\text{FIRST}(a_k \zeta_k)$, and then $\text{FIRST}(a_k \zeta_k) = \{a_k\}$

(b)   if the first symbol of the right-hand string ξ_k is a non-terminal then $\text{FIRST}(\xi_k)$ is of the form $\text{FIRST}(B_k \zeta_k)$. If B_k is a non-terminal with the derivation rule

$$B_k \to \alpha_{k1} \mid \alpha_{k2} \mid \ldots \mid \alpha_{kn}$$

then $\text{FIRST}(B_k \zeta_k) = \text{FIRST}(\alpha_{k1}) \cup \text{FIRST}(\alpha_{k2}) \cup \ldots \cup \text{FIRST}(\alpha_{kn})$

We can demonstrate this with another toy grammar, rather similar to the one of the last section. Suppose we have

$$G = \{N, T, S, P\}$$
$$N = \{A, B, C\}$$
$$T = \{x, y, z\}$$
$$S = A$$
$$P =$$

$A \to B$	(1)
$A \to C$	(2)

$$B \rightarrow xB \qquad (3)$$
$$B \rightarrow y \qquad (4)$$
$$C \rightarrow xC \qquad (5)$$
$$C \rightarrow z \qquad (6)$$

This generates exciting sentences with any number of x's, followed by a single y or z. On looking at the alternatives for the non-terminal A we see that

$$\text{FIRST}(B) = \text{FIRST}(xB) \cup \text{FIRST}(y) = \{x, y\}$$
$$\text{FIRST}(C) = \text{FIRST}(xC) \cup \text{FIRST}(z) = \{x, z\}$$

so that Rule 1 is violated, as both $\text{FIRST}(B)$ and $\text{FIRST}(C)$ have x as a member.

We have already commented that ε-productions might cause difficulties in parsing. Indeed, Rule 1 is not enough to prevent another source of trouble, which may arise if such productions are used. Consider the silly grammar

$$G = \{N, T, S, P\}$$
$$N = \{A, B\}$$
$$T = \{x\}$$
$$S = A$$
$$P =$$
$$\qquad A \rightarrow Bx \qquad (1)$$
$$\qquad B \rightarrow x \qquad (2)$$
$$\qquad B \rightarrow \varepsilon \qquad (3)$$

If we try to parse the string x we may come unstuck

Sentential form $S = A$	Input string x
Sentential form Bx	Input string x

As we are working from left to right and have a non-terminal on the left we substitute for B to get, perhaps,

Sentential form xx	Input string x

which is clearly wrong. We should have used (3), not (2), but we had no way of telling this on the basis of looking at only the next terminal in the input.

This situation is called the **null string problem**, and it arises only for productions which can generate the null sequence. One might try to rewrite the grammar avoiding ε-productions, but in fact that is not always necessary, and, as we have commented, it is sometimes highly inconvenient.

To overcome the problem we postulate

Rule 2

For every non-terminal A which can generate the null string, the set $\text{FIRST}(A)$ of the initial symbols which can be derived by using any alternative productions for A must be disjoint from the set $\text{FOLLOW}(A)$ of symbols that may follow any sequence generated from A, that is

$$\text{FIRST}(A) \cap \text{FOLLOW}(A) = \phi.$$

where the set FOLLOW(A) is computed by considering every production P_k of the form

$$P_k \rightarrow \xi_k A \zeta_k$$

and forming the sets FIRST(ζ_k), when

$$\text{FOLLOW}(A) = \text{FIRST}(\zeta_1) \cup \text{FIRST}(\zeta_2) \cup \ldots \cup \text{FIRST}(\zeta_n)$$

with the addition that if at least one ζ_k is capable of generating the null string, then the set FOLLOW(P_k) has to be included in the set FOLLOW(A) as well.

In the above example this rule is violated because

$$\text{FIRST}(B) = \text{FOLLOW}(B) = \{x\}$$

These two rules are sometimes found stated in other ways. For example, Griffiths (Bauer and Eickel, 1976, page 62) introduces the concept of **director sets**. Given a non-terminal A which admits to alternative productions of the form

$$A \rightarrow \alpha_1 \mid \alpha_2 \mid \ldots \mid \alpha_n$$

we define DS(A, α_k) for each alternative to be the set which helps choose whether to use the alternative; when the input string contains the terminal a we choose α_k such that $a \in \text{DS}(P, \alpha_k)$. The LL(1) condition is then

$$\text{DS}(P_m, \alpha_k) \cap \text{DS}(P_m, \alpha_j) = \phi \quad \text{for } k \neq j, m = 1, n$$

The director sets are found from the relation

$$a \in \text{DS}(P, \alpha) \quad \text{if} \quad \text{either } a \in \text{FIRST}(\alpha)$$
$$\text{or} \quad a \in \text{FOLLOW}(P) \quad (\text{if } \alpha \Rightarrow^* \varepsilon)$$

This may all seem rather complicated, and the reader can probably foresee that in a really large grammar one might have to make many iterations over the productions in forming all the FIRST and FOLLOW sets and in checking the applications of all these rules.

6.5 The effect of the LL(1) conditions on language design

There are some immediate implications which follow from the rules of the last section as regards language design and specification. Alternative right-hand sides for productions are very common; we cannot hope to avoid their use in practice. Let us consider some common situations where problems might arise, and see whether we can ensure that the conditions are met.

Firstly, we should note that we cannot hope to transform every non-LL(1) grammar into a equivalent LL(1) grammar. To take an extreme example, an ambiguous grammar must have two parse trees for at least one input sentence, and if we really want to allow this we shall not be able to use a parsing method which is capable of finding only one parse tree, as deterministic parsers must do. We can argue that an ambiguous grammar is of little interest, but the reader should not go away with the impression that it is just a matter of trial and error before an equivalent LL(1) grammar is found for an arbitrary grammar.

Often a combination of substitution and refactorization will resolve problems. For example, it is almost trivially easy to find a grammar for the toy language of the last section that satisfies Rule 1. Once we have seen the types of strings the language contains, then we shall probably also see that all we have to do is to find productions which deal with leading strings of x's and delay introducing y and z as long as possible. Thus we could be led to productions of the form

$$A \to xA \mid C$$
$$C \to y \mid z$$

Alternative productions are often found in specifying the kinds of ⟨statement⟩ a language may have. Rule 1 suggests that if we wish to parse programs in such a language using LL(1) techniques we design the language so that each statement type begins with a different reserved word. (As we have already commented, reserved words are terminals in most high-level languages.) This is what is attempted in several languages, but it is not always convenient. In such cases we may often get round the problem by factoring the grammar differently.

As a rather more realistic example, in a later extension to the language of Section 5.11 we shall suggest introducing **repeat** loops in one of two forms

    repeat ⟨statement sequence⟩ **until** ⟨condition⟩

and

    repeat ⟨statement sequence⟩ **forever**

Both of these start with the reserved word **repeat**. However, if we define

    ⟨repeatstatement⟩ ::= **repeat** ⟨statement sequence⟩ ⟨rest repeatstmt⟩
    ⟨rest repeatstmt⟩ ::= **until** ⟨condition⟩ | **forever**

parsing can proceed quite happily. Another case which probably comes to mind is provided by the statements

    if ⟨condition⟩ **then** ⟨statement⟩

and

    if ⟨condition⟩ **then** ⟨statement⟩ **else** ⟨statement⟩

Factorization on the same lines as for the **repeat** loop is less successful. We might be tempted to try

    ⟨ifstatement⟩ ::= **if** ⟨condition⟩ **then** ⟨statement⟩ ⟨rest ifstmt⟩
    ⟨rest ifstmt⟩ ::= **else** ⟨statement⟩ | ε

but then we run foul of Rule 2. A little reflection shows that

    FIRST(⟨rest ifstmt⟩) = {**else**}

while

$$FOLLOW(\langle rest\ ifstmt\rangle) = FOLLOW(\langle ifstatement\rangle)$$
$$= FOLLOW(\langle statement\rangle)$$

which includes **else**.

The reader will recognize this as the 'dangling **else**' problem again. We have already remarked that we can find ways of expressing this construct unambiguously; but in fact the more usual solution is just to impose the semantic meaning that the **else** is attached to the most recent unmatched **then**, which, as the reader will discover, is handled trivially easily by a recursive descent parser. (Semantic overtones are quite often used to resolve tricky points in recursive descent parsers, as we shall see.)

Perhaps not quite so obviously, Rule 1 eliminates the possibility of using left recursion to specify syntax. This is a very common way of expressing a repeated pattern of symbols in BNF. For example, the two productions

$$A \rightarrow B \mid AB$$

describe the set of sequences $B, BB, BBB \ldots$. Their use is now ruled out by Rule 1, because

$$FIRST(AB) = FIRST(B) \cup FIRST(AB)$$
$$= FIRST(B)$$

Direct left recursion can be avoided by using right recursion, but care must be taken, as sometimes the resulting grammar is still unsuitable. For example, the productions above are equivalent to

$$A \rightarrow B \mid BA$$

but this still more clearly violates Rule 1. The secret lies in deliberately introducing extra non-terminals. A non-terminal that admits to left recursive productions will in general have two alternative productions, of the form

$$A \rightarrow AX \mid Y$$

By expansion we can see that this leads to sentential forms like

$$Y, YX, YXX, YXXX$$

and these can easily be derived by the equivalent grammar

$$A \rightarrow YZ$$
$$Z \rightarrow \varepsilon \mid XZ$$

The example given earlier is easily dealt with in this way by writing $X = Y = B$.

$$A \rightarrow BZ$$
$$Z \rightarrow \varepsilon \mid BZ$$

The astute reader might complain that the limitation on two alternatives for A is too severe. This is not really true, as suitable factorization can allow X and Y to have alternatives, none of which starts with A. For example, the set

$$A \rightarrow Ab \mid Ac \mid d \mid e$$

can obviously be recast as

$$A \rightarrow AX \mid Y$$
$$X \rightarrow b \mid c$$
$$Y \rightarrow d \mid e$$

(Indirect left recursion, for example

$$A \rightarrow B$$
$$B \rightarrow C \ldots$$
$$C \rightarrow A \ldots$$

is harder to handle, and is, fortunately, not very common in practice.)

This might not be quite as useful as it first appears. For example, the problem with

$$\langle \text{expression} \rangle ::= \langle \text{expression} \rangle + \langle \text{term} \rangle \mid \langle \text{term} \rangle$$

can readily be removed by using right recursion

$$\langle \text{expression} \rangle \quad ::= \langle \text{term} \rangle \langle \text{restexpression} \rangle$$
$$\langle \text{restexpression} \rangle ::= \varepsilon \mid + \langle \text{term} \rangle \langle \text{restexpression} \rangle$$

but this may have the side-effect of altering the implied order of evaluation of an $\langle \text{expression} \rangle$. For example, adding the productions

$$\langle \text{term} \rangle ::= X \mid Y \mid Z$$

to the above would mean that with the former production for $\langle \text{expression} \rangle$, a string of the form $X + Y + Z$ would be evaluated as $(X + Y) + Z$, but with the latter production it might be evaluated as $X + (Y + Z)$ – which in a machine with fixed real precision might result in differing answers.

The way to handle this situation would be to write the parsing algorithms to use iteration, as introduced earlier, for example

$$\langle \text{expression} \rangle ::= \langle \text{term} \rangle \{ + \langle \text{term} \rangle \}$$

Although this is merely another way of expressing the right recursive productions used above, it may be easier for the reader to follow, and carries the advantage of more easily retaining left associativity which the $+$ terminal clearly implies.

It might be tempting to try to use such iteration to remove all the problems associated with recursion, but care must be taken since this action often implies that ε-productions either explicitly or implicitly enter the grammar. For example, the construction

$$A \rightarrow \{B\}$$

actually implies, and can be written

$$A \rightarrow \varepsilon \mid BA$$

but can only be handled if $\text{FIRST}(B) \cap \text{FOLLOW}(A) = \phi$. The astute reader might already have realized that all our manipulations to handle $\langle \text{expression} \rangle$ would come to naught if $+$ could follow $\langle \text{expression} \rangle$ in other productions of the grammar.

It is of interest to relate this discussion to the grammars derived in Section 6.1 for a sequence of variable declarations followed by a statement sequence.

We should now be able to see that grammars G1, G2 and G5 are immediately ruled out because of Rule 1. G3, G4, G6 and G7 bear closer scrutiny. G3 is ruled out because

$$FIRST(\langle restoflist \rangle) = FOLLOW(\langle restoflist \rangle)$$
$$= FOLLOW(\langle varlist \rangle) = \{ ; \}.$$

Since G4 is just an iterative equivalent of G3 it must be ruled out as well. Put in another way, one cannot tell from looking at the next semicolon whether it should be treated as the separator between the $\langle declarationpart \rangle$ and the $\langle statementpart \rangle$, or whether it is the sign to embark on another iteration of the $\{ ; \langle varlist \rangle \}$ kind.

G6 and G7, however, are satisfactory. Although G6 has an ε-production for $\langle restoflist \rangle$ we see that

$$FIRST(\langle restoflist \rangle) = FIRST(\langle varlist \rangle) = FIRST(\langle onevar \rangle)$$
$$= FIRST(\langle identifier \rangle)$$

while

$$FOLLOW(\langle restoflist \rangle) = FOLLOW(\langle declarationpart \rangle)$$
$$= FIRST(\langle statementpart \rangle)$$
$$= \{ \textbf{begin} \}$$

In Pascal the semicolon is usually considered to be a separator, and indeed it is, in the context of statements. We can now see that in the context of declarations it is actually a terminator.

Exercises

6.2 Determine the FIRST and FOLLOW sets for the following non-terminals of the grammar defined in various ways in Section 5.11, and comment on which formulations may be parsed using LL(1) techniques.

> $\langle block \rangle$
> $\langle constdeclarations \rangle$
> $\langle vardeclarations \rangle$
> $\langle statement \rangle$
> $\langle expression \rangle$
> $\langle factor \rangle$
> $\langle term \rangle$

6.3 What are the semantic implications of using the productions suggested in Section 5.5 for the **if...then** and **if...then...else** statements?

6.4   Whether to regard the semicolon as a separator or as a terminator has been a matter of some controversy. Do we need semicolons at all in a language like the one suggested in Section 6.1? Try writing productions for a version of the language where they are simply omitted, and check that the grammar you produce satisfies the LL(1) conditions.

You might like to follow up the semicolon controversy a little further. See the discussions in the books by Horowitz (1984) (page 69) or Ledgard and Marcotty (1981) (page 34), and references quoted there.

6.5   A close look at the syntax of Pascal or the language of Section 5.11 shows that an ε-production is allowed for ⟨statement⟩. Can you think of any reasons at all why one should not simply forbid empty statements?

6.6 Construction of simple recursive descent parsers

We turn now to a consideration of the actual implementation of a parser for the kind of language which satisfies the rules mentioned earlier. This is, in fact, remarkably easy. The syntax of the language is governed by production rules of the form

⟨non-terminal⟩ → allowable string

where the allowable string is a concatenation derived from

(a)   the basic symbols or terminals of the language
(b)   other non-terminals
(c)   the actions of meta-symbols such as { and |.

We aim to express the effect of using each production by writing a **procedure** to which we shall give the name of the non-terminal. The action of this procedure will be to analyse a sequence of symbols (which will be supplied on request from a suitable lexical analyser), and verify that it is of the correct form, reporting errors if it is not. More precisely, the procedure corresponding to a non-terminal S

(a)   will assume that it has been called after some (globally accessible) variable SYM has been found to contain one of the terminals in FIRST(S);
(b)   will then parse a complete sequence of terminals which can be derived from S, reporting an error if no such sequence is found (in doing this it may have to call on similar procedures to handle sub-sequences);
(c)   will relinquish parsing leaving SYM with the first terminal it finds which cannot be derived from S, that is to say, one of the set FOLLOW(S).

The shell of each parsing procedure will thus be

```
procedure S;
  begin
  (*assert SYM ∈ FIRST(S) *)
  T(string)
  (*assert SYM ∈ FOLLOW(S) *)
end
```

The transformation T(string) is governed by the following rules:

(a) If the production yields a single terminal, then the action of T is to report an error if it is incorrect, or (more optimistically) to accept it, and then to scan to the next symbol.

```
T(terminal) →
  if terminal correct
    then get next symbol SYM
    else report error
```

(b) If we are dealing with a 'single' production, then the action of T is a simple invocation of the corresponding procedure

$$T(singleproduction\langle A \rangle) \rightarrow A$$

This is a rather trivial case, just mentioned here for completeness. Single productions do not really need special mention, except where they form part of longer strings, as discussed below.

(c) If the production allows a number of alternative forms, then the action can be expressed as a **case** selection

```
T(α₁ | α₂ | ... αₙ) →
  case SYM of
    FIRST(α₁) : T(α₁);
    FIRST(α₂) : T(α₂);
    ......
    FIRST(αₙ) : T(αₙ)
end
```

in which we see immediately the relevance of Rule 1. In fact we can go further to see the relevance of Rule 2, for to the above we should add the action to be taken if one of the alternatives of T is empty. Here we do nothing to advance SYM – an action which must leave SYM, as we have seen, as one of the set FOLLOW(S) – so that we may augment the above as

```
T(α₁ | α₂ | ... αₙ) →
  case SYM of
    FIRST(α₁)   : T(α₁);
    FIRST(α₂)   : T(α₂);
    ......
    FIRST(αₙ)   : T(αₙ);
    FOLLOW(S): {do nothing}
end
```

(d)   If the production allows for possible repetition, the transformation involves a loop, often of the form

$T(\{string\}) \rightarrow$ **while** SYM **in** FIRST(string) **do** T(string)

Note the importance of Rule 2 here again. Some repetitions are of the form

$S \rightarrow A\{A\}$

which transforms to

begin $T(A)$; **while** SYM **in** FIRST(A) **do** $T(A)$ **end**

On occasions this may be better written

repeat $T(A)$ **until not** (SYM **in** FIRST(A))

(e)   Most commonly, the production generates a sequence of terminals and non-terminals. The action is then a sequence derived from (a) and (b), namely

$T(\alpha_1 \alpha_2 \dots \alpha_n) \rightarrow$ **begin** $T(\alpha_1)$; $T(\alpha_2)$; $\dots$ $T(\alpha_n)$ **end**

To illustrate these ideas further, we present a rather simple grammar, chosen to illustrate these various options.

$G = \{N, T, S, P\}$
$N = \{A, B, C, D\}$
$T = \{(,), +, x, [,], .\}$
$S = A$
$P =$

$A \rightarrow B.$	(1)
$B \rightarrow x \mid (C) \mid [B] \mid \varepsilon$	(2,3,4,5)
$C \rightarrow BD$	(6)
$D \rightarrow \{ \mid D\}$	(7)

We first check that this language satisfies the requirements for LL(1) parsing.

We can easily see that Rule 1 is satisfied. The only production for which there are alternatives is that for B, and each alternative starts with a different terminal.

To check Rule 2 we note that B and D can both generate the null string. We readily compute

FIRST(B) = $\{x, (, [\}$
FIRST(D) = $\{+\}$

The computation of the FOLLOW sets is a little trickier. That for A is easily seen to be ϕ. FOLLOW(C) likewise is easily seen to be $\{) \}$.

For FOLLOW(B) we use the rules of the previous section. We check productions of the form $\xi B \zeta$ – these are the ones for A and C and the third alternative for B itself. This seems to indicate that

FOLLOW(B) = $\{ .,] \} \cup$ FIRST(D).
             = $\{ .,], + \}$

We must be more careful. Further inspection reveals that the production for D

can generate a null string. This means that we must augment FOLLOW(B) by
FOLLOW(C) to give

$$FOLLOW(B) = \{ . ,] , + \} \cup \{) \}$$
$$= \{ . ,] , + ,) \}$$

The only production in which D appears on the right is that for C, so that
FOLLOW(D) = FOLLOW(C) = {) }.

Since FIRST(B)∩FOLLOW(B) = ϕ and FIRST(D)∩FOLLOW(D)
= ϕ, Rule 2 is satisfied as well.

A Pascal program for a parser follows. The terminals of the language are all
single characters, so that we do not have to make any special arrangements for
character handling (a simple *read* statement suffices) or for lexical analysis.

Listing 6   Simple recursive descent parser

```
1    program PARSER (INPUT, OUTPUT);
2    (*Simple Recursive Descent Parser for the language
3            G = { N , T , S , P }
4            N = { A , B , C , D }
5            T = { ( , ) , + , x , [ , ] , . }
6            S = A
7            P =
8              A ::= B .
9              B ::= x  |  ( C )  |  [ B ]  |  null
10             C ::= B D
11             D ::= { + B }
12
13   ++++++++++++++++++++++++++++++++++++++++++++++++++++++++++++++++++
14
15   NOTE that the comments above require that your Pascal system
16        allow nesting of comments with alternative brackets
17   NOTE that we use a non-standard HALT procedure to abort
18
19   ++++++++++++++++++++++++++++++++++++++++++++++++++++++++++++++++++
20
21   P.D. Terry,  31 January 1985   *)
22
23   var
24     SYM : CHAR (*source token*);
25
26   procedure ACCEPT (TERMINAL : CHAR);
27     begin
28       if SYM = TERMINAL
29         then READ(INPUT, SYM)
30         else begin WRITELN(OUTPUT, 'Error'); HALT end
31     end (*ACCEPT*);
```

```
32
33      procedure B;
34
35        procedure D;
36          begin
37            while SYM = '+' do begin ACCEPT('+'); B end
38          end (*D*);
39
40        procedure C;
41          begin
42            B; D
43          end (*C*);
44
45        begin (*B*)
46          case SYM of
47            'x' : ACCEPT('x');
48            '(' : begin ACCEPT('('); C; ACCEPT(')') end;
49            '[' : begin ACCEPT('['); B; ACCEPT(']') end;
50            ')', ']', '+', '.' : (*followers of B*)
51          end
52        end (*B*);
53
54      procedure A;
55        begin
56          B; ACCEPT('.')
57        end (*A*);
58
59      begin (*PARSER*)
60        READ(INPUT, SYM); A; WRITELN(OUTPUT, 'Successful')
61      end (*PARSER*).
```

When writing recursive descent parsers, construction of syntax diagrams may be of great assistance, as they essentially provide flowcharts for the procedures. In addition, the determination of the FIRST and FOLLOW sets may be quite easily made by inspecting the branches. As before, care must be taken to retain the equivalence of the grammars.

Although recursive descent parsers are suitable for handling languages which satisfy the LL(1) conditions, we should remark that they may be used, often with relatively simple modifications, to handle languages which, strictly, do not satisfy them.

Some care must be taken with the relative ordering of the declaration of procedures, which in this example, and in general, are recursive in nature. It should now be clear why this method of parsing is called 'Recursive Descent', and that such parsers are only really easy to implement in languages which support recursion directly. A little reflection shows that one can often combine procedures (this corresponds to reducing the number of productions used to define the grammar) and produce a shorter program – of course, precautions must be taken to ensure that the two grammars, and any implicit semantic overtones are truly equivalent. An equivalent grammar to the above one is

$$G = \{N, T, S, P\}$$
$$N = \{A, B\}$$
$$T = \{(,), +, x, [,], . \}$$
$$S = A$$
$$P =$$
$$A \rightarrow B. \tag{1}$$
$$B \rightarrow x \mid (B \{ + B \}) \mid [B] \mid \varepsilon \tag{2,3,4,5}$$

leading to a parser

```
program PARSER (INPUT, OUTPUT);
(*Simple Recursive Descent Parser for the same language
  using an equivalent but different grammar *)
var
  SYM : CHAR (*source token*);

procedure ACCEPT (TERMINAL : CHAR);
  begin
    if SYM = TERMINAL
      then READ(INPUT, SYM)
      else begin WRITELN(OUTPUT, 'Error'); HALT end
  end (*ACCEPT*);

procedure A;

  procedure B;
    begin
      case SYM of
        'x' : ACCEPT('x');
        '(' : begin
                ACCEPT('('); B;
                while SYM = '+' do
                  begin ACCEPT('+'); B end;
                ACCEPT(')')
              end;
        '[' : begin ACCEPT('['); B; ACCEPT(']') end;
        ')', ']', '+', '.' : (*followers of B*)
      end
    end (*B*);

  begin (*A*)
    B; ACCEPT('.')
  end (*A*);

begin (*PARSER*)
  READ(INPUT, SYM); A; WRITELN(OUTPUT, 'Successful')
end (*PARSER*).
```

Recursive descent parsers are easily written, provided a satisfactory grammar can be found. Being simple, they may be developed manually quite quickly, and since the code tends to match the grammar very closely, they can be written quite accurately. There are some disadvantages in the method. The overheads involved in making many procedure calls, and in demanding that these can be recursive, can make the parser 'inefficient' (the reader will be better placed to appreciate this when we discuss the implementation of recursive procedures in a later chapter). Secondly, there is a great temptation – indeed it is the obvious course of action – to supplement the parser with the semantic analysis and code generation phases in developing a complete compiler, and this can make the program steadily more difficult to maintain, to understand, and to keep in a 'portable' form.

The astute reader may have wondered at the fact that the parsing methods we have advocated all look 'ahead', and never seem to make use of what has already been achieved, that is, of information which has become embedded in the previous history of the parse. We have also made no mention at all of context-sensitive features of languages in this chapter, and yet we pointed out in Chapter 5 that there are features of programming languages which cannot be specified in a context-free grammar (such as the requirement in Pascal that variables must be declared before use, and that expressions may be formed only when terms and factors are of the correct types). In practice, of course, a parser is usually combined with a semantic analyser; in a sense some of the past history of the parse is recorded in such devices as symbol tables which the semantic analysis needs to maintain, and this information may often be used to help overcome problems which strictly render the grammar non-LL(1).

Exercises

6.6 Check the LL(1) conditions for the equivalent grammar used in the second of the Pascal programs above.

6.7 Rework the example by checking the director sets for the productions.

6.8 We could have written the productions for D in this language as

$$D \rightarrow \varepsilon \mid + BD$$

Check that the rules for LL(1) parsing are still satisfied, and modify the program to reflect this alternative approach.

6.9 Suppose we wished the language to be such that spaces in the input file were irrelevant. How could this be done?

6.10 Draw the equivalent syntax diagrams for the above grammars, and confirm the allegations made above about their use as procedural flowcharts.

6.11 Construct a recursive descent parser for the language of Section 6.1.

6.7   LR parsing

Although space does not permit of a full description, no modern text on translators would be complete without some mention of so-called **LR(k) parsing**. The terminology here comes from the notion that we scan the input string from Left to right (the L), applying reductions so as to yield a Rightmost parse (the R), by looking as far ahead as the next k terminals to help decide which production to apply. (In practice k is never more than 1, and may be zero.)

The technique is **bottom-up** rather than **top-down**. Starting from the input sentence, and making **reductions**, we aim to end up with the goal symbol. The reduction of a sentential form is achieved by substituting the left side of a production for a string (appearing in the sentential form) which matches the right side, rather than by substituting the right side of a production whose left side appears as a non-terminal in the sentential form.

A bottom-up parsing algorithm might employ a **parse stack**, which contains part of a possible sentential form of terminals and/or non-terminals. As we read each terminal from the input string we push it onto the parse stack, and then examine the top elements of this to see whether we can make a reduction. Some terminals may remain on the parse stack quite a long time before they are finally pushed off and discarded. (By way of contrast, a top-down parser can discard the terminals immediately after reading them. Furthermore, a recursive descent parser stores the non-terminal components of the partial sentential form only implicitly, as a chain of as yet uncompleted calls to the procedures which handle each non-terminal.)

Perhaps an example will help to make this clearer. Suppose we have a highly simplified (non-LL(1)) grammar for expressions, defined by

$\langle$goal$\rangle$	$::= \langle$expression$\rangle$	(1)
$\langle$expression$\rangle$	$::= \langle$expression$\rangle + \langle$term$\rangle \mid \langle$term$\rangle$	(2,3)
$\langle$term$\rangle$	$::= a$	(4)

and are given the string '$a + a + a$ ' to parse.

The sequence of events could be summarized as shown in Table 6.1. At the end of the summary we have reached $\langle$goal$\rangle$ and can conclude that the sentence is valid.

The reader will declare that we have cheated somewhat. Why did we not use the production $\langle$goal$\rangle ::= \langle$expression$\rangle$ when we had reduced the string a to $\langle$expression$\rangle$ after step 3? To apply a reduction it is, of course, necessary that the right side of a production be currently on the parse stack, but this in itself is insufficient. Faced with a choice of right-hand sides which match the top elements on the parse stack, a practical parser will have to employ some strategy, perhaps of looking ahead in the input string, to decide which to apply.

Such parsers are invariably table driven, with the particular strategy at any stage being determined by looking up an entry in a rectangular matrix indexed by two variables, one representing the current 'state' of the parse (the position the parser has reached within the productions of the grammar) and the other representing the current 'input symbol' (which is one of the terminals or non-

Table 6.1

Step	Action	Using production	Stack
1	read *a*		*a*
2	reduce	4	⟨term⟩
3	reduce	3	⟨expression⟩
4	read +		⟨expression⟩ +
5	read *a*		⟨expression⟩ + *a*
6	reduce	4	⟨expression⟩ + ⟨term⟩
7	reduce	2	⟨expression⟩
8	read +		⟨expression⟩ +
9	read *a*		⟨expression⟩ + *a*
10	reduce	4	⟨expression⟩ + ⟨term⟩
11	reduce	2	⟨expression⟩
12	reduce	1	⟨goal⟩

terminals of the grammar). The entries in the table specify whether the parser is to
accept the input string as correct, **reject** as incorrect, **shift** to another state, or
reduce by applying a particular production. Rather than stack the symbols of the
grammar, as was implied by the trace above, the parsing algorithm pushes or
pops elements representing states of the parse – a *shift* operation pushing the
newly reached state onto the stack, and a *reduce* operation popping as many
elements as there are symbols on the right side of the production being applied.
The algorithm can be expressed:

```
INPUTSYMBOL ← first SYM in sentence
STATE ← 1; PUSH(STATE); PARSING ← TRUE
repeat
  determine ACTION from TABLE[STATE, INPUTSYMBOL]
  case ACTION of
    SHIFT:
      STATE ← NEXTSTATE as specified in TABLE; PUSH(STATE)
      if INPUTSYMBOL is a terminal then GETSYM (*accept it*)
      INPUTSYMBOL ← SYM
    REDUCE:
      POP N elements from stack, where N  is length of right side
          of production being applied (as specified in TABLE)
      STATE ← STATE now on top of stack
      INPUTSYMBOL ← left side of production being applied
    REJECT:
      report error; PARSING ← FALSE
    ACCEPT:
      report successful; PARSING ← FALSE
until not PARSING
```

Although the algorithm itself is very simple, construction of the parsing table is considerably more difficult. We shall not go into how this is done here, but simply note that for the simple example given above the parsing table might appear as shown in Table 6.2 (we have left the *reject* entries blank for clarity).

Table 6.2

	Symbol					
State	⟨goal⟩	⟨expression⟩	⟨term⟩	*a*	+	.
1	Accept	Shift 2	Shift 3	Shift 4		
2					Shift 5	Reduce 1
3					Reduce 3	Reduce 3
4					Reduce 4	Reduce 4
5			Shift 6	Shift 4		
6					Reduce 2	Reduce 2

Given this table, a parse of the string '*a + a + a* .' would proceed as shown in Table 6.3. Notice that the period has been introduced merely to make recognizing the end of the string somewhat easier.

Table 6.3

State	*Symbol*	*Stack*	*Action*
1	*a*	1	Shift to state 4, accept *a*
4	+	1 4	Reduce by (4) ⟨term⟩ ::= *a*
1	⟨term⟩	1	Shift to state 3
3	+	1 3	Reduce by (3) ⟨expression⟩ ::= ⟨term⟩
1	⟨expression⟩	1	Shift to state 2
2	+	1 2	Shift to state 5, accept +
5	*a*	1 2 5	Shift to state 4, accept *a*
4	+	1 2 5 4	Reduce by (4) ⟨term⟩ ::= *a*
5	⟨term⟩	1 2 5	Shift to state 6
6	+	1 2 5 6	Reduce by (2) ⟨expression⟩ ::= ⟨expression⟩ + ⟨term⟩
1	⟨expression⟩	1	Shift to state 2
2	+	1 2	Shift to state 5, accept +
5	*a*	1 2 5	Shift to state 4, accept *a*
4	.	1 2 5 4	Reduce by (2) ⟨term⟩ ::= *a*
5	⟨term⟩	1 2 5	Shift to state 6
6	.	1 2 5 6	Reduce by (2) ⟨expression⟩ ::= ⟨expression⟩ + ⟨term⟩
1	⟨expression⟩	1	Shift to state 2
2	.	1 2	Reduce by 1 ⟨goal⟩ ::= ⟨expression⟩
1	⟨goal⟩	1	Accept – completed

Fully refined, for a grammar with very simple single character symbols, the algorithm might be developed into a Pascal program such as that given below with notes following.

Listing 7   Simple table-driven LR parser

```
1 program LRPARSER (INPUT, OUTPUT);
2 (*Simple table driven LR parser.  P.D. Terry, August 15th, 1985 *)
3 const
4    ENDSTRING = '.'        (*terminate sentences*);
5    LOWEST = 0             (*ASCII ordinal value*);
6    HIGHEST = 127          (*ASCII ordinal value*);
7    MAXPRODUCTIONS = 15 (*limit on number of productions*);
8    MAXSTATES = 15         (*limit on number of states*);
9    MAXLENGTH = 15         (*limit on length of right side of productions*);
10 type
11    STATES = 0 .. MAXSTATES;
12    PRODUCTIONS = 0 .. MAXPRODUCTIONS;
13    ACTIONS = (ACCEPT, REJECT, SHIFT, REDUCE);
14    TABLEENTRIES = record  (*parser table entries*)
15                    case ACTION : ACTIONS of
16                       SHIFT  : (NEXTSTATE : STATES);
17                       REDUCE : (TOBEAPPLIED : PRODUCTIONS)
18                  end (*TABLEENTRIES*);
19    RULES = record (*production rules*)
20          LENGTH    : 0 .. MAXLENGTH;
21          RIGHTSIDE : array [0 .. MAXLENGTH] of CHAR;
22          LEFTSIDE  : CHAR
23        end (*RULE*);
24 var
25    (*some implementations require INPUT, OUTPUT : TEXT; *)
26    RULE  : array [PRODUCTIONS] of RULES        (*the productions*);
27    TABLE : array [STATES, CHAR] of TABLEENTRIES (*the parser table*);
28    MAP   : array [CHAR] of ACTIONS             (*convert chars to actions*);
29    NPRODUCTIONS : PRODUCTIONS                  (*number of productions*);
30    TERMINALS : set of CHAR                     (*UPPER CASE are non-terminals*);
31
32 procedure INITIALIZE;
33 (*Assimilate production rules and parser table*)
34    var
35    C : CHAR;
36    I : INTEGER;
37
```

```
38   procedure READPRODUCTIONS;
39   (*Supplied one to a line, in form <lhs> <blank> <rhs> <crlf> for example
40          S E
41          E T+F
42     use CAPITAL letters for non-terminals, others for terminals.
43          Terminate list with ENDSTRING in first column                    *)
44     var
45       BLANK, CH : CHAR;
46     begin
47       NPRODUCTIONS := 0; READ(INPUT, CH);
48       while CH <> ENDSTRING do
49         begin
50           NPRODUCTIONS := NPRODUCTIONS + 1;
51           with RULE[NPRODUCTIONS] do
52             begin
53               LENGTH := 0; LEFTSIDE := CH; READ(INPUT, BLANK);
54               while not EOLN(INPUT) do
55                 begin LENGTH := LENGTH + 1; READ(INPUT, RIGHTSIDE[LENGTH]) end
56             end;
57           READLN(INPUT); READ(INPUT, CH)
58         end;
59       READLN(INPUT)
60     end (*READPRODUCTIONS*);
61
62   procedure READTABLE;
63   (*Parser table entries one line per entry, of form
64     <state> <symbol> <blank> <action> <number>   for example
65                1S A0    State 1, symbol S, A(ccept, next state 0
66                2+ S7    State 2, symbol +, S(hift,  next state 7
67                6+ R4    State 6, symbol +, R(educe, by production 4
68                0.
69       Terminate with line reading 0  (0 is not a valid state number).
70       All unspecified entries will be set up as E(rror entries  *)
71     var
72       SYMBOL, BLANK, ACTIONCODE : CHAR;
73       STATE, NUMBER : INTEGER;
74     begin
75       READ(INPUT, STATE);
76       while STATE > 0 do
77         begin
78           READ(INPUT, SYMBOL, BLANK, ACTIONCODE, NUMBER);
79           with TABLE[STATE, SYMBOL] do
80             begin
81               ACTION := MAP[ACTIONCODE];
82               case ACTION of
```

```
83                    SHIFT  : NEXTSTATE   := NUMBER;
84                    REDUCE : TOBEAPPLIED := NUMBER;
85                    ACCEPT : (*no further action*)
86                end
87              end;
88          READLN(INPUT); READ(INPUT, STATE)
89        end;
90      READLN(INPUT)
91    end (*READTABLE*);
92
93  begin (*INITIALIZE*)
94    TERMINALS := [CHR(LOWEST + 1) .. CHR(HIGHEST)] - ['A'..'Z'];
95    for I := 1 to MAXSTATES do
96      for C := CHR(LOWEST) to CHR(HIGHEST) do
97        with TABLE[I, C] do ACTION := REJECT;
98      for C := CHR(LOWEST) to CHR(HIGHEST) do MAP[C] := REJECT;
99    MAP['S'] := SHIFT;  MAP['s'] := SHIFT;
100   MAP['A'] := ACCEPT; MAP['a'] := ACCEPT;
101   MAP['R'] := REDUCE; MAP['r'] := REDUCE;
102   READPRODUCTIONS; READTABLE
103 end (*INITIALIZE*);
104
105 procedure PARSESTRING;
106   const
107     LINEMAX = 120              (*limit on line length*);
108     STACKMAX = 100             (*limit on stack depth*);
109   type
110     LINEINDEX  = 0 .. LINEMAX;
111     STACKINDEX = 0 .. STACKMAX;
112     ELEMENTS   = (SYMBOLIC, NUMERIC)  (*type of entries on stack*);
113   var
114     CURRENTENTRY : TABLEENTRIES      (*current entry used in parser table*);
115     CURRENTSTATE : STATES            (*current state of parse*);
116     INPUTSYMBOL, SYM : CHAR          (*driver and latest input terminal*);
117     TOP : STACKINDEX                 (*stack pointer*);
118     STACK : array [STACKINDEX] of    (*parse stack*)
119               record
120                 case TIPE : ELEMENTS of
121                   SYMBOLIC : (SYMBOL : CHAR);
122                   NUMERIC :  (STATE  : STATES)
123                 end (*STACK*);
124     LL, CC : LINEINDEX               (*line length, character count*);
125     STRING : array [LINEINDEX] of CHAR (*being parsed*);
126
127   procedure READSTRING;
```

```
128    (*Read STRING to be parsed and append end marker*)
129      begin
130        LL := 0; CC := 0;
131        while not EOLN(INPUT) do
132          begin LL := LL + 1; READ(INPUT, STRING[LL]) end;
133        LL := LL + 1; STRING[LL] := ENDSTRING; READLN(INPUT)
134      end (*READSTRING*);
135
136    procedure GETNEXTTERMINAL;
137    (*Scan and ignore blanks until next terminal SYM found*)
138      begin
139        repeat CC := CC + 1; SYM := STRING[CC] until SYM <> ' ';
140        if not (SYM in TERMINALS) then SYM := CHR(LOWEST) (*forced*)
141      end (*GETNEXTTERMINAL*);
142
143    procedure PUSH (ELEMENT : ELEMENTS);
144    (*Push either a state or a symbol onto parse stack*)
145      begin
146        TOP := TOP + 1; STACK[TOP].TIPE := ELEMENT;
147        case ELEMENT of
148          SYMBOLIC : STACK[TOP].SYMBOL := INPUTSYMBOL;
149          NUMERIC  : STACK[TOP].STATE  := CURRENTSTATE
150        end
151      end (*PUSH*);
152
153    procedure POP (N : INTEGER);
154    (*Pop N items off parse stack*)
155      begin TOP := TOP - N end;
156
157    procedure DUMPSTACK;
158    (*Show state of parse stack for demonstration purposes*)
159      var
160        LOOP : INTEGER;
161      begin
162        WRITE(OUTPUT, 'Input symbol ', INPUTSYMBOL, ' Parse stack: ');
163        for LOOP := 1 to TOP do
164          with STACK[LOOP] do case TIPE of
165            SYMBOLIC : WRITE(OUTPUT, SYMBOL:2);
166            NUMERIC  : WRITE(OUTPUT, STATE:2)
167          end;
168        WRITELN(OUTPUT)
169      end (*DUMPSTACK*);
170
171    begin (*PARSESTRING*)
172      READSTRING; GETNEXTTERMINAL; INPUTSYMBOL := SYM;
```

```
173     TOP := 0; CURRENTSTATE := 1; PUSH(NUMERIC); DUMPSTACK;
174     while TABLE[CURRENTSTATE, INPUTSYMBOL].ACTION in [SHIFT, REDUCE] do
175       begin
176         CURRENTENTRY := TABLE[CURRENTSTATE, INPUTSYMBOL];
177         with CURRENTENTRY do case ACTION of
178           SHIFT:
179             begin
180               WRITELN(OUTPUT, 'Shift to ', NEXTSTATE);
181               PUSH(SYMBOLIC) (*the INPUTSYMBOL*);
182               CURRENTSTATE := NEXTSTATE; PUSH(NUMERIC) (*the CURRENTSTATE*);
183               if INPUTSYMBOL in TERMINALS then GETNEXTTERMINAL (*accept*);
184               INPUTSYMBOL := SYM
185             end;
186           REDUCE:
187             begin
188               WRITELN(OUTPUT, 'Reduce by ', TOBEAPPLIED);
189               POP(2 * RULE[TOBEAPPLIED].LENGTH);
190               CURRENTSTATE := STACK[TOP].STATE;
191               INPUTSYMBOL := RULE[TOBEAPPLIED].LEFTSIDE
192             end
193         end (*case*);
194         DUMPSTACK
195       end;
196     for LL := 1 to LL - 1 do WRITE(OUTPUT, STRING[LL]); WRITELN(OUTPUT);
197     case TABLE[CURRENTSTATE, INPUTSYMBOL].ACTION of
198       ACCEPT : WRITELN(OUTPUT, 'String parsed correctly');
199       REJECT : WRITELN(OUTPUT, ' ':CC, 'Error in parsing string')
200     end
201   end (*PARSESTRING*);
202
203 begin
204   (*open and RESET(INPUT), REWRITE(OUTPUT) as appropriate*)
205   INITIALIZE;
206   while not EOF(INPUT) do PARSESTRING;
207   (*close OUTPUT file if necessary*)
208 end (*LRPARSER*).
```

Notes

(a)   The simplicity of the parsing algorithm is rather overwhelmed by all the code required to read in the productions (lines 38–60) and the elements of the parsing tables (lines 62–91). The main body of the parsing algorithm only occupies some thirty lines (171–201).

(b)   We assume the existence of an implementation which can support a large character set, and `set of CHAR`. The symbols in the grammar are all assumed to be single characters, with upper case letters reserved for non-terminals, and the rest of the character set available for terminals, with the exception of the period, which is appended to the input string so as to demarcate its end. A simple modification (say by reserving A through H for non-terminals) would allow the program to be executed on a machine with a smaller character set.

(c)   The data for the productions and parsing table is supplied in fixed format, with one production, or one table entry per line.

(d)   No attempt has been made to detect errors in the data specifying the table and the productions, although this would be well worth doing. In fact the strings specifying the right sides of productions are not used for anything other than to determine their length.

(e)   It is convenient to read in a complete sentence before parsing is attempted, and to provide a simple character handler (lines 127–141) to strip blanks from this and to record the last terminal scanned for reporting errors. As upper case letters are reserved for non-terminals, a simple check that these do not appear in the input sentence is easily made (line 140).

(f)   The reader will have noticed that the parsing table for the toy example is very sparsely filled. The use of fixed size arrays for this, for the production lists and for the parse stack is clearly non-optimal. One of the great problems in using the LR method in real applications is the amount of storage these structures require, and considerable research has been done in finding ways to minimize this.

(g)   Use has also been made of a variant record to handle the entries in the parse table, even though both variants have the same intrinsic structure.

(h)   In the original explanation of the method we demonstrated the use of a stack which contained symbols; in the later discussion we commented that the algorithm could merely stack states. However, for demonstration purposes it is convenient to show both these structures, and so in the program we have made use of a **variant record** for handling a parse stack (lines 118–123), which can accommodate elements which represent symbols as well as ones which represent parse states. An alternative method would be to use two separate stacks, as is outlined by Hunter (1981) (page 104).

As in the case of LL(1) parsers it will be necessary to ensure that productions are of the correct form before we can write a deterministic parser using such algorithms. It turns out that LR(k) parsing is much more powerful than LL(k) parsing; in practice the difficult task of producing the parse table for a large grammar with many productions and many states is usually left to so-called **parser generator** programs. A discussion of these, and of their underlying algorithms is, perhaps regrettably, beyond the scope of this book. In any case the rest of our treatment is all presented in terms of the recursive descent technique, which is far more suitable for hand-crafted compilers.

Further reading

Good treatments of the material in this chapter may be found at a comprehensible level in the books by Wirth (1976), pages 283–287 and 291–295; Welsh and McKeag (1980), pages 83–87; Bornat (1979), Chapter 16; Hunter (1981), Chapter 4; Davie and Morrison (1981), Chapters 3.7 and 4; and Tremblay and Sorenson (1985), Chapter 6.

Algorithms exist for the detection and elimination of useless productions; for a discussion of these the reader is referred to the books by Backhouse (1979), pages 40–56, and Tremblay and Sorenson (1985), pages 57–63.

Davie and Morrison (1981), page 17, give a brief history and bibliography for LL(1) and recursive descent parsing.

Our treatment of the LL(1) conditions may have left the reader wondering whether the process of checking them – especially the second one – ever converges for a grammar with anything like the number of productions needed to describe a real programming language. In fact, a little thought should suggest that, even though the number of sentences which they can generate might be infinite, since the number of productions is finite, convergence should be guaranteed. In fact the process of checking the LL(k) conditions can be automated, and algorithms for doing this and further discussion of convergence can be found in the books by Backhouse (1979), Chapter 3; Hunter (1981), pages 71–77; Bauer and Eickel (1976), pages 64–67; and Davie and Morrison (1981), pages 55–59.

Several texts have good discussions of what action can be taken to try to transform non-LL(k) grammars into LL(k) ones. The reader might like to consult the books by Hunter (1981), pages 79–84 and Bornat (1979), pages 277–302.

More sophisticated parsing methods may be found for languages which satisfy the LL(k) conditions, in particular by writing 'table-driven' parsers. Here, as in the LR parser discussed briefly earlier, the parser itself becomes essentially language independent, relying on an input description of the grammar (perhaps in textual form representing the BNF productions themselves) from which tables can be constructed which drive the parser as it handles the string to be parsed. We shall not attempt to discuss this here.

Introductions to the topic may be found in the books by Wirth (1976), pages 295–306 and Hunter (1981), pages 84–94.

Good discussions of LR(k) parsing and its variations such as SLR (Simple LR) and LALR (Look Ahead LR) appear in many of the sources mentioned. Introductory treatments are found in the books by Hunter (1981), Chapter 5 and Bornat (1979), Chapter 18.

More advanced treatments of these and other parsing methods may be found in the books by Aho and Ullman (1977), Barrett and Couch (1979), Bauer and Eickel (1976), Tremblay and Sorenson (1985), and Backhouse (1979).

Chapter 7 A simple compiler

At this point it may be of interest to consider the construction of a compiler for a simple programming language, specifically that of Section 5.11. The technique we shall follow is one of slow refinement; in later chapters we shall extend this language to illustrate other important points.

Apart from the treatment found in the books by Wirth (1976, Chapter 5) and Welsh and McKeag (1980, Chapter 2), few texts on compilers seem to illustrate their discussion with complete case studies. In a text of this nature it is impossible to discuss a full-blown compiler, and the value of our treatment may arguably be reduced by the fact that in dealing with a toy language and toy compiler we are evading many of the real issues a compiler writer has to face. However, we hope the reader will find the ensuing discussion of interest, and that it will serve as a useful preparation for the study of a much larger compiler. To this end we shall supplement the discussion with numerous asides on issues raised in compiling larger languages.

In Chapter 2 we commented that a compiler was often developed as a sequence of phases, of which syntactic analysis is only one. Although the recursive descent parsing phase is easily written by applying the ideas of the last chapter, it should be clear that consideration will have to be given to the relationship of this to the other phases. We can think of a compiler with a recursive descent core as having the structure shown in Figure 7.1.

When speaking of 'phases' we should recall that these need not be sequential, as 'passes' would be, but may be interleaved. In a recursive descent

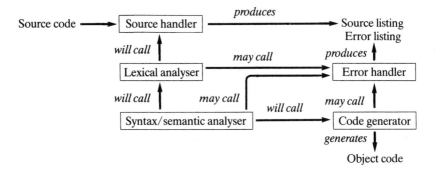

Figure 7.1

compiler the phases of syntax analysis, semantic analysis and code generation are almost invariably interleaved, especially if the language is designed in such a way as to permit one-pass compilation. Nevertheless, it is useful to think of developing these components in a modular way, with clear simple interfaces between them.

For example, character handling is notoriously device dependent, and probably profits from isolation from the phases which follow, especially if one is interested in developing portable compilers. Similarly, although lexical analysis is just a variation on syntax analysis – the rules for <identifier> and <number> can be expressed in BNF just as we express the rules for <statement> and <expression> – it is convenient to confine lexical analysis for a language such as we are discussing to a separate phase, because an <identifier> or <number> almost has the status of a terminal as far as productions for <statement> and <expression> are concerned; in practice many of the terminals like begin and end are, lexically speaking, indistinguishable from an <identifier> anyway.

7.1 Source handling

The source handler has the task of transmitting the source, character by character, to the lexical analyser (which will assemble it into symbols for subsequent parsing by the syntax analyser). Ideally the handler should only have to scan the source once, from start to finish – in a one-pass compiler that should always be the case. It is usual to let it have the further task of producing the source listing, and even of producing the error listing, because all this will be input/output device dependent. The interface needed between source handler and lexical analyser is simple, and can be supplied by a suitable procedure for returning the next character. It is useful also to add to this interface a means of knowing the position (in the source) of the character returned, so that error reporting may be done with reference to this position, and a means of knowing when the end of an input line has been reached, since line ends often have peculiar significance. Accordingly we introduce the declarations

```
var
  CH      : CHAR    (*latest character read*);
  CC      : INTEGER (*character pointer*);
  ENDLINE : BOOLEAN (*true at end of line*);

procedure GETCH;
(*Get next CH from SOURCE and form source listing*)
```

In fact, we shall have to make more declarations at the global level, as non-global variables in Pascal 'exist' only so long as the procedure that declares them is active. In this way we come up with

```
const
  LINEMAX = 120 (*max characters in source line*);
```

```
type
  LINEINDEX = 0 .. LINEMAX;
var
  CH      : CHAR              (*latest character read*);
  CC,                         (*character pointer*)
  LL      : LINEINDEX         (*line length*);
  ENDLINE : BOOLEAN           (*true when CC = LL*);
  LINE    : array [LINEINDEX] of CHAR (*latest line read*);
```

The source handler has little autonomy, but it might be made responsible for detecting that the input stream has terminated prematurely – this is presumably a fairly serious error, requiring abortive action. With these points in mind a simple input handler is easily written on the lines of the code in lines 54–69 of Listing 8.

In keeping with this, a very simple form of error reporting might be implemented with reference to a list of error numbers, by calls on

```
procedure ERROR (ERRORCODE : INTEGER);
  begin
    WRITELN(OUTPUT, ' ↑':CC , ERRORCODE:1)
  end (*ERROR*);
```

However, we shall have a lot more to say on errors later, and so will leave the subject for the present.

Notes

(a) The source is scanned and reflected a whole line at a time, no thin make s subsequent error reporting much easier.

(b) The handler effectively inserts an extra blank at the end of each line (line 66). This ensures that no word or number can be carried over from one line to the next. (Although this is allowed in some languages, it is visually deceptive, and best avoided.)

Exercises

7.1 The GETCH routine will be called once for every character in the source text. This can represent a considerable bottleneck, especially as programs in Pascal-like languages are often prepared with a great many blanks at the starts of indented lines (and, on some systems, with a great number of trailing blanks as well). Can you think of any way in which this overhead might be reduced?

7.2 We set ENDLINE on every call on GETCH. Since ENDLINE is not likely to be tested after every call to GETCH, there must be a better way. Suggest one.

7.3 A problem with 'global' variables like CH, CC and ENDLINE is that the programmer may tamper with them, either accidentally (by forgetting to declare a local variable CH somewhere else, perhaps) or deliberately (the modular approach suggests that the prerogative of assigning to these variables should rest with GETCH). Suggest a way of preventing this.

7.4 Some systems allowing an ASCII character set (with ordinal values in the range 0 ... 127) are used with input devices which generate characters having ordinal values in the range 0 ... 255 – typically the 'eighth bit' might always be set, or used or confused with parity checking. How and where could this bit be discarded?

7.2 Lexical analysis

In a sense, a lexical analyser may be thought of as just another syntax analyser. It handles a grammar with productions relating non-terminals such as <identifier>, <number> and <relop> with the obvious terminals supplied as the single characters of the source text. In this case there is, of course, no special goal symbol – the task of the lexical analyser is very much bottom-up rather than top-down, and its task ends when it has reduced a string of terminals to a single non-terminal, without preconceived ideas of what that should be. As we have already commented, these non-terminals can then be regarded as terminals by the higher level recursive descent parser which handles <block>, <statement>, <expression> and so on.

There are at least five reasons for wishing to draw this special distinction:

(a) The productions involved are so simple that the parsing is easily done without recourse to devices like recursive descent.

(b) A symbol like an <identifier> is lexically equivalent to a 'reserved word'; the distinction may sensibly be made as soon as the basic 'word' has been assembled.

(c) The character set may vary from one machine to another, and this variation is easily isolated in this phase.

(d) The semantic analysis of a numeric constant (deriving the internal representation of its value from the characters) is easily performed in parallel with lexical analysis.

(e) The lexical analyser can be made responsible for screening out superfluous separators, like blanks and comments, which are rarely of interest in the formulation of the higher level grammar.

The interface between lexical analyser and the syntax analyser that calls on it is conveniently provided by a globally accessible variable SYM of enumerated scalar type, and a procedure for determining this from the source text.

```
type
  SYMBOLS =
    (UNKNOWN, IDENT, NUMBER, STRINGSYM, PLUS, MINUS, TIMES, SLASH, ODDSYM,
    EQLSYM, NEQSYM, LSSSYM, LEQSYM, GTRSYM, GEQSYM, LPAREN, RPAREN,
    COMMA, SEMICOLON, PERIOD, BECOMES, BEGINSYM, ENDSYM, IFSYM, THENSYM,
    WHILESYM, DOSYM, READSYM, WRITESYM, CONSTSYM, VARSYM, PROCSYM);
var
  SYM : SYMBOLS (*latest symbol read*);

procedure GETSYM;
(*Get next SYM from SOURCE*)
```

The SYM interface is adequate for syntax analysis, but the process of semantic analysis will require further details of the symbol scanned, and we may as well look ahead and incorporate the ability to provide them here. We shall need the value of a number, the spelling of an identifier, and the actual characters in a string. These interfaces are readily added by introducing global declarations

```
const
  ALENG = 8 (*significant length of identifiers*);
type
  ALFA = packed array [1 .. ALENG] of CHAR;
var
  ID   : ALFA                      (*latest identifier read*);
  NUM  : INTEGER                   (*latest number read*);
  STRINGTEXT : array [LINEINDEX] of CHAR (*latest string read*);
```

As before, we shall need to make use of further global declarations, for objects that need to remain in existence throughout compilation. We shall need tables of reserved words and their corresponding symbols, and an array of symbols for single character terminals.

```
const
  LOWEST  = 0    (*ASCII ordinal value - system dependent*);
  HIGHEST = 127  (*ASCII ordinal value*);
  KEYWORDS = 12  (*number of reserved words*);
var
  WORD : array [1 .. KEYWORDS] of ALFA    (*reserved words*);
  WSYM : array [1 .. KEYWORDS] of SYMBOLS (*matching symbols*);
  CSYM : array [CHAR] of SYMBOLS          (*one character symbols*);
```

The arrays WORD, WSYM and CSYM must be initialized before use. WORD and WSYM are easily set up, but the initialization of CSYM is more difficult, as it depends on the underlying character set. The initialization is to be found in lines 153–179 of Listing 8.

A lexical analyser is readily programmed for this language in terms of a case selection. In common with the parsing strategy suggested in the last chapter, GETSYM will scan as many terminals (characters) as it needs to recognize a basic symbol, and will relinquish parsing with CH set to the first character it finds that does not form part of that basic symbol.

The code may be found in lines 73–151 of Listing 8.

Notes

(a) Identifiers are regarded as distinct over their first ALENG characters only.

(b) We have chosen to use a binary search to recognize the reserved words (lines 102–108).

(c) Note the way in which parsing of a string is effected (lines 139–146). A repeated quote within a string is used (as in Pascal) to denote a single quote, so that the end of a string is detected only when an odd number of quotes is followed by a non-quote.

(d) Note the rather dubious use of NUM to denote either the value of a <number> or the length of a <string>.

(e) The UNKNOWN option for SYM is to cater for erroneous characters like # and ? which do not really form part of the terminal alphabet. Rather than take action, the humble lexical analyser just returns the symbol without comment, and leaves the syntax analyser to cope.

(f) We have assumed that the host Pascal system can support a large character set, including upper and lower case, and also that it can support set of CHAR. The changes needed if this is not true are easily made to the routines NOTLETTER, NOTDIGIT, DIGIT, and to the case list in GETSYM.

Exercises

7.5 GETSYM suffers from the same defect as did GETCH in the last section – the unsuspecting or unscrupulous programmer might alter the value of SYM, ID or NUMBER elsewhere in the program. Can this be avoided?

7.6 We have chosen to declare SYM, ID, NUM and STRINGTEXT as separate variables. Perhaps we should have defined SYM along the following lines

```
var
  SYM : record
          TERMINAL : SYMBOLS;
          ID       : ALFA;
          NUM      : INTEGER;
          STRING   : STRINGTEXT : array [LINEINDEX] of CHAR
        end (*SYM*)
```

or even

```
var
  SYM : record
          case TERMINAL : SYMBOLS of
            IDENT     : (ID : ALFA);
            NUMBER    : (NUM : INTEGER);
            STRINGSYM : (STRINGTEXT : array [LINEINDEX] of CHAR)
          end (*SYM*)
```

What advantages or disadvantages can you see in the three alternatives?

7.7   The only screening this analyser does is to strip blanks separating symbols. How would you arrange for it to strip comments

(a)   of the form {comment in curly braces}

(b)   of the form (*comment in Pascal braces*)

(c)   of the form -- comment to end of the line as in Ada

(d)   of either or both of forms (a) and (b), allowing for nesting?

7.8   Pascal-like comments are actually dangerous. If not properly closed, they may 'consume' valid source code. One way of assisting the coder is to issue a warning if a semicolon is found within a comment. How could this be implemented as part of the answer to Exercise 7.7?

7.9   The version of the binary search used here is taken from Wirth (1976) (page 315) and differs from that used in the assembler given earlier. Which of the two versions is 'better', and why?

7.10   Arranging the reserved words in alphabetic order and checking the table using a binary search is only one of several ideas which try to be 'efficient'. Two others are

(a)   Arrange in length order, and search sequentially among those that have the same length as the word just assembled. This is suggested in the texts by Welsh and McKeag (1980), page 75 and by Pemberton and Daniels (1982), page 22.

(b)   Arrange in alphabetic order, and scan sequentially among those that have the same initial letter as the word just assembled.

Which of the methods is actually the best (a) for the reserved word list of CLANG and (b) for the reserved word list of Pascal? Which leads to the simplest algorithms for searching?

7.11   Identifiers are truncated to eight letters. While it is unreasonable to expect compilers (especially written in Pascal, which does not have dynamic strings as standard types) to cater for any length, can you think of any way of using a packed array [1 .. ALENG] of CHAR to represent more than ALENG characters, with only a small possibility of aliasing beyond the first ALENG - 1 characters?

7.12 Although it does not arise in the case of CLANG, how do you suppose a Pascal compiler might be able to distinguish between a real NUMBER of the form 3.4 and a subrange selector of the form 3..4, where no spaces delimit the '..', as is quite legal (Pemberton and Daniels (1982), page 29)? Can you think of an alternative syntax which avoids the issue altogether? Why do you suppose Pascal does not use such a syntax?

7.13 Some languages, like Modula-2, allow strings to be delimited by either single or double quotes, but not to contain the delimiter as a member of the string (so that we could write "David's Helen's brother" or 'He said "Hello"', but not 'He said "That's awkward!"'). How would you modify the lexical analyser to handle this? Do advantages outweigh disadvantages?

7.14 Pascal does not allow non-printable (control) character constants, so the case statement given is strictly inadequate for handling source programs which (accidentally) contain such characters. How could you modify it to work under all circumstances?

Further reading

Several texts treat lexical analysis in far more detail than we have done; justifiably, since for larger languages there are considerably more problem areas than our simple one raises. Good discussions are found in Chapter 7 of Davie and Morrison (1981) and Chapter 3 of Hunter (1981). Chapter 1 of the book by Pemberton and Daniels has a very detailed discussion of the much larger lexical analyser found in the Pascal-P compiler.

7.3 Syntax analysis

The rest of the parser now presents few problems, and follows the ideas developed in the previous chapter. The code is to be found in lines 190–303 of Listing 8, and we need draw attention only to the fact that at this stage we are content to stop parsing as soon as the first error is detected. Although at least one highly successful microcomputer Pascal compiler (TurboPascal, by Borland International) uses this strategy, it is rarely satisfactory for compilers used in a batch environment, or even in most interactive ones. We return to this problem in the next section, where it will be seen that attempts to overcome it lead to an immediate dramatic increase in the size and complexity of the parser.

Exercises

Before we go on to see how the parser needs to be modified to handle the erroneous programs that will inevitably be presented to it by over-confident users, the reader might like to consider the following.

7.15 How might one add the repeat ... until loop, the for loop, and the case statement on the lines of those found in Pascal?

7.16 What happens when one tries to add the if ... then ... else statement?

Listing 8   Recursive descent parser for CLANG level 1

```
1  program SIMPLEPARSER (INPUT, OUTPUT, SOURCE);
2  (*Simple parser for CLANG level 1, without error recovery
3    P.D. Terry, January 22 1985     *)
4  const
5    VERSION = '0.0'            (*level.release*);
6    LOWEST  = 0                (*ASCII ordinal value*);
7    HIGHEST = 127              (*ASCII ordinal value*);
8    KEYWORDS = 12              (*number of reserved words*);
9    LINEMAX  = 120             (*max characters on source line*);
10   ALENG    = 8               (*length of identifiers*);
11 type
12   SYMBOLS =
13     (UNKNOWN, IDENT, NUMBER, STRINGSYM, PLUS, MINUS, TIMES, SLASH, ODDSYM,
14      EQLSYM, NEQSYM, LSSSYM, LEQSYM, GTRSYM, GEQSYM, LPAREN, RPAREN,
15      COMMA, SEMICOLON, PERIOD, BECOMES, BEGINSYM, ENDSYM, IFSYM, THENSYM,
16      WHILESYM, DOSYM, READSYM, WRITESYM, CONSTSYM, VARSYM, PROCSYM);
17   ALFA      = packed array [1 .. ALENG] of CHAR;
18   LINEINDEX = 0 .. LINEMAX;
19 var
20
21 (* +++++++++++++++++ used by the character and option handler +++++++ *)
22
23   (*some implementations require INPUT, OUTPUT : TEXT*)
24   SOURCE  : TEXT;
25   CH      : CHAR                (*latest character read*);
26   CC,                           (*character pointer*)
27   LL      : LINEINDEX           (*line length*);
28   ENDLINE : BOOLEAN             (*true when CC = LL*);
29   LINE    : array [LINEINDEX] of CHAR   (*latest line read*);
30
31 (* +++++++++++++++++ used by the lexical analyser +++++++++++++++++ *)
32
```

```
33   SYM  : SYMBOLS                 (*latest symbol read*);
34   ID   : ALFA                    (*latest identifier read*);
35   NUM  : INTEGER                 (*latest number read*);
36   STRINGTEXT : array [LINEINDEX] of CHAR  (*latest string read*);
37   WORD : array [1 .. KEYWORDS] of ALFA    (*reserved words*);
38   WSYM : array [1 .. KEYWORDS] of SYMBOLS (*matching symbols*);
39   CSYM : array [CHAR] of SYMBOLS          (*one character symbols*);
40
41 procedure QUIT (N : INTEGER);
42 (* ++++++++ Implementation dependent for aborting program ++++++++++++ *)
43   begin
44     WRITELN(OUTPUT);
45     case N of
46       3 : WRITELN(OUTPUT, ' Program Incomplete - Unexpected EOF');
47       9 : WRITELN(OUTPUT, ' Syntax errors - parsing abandoned');
48     end;
49     (*close OUTPUT file if necessary and abort program*)
50   end (*QUIT*);
51
52 (* +++++++++++++++++++++++++++ Source Handler +++++++++++++++++++++++ *)
53
54 procedure GETCH;
55 (*Get next character from SOURCE, form source listing*)
56   begin
57     if CC = LL then
58       begin
59         if EOF(SOURCE) then QUIT(3);
60         LL := 0; CC := 0;
61         while not EOLN(SOURCE) do
62           begin
63             LL := LL + 1; READ(SOURCE, CH); WRITE(OUTPUT, CH);
64             LINE[LL] := CH
65           end;
66         WRITELN(OUTPUT); READLN(SOURCE); LL := LL + 1; LINE[LL] := ' '
67       end (*new line*);
68     CC := CC + 1; CH := LINE[CC]; ENDLINE := CC = LL
69   end (*GETCH*);
70
71 (* +++++++++++++++++++++++++++ Lexical Analyser +++++++++++++++++++++++ *)
72
73 procedure GETSYM;
74 (*Get next SYM from SOURCE, with its attributes*)
75   var
76     I, J, K  : INTEGER;
77     ENDSTRING : BOOLEAN;
78
```

```
79   function NOTLETTER : BOOLEAN;
80     begin NOTLETTER := not (CH in ['A' .. 'Z', 'a' .. 'z']) end (*NOTLETTER*);
81
82   function NOTDIGIT : BOOLEAN;
83     begin NOTDIGIT := not (CH in ['0' .. '9']) end (*NOTDIGIT*);
84
85   function DIGIT : INTEGER;
86     begin DIGIT := ORD(CH) - ORD('0') end (*DIGIT*);
87
88   begin (*GETSYM*)
89     while CH = ' ' do GETCH (*Skip blanks*);
90     SYM := CSYM[CH] (*initial assumption*);
91     case CH of
92       'a', 'b', 'c', 'd', 'e', 'f', 'g', 'h', 'i', 'j', 'k', 'l', 'm',
93       'n', 'o', 'p', 'q', 'r', 's', 't', 'u', 'v', 'w', 'x', 'y', 'z',
94       'A', 'B', 'C', 'D', 'E', 'F', 'G', 'H', 'I', 'J', 'K', 'L', 'M',
95       'N', 'O', 'P', 'Q', 'R', 'S', 'T', 'U', 'V', 'W', 'X', 'Y', 'Z':
96         begin (*identifier or reserved word*)
97           K := 1; ID := '          ';
98           repeat
99             if CH in ['a'..'z'] then CH := CHR(ORD(CH) - ORD('a') + ORD('A'));
100            if K <= ALENG then begin ID[K] := CH; K := K + 1 end; GETCH
101          until NOTLETTER and NOTDIGIT;
102          I := 1; J := KEYWORDS;
103          repeat (*binary search*)
104            K := (I + J) div 2;
105            if ID < WORD[K] then J := K - 1;
106            if ID >= WORD[K] then I := K + 1
107          until I > J;
108          if I - 1 > J then SYM := WSYM[K] else SYM := IDENT
109        end;
110      '0', '1', '2', '3', '4', '5', '6', '7', '8', '9':
111        begin
112          NUM := 0; SYM := NUMBER;
113          repeat
114            NUM := 10 * NUM + DIGIT; GETCH
115          until NOTDIGIT
116        end;
117      ':':
118        begin
119          GETCH;
120          if CH = '=' then begin SYM := BECOMES; GETCH end
121        end;
122      '<':
123        begin
124          GETCH;
```

```
125          if CH = '='
126            then begin SYM := LEQSYM; GETCH end
127            else
128              if CH = '>'
129                then begin SYM := NEQSYM; GETCH end
130                else SYM := LSSSYM
131          end;
132        '>':
133          begin
134            GETCH;
135            if CH = '='
136              then begin SYM := GEQSYM; GETCH end
137              else SYM := GTRSYM
138          end;
139        '''':
140          begin (*string*)
141            NUM := 0; GETCH; SYM := STRINGSYM; ENDSTRING := FALSE;
142            repeat
143              if CH = '''' then begin GETCH; ENDSTRING := CH <> '''' end;
144              if not ENDSTRING then GETCH
145            until ENDSTRING
146          end;
147        '*', '+', '-', '#', '=', '/', ')', '[', ']', ',', ';', '↑', '&', '@',
148        '{', '}', '(', '$', '.', '_', '%', '?', '"', '!', '|', '¬':
149          begin SYM := CSYM[CH]; GETCH end (*implementation defined*);
150      end (*case*)
151    end (*GETSYM*);
152
153 procedure INITIALIZE;
154    var
155      C : CHAR;
156
157    procedure RESERVEDWORDS;
158      begin
159        WORD[ 1] := 'BEGIN   ' ; WORD[ 2] := 'CONST   ' ; WORD[ 3] := 'DO      ' ;
160        WORD[ 4] := 'END     ' ; WORD[ 5] := 'IF      ' ; WORD[ 6] := 'ODD     ' ;
161        WORD[ 7] := 'PROGRAM ' ; WORD[ 8] := 'READ    ' ; WORD[ 9] := 'THEN    ' ;
162        WORD[10] := 'VAR     ' ; WORD[11] := 'WHILE   ' ; WORD[12] := 'WRITE   ' ;
163        WSYM[ 1] := BEGINSYM   ; WSYM[ 2] := CONSTSYM   ; WSYM[ 3] := DOSYM      ;
164        WSYM[ 4] := ENDSYM     ; WSYM[ 5] := IFSYM      ; WSYM[ 6] := ODDSYM     ;
165        WSYM[ 7] := PROCSYM    ; WSYM[ 8] := READSYM    ; WSYM[ 9] := THENSYM    ;
166        WSYM[10] := VARSYM     ; WSYM[11] := WHILESYM   ; WSYM[12] := WRITESYM
167      end (*RESERVEDWORDS*);
168
169    begin
170      WRITELN(OUTPUT, 'CLANG Parser Mark ', VERSION); WRITELN(OUTPUT);
```

```
171      RESERVEDWORDS;
172      for C := CHR(LOWEST) to CHR(HIGHEST) do CSYM[C] := UNKNOWN;
173      CSYM['+'] := PLUS   ; CSYM['-'] := MINUS  ; CSYM['*'] := TIMES;
174      CSYM['/'] := SLASH  ; CSYM['('] := LPAREN ; CSYM[')'] := RPAREN;
175      CSYM['='] := EQLSYM ; CSYM[','] := COMMA   ; CSYM['.'] := PERIOD;
176      CSYM['<'] := LSSSYM ; CSYM['>'] := GTRSYM ; CSYM[';'] := SEMICOLON;
177      (*initialize lexical analyser*)
178      CC := 0; LL := 0; CH := ' '; GETSYM
179    end (*INITIALIZE*);
180
181  (* +++++++++++++++++++++++++++++++ Syntax Analyser +++++++++++++++++++ *)
182
183  procedure ACCEPT (S : SYMBOLS);
184    begin
185      if SYM = S
186        then GETSYM
187        else begin WRITELN (OUTPUT, '↑':CC , 'Error'); QUIT(9) end
188    end (*ACCEPT*);
189
190  procedure BLOCK;
191
192    procedure CONSTDECLARATION;
193      begin
194        ACCEPT(CONSTSYM);
195        repeat
196          ACCEPT(IDENT); ACCEPT(EQLSYM); ACCEPT(NUMBER); ACCEPT(SEMICOLON)
197        until SYM <> IDENT
198      end (*CONSTDECLARATION*);
199
200    procedure VARDECLARATION;
201      begin
202        ACCEPT(VARSYM);
203        ACCEPT(IDENT);
204        while SYM = COMMA do begin ACCEPT(COMMA); ACCEPT(IDENT) end;
205        ACCEPT(SEMICOLON)
206      end (*VARDECLARATION*);
207
208  (* +++++++++++++++++++++++++++++++++++ Statement part +++++++++++++++++ *)
209
210    procedure COMPOUNDSTATEMENT;
211
212      procedure STATEMENT;
213
214        procedure EXPRESSION;
215
216          procedure TERM;
```

```
217
218        procedure FACTOR;
219          begin
220            if SYM in [IDENT, NUMBER]
221              then GETSYM
222              else begin ACCEPT(LPAREN); EXPRESSION; ACCEPT(RPAREN) end
223          end (*FACTOR*);
224
225        begin (*TERM*)
226          FACTOR;
227          while SYM in [TIMES, SLASH] do begin GETSYM; FACTOR end
228        end (*TERM*);
229
230      begin (*EXPRESSION*)
231        if SYM in [PLUS, MINUS] then GETSYM;
232        TERM;
233        while SYM in [PLUS, MINUS] do begin GETSYM; TERM end
234      end (*EXPRESSION*);
235
236    procedure CONDITION;
237      begin
238        if SYM = ODDSYM
239          then begin GETSYM; ACCEPT(LPAREN); EXPRESSION; ACCEPT(RPAREN) end
240          else begin EXPRESSION; GETSYM; EXPRESSION end
241      end (*CONDITION*);
242
243    procedure IFSTATEMENT;
244      begin
245        ACCEPT(IFSYM); CONDITION; ACCEPT(THENSYM); STATEMENT
246      end (*IFSTATEMENT*);
247
248    procedure WHILESTATEMENT;
249      begin
250        ACCEPT(WHILESYM); CONDITION; ACCEPT(DOSYM); STATEMENT
251      end (*WHILESTATEMENT*);
252
253    procedure WRITESTATEMENT;
254      begin
255        ACCEPT(WRITESYM);
256        if SYM = LPAREN then
257          begin
258            repeat
259              GETSYM; if SYM <> STRINGSYM then EXPRESSION else GETSYM
260            until SYM <> COMMA;
261            ACCEPT(RPAREN)
262          end
263      end (*WRITESTATEMENT*);
```

```
264
265      procedure READSTATEMENT;
266        begin
267          ACCEPT(READSYM);
268          ACCEPT(LPAREN);
269          ACCEPT(IDENT);
270          while SYM = COMMA do begin ACCEPT(COMMA); ACCEPT(IDENT) end;
271          ACCEPT(RPAREN)
272        end (*READSTATEMENT*);
273
274      begin (*STATEMENT*)
275        case SYM of
276          IDENT    : begin ACCEPT(IDENT); ACCEPT(BECOMES); EXPRESSION end;
277          IFSYM    : IFSTATEMENT;
278          BEGINSYM : COMPOUNDSTATEMENT;
279          WHILESYM : WHILESTATEMENT;
280          WRITESYM : WRITESTATEMENT;
281          READSYM  : READSTATEMENT;
282        end
283      end (*STATEMENT*);
284
285    begin (*COMPOUNDSTATEMENT*)
286      ACCEPT(BEGINSYM);
287      STATEMENT;
288      while SYM = SEMICOLON do begin ACCEPT(SEMICOLON); STATEMENT end;
289      ACCEPT(ENDSYM)
290    end (*COMPOUNDSTATEMENT*);
291
292  begin (*BLOCK*)
293    if SYM = CONSTSYM then CONSTDECLARATION;
294    if SYM = VARSYM then VARDECLARATION;
295    COMPOUNDSTATEMENT
296  end (*BLOCK*);
297
298  procedure PROGRAMME;
299    begin
300      ACCEPT(PROCSYM); ACCEPT(IDENT); ACCEPT(SEMICOLON);
301      BLOCK;
302      if SYM <> PERIOD then begin WRITELN(OUTPUT, '↑':CC, 'Error'); QUIT(9) end
303    end (*PROGRAMME*);
304
305  begin (*SIMPLEPARSER*)
306    (*open and RESET(SOURCE) and OUTPUT files as appropriate*)
307    INITIALIZE;
308    PROGRAMME;
309    (*close OUTPUT file if necessary*)
310  end (*SIMPLEPARSER*).
```

7.4 Error detection and recovery

7.4.1 Context-free errors

Up to this point the parser has been content merely to stop if a syntactic error is detected. In the case of a real compiler this is probably unacceptable. If we modify the parser of Listing 8 so as simply not to stop after detecting an error, the result will be pretty chaotic, as the analysis process will get out of step with the set of symbols being scanned, and in all likelihood will then detect a plethora of spurious errors.

We should note, however, that one useful feature of the compilation technique we are using is that the parser can detect a syntactically incorrect structure after reading the first 'unexpected' terminal. This is not necessarily at the point where the error really occurred. For example, in parsing the sequence

```
begin if A > 6 do B := 2; C := 5 end end
```

we could hope for a sensible error message when do is found where then is expected. Even if it does not get out of step, we would get a less helpful message when the second end is found – the compiler can have little idea where the missing begin should have been.

A production quality compiler should aim to issue appropriate diagnostic messages for all the 'genuine' errors, and for as few 'spurious' errors as possible. This is only possible if it can make some likely assumption about the nature of each error and the probable intention of the author, or if it skips over some part of the malformed text, or both. Various approaches may be made to handling the problem. Some compilers go so far as to try to correct the error, and continue to produce object code for the program. **Error correction** is a little dangerous, except in some trivial cases, and we shall discuss it no further here. Many systems confine themselves to attempting **error recovery**, which is the term used to describe the process of simply trying to get the parser back into step with the source code presented to it. For hand-crafted compilers, the art of doing this is rather intricate, and relies on a mixture of fairly well defined methods and intuitive experience, both with the language being compiled and with the class of user of the same.

Recursive descent parsers are constructed as a set of procedures, each of which tackles a sub-goal on behalf of its caller. A fairly obvious place to try to regain lost synchronization is at the entry to and exit from these procedures, where the effects of getting out of step can be confined to a small range of known FIRST and FOLLOW symbols. To enforce synchronization at the start of the procedure for a non-terminal S we could employ a strategy like

```
if not SYM in FIRST(S)
   then report an error and SKIPTO(FIRST(S))
```

where SKIPTO is an operation that simply calls on GETSYM until one of the set FIRST(S) is found. Unfortunately this is not quite adequate, as if the leading terminal has been omitted we may then skip over symbols that should have been processed by the procedure which called S.

At procedure exit we have postulated that SYM should be one of FOLLOW(S) for the non-terminal parsed by S. This set may not be known to S, but should be known to the procedure that calls S, so that it may conveniently be passed to S as a parameter. This suggests that we should employ a strategy like

```
if not SYM in FOLLOW(S)
    then report an error and SKIPTO(FOLLOW(S))
```

The use of FOLLOW(S) also allows us to avoid the danger mentioned earlier of skipping too far at procedure entry, by employing a strategy like

```
if not SYM in FIRST(S)
    then report an error and SKIPTO(FIRST(S) ∪ FOLLOW(S))
if SYM in FIRST(S)
    then parse the body of the procedure
        if not SYM in FOLLOW(S)
            then report an error and SKIPTO(FOLLOW(S))
```

Although the FOLLOW set for a non-terminal is quite easy to determine, the legitimate follower may itself have been omitted, and this may lead to too many symbols being skipped at procedure exit. A parser using this approach usually passes to each sub-parser a parameter FOLLOWERS, of Pascal set type, which is constructed so as to include

(a)   the syntactically correct set FOLLOW(S),

(b)   symbols that have already been passed as FOLLOWERS to the calling procedure,

(c)   so-called BEACON symbols, which are on no account to be passed over, even though their presence would be quite out of context. In this way we can often avoid skipping large sections of possibly important code.

On return from a sub-parser we can then be fairly certain that SYM contains a terminal which is either expected (if it is in FOLLOW(S)) or which can be used to regain synchronization (if it is one of the BEACONS or the FOLLOW set for the caller). A further test will be needed in the calling procedure to see which of these conditions has arisen.

The system is conveniently implemented by defining a procedure on the lines of

```
procedure TEST (ALLOWED, BEACONS : SYMSET; ERRORCODE : INTEGER);
    begin
        if not (SYM in ALLOWED) then
            begin ERROR(ERRORCODE); while not (SYM in ALLOWED + BEACONS) do GETSYM end
    end (*TEST*);
```

and the way in which this could be used is exemplified in a procedure for handling variable declarations, for which the FIRST and FOLLOW sets are easily determined.

```
procedure VARDECLARATION (FOLLOWERS : SYMSET);
  begin
    GETSYM (*get past the 'var'*);
    TEST([IDENT], FOLLOWERS, 6);
    if SYM = IDENT then
      begin
        GETSYM;
        while SYM = COMMA do begin GETSYM; ACCEPT(IDENT, 6) end;
        ACCEPT(SEMICOLON, 2);
        TEST(FOLLOWERS, [], 34)
      end
  end (*VARDECLARATION*);
```

The FOLLOWERS passed to VARDECLARATION should include as BEACONS the members of FIRSTSTATEMENT – symbols that could start a <statement> (in case begin was omitted) – and the symbols that could follow a <block>, such as a period.

To use this system we must amend the ACCEPT procedure to read

```
procedure ACCEPT (EXPECTED : SYMBOLS; ERRORCODE : INTEGER);
  begin
    if SYM = EXPECTED then GETSYM else ERROR(ERRORCODE)
  end (*ACCEPT*);
```

Note that ACCEPT does not try to regain synchronization in any way.

Calling VARDECLARATION might be done from within BLOCK on the lines of

```
if SYM = VARSYM then
  begin
    VARDECLARATION([BEGINSYM] + FIRSTSTATEMENT + FOLLOWERS);
    if SYM <> BEGINSYM then ERROR(34)
  end
```

Too rigorous an implementation of this scheme will result in some spurious errors, and in the augmented parser in Listing 9 we have adapted it somewhat. As mentioned earlier, one gains from experience when dealing with learners, and some concession to likely mistakes is perhaps a good thing. Accordingly, recognizing that beginners are likely to confuse := and =, and also then and do after if, and to confuse the order of declarations, the parser might make concessions in this direction.

Clearly it is impossible to recover from all possible contortions of code, but one should guard against the cardinal sins of not reporting errors when they are present, or of collapsing completely when trying to recover from an error, either by giving up prematurely, or by getting the parser caught in an infinite loop reporting the same error.

Notes

(a)   A good example of the use of a concessionary strategy is in the parsing of COMPOUNDSTATEMENT, since semicolons in our language (as in Pascal) will doubtless be omitted by some beginners. We have arranged for the FOLLOWERS passed to COMPOUNDSTATEMENT to include as BEACONS the members of the set FIRSTSTATEMENT. In fact the elements of FIRSTBLOCK and FIRSTSTATEMENT (see lines 118–119) are members of all FOLLOWERS sets, by virtue of the first call on BLOCK (line 377).

(b)   A similar concessionary strategy has been used in FACTOR (line 239) to try to deal kindly with missing operators in expressions.

(c)   A further concessionary strategy has been employed in BLOCK (lines 359–363) to try to deal with declarations made in the incorrect order.

(d)   Many sub-parsers do not make use of TEST. In particular, there is no need to do this in procedures like IFSTATEMENT, WHILESTATEMENT and so on, which have been defined merely for enhanced modularity of STATE-MENT.

(e)   BLOCK might have been nested within PROGRAMME. This was not done, so as to keep the deepest level of nesting (for FACTOR) as low as possible. Some Pascal compilers impose a limit on the depth to which procedures may be nested, for reasons which will become clearer in the next chapter.

(f)   We cannot make use of ACCEPT to handle the final PERIOD in PROGRAMME, for there will, almost invariably, be no symbol following it (line 378)

(g)   The usefulness of the Pascal set type should be obvious. We should mention, however, that some Pascal implementations restrict the size of sets to such an extent that the techniques we have used would require drastic recoding. In particular, we have assumed that the system can support sets with as many elements as there are values for type SYMBOLS. At present this is only 32, but later versions of the system will extend this considerably.

(h)   We introduce the set type needed for recovery in line 13, and variables of this type in line 25, and initialize them in lines 117–120.

(i)   The FOLLOWERS parameters must all be passed 'by value'.

(j)   Procedure ERROR (lines 44–76) is straightforward, using a case selector to choose an appropriate error message according to the value of its parameter.

7.4.2   Context-sensitive errors

We have already had cause to remark that the boundary between syntactic and semantic errors can be rather vague, and that there are features of real computer languages that cannot be readily described by context-free grammars. Typical of these are the requirements, familiar to all Pascal programmers, that all identifiers must be declared before they are used. Our language seems, perhaps, to insist on this by placing obvious 'declaration' clauses before obvious 'statement' clauses in the programs it allows, but that is illusory, for nothing we have said in the grammar requires that only those identifiers which have appeared in such declarations (so-called **defining occurrences**) appear in the statements (in so-called **applied occurrences**). We could attempt to use a context-sensitive grammar to overcome this problem, but that turns out to be unnecessarily complicated, for it is easily handled by using a symbol table.

The fact that the semantic attributes of identifiers cannot be distinguished by a context-free language can be handled by the same device. At this stage these semantic attributes are simple. Identifiers come in various classes – namely 'constant', 'variable' and 'program' – all of which are lexically equivalent. A parser may be able to distinguish them by context, but that is a messy process, and may result in a lot of backtracking. Demanding that they be declared is simple enough, and not nearly as tedious as it might at first seem to be. It is clearly a 'semantic' activity, although the division into semantic classes is made precise by the purely syntactic association with reserved words like const, var and program.

We have previously pointed out the great strength a recursive descent algorithm has in being able to handle the parsing process in a top-down, one-pass manner. If we wish to retain the advantages of one-pass compilation when we include semantic analysis, we shall, fairly obviously, have to insist on the 'declaration' part coming before the 'statement' part. This is easily enforced by the context-free grammar, all very familiar to a Pascal-trained programmer, and seems quite natural after a while.

Setting up a symbol table may be done in many ways. For the moment it will suffice to introduce

```
const
  TABLEMAX = 100 (*length of identifier table*);
type
  TABLEINDEX = 0 .. TABLEMAX;
  CLASSES    = (CONSTANT, VARIABLE, PROG);
  CLASSSET   = set of CLASSES;
var
  TABLE : array [TABLEINDEX] of record (*symbol table entries*)
                          NAME  : ALFA;
                          CLASS : CLASSES
                        end (*TABLE*);
```

and simply to enter the identifiers sequentially into TABLE when they are first recognized by the procedures for CONSTDECLARATION and VARDECLARATION. Before identifiers are accepted by FACTOR and STATEMENT they are checked against this table both for non-declaration of NAME and for abuse of CLASS (this can conveniently be done in the same procedure).

The code for handling declarations and for searching the symbol table can be found in lines 162–220 of Listing 9.

Notes

(a) The symbol table is set up so that the zero entry can be used as a sentinel in a simple sequential search by SEARCHID. Although this is inefficient, it is adequate for experimental use of the toy system.

(b) A call to SEARCHID will always return with a value for ENTRY which matches the position of ID in TABLE, even if it is strictly 'undeclared'.

(c) As a consequence of the way in which the program name is entered into the table (lines 372–373), undeclared identifiers will seem to have an effective CLASS = PROG, which will always be semantically unacceptable.

(d) Procedures that need to identify an entry in the symbol table always follow this by looking at the next terminal, so a call to GETSYM has been incorporated directly into SEARCHID.

(e) We might consider letting the lexical analyser interact with the symbol table, but this is rarely done. The lexical analyser has very little autonomy.

7.4.3 Other errors

Our initial parser was somewhat naïve, in that the lexical analyser attempted no error detection. There are two areas where this should be added.

Although the syntactic description of the language does not demand it, practical considerations require that the value of a numeric constant should be within the range of the machine. This is somewhat tricky to ensure in the case of cross-compilers, where the range on the host and target machines may be different, and some authors go so far as to suggest that this semantic activity be divorced from lexical analysis for that reason. The code on lines 86–94 of Listing 9 shows how range checking can be handled for a self-resident compiler.

Not only does Pascal insist that no identifier (or number) be carried across a line break, it does this for strings as well. This is done, presumably, to help guard against the chaos that would arise were a closing quote to be omitted – further code would become string text, and future string text would become code! The limitation that a string be confined to one source line is, in practice, rarely a handicap; a way of enforcing it is suggested on lines 95–104 of Listing 9.

The effectiveness of the parser may be partially judged by looking at the following typical output.

```
CLANG Parser Mark 1.0

program TEST
const
```

```
      ↑; EXPECTED
  TOOBIGANUMBER = 328000;
                        ↑NUMBER OUT OF RANGE
  ZERO := 0;
        ↑:= IN WRONG CONTEXT
var
  VALU, SMALLEST, LARGEST, TOTAL;
const
      ↑BEGIN EXPECTED
  MIN = ZERO;
            ↑NUMBER EXPECTED
            ↑; EXPECTED
            ↑= EXPECTED
begin
  TOTAL := ZERO;
  read (VALU); if VALU > MIN do write(VALU);
                              ↑THEN EXPECTED
  LARGEST := VALU; SMALLEST = VALU;
                            ↑:= EXPECTED
  while VALU <> ZERO do
    begin
      TOTAL := TOTAL + VALU
      if VALU > = LARGEST then LARGEST := VALUE;
        ↑; EXPECTED
              ↑INVALID START TO FACTOR
                                      ↑UNDECLARED
      if VALU < SMALLEST then SMALLEST := VALU;
      readln(VALU); if VALU > ZERO then write(VALU)
            ↑UNDECLARED
            ↑:= EXPECTED
    end;
  write ('TOTAL:', TOTAL, ' LARGEST:', LARGEST, 'SMALLEST: , SMALLEST)
                                                      ↑STRING INCOMPLETE
end.
  ↑, OR ) EXPECTED
```

Symbol table

```
    1 TEST      PROGRAM
    2 TOOBIGAN  CONSTANT
    2 ZERO      CONSTANT
    3 VALU      VARIABLE
    4 SMALLEST  VARIABLE
    5 LARGEST   VARIABLE
    6 TOTAL     VARIABLE
    7 MIN       CONSTANT
    8 ZERO      CONSTANT
```

Exercises

7.17 Is there any real need to insist on const declarations coming before var declarations in CLANG? How could you relax this? Why do you suppose the order label, const, type, var is required in Pascal?

7.18 At present the error messages are given out at the end of the symbol after the point where the error was detected. Can you find an easy way of improving on this?

7.19 A disadvantage of the error recovery scheme used here is that a user may not realize which symbols have been skipped. Can you find a way to mark some or all of the symbols skipped by TEST? Has TEST been used in the best possible way to facilitate error recovery?

7.20 Another weakness is that, in effecting error recovery, several errors may be reported at one point (in the example above this has happened with the erroneous line MIN = ZERO). It is quite easy to suppress all messages after the first at a given point (try it). However, one might then find that the quality of error message deteriorates. For example, if one terminates the program with end; rather than end., the message INVALID SYMBOL AFTER BLOCK will be given out (by virtue of the call to TEST from within BLOCK at line 366) rather than the more helpful . EXPECTED (because of the test within PROGRAMME after the call to BLOCK at line 377). Can you implement a better method than the one we have? (Notice that the FOLLOWERS parameter passed to a sub-parser for S includes not only the genuine FOLLOW(S) symbols, but further BEACONS.)

7.21 What happens if the parser is given erroneous code like

```
program TEST;
  const
    A = 8
    B = 9
  var
    P, Q, , X Y Z ; K ;
  begin
    P := Q + A + K K
    Q := Q + B * * Z
  end.
```

Can you find a way to effect any improvements which may be needed? Is it a good idea to have IDENT in all FOLLOWERS sets?

7.22 Examine critically the quality of the error recovery in our parser for erroneous lists in read and write statements, and if necessary improve on it.

7.23 Although not strictly illegal, the appearance of a semicolon in a program immediately following a do or then, or immediately preceding an end may be symptomatic of omitted code. Is it possible to warn the user when this has occurred, and, if so, how?

7.24 The error handler makes no distinction between context-free and semantic or context-sensitive errors. Do you suppose it would be an improvement to try to do this, and, if so, how could it be done?

7.25 How would you parse the repeat ... until and if ... then ... else statements, incorporating error recovery?

7.26 How would you parse a Pascal-like case statement, incorporating error recovery? The standard Pascal case statement does not have an else or otherwise option. Suggest how this could be added, and modify the parser accordingly. Is it a good idea to use otherwise or else for this purpose – assuming that you already have an if ... then ... else construct?

7.27 How would you reliably parse a Pascal-like for loop? One school of thought maintains that in this construction the 'control' variable should be implicitly declared at the start of the loop, so that it is truly local to the loop. It should also not be possible to alter the value of the control variable within the loop. How can these ideas be handled?

7.28 The while, for and repeat loops of Pascal are structured – they have only one entry point, and only one exit point. Some languages allow a slightly less structured loop, which has only one entry point, but which allows exit from various places within the loop body. An example of this might be as follows

```
begin
  loop
    read(A);  if A > 100 then exit;  ─────────────────┐
    loop                                               │
      write(A); read(B);                               │
      if B > 10 then begin write('last '); exit end;   ▼
      A := A + B;
      if odd(A) then exit ─────────────┐        │
    end;                                │        │
    write('Total ',A);  ◄───────────────┘        │
  end;                                           │
  write('Finished') ◄───────────────────────────┘
end.
```

Loop statements can be nested; a breakout made with an exit is to the statement following the nearest closing end. Exit statements may only appear within loop sequences.

Describe as many of the properties of the loop and exit statements as you can in a form suitable for parsing, and then modify the parser to handle correct and incorrect attempts at using the construction.

7.29 In our parser the name TEST for the main program is used to request a symbol table dump. Several Pascal compilers make use of **pragmatic comments** as **compiler directives** to make such demands of the system – for example a comment of the form (*$L-*) requests that the listing be switched off, and one of the form (*$L+*) that it be reinstated. These requests are usually handled by the lexical analyser. Implement such facilities for controlling listing of the source program, and dumping the symbol table (for example, using (*$T+*) to request a symbol table dump). What action should be taken if the listing has been suppressed, and if errors are discovered?

7.30 A frequent (and very useful) pragmatic comment in Pascal compilers takes the form (*$I FILENAME*) and indicates that the compiler should switch to reading source code from the external file specified by FILENAME, later switching back to the original file when the new file is exhausted. Why is it not possible to do this with a compiler written in standard Pascal? Can you find a way of doing it on the Pascal implementation you have available?

7.31 Check that no identifier is declared more than once.

7.32 Perhaps in a language as simple as this one could assume that all undeclared identifiers be treated as variables, and entered as such in the symbol table at the point of first reference. Is this a good idea? Can it be easily implemented?

7.33 Is it worth implementing more sophisticated ways of maintaining the symbol table – say as a binary tree, using Pascal dynamic variables? Try it anyway!

7.34 Add the ability to declare signed constants, and ones defined in terms of previously named constants, as for example

```
const
   MAX   = +456;
   MIN   = -456;
   LOWER = -MAX;
```

The cynic might contend that if a language has features that are the cause of numerous beginners' errors then one should redesign the language. Consider a selection of the following:

7.35 Suppose the syntax for if and while statements was to be changed to

       if <condition> then <statement> { ; <statement> } end

and

       while <condition> do <statement> { ; <statement> } end

How would this alter the parser and error recovery? Do you think it has advantages or disadvantages over the original syntax from the viewpoint of either the compiler writer or the program writer? How should the if ... then ... else statement best be introduced in this scheme?

7.36 Bailes (1984) makes a plea for the introduction of a 'Rational Pascal'. According to him, the keywords do (in while and for statements), then (in if statements) and the semicolons used as terminators at the ends of declarations and as statement separators should all be discarded. (He has a few other ideas, some even more contentious.) Can you produce a description of a version of our mini-language with the same excisions, and then write a reliable recursive descent parser for it? What are the merits and demerits of his suggestions from the viewpoint of the compiler writer and the program writer?

7.37 The problems with if ... then and if ... then ... else statements are such that some languages introduce a construct which can be exemplified

```
if <condition> then <statement>
  elsif <condition> then <statement>
  elsif <condition> then <statement>
  . . .
  else <statement>
```

or

```
if <condition> then <statementsequence>
  elsif <condition> then <statementsequence>
  elsif <condition> then <statementsequence>
  . . .
  else <statementsequence>
end
```

Describe these more formally in BNF and in EBNF, and discuss whether they might easily be handled by extensions to our parser. Do they have any advantages over the standard if ... then ... else arrangement? In particular, do they resolve the 'dangling else' problem neatly?

7.38 The language Edison introduces an extended form of the while loop. In his book, Brinch Hansen (1983) (page 30) describes this as having the form

```
while <condition1> do <statementsequence1>
  else <condition2> do <statementsequence2>
  . . .
  else <conditionN> do <statementsequenceN>
end
```

The conditions are evaluated one at a time in the order written until one is found to be true, when the matching <statementsequence> is executed, after which the process is repeated. If no <condition> is true, the loop terminates. How could this be parsed reliably?

7.39 Brinch Hansen does not like Pascal's empty statement. What is this, is it ever of use, and, if so, why should an explicit statement (like the skip suggested by Brinch Hansen) be any improvement over Pascal?

7.40 Brinch Hansen has incorporated only one form of loop into Edison – the while loop – arguing that the repeat and for loops are unnecessary. What particular advantages and disadvantages do these loops have from the points of view of a compiler writer and a compiler user respectively?

Further reading

Good treatments of the material of this section may be found in the books by Welsh and McKeag (1980) (pages 91–103); Wirth (1976) (pages 320–329) and Davie and Morrison (1981) (pages 101–108; they also suggest alternative approaches). A much higher level treatment is given in Chapter 6 of Backhouse (1979), while a rather simplified version is given by Brinch Hansen (1983) (pages 299–303). Papers by Pemberton (1980) and by Topor (1982) are also worth exploring. Brinch Hansen (1983) (pages 25–34), in discussing the rationale for the language Edison, makes interesting comments on the forms that sequential control statements should have for easy parsing.

Listing 9 Shell of CLANG parser with syntactic and semantic error handling

```
1  program PARSER(INPUT, OUTPUT, SOURCE);
2  (*Simple parser for CLANG level 1, without code generation
3     P.D. Terry,   January 22, 1985      *)
4  const
5    (*mostly as before, with additions*)
6    VERSION  = '1.0'        (*level.release*);
7    TABLEMAX = 100          (*length of identifier table*);
8  type
9    (*mostly as before, with additions*)
10   TABLEINDEX = 0 .. TABLEMAX;
11   CLASSES    = (CONSTANT, VARIABLE, PROG);
12   CLASSSET   = set of CLASSES;
```

```
13    SYMSET      = set of SYMBOLS;
14  var
15    (* ++++++++++ used by the character and option handler ++++++++++ *)
16    (*mostly as before, with additions*)
17    TABLES : BOOLEAN                  (*request tables*);
18
19    (* ++++++++++ used by the lexical analyser ++++++++++++++++++++ *)
20    (*as before*)
21
22    (* ++++++++++ used by the syntax analyser +++++++++++++++++++++++ *)
23
24    ERRORS : BOOLEAN                  (*whether we have any*);
25    FIRSTBLOCK, FIRSTSTATEMENT, FIRSTFACTOR, RELOPSYMS : SYMSET;
26    TABLE : array [TABLEINDEX] of record (*symbol table entries*)
27                             NAME  : ALFA;
28                             CLASS : CLASSES
29                             end (*TABLE*);
30
31  procedure QUIT (N : INTEGER);
32  (* +++++ Implementation dependent for handling fatal errors +++++ *)
33    begin
34      WRITELN (OUTPUT);
35      case N of
36        3: WRITELN(OUTPUT, 'Program Incomplete - Unexpected EOF');
37        4: WRITELN(OUTPUT, 'Too many identifiers');
38      end;
39      (*close OUTPUT file if necessary and abort program*)
40    end (*QUIT*);
41
42  (* +++++++++++++++++++++++++++++ Source Handler +++++++++++++++++++++++++++++ *)
43
44  procedure ERROR (ERRORCODE : INTEGER);
45    begin
46      ERRORS := TRUE; WRITE(OUTPUT, '↑': CC);
47      case ERRORCODE of
48         0: WRITE(OUTPUT, 'NUMBER OUT OF RANGE');
49         1: WRITE(OUTPUT, 'STRING INCOMPLETE');
50         2: WRITE(OUTPUT, '; EXPECTED');
51         3: WRITE(OUTPUT, 'INVALID SEQUENCE');
52         5: WRITE(OUTPUT, 'UNDECLARED');
53         6: WRITE(OUTPUT, 'IDENTIFIER EXPECTED');
54         7: WRITE(OUTPUT, ':= IN WRONG CONTEXT');
55         8: WRITE(OUTPUT, 'NUMBER EXPECTED');
56         9: WRITE(OUTPUT, '= EXPECTED');
57        13: WRITE(OUTPUT, ', OR ) EXPECTED');
58        14: WRITE(OUTPUT, 'INVALID START TO FACTOR');
```

```
59        17: WRITE(OUTPUT, ') EXPECTED');
60        18: WRITE(OUTPUT, '( EXPECTED');
61        19: WRITE(OUTPUT, 'RELATIONAL OPERATOR EXPECTED');
62        20: WRITE(OUTPUT, 'INVALID ASSIGNMENT');
63        21: WRITE(OUTPUT, ':= EXPECTED');
64        22: WRITE(OUTPUT, 'INVALID CLASS');
65        23: WRITE(OUTPUT, 'THEN EXPECTED');
66        24: WRITE(OUTPUT, 'END EXPECTED');
67        25: WRITE(OUTPUT, 'DO EXPECTED');
68        28: WRITE(OUTPUT, 'CANNOT BE READ');
69        32: WRITE(OUTPUT, 'INVALID SYMBOL AFTER A STATEMENT');
70        34: WRITE(OUTPUT, 'BEGIN EXPECTED');
71        35: WRITE(OUTPUT, 'INVALID SYMBOL AFTER BLOCK');
72        36: WRITE(OUTPUT, 'PROGRAM EXPECTED');
73        37: WRITE(OUTPUT, '. EXPECTED');
74      end (*case*);
75      WRITELN(OUTPUT)
76    end (*ERROR*);
77
78  procedure GETCH;
79    (*as before*)
80
81  (* +++++++++++++++++++++++++++++ Lexical Analyser +++++++++++++++++++++ *)
82
83  procedure GETSYM;
84    (*mostly as before, but with the following alterations to some options*)
85
86      '0', '1', '2', '3', '4', '5', '6', '7', '8', '9':
87        begin
88          NUM := 0; SYM := NUMBER;
89          repeat
90            if NUM <= (MAXINT - DIGIT) div 10   (*check imminent overflow*)
91              then NUM := 10 * NUM + DIGIT else ERROR(0);
92            GETCH
93          until NOTDIGIT
94        end;
95      '''':
96        begin (*string*)
97          NUM := 0; GETCH; SYM := STRINGSYM; ENDSTRING := FALSE;
98          repeat
99            if CH = '''' then begin GETCH; ENDSTRING := CH <> '''' end;
100           if not ENDSTRING then
101             begin NUM := NUM + 1; STRINGTEXT[NUM] := CH; GETCH end
102         until ENDSTRING or ENDLINE;
103         if not ENDSTRING then begin NUM := 0; ERROR(1) end
104       end;
```

```
105
106   end (*GETSYM*);
107
108 procedure INITIALIZE;
109   var
110     C : CHAR;
111
112   procedure RESERVEDWORDS;
113     (*as before*)
114
115   begin
116     (*as before, with additions*)
117     RELOPSYMS     := [EQLSYM, NEQSYM, GTRSYM, GEQSYM, LSSSYM, LEQSYM];
118     FIRSTBLOCK    := [CONSTSYM, VARSYM, BEGINSYM];
119     FIRSTSTATEMENT := [IDENT, BEGINSYM, IFSYM, WHILESYM, WRITESYM, READSYM];
120     FIRSTFACTOR   := [IDENT, NUMBER, LPAREN];
121     ERRORS := FALSE;
122   end (*INITIALIZE*);
123
124 (* +++++++++++++++++++++ Syntax and Semantic Analyser +++++++++++++++++++++ *)
125
126 procedure ACCEPT (EXPECTED : SYMBOLS; ERRORCODE : INTEGER);
127   begin
128     if SYM = EXPECTED then GETSYM else ERROR(ERRORCODE)
129   end (*ACCEPT*);
130
131 procedure BLOCK (FOLLOWERS : SYMSET);
132   var
133     LASTENTRY : TABLEINDEX (*index into symbol table*)
134
135   procedure PRINTSYMBOLTABLE;
136   (*List current entries in symbol table*)
137     var
138       I : TABLEINDEX;
139     begin
140       for I := 1 to LASTENTRY do with TABLE[I] do
141         begin
142           WRITE(OUTPUT, I:10, NAME:9);
143           case CLASS of
144             CONSTANT : WRITELN(OUTPUT, '  CONSTANT ');
145             VARIABLE : WRITELN(OUTPUT, '  VARIABLE ');
146             PROG     : WRITELN(OUTPUT, '  PROGRAM ');
147           end (*case*)
148         end
149     end (*PRINTSYMBOLTABLE*);
150
```

```
151    procedure TEST (ALLOWED, BEACONS : SYMSET; ERRORCODE : INTEGER);
152    (*Test to see whether current SYM is ALLOWED and recover if not*)
153      begin
154        if not (SYM in ALLOWED) then
155          begin
156            ERROR(ERRORCODE); while not (SYM in ALLOWED + BEACONS) do GETSYM
157          end
158      end (*TEST*);
159
160 (* ++++++++++++++++++++++++++ Declaration Part ++++++++++++++++++++++++++ *)
161
162    procedure ENTER (C : CLASSES);
163    (*Enter object of class C into symbol table*)
164      begin
165        if LASTENTRY = TABLEMAX then QUIT(4) (*symbol table overflow*);
166        LASTENTRY := LASTENTRY + 1;
167        with TABLE[LASTENTRY] do begin NAME := ID; CLASS := C end
168      end (*ENTER*);
169
170
171    procedure SEARCHID (var ENTRY : TABLEINDEX; ALLOWED : CLASSSET;
172                        ERRORCODE : INTEGER);
173    (*Find identifier ID in table at location ENTRY, check ALLOWED class*)
174      begin
175        TABLE[0].NAME := ID; ENTRY := LASTENTRY;
176        while TABLE[ENTRY].NAME <> ID do ENTRY := ENTRY - 1;
177        if ENTRY = 0 (*not really there*)
178          then ERROR(5)
179          else if not (TABLE[ENTRY].CLASS in ALLOWED) then ERROR(ERRORCODE);
180        GETSYM (*side-effect*)
181      end (*SEARCHID*);
182
183    procedure CONSTDECLARATION;
184    (*Handle declaration of named constants*)
185      begin
186        GETSYM;
187        TEST([IDENT], FOLLOWERS, 6);
188        while SYM = IDENT do
189          begin
190            ENTER(CONSTANT); GETSYM;
191            if SYM in [EQLSYM, BECOMES]
192              then
193                begin
194                  if SYM = BECOMES then ERROR(7); GETSYM;
195                  ACCEPT(NUMBER, 8)
196                end
```

```
197              else ERROR(9);
198            ACCEPT(SEMICOLON, 2)
199          end (*while*)
200      end (*CONSTDECLARATION*);
201
202   procedure VARDECLARATION;
203   (*Handle declaration of variables*)
204
205      procedure ENTERVARIABLE;
206        begin
207          if SYM <> IDENT then ERROR(6) else
208            begin ENTER(VARIABLE); GETSYM end
209        end (*ENTERVARIABLE *);
210
211      begin (*VARDECLARATION*)
212        GETSYM;
213        TEST([IDENT], FOLLOWERS, 6);
214        if SYM = IDENT then
215          begin
216            ENTERVARIABLE;
217            while SYM = COMMA do begin GETSYM; ENTERVARIABLE end;
218            ACCEPT(SEMICOLON, 2)
219          end
220      end (*VARDECLARATION*);
221
222   (* ++++++++++++++++++++++++++++ Statement Part ++++++++++++++++++++++++++ *)
223
224      procedure COMPOUNDSTATEMENT (FOLLOWERS : SYMSET);
225
226        procedure STATEMENT (FOLLOWERS : SYMSET);
227          var
228            IDENTRY : TABLEINDEX;
229
230          procedure EXPRESSION (FOLLOWERS : SYMSET);
231
232            procedure TERM (FOLLOWERS : SYMSET);
233
234              procedure FACTOR (FOLLOWERS : SYMSET);
235                var
236                  IDENTRY : TABLEINDEX;
237                begin
238                  TEST(FIRSTFACTOR, FOLLOWERS, 14);
239                  while SYM in FIRSTFACTOR do
240                    begin
241                      case SYM of
242                          IDENT : SEARCHID(IDENTRY, [CONSTANT, VARIABLE], 14);
```

```
243                    NUMBER: GETSYM;
244                    LPAREN:
245                      begin
246                        GETSYM; EXPRESSION([RPAREN] + FOLLOWERS);
247                        ACCEPT(RPAREN, 17)
248                      end
249                  end (*case SYM*);
250                  TEST(FOLLOWERS - FIRSTFACTOR, FIRSTFACTOR, 3)
251                end (*while*)
252            end (*FACTOR*);
253
254        begin (*TERM*)
255          FACTOR([TIMES, SLASH] + FOLLOWERS);
256          while SYM in [TIMES, SLASH] do
257            begin GETSYM; FACTOR([TIMES, SLASH] + FOLLOWERS) end
258        end (*TERM*);
259
260      begin (*EXPRESSION*)
261        if SYM in [PLUS, MINUS] then GETSYM;
262        TERM([PLUS, MINUS] + FOLLOWERS);
263        while SYM in [PLUS, MINUS] do
264          begin GETSYM; TERM([PLUS, MINUS] + FOLLOWERS) end
265      end (*EXPRESSION*);
266
267    procedure CONDITION (FOLLOWERS : SYMSET);
268      begin
269        if SYM = ODDSYM
270          then
271            begin
272              GETSYM; ACCEPT(LPAREN, 18);
273              EXPRESSION([RPAREN] + FOLLOWERS); ACCEPT(RPAREN, 17)
274            end
275          else
276            begin
277              EXPRESSION(RELOPSYMS + FOLLOWERS);
278              if not (SYM in RELOPSYMS) then ERROR(19)
279                else begin GETSYM; EXPRESSION(FOLLOWERS) end
280            end;
281        TEST(FOLLOWERS, [], 3)
282      end (*CONDITION*);
283
284    procedure IFSTATEMENT;
285      begin
286        GETSYM; CONDITION([THENSYM, DOSYM] + FOLLOWERS);
287        if SYM = THENSYM then GETSYM
288          else begin ERROR(23); if SYM = DOSYM then GETSYM end;
```

```
289              STATEMENT(FOLLOWERS)
290          end (*IFSTATEMENT*);
291
292      procedure WHILESTATEMENT;
293        begin
294          GETSYM; CONDITION([DOSYM] + FOLLOWERS); ACCEPT(DOSYM, 25);
295          STATEMENT(FOLLOWERS)
296        end (*WHILESTATEMENT*);
297
298      procedure WRITESTATEMENT;
299        begin
300          GETSYM;
301          if SYM = LPAREN then
302            begin
303              repeat
304                GETSYM;
305                if SYM <> STRINGSYM
306                  then begin EXPRESSION([COMMA, RPAREN] + FOLLOWERS) end
307                  else GETSYM
308              until SYM <> COMMA;
309              ACCEPT(RPAREN, 13)
310            end
311        end (*WRITESTATEMENT*);
312
313      procedure READSTATEMENT;
314        begin
315          GETSYM;
316          if SYM <> LPAREN then ERROR(18) else
317            begin
318              repeat
319                GETSYM;
320                if SYM <> IDENT then ERROR(6) else
321                  SEARCHID(IDENTRY, [VARIABLE], 28);
322              until SYM <> COMMA;
323              ACCEPT(RPAREN, 13)
324            end
325        end (*READSTATEMENT*);
326
327      begin (*STATEMENT*)
328        if SYM in FIRSTSTATEMENT then
329          case SYM of
330            IDENT:
331              begin
332                SEARCHID(IDENTRY, [VARIABLE], 20);
333                if SYM = BECOMES then GETSYM else
334                  begin ERROR(21); if SYM = EQLSYM then GETSYM end;
```

```
335                   EXPRESSION(FOLLOWERS)
336                end (*IDENT*);
337           IFSYM     : IFSTATEMENT;
338           BEGINSYM : COMPOUNDSTATEMENT(FOLLOWERS);
339           WHILESYM : WHILESTATEMENT;
340           WRITESYM : WRITESTATEMENT;
341           READSYM  : READSTATEMENT;
342         end (*case SYM*);
343       TEST(FOLLOWERS, [], 32)
344     end (*STATEMENT*);
345
346    begin (*COMPOUNDSTATEMENT*)
347      ACCEPT(BEGINSYM, 34);
348      STATEMENT([SEMICOLON, ENDSYM] + FOLLOWERS);
349      while SYM in [SEMICOLON] + FIRSTSTATEMENT do
350        begin
351          ACCEPT(SEMICOLON, 2); STATEMENT([SEMICOLON, ENDSYM] + FOLLOWERS)
352        end;
353      ACCEPT(ENDSYM, 24)
354    end (*COMPOUNDSTATEMENT*);
355
356  begin (*BLOCK*)
357    LASTENTRY := 1 (*Initialize symbol table*);
358    TEST(FIRSTBLOCK, FOLLOWERS, 3);
359    repeat
360      if SYM = CONSTSYM then CONSTDECLARATION;
361      if SYM = VARSYM then VARDECLARATION;
362      TEST([BEGINSYM], FOLLOWERS, 34)
363    until SYM in FIRSTSTATEMENT + [PERIOD];
364    if TABLES then PRINTSYMBOLTABLE (*demonstration purposes*);
365    COMPOUNDSTATEMENT(FOLLOWERS);
366    TEST(FOLLOWERS, [], 35)
367  end (*BLOCK*);
368
369  procedure PROGRAMME;
370    begin
371      ACCEPT(PROCSYM, 36);
372      with TABLE[0] do begin NAME := ID; CLASS := PROG end;
373      TABLE[1] := TABLE[0]  (*enter program name*);
374      if SYM <> IDENT then ERROR(6) else
375        begin TABLES := ID = 'TEST    '; GETSYM end;
376      ACCEPT(SEMICOLON, 2);
377      BLOCK([PERIOD] + FIRSTBLOCK + FIRSTSTATEMENT);
378      if SYM <> PERIOD then ERROR(37)
379    end (*PROGRAMME*);
380
```

```
381  begin (*PARSER*)
382    (*open and RESET(SOURCE) and OUTPUT files as appropriate*)
383    INITIALIZE;
384    PROGRAMME;
385    if not ERRORS then WRITELN(OUTPUT, 'Program parsed correctly');
386    (*close OUTPUT file if necessary*)
387  end (*PARSER*).
```

7.5 The code-generation interface

In an earlier section we claimed that it would be advantageous to split our
compiler into distinct syntax/semantic and code-generation phases. One good
reason for doing this is to isolate the machine-dependent part of compilation as
far as possible from the language analysis – the degree of our success may be
measured by the fact that we have not yet made any mention of what sort of
object code we are trying to generate. The critical reader will, perhaps, observe
that code generation, of any form, implies that we consider semantics of our
language in far more detail than we have done until now. Indeed, we have
made no real attempt to discuss what programs written in our language 'mean',
although we have tacitly assumed that the reader has quite an extensive
knowledge of Pascal-like languages, and that we could safely draw on this.

In considering the interface between analysis and code generation it will
again pay to aim for some degree of machine independence. Generation of
code should take place without too much, if any, knowledge of how the
analyser works. A common technique for achieving this seemingly impossible
task is to define a hypothetical machine with architecture and instruction set
convenient for the execution of programs of the source language, without being
too far removed from the actual system for which the compiler is required. The
action of the interface procedures will be to translate the source program into
an equivalent sequence of operations for the hypothetical machine; calls to
these procedures can be embedded in the analyser so far developed without
overmuch concern for how the final generator will turn the operations into
object code for the target machine. (Indeed, some interpretive systems, as we
have already mentioned, hand such operations over directly to an interpreter,
without native machine code ever being produced.)

Of course, any interface must take cognisance of data-related concepts
like 'storage', 'addresses' and 'data representation', as well as control-related
ones like 'program counter', 'sequential execution' and 'branch instruction',
which are fundamental to nearly all machines on which programs in Pascal-like
languages execute. Typically, machines allow some operations that simulate
arithmetic or logical operations on data bit patterns that simulate numbers or
characters, these patterns being stored in an array-like structure of 'memory',
whose elements are distinguished by 'addresses'. In high-level languages these
addresses are usually given mnemonic names. The syntax of many high-level
languages, as it happens, rarely draws the distinction between the 'address' for

a 'variable' and the 'value' associated with that variable and stored at its address. Thus we find statements like

```
X := X + 4
```

in which the X on the left of the := operator actually represents an address, (sometimes called the **L-value** of X) while the X on the right (sometimes called the **R-value** of X) actually represents the value of the quantity currently residing at the same address. Small wonder that mathematically trained beginners find the assignment notation strange! After a while it usually becomes second nature – by which time notations in which the distinction is made clearer possibly only confuse still further, as witness the problems beginners often have with pointer types in Pascal, where P↑ may be regarded as the explicit value residing at the explicit address P.

To perform its task, the interface will have to allow the extraction of information associated with user-defined identifiers and best kept in the symbol table. In the case of the system under discussion most of this has already been provided, with one major exception – we have yet to specify the addresses of variables. If we can assume that our machine incorporates the 'linear array' model of 'memory', this information is easily added as the variables are declared, if we modify the symbol table to be of the form

```
TABLE : array [TABLEINDEX] of record
                        NAME    : ALFA;
                        CLASS   : CLASSES;
                        ADDRESS : INTEGER
                    end (*TABLE*);
```

and alter VARDECLARATION to set the ADDRESS field as below

```
procedure ENTERVARIABLE;
  begin
    if SYM <> IDENT then ERROR(6) else
      begin
        ENTER(VARIABLE); GETSYM;
        TABLE[LASTENTRY].ADDRESS := OFFSET; OFFSET := OFFSET + 1
      end
  end (*ENTERVARIABLE*);
```

Here OFFSET, a simple count, which is initialized to zero before parsing of the block commences, keeps track of the number of variables declared, and also serves to set the addresses these variables will have relative to the start of memory when the program runs. (A trivial modification gets round the problem if it is impossible or inconvenient to use zero-based addresses in the real machine.)

For constants the ADDRESS field can be used to store the value of the constant; this value is not necessarily the 'address' of anything.

As we have already remarked, the concepts of the meaning of an expression, and of assignment of the 'values' of expressions to locations in memory labelled with the 'addresses' of variables are probably well understood by the reader. As it happens, such operations are most easily handled for our sort of language by assuming that the hypothetical machine is stack-based, and translating the normal **infix** notation used in describing expressions into a **postfix** or **Polish** equivalent, which is easily handled with the aid of an evaluation stack, the elements of which are either addresses of storage locations or the values found at such addresses. These ideas will probably be familiar to readers already acquainted with stack-based machines like the Hewlett-Packard calculator.

Code for data manipulation on such a machine can be generated by making calls on procedures like

```
procedure STACKCONSTANT (NUM : INTEGER);
(*generate code to push NUM onto evaluation stack*)

procedure STACKADDRESS (ADDRESS : INTEGER);
(*generate code to push ADDRESS onto evaluation stack*)

procedure DEREFERENCE;
(*generate code to replace top of evaluation stack by VALUE
  found at the ADDRESS currently on top of the stack*)
```

for storage access; by calls to procedures like

```
procedure NEGATEINTEGER;
(*generate code to negate integer value on top of evaluation stack*)

procedure BINARYINTEGEROPERATION (OP : SYMBOLS);
(*generate code to pop two values A,B from evaluation stack and push
  value A OP B *)
```

to allow for simple arithmetic; and finally by calls to a procedure

```
procedure ASSIGN;
(*generate code to store value currently on top-of-stack on address
  given by next-to-top, pop two elements*)
```

to handle the familiar assignment process.

Thus, for example, a statement of the form

```
A := 4 + C
```

should produce the sequence of code-generating procedure calls

```
STACKADDRESS(address of A)
  STACKCONSTANT(4)
  STACKADDRESS(address of C); DEREFERENCE
  BINARYINTEGEROPERATION(PLUS)
ASSIGN
```

The sequence STACKADDRESS(ADDRESS); DEREFERENCE occurs so often that it suggests easy optimization by introducing an alternative procedure

```
procedure LOADVARIABLE (ADDRESS : INTEGER);
(*generate code to store value at ADDRESS directly on top of stack*)
```

We shall not make use of this optimization, but leave it to the reader to incorporate it as an easy exercise. Nor shall we call on STACKADDRESS directly, but via a procedure

```
procedure ADDRESSFOR (I : TABLEINDEX);
(*generate code to push onto the evaluation stack the address for the
  variable described in position I in TABLE *)
```

This will allow for easier expansion later; for the moment we note that this procedure is simply

```
procedure ADDRESSFOR (I : TABLEINDEX);
  begin with TABLE[I] do STACKADDRESS(ADDRESS) end;
```

For simple I/O operations we can call on procedures

```
procedure INPUTOPERATION (OP : TRANSFERS);
(*generate code to read value; store on address found on top of stack*)

procedure OUTPUTOPERATION (OP : TRANSFERS);
(*generate code to output value from top of stack*)
```

where OP controls the choice of the somewhat complicated code needed to handle conversion from internal to external form for various kinds of data, like strings, numbers, and so on.

Control statements are a little trickier. In the typical machine being considered, machine code is assumed to be executed in the order in which it was generated, except where explicit 'branch' operations occur. Although our simple language does not incorporate the somewhat despised goto statement, this maps very closely onto real machine code, and must form the basis of code generated by higher level control statements. The transformation is, of course, easily automated, save for the familiar problem of forward references. In our case there are two source statements that can give rise to these.

```
if CONDITION then STATEMENT
```

must produce object code of the more fundamental form

```
        code for CONDITION
        if not CONDITION then goto LAB
        code for STATEMENT
LAB     continue
```

and the problem is that when we get to the stage of generating goto LAB we do not know where LAB will be. Similarly, the source code

```
while CONDITION do STATEMENT
```

must produce object code of the form

```
LAB     code for CONDITION
        if not CONDITION then goto EXIT
        code for STATEMENT
        goto LAB
EXIT    continue
```

Here we should know the address of LAB as we start to generate the 'code for CONDITION', but we shall not know the address of EXIT when we get to the stage of generating goto EXIT.

In general the solution to this problem may require the use of a two-pass system. Here, however, we shall assume that we are developing a one-pass load-and-go compiler, and that the generated code is all in memory, or at least on a random access file, so that modification of addresses in branch instructions can easily be effected. In this case we can solve the problem with the aid of

```
procedure JUMP (LAB : INTEGER);
(*generate unconditional branch to instruction at LAB*)

procedure JUMPONFALSE (LAB : INTEGER);
(*generate branch to instruction at LAB, conditional on
  the Boolean value on top of the evaluation stack*)
```

When we call on these routines we may not know the values of parameter LAB, and so we introduce two auxiliary procedures

```
procedure STORELABEL (var LAB : INTEGER);
(*store address of next instruction in LAB for use in backpatching*)

procedure BACKPATCH (LOCATION, ADDRESS : INTEGER);
(*fill in ADDRESS as address field of branch instruction at LOCATION*)
```

To allow comparisons to be effected we can call on

```
procedure COMPARISON (OP : SYMBOLS);
(*generate code to pop two integer values A,B from stack; push Boolean
  value A OP B*)
```

The exceptional case generated by the Boolean function *odd* can be dealt with by

```
procedure CODEFORODD;
(*generate code to replace top-of-stack by true/false according as it
  is odd/even*)
```

We have so far made no mention of the branch ahead tables which the reader may be dreading. In fact we can leave the system to sort these out implicitly, pointing to yet another advantage of the recursive descent method. A little thought should show that a side-effect of supplying only the while and if statements is that we do not need explicit labels, and that we need the same number of implicit labels for each instance of the construction. These labels may be handled by declaring appropriate variables local to parsing procedures like STATEMENT; each time a recursive call is made to STATEMENT new variables will come into existence, and remain there just so long as it takes to complete parsing of the construction, after which they may be discarded. Thus, for example, in compiling an if statement we may use a technique such as the following (shown devoid of error handling for simplicity)

```
procedure IFSTATEMENT;
  var
```

```
      TESTLABEL : INTEGER;
   begin
      GETSYM                           (*scan past if*);
      CONDITION                        (*generates code to evaluate <condition>*);
      STORELABEL(TESTLABEL)            (*remember address of next branch
                                         instruction in a local variable*);
      JUMPONFALSE(0)                   (*generate it incompletely*);
      ACCEPT(THENSYM)                  (*scan past then*);
      STATEMENT                        (*all code for intervening statement(s)*);
      BACKPATCH(TESTLABEL, NEXTCODE)   (*using same local TESTLABEL as was used
                                         in STORELABEL above*)
   end (*IFSTATEMENT*);
```

If the interior call to STATEMENT needs to parse an inner IFSTATEMENT, a further instance of TESTLABEL will be created for the purpose. In writing such parsers and compilers, clearly, great care has to be taken to ensure that the variables associated with handling implicit forward references are correctly declared, or chaos will ensue.

Finally, we may need to generate special housekeeping code as we enter or leave a block. This may not be apparent in the case of a single block program – which is all our language allows at present – but will certainly be the case when we extend the language to allow procedures. This code can be handled by

```
procedure ENTERBLOCK (BLOCKCLASS : CLASSES);
(*generate code needed as we start execution of a block*)

procedure LEAVEBLOCK (BLOCKCLASS : CLASSES);
(*generate code needed as we leave a block*)
```

The way in which these procedure calls may be incorporated in the analyser developed previously is shown in Listing 10 below. For convenience we list the code for BLOCK almost in its entirety, with the refinements in sloping type.

Notes

(a) We assume that the address of the next instruction to be generated is stored in a global variable NEXTCODE.

(b) Note how easily the reverse Polish form of the expression manipulation is accomplished simply by delaying the calls for 'operation' code generation until after the second 'operand' code generation has taken place, as, for example, in procedure TERM (lines 118–125).

(c) It will turn out useful for debugging purposes, and fully to understand the way in which our machine works, to be able to print out the evaluation stack at any point in the program. This we can do by introducing

```
procedure CODEFORDUMP;
(*generate code to dump the current state of the evaluation stack*)
```

The way in which this will be done is by introducing a new reserved word into the language, stackdump, which can appear as a simple statement. The changes needed to the initialization and analysis routines are trivial, and need not be given in full here.

Exercises

7.41 Modify the analyser to cater for the repeat ... until statement, and the if ... then ... else statement, with the 'dangling else' ambiguity resolved as in Pascal.

7.42 How would you introduce a Pascal-like for loop? Make sure you fully understand the semantics of this. Try to add the refinements suggested in Exercise 7.27. Why do you suppose the Pascal for loop terminates with its control variable 'undefined'?

7.43 How would you introduce a Pascal-like case statement? If a case statement is introduced, what should be done about an otherwise option, or the action to be taken when the case selector does not match any of the case labels?

7.44 At present the write statement is rather like the Pascal writeln. Change the language and the compiler to provide an explicit writeln statement, and, similarly, an explicit readln statement, with semantics as in Pascal.

7.45 It might be useful to add 'character' data to the language. An easy way to do this would be simply to extend the write statements so that they could give the ASCII equivalents of the data being written, and the read statements so that they could convert the character being read into its equivalent ordinal value. This might be done, for example, by coding

```
read (A$, B$, C)
```

meaning 'read A and B as the next two characters, C as the next integer', with a similar idea for output. How easy is this to implement? You should regard the $ as a new terminal, not as part of an identifier.

7.46 Code generation for the loop ... exit ... end construction suggested in Exercise 7.28 provides quite an interesting exercise. Since we may have several exit statements in a loop, we seem to have a severe forward reference problem. This may be avoided in several ways. For example, we could generate code of the form

```
              goto STARTLOOP
EXITPOINT     goto LOOPEXIT
```

```
STARTLOOP   code for loop body

            . . .

            goto EXITPOINT      (from an exit statement)

            . . .

            goto STARTLOOP
LOOPEXIT    code which follows loop
```

With this idea, all exit statements can branch back to EXITPOINT, and we have only to backpatch the one instruction at EXITPOINT when we reach the end of the loop. (This is marginally 'inefficient', but an extra goto statement adds very little.)

Another idea is to generate code like

```
STARTLOOP   code for loop body

            . . .

            goto EXIT1     (from an exit statement)

            . . .

EXIT1       goto EXIT2     (from an exit statement)

            . . .

EXIT2       goto LOOPEXIT  (from an exit statement)

            . . .

            goto STARTLOOP
LOOPEXIT    code which follows end
```

In this case, every time another exit is encountered, the previously incomplete one is backpatched to branch to the incomplete instruction which is just about to be generated· when the end is encountered, the last one is backpatched to leave the loop. (A loop ... end structure may, unusually, have no exit statements, but this is easily handled.) This solution is even less efficient than the last. An ingenious modification can lead to much better code. Suppose we generate code which at first appears quite incorrect, on the lines of

```
STARTLOOP   code for loop body

            . . .

EXIT0       goto 0         (incomplete – from an exit statement)

            . . .

EXIT1       goto EXIT0     (from an exit statement)

            . . .

EXIT2       goto EXIT1     (from an exit statement)

            . . .
```

with an auxiliary variable EXIT that contains the address of the most recent of the goto instructions so generated. (In the above example this would contain the address of the instruction labelled EXIT2.) We have used only backward references so far, so no real problems arise. When we encounter the end, we refer to the instruction at EXIT2, alter its address field to the now known forward address, and use the old backward address to find the address of the next instruction to modify, repeating this process until the goto 0 is encountered, which stops the chaining process (we are, of course, doing nothing other than constructing a linked list temporarily within the generated code).

Try out one or other of these schemes, or come up with your own ideas. (All of these schemes need modification when one adds the possibility of having nested loop ... end structures, which you should allow.)

7.47   If you have written parsers that handle the ideas of Exercises 7.35 and 7.37, write appropriate code generation interfaces for them.

7.48   Implement the extended while construct suggested by Brinch Hansen (1983), and discussed in Exercise 7.38.

7.49   Add the mod operator, as in Pascal, for use in forming expressions.

7.50   Add an exceptional halt statement, as a variation on the write statement, which first prints the values of its parameters and then stops execution.

7.51   How would you handle the goto statement, assuming you were to add it to the language? If you also include the for loop, what restrictions or precautions should you take when combining the two constructs?

Further reading

The hypothetical stack machine has been widely used in the development of Pascal compilers. A treatment on which our own is partly based can be found in Welsh and McKeag (1980) (pages 145–173). The discussion in the book by Wirth (1976) (pages 334–347) is also relevant, although, as is typical in several systems like this, no real attempt is made to specify an interface to the code generation, which is simply overlaid directly onto the analyser in a machine-dependent way. The discussion of the Pascal-P compiler in the book by Pemberton and Daniels (1982) is, as usual, extensive. However, code generation for a language supporting a variety of data types (something we have so far assiduously avoided introducing), when layered onto an already large system, tends to obscure many principles.

Various approaches can be taken to compiling the case statement (Exercise 7.43). The reader might like to consult the articles by Sale (1981) and by Hennessy and Mendelsohn (1982) as well as the descriptions in the books by Pemberton and Daniels (1982) and by Berry (1982).

Listing 10   Enhanced analyser with code-generation interface

```
1  procedure BLOCK (FOLLOWERS : SYMSET);
2  var
3    LASTENTRY : TABLEINDEX (*index into symbol table*);
4    OFFSET    : INTEGER    (*variable address offset*);
5
6  procedure PRINTSYMBOLTABLE;
7    (* essentially as before *)
8
9  procedure TEST (ALLOWED, BEACONS : SYMSET; ERRORCODE : INTEGER);
10   (* as before *)
11
12 (* ++++++++++++++++++++++++ Declaration Part +++++++++++++++++++++++++ *)
13
14 procedure ENTER (C : CLASSES);
15   (* as before *)
16
17 procedure SEARCHID (var ENTRY : TABLEINDEX; ALLOWED : CLASSSET;
18                     ERRORCODE : INTEGER);
19   (* as before *)
20
21 procedure CONSTDECLARATION;
22 (*Handle declaration of named constants*)
23   begin
24     GETSYM;
25     TEST([IDENT], FOLLOWERS, 6);
26     while SYM = IDENT do
27       begin
28         ENTER(CONSTANT); GETSYM;
29         if SYM in [EQLSYM, BECOMES]
30           then
31             begin
32               if SYM = BECOMES then ERROR(7); GETSYM;
33               if SYM <> NUMBER then ERROR(8) else
34                 begin TABLE[LASTENTRY].ADDRESS := NUM; GETSYM end
35             end
36           else ERROR(9);
37         ACCEPT(SEMICOLON, 2)
38       end (*while*)
39   end (*CONSTDECLARATION*);
40
41 procedure VARDECLARATION;
42 (*Handle declaration of variables*)
43
44   procedure ENTERVARIABLE;
```

```
45        begin
46          if SYM <> IDENT then ERROR(6) else
47            begin
48              ENTER(VARIABLE); GETSYM;
49              TABLE[LASTENTRY].ADDRESS := OFFSET; OFFSET := OFFSET + 1
50            end
51        end (*ENTERVARIABLE *);
52
53    begin (*VARDECLARATION*)
54      GETSYM;
55      TEST([IDENT], FOLLOWERS, 6);
56      if SYM = IDENT then
57        begin
58          ENTERVARIABLE;
59          while SYM = COMMA do begin GETSYM; ENTERVARIABLE end;
60          ACCEPT(SEMICOLON, 2)
61        end
62    end (*VARDECLARATION*);
63
64 (* ++++++++++++++++++++++++++ Statement Part ++++++++++++++++++++++++++ *)
65
66  procedure COMPOUNDSTATEMENT (FOLLOWERS : SYMSET);
67
68    procedure STATEMENT (FOLLOWERS : SYMSET);
69      var
70        IDENTRY : TABLEINDEX;
71        TESTLABEL, STARTLOOP : INTEGER;
72
73      procedure ADDRESSFOR (I : TABLEINDEX);
74      (*load address for identifier at table entry I *)
75        begin
76          with TABLE[I] do STACKADDRESS(ADDRESS)
77        end (*ADDRESSFOR*);
78
79      procedure EXPRESSION (FOLLOWERS : SYMSET);
80        var
81          ADDOP : SYMBOLS;
82
83        procedure TERM (FOLLOWERS : SYMSET);
84          var
85            MULOP : SYMBOLS;
86
87          procedure FACTOR (FOLLOWERS : SYMSET);
88            var
89              IDENTRY : TABLEINDEX;
90            begin
```

```
91                TEST(FIRSTFACTOR, FOLLOWERS, 14);
92                while SYM in FIRSTFACTOR do
93                  begin
94                    case SYM of
95                      IDENT:
96                        begin
97                          SEARCHID(IDENTRY, [CONSTANT, VARIABLE], 14);
98                          with TABLE[IDENTRY] do
99                            case CLASS of
100                             CONSTANT : STACKCONSTANT(ADDRESS);
101                             VARIABLE :
102                               begin ADDRESSFOR(IDENTRY); DEREFERENCE end;
103                             PROG     : (*error already reported*)
104                            end (*case CLASS*)
105                        end;
106                      NUMBER:
107                        begin STACKCONSTANT(NUM); GETSYM end;
108                      LPAREN:
109                        begin
110                          GETSYM; EXPRESSION([RPAREN] + FOLLOWERS);
111                          ACCEPT(RPAREN, 17)
112                        end
113                    end (*case SYM*);
114                    TEST(FOLLOWERS - FIRSTFACTOR, FIRSTFACTOR, 3)
115                  end (*while*)
116              end (*FACTOR*);
117
118        begin (*TERM*)
119          FACTOR([TIMES, SLASH] + FOLLOWERS);
120          while SYM in [TIMES, SLASH] do
121            begin
122              MULOP := SYM; GETSYM; FACTOR([TIMES, SLASH] + FOLLOWERS);
123              BINARYINTEGEROP(MULOP)
124            end
125        end (*TERM*);
126
127    begin (*EXPRESSION*)
128      if SYM in [PLUS, MINUS]
129        then
130          begin
131            ADDOP := SYM; GETSYM; TERM([PLUS, MINUS] + FOLLOWERS);
132            if ADDOP = MINUS then NEGATEINTEGER
133          end
134        else TERM([PLUS, MINUS] + FOLLOWERS);
135      while SYM in [PLUS, MINUS] do
136        begin
```

```
137                ADDOP := SYM; GETSYM; TERM([PLUS, MINUS] + FOLLOWERS);
138                BINARYINTEGEROP(ADDOP)
139            end
140       end (*EXPRESSION*);
141
142   procedure CONDITION (FOLLOWERS : SYMSET);
143      var
144        RELOP : SYMBOLS;
145      begin
146        if SYM = ODDSYM
147        then
148          begin
149            GETSYM; ACCEPT(LPAREN, 18);
150            EXPRESSION([RPAREN] + FOLLOWERS); ACCEPT(RPAREN, 17);
151            CODEFORODD
152          end
153        else
154          begin
155            EXPRESSION(RELOPSYMS + FOLLOWERS);
156            if not (SYM in RELOPSYMS) then ERROR(19) else
157              begin
158                RELOP := SYM; GETSYM; EXPRESSION(FOLLOWERS);
159                COMPARISON(RELOP)
160              end
161          end;
162        TEST(FOLLOWERS, [], 3)
163      end (*CONDITION*);
164
165   procedure IFSTATEMENT;
166      begin
167        GETSYM; CONDITION([THENSYM, DOSYM] + FOLLOWERS);
168        if SYM = THENSYM then GETSYM
169          else begin ERROR(23); if SYM = DOSYM then GETSYM end;
170        STORELABEL(TESTLABEL); JUMPONFALSE(0) (*Incomplete*);
171        STATEMENT(FOLLOWERS);
172        BACKPATCH(TESTLABEL, NEXTCODE)
173      end (*IFSTATEMENT*);
174
175   procedure WHILESTATEMENT;
176      begin
177        STORELABEL(STARTLOOP);
178        GETSYM; CONDITION([DOSYM] + FOLLOWERS); ACCEPT(DOSYM, 25);
179        STORELABEL(TESTLABEL); JUMPONFALSE(0) (*Incomplete*);
180        STATEMENT(FOLLOWERS); JUMP(STARTLOOP);
181        BACKPATCH(TESTLABEL, NEXTCODE)
182      end (*WHILESTATEMENT*);
```

```
183
184      procedure WRITESTATEMENT;
185        begin
186          GETSYM;
187          if SYM = LPAREN then
188            begin
189              repeat
190                GETSYM;
191                if SYM <> STRINGSYM
192                  then
193                    begin
194                      EXPRESSION([COMMA, RPAREN] + FOLLOWERS);
195                      OUTPUTOPERATION(NUMBERS)
196                    end
197                  else
198                    begin OUTPUTOPERATION(STRINGS); GETSYM end (*string*)
199              until SYM <> COMMA;
200              ACCEPT(RPAREN, 13)
201            end;
202          OUTPUTOPERATION(NEWLINE)
203        end (*WRITESTATEMENT*);
204
205      procedure READSTATEMENT;
206        begin
207          GETSYM;
208          if SYM <> LPAREN then ERROR(10) else
209            begin
210              repeat
211                GETSYM;
212                if SYM <> IDENT then ERROR(6) else
213                  begin
214                    SEARCHID(IDENTRY, [VARIABLE], 28);
215                    ADDRESSFOR(IDENTRY);
216                    INPUTOPERATION(NUMBERS)
217                  end
218              until SYM <> COMMA;
219              ACCEPT(RPAREN, 13)
220            end
221        end (*READSTATEMENT*);
222
223      begin (*STATEMENT*)
224        if SYM in FIRSTSTATEMENT then
225          case SYM of
226            IDENT:
227              begin
228                SEARCHID(IDENTRY, [VARIABLE], 20);
```

```
229                  ADDRESSFOR(IDENTRY);
230                  if SYM = BECOMES then GETSYM
231                     else begin ERROR(21); if SYM = EQLSYM then GETSYM end;
232                  EXPRESSION(FOLLOWERS);
233                  ASSIGN
234                end (*IDENT*);
235           IFSYM    : IFSTATEMENT;
236           BEGINSYM : COMPOUNDSTATEMENT(FOLLOWERS);
237           WHILESYM : WHILESTATEMENT;
238           WRITESYM : WRITESTATEMENT;
239           READSYM  : READSTATEMENT;
240           STACKSYM : begin CODEFORDUMP; GETSYM end
241         end (*case SYM*);
242       TEST(FOLLOWERS, [], 32)
243     end (*STATEMENT*);
244
245   begin
246     ACCEPT(BEGINSYM, 34);
247     STATEMENT([SEMICOLON, ENDSYM] + FOLLOWERS);
248     while SYM in [SEMICOLON] + FIRSTSTATEMENT do
249       begin
250         ACCEPT(SEMICOLON, 2); STATEMENT([SEMICOLON, ENDSYM] + FOLLOWERS)
251       end;
252     ACCEPT(ENDSYM, 24)
253   end (*COMPOUNDSTATEMENT*);
254
255 begin (*BLOCK*)
256   LASTENTRY := 1 (*Initialize symbol table*);
257   OFFSET := 0 (*Initialize address allocations*);
258   ENTERBLOCK(PROG) (*actually a null call here*);
259   TEST(FIRSTBLOCK, FOLLOWERS, 3);
260   repeat
261     if SYM = CONSTSYM then CONSTDECLARATION;
262     if SYM = VARSYM then VARDECLARATION;
263     TEST([BEGINSYM], FOLLOWERS, 34)
264   until SYM in FIRSTSTATEMENT + [PERIOD];
265   OPENSTACKFRAME(OFFSET) (*reserve space for variables*);
266   COMPOUNDSTATEMENT(FOLLOWERS);
267   if TABLES then PRINTSYMBOLTABLE (*demonstration purposes*);
268   LEAVEBLOCK(PROG);
269   TEST(FOLLOWERS, [], 35)
270 end (*BLOCK*);
```

7.6 Code generation for a simple stack machine

The problem of code generation for a real machine is, in general, complex, and very specialized. Here we shall content ourselves with completing the compiler, under the assumption that we wish to generate code for the stack machine described in Chapter 2. Such a machine does not exist, but, as we saw, it may be simulated by a simple interpreter. Indeed, if the INTERPRET procedure from the program in Listing 1 is added to the compiler, an implementation of the language quite suitable for experimental work is readily produced.

To allow code to be generated for this machine, we add to the declarations so far introduced

```
const
  CODEMAX = 1000              (*max size of code*);
type
  SHORTSTRING = packed array [1 .. 3] of CHAR;
  OPCODES     = (LDI, LDA, INT, BRN, BZE, NEG, ADD, SUB, MUL, DVD, OD, EQL, NEQ,
                 LSS, GEQ, GTR, LEQ, STK, STO, HLT, INN, PRN, PRS, NLN, LDV);
  INSTRUCTIONS = packed record
                   F : OPCODES (*function code*);
                   A : INTEGER (*address*)
                 end (*INSTRUCTIONS*);
  TRANSFERS = (NUMBERS, STRINGS, NEWLINE);
var
  MNEMONIC : array [OPCODES] of SHORTSTRING    (*opcodes*);
  NEXTCODE : INTEGER                           (*code location counter*);
  PCODE : array [0 .. CODEMAX] of INSTRUCTIONS (*generated code*);
  CODEISTOBEGENERATED : BOOLEAN                 (*not after errors*);
  HASADDRESSFIELD : set of OPCODES              (*record which use A field*);
```

The array MNEMONIC and the set HASADDRESSFIELD must be initialized: this is easily done (notice that the order in which OPCODES is defined is important)

```
MNEMONIC[LDI] := 'LDI'; MNEMONIC[LDA] := 'LDA'; MNEMONIC[LDV] := 'LDV';
MNEMONIC[INT] := 'INT'; MNEMONIC[BRN] := 'BRN'; MNEMONIC[BZE] := 'BZE';
MNEMONIC[NEG] := 'NEG'; MNEMONIC[ADD] := 'ADD'; MNEMONIC[SUB] := 'SUB';
MNEMONIC[MUL] := 'MUL'; MNEMONIC[DVD] := 'DVD'; MNEMONIC[OD ] := 'ODD';
MNEMONIC[EQL] := 'EQL'; MNEMONIC[NEQ] := 'NEQ'; MNEMONIC[LSS] := 'LSS';
MNEMONIC[GEQ] := 'GEQ'; MNEMONIC[GTR] := 'GTR'; MNEMONIC[LEQ] := 'LEQ';
MNEMONIC[STK] := 'STK'; MNEMONIC[STO] := 'STO'; MNEMONIC[HLT] := 'HLT';
MNEMONIC[INN] := 'INN'; MNEMONIC[PRN] := 'PRN'; MNEMONIC[PRS] := 'PRS';
MNEMONIC[NLN] := 'NLN';
HASADDRESSFIELD := [LDI .. BZE];
```

The code to be generated is stored in the array PCODE, and before we start to generate code we initialize

```
NEXTCODE := 0; CODEISTOBEGENERATED := TRUE;
```

Here CODEISTOBEGENERATED is a Boolean variable which will allow us to abort code generation if errors are discovered. This is useful in preventing gross errors (for example in backpatching), which could arise from badly malformed code sequences.

The main part of the code generation is done in terms of calls to a procedure

```
procedure GEN (OP : OPCODES; ADDRESS : INTEGER);
(*Code generator for instructions with address field*)
  begin
    if NEXTCODE > CODEMAX then QUIT(2) (*program too long*);
    if CODEISTOBEGENERATED then
      begin
      with PCODE[NEXTCODE] do begin F := OP; A := ADDRESS end;
      NEXTCODE := NEXTCODE + 1
      end
  end (*GEN*);
```

but instructions without address fields will occur so frequently that it is useful to introduce an auxiliary procedure

```
procedure EMIT (OP : OPCODES);
(*Code generator with no address field*)
  begin GEN(OP, 0) end;
```

In terms of these procedures, the ones defined previously are easily introduced, and can be studied in Listing 11. Note how easy the code generation is for a stack oriented language – it is much more difficult for a machine with no stack, and only a few registers and addressing modes.

The only complication not mentioned earlier is the following. Since the stack memory is used to store 'variables' in its first few positions, space for these must be allocated after the variable declarations have been processed. This is done by introducing a call to a procedure OPENSTACKFRAME just before we parse COMPOUNDSTATEMENT.

It is useful to produce a listing of the generated code. This can be done by a procedure like DUMPCODE (lines 104–115).

It may of interest to show the code generated for a simple program, which shows most features of the language. In producing this listing the source handler has been augmented to list the generated code addresses – this is useful for execution error reporting.

```
0 program TEST;
0 const
0   ZERO = 0;
0 var
0   VALUE, LARGEST, TOTAL;
0
0 begin
1   TOTAL := ZERO;
```

```
 4   read(VALUE);
 6   LARGEST := VALUE;
10   while VALUE <> ZERO do
15     begin
15       TOTAL := TOTAL + VALUE;
22       if VALUE > LARGEST then LARGEST := VALUE;
32       read(VALUE)
34     end;
35   write('TOTAL: ', TOTAL, ' LARGEST: ', LARGEST);
63 end.
```

<u>Symbol table</u>

	Identifier	Class	Address
1	TEST	PROGRAM	0
2	ZERO	CONSTANT	0
3	VALUE	VARIABLE	0
4	LARGEST	VARIABLE	1
5	TOTAL	VARIABLE	2

<u>Generated code</u>

```
 0 INT 3   reserve VALUE,LARGEST,TOTAL    32 LDA 0
 1 LDA 2                                  33 INN     read (VALUE)
 2 LDI 0   TOTAL := ZERO                  34 BRN 10
 3 STO                                    35 LDI 84  (these values are internal
 4 LDA 0                                  36 LDI 79  ASCII equivalents of the
 5 INN     read (VALUE)                   37 LDI 84  letters T O T A L : and
 6 LDA 1                                  38 LDI 65  "space" )
 7 LDA 0                                  39 LDI 76
 8 LDV                                    40 LDI 58
 9 STO     LARGEST := VALUE               41 LDI 32
10 LDA 0                                  42 LDI 7   (7 characters to print)
11 LDV                                    43 PRS     write ('TOTAL: '
12 LDI 0                                  44 LDA 2
13 NEQ                                    45 LDV
14 BZE 35  while VALUE <> ZERO do         46 PRN             TOTAL,
15 LDA 2                                  47 LDI 32
16 LDA 2                                  48 LDI 76
17 LDV                                    49 LDI 65
18 LDA 0                                  50 LDI 82
19 LDV                                    51 LDI 71
20 ADD                                    52 LDI 69
21 STO     TOTAL := TOTAL + VALUE         53 LDI 83
22 LDA 0                                  54 LDI 84
23 LDV                                    55 LDI 58
24 LDA 1                                  56 LDI 32
25 LDV                                    57 LDI 10  (10 characters to print)
26 GTR     if VALUE > LARGEST then        58 PRS         ' LARGEST: '
```

```
27 BZE 32                          59 LDA 1
28 LDA 1                           60 LDV
29 LDA 0                           61 PRN          LARGEST)
30 LDV                             62 NLN
31 STO    LARGEST := VALUE         63 HLT
```

Exercises

7.52 Complete Exercise 7.42 by generating code for the for loop for this machine. Would you have to introduce further opcodes to the machine set, or could you make do with what we have?

7.53 Complete Exercise 7.43 by generating code for the case statement. Make any additions or alterations needed to the machine code set, and to the interpreter of Chapter 2. What action should be taken when the case selector does not match any of the case labels?

7.54 Generate code for if ... then ... else and repeat ... until statements.

7.55 Complete Exercise 7.45 by generating code and altering the interpreter so as to be able to read and write character data.

7.56 Complete Exercise 7.51 by generating code for goto statements.

7.57 We have already commented that the sequence STACKADDRESS; DEREFERENCE occurs so often that it is worth trying to replace it with more optimal code. Investigate this in more detail. Is it also possible to optimize the code associated with assignment and reading operations?

7.58 Most of the codes emitted for our pseudo-machine have only an opcode field; comparatively few have an address field. Surely this calls for optimization in the size of the codefile produced? Investigate the possibility of reducing the number of bytes of code generated, and modifying the interpreter from Chapter 2 accordingly. Measure the effect of the improvement on a few simple programs.

7.59 At present we abort compilation if we try to generate too much code. Can you think of a better strategy, and implement it?

7.60 Suppose that we wished to use relative branch instructions, rather than absolute branch instructions. How would code generation be affected?

Listing 11   Stack machine code generator

```
1    procedure GEN (OP : OPCODES; ADDRESS : INTEGER);
2    (*Code generator for instruction with address field*)
3      begin
4        if NEXTCODE > CODEMAX then QUIT(2) (*program too long*);
5        if CODEISTOBEGENERATED then
6          begin
7            with PCODE[NEXTCODE] do begin F := OP; A := ADDRESS end;
8            NEXTCODE := NEXTCODE + 1
9          end
10     end (*GEN*);
11
12   procedure EMIT (OP : OPCODES);
13   (*Code generator with no address field*)
14     begin GEN(OP, 0) end;
15
16   procedure NEGATEINTEGER;
17     begin EMIT(NEG) end;
18
19   procedure BINARYINTEGEROP (OP : SYMBOLS);
20     begin
21       case OP of
22         TIMES : EMIT(MUL);
23         SLASH : EMIT(DVD);
24         PLUS  : EMIT(ADD);
25         MINUS : EMIT(SUB)
26       end
27     end (*BINARYINTEGEROP*);
28
29   procedure COMPARISON (OP : SYMBOLS);
30     begin
31       case OP of
32         EQLSYM : EMIT(EQL);
33         NEQSYM : EMIT(NEQ);
34         LSSSYM : EMIT(LSS);
35         LEQSYM : EMIT(LEQ);
36         GTRSYM : EMIT(GTR);
37         GEQSYM : EMIT(GEQ)
38       end
39     end (*COMPARISON*);
40
41   procedure INPUTOPERATION (OP : TRANSFERS);
42     begin
43       case OP of
44         NUMBERS        : EMIT(INN);
```

```
45          STRINGS, NEWLINE : (*not used*)
46        end
47      end (*INPUTOPERATION*);
48
49    procedure STACKSTRING;
50      var
51        I : INTEGER;
52      begin
53        for I := 1 to NUM do GEN(LDI, ORD(STRINGTEXT[I])); GEN(LDI, NUM)
54      end (*STACKSTRING*);
55
56    procedure OUTPUTOPERATION (OP : TRANSFERS);
57      begin
58        case OP of
59          STRINGS : begin STACKSTRING; EMIT(PRS) end;
60          NUMBERS : EMIT(PRN);
61          NEWLINE : EMIT(NLN)
62        end
63      end (*OUTPUTOPERATION*);
64
65    procedure STACKCONSTANT (NUM : INTEGER);
66      begin GEN(LDI, NUM) end;
67
68    procedure STACKADDRESS (OFFSET : INTEGER);
69      begin GEN(LDA, OFFSET) end;
70
71    procedure DEREFERENCE;
72      begin EMIT(LDV) end;
73
74    procedure ASSIGN;
75      begin EMIT(STO) end;
76
77    procedure OPENSTACKFRAME (SIZE : INTEGER);
78      begin GEN(INT, SIZE) end;
79
80    procedure JUMP (LAB : INTEGER);
81      begin GEN(BRN, LAB) end;
82
83    procedure JUMPONFALSE (LAB : INTEGER);
84      begin GEN(BZE, LAB) end;
85
86    procedure ENTERBLOCK (BLOCKCLASS : CLASSES);
87      begin (*not used here*) end;
88
89    procedure LEAVEBLOCK (BLOCKCLASS : CLASSES);
90      begin EMIT(HLT) end;
```

```
91
92    procedure CODEFORODD;
93      begin EMIT(OD) end;
94
95    procedure CODEFORDUMP;
96      begin EMIT(STK) end;
97
98    procedure STORELABEL (var LAB : INTEGER);
99      begin LAB := NEXTCODE end;
100
101   procedure BACKPATCH (LOCATION, ADDRESS : INTEGER);
102     begin PCODE[LOCATION].A := ADDRESS end;
103
104   procedure DUMPCODE;
105   (*List code for the program*)
106     var
107       I : INTEGER;
108     begin
109       (*open and REWRITE(CODEFILE) as appropriate*)
110       for I := 0 to NEXTCODE - 1 do with PCODE[I] do
111         if F in HASADDRESSFIELD
112           then WRITELN(CODEFILE, I:10, MNEMONIC[F]:4, ' ', A:1);
113           else WRITELN(CODEFILE, I:10, MNEMONIC[F]:4);
114       (*close CODEFILE if necessary*)
115     end (*DUMPCODE*)
```

7.7   Code generation for a more conventional machine

As the reader may have realized, what we have done in this chapter has been rather simple. The hypothetical stack machine is, in some ways, 'ideal' for our language (as witness the simplicity of the code generator in Listing 11), but may differ rather markedly from a real machine. Nevertheless, it has been widely used in the development of Pascal compilers.

It is rather awkward to describe code generation for a real machine in a general text. It inevitably becomes machine specific, and the principles may become obscured behind a lot of detail for an architecture with which the reader may be completely unfamiliar. To try to minimize these difficulties, while at the same time trying to illustrate some key issues, we shall consider just a few points, using features of a relatively simple processor, which are probably sufficiently similar to processors familiar to the reader not to cause confusion.

The Zilog Z80 processor which we shall use as a model is typical of several 8-bit microprocessors. It has a single 8-bit accumulator (denoted by A), several internal 8-bit registers (denoted by B, C, D, E, H and L), a 16-bit program counter (PC), two 16-bit index registers (IX and IY), a 16-bit stack pointer

(SP), an 8-bit data bus, and a 16-bit address bus to allow access to 64 Kbytes of memory. With the exception of the BRN opcode (and, perhaps, the HLT opcode), our hypothetical machine instructions do not map one-for-one onto Z80 opcodes. The disparity between the two processors, and the ways in which we might adapt our code-generating interface procedures to generate code for the Z80, are quite well illustrated by the very areas in which the difficulty might seem most acute – simple arithmetic. At first sight the Z80 would appear to be ill suited to supporting a high-level language at all, since operations on a single 8-bit accumulator only provide for handling numbers between -128 and $+127$, scarcely of much use in arithmetic calculations. 16-bit arithmetic is probably adequate for quite a number of operations, as it allows for numbers in the range -32768 to $+32767$. In the Z80 a limited number of operations are allowed on 16-bit register pairs. These are denoted BC, DE and HL, and are formed by simply concatenating the 8-bit registers mentioned earlier. For example, 16-bit constants may be loaded immediately into a register pair, pairs may be pushed and popped from the stack, and may be transferred directly to and from memory. In addition, the HL pair may be used as a 16-bit accumulator into which may be added and subtracted the other pairs, and may also be used to perform register-indirect addressing of bytes. On the Z80 the 16-bit operations stop short of multiplication, division, logical operations and even comparison against zero, all of which are found on more modern 16-bit processors. We do not propose to describe the instruction set in any detail; hopefully the reader will be able to follow the code fragments below from the Pascal-like commentary which accompanies them.

As an example, let us consider Z80 code for the simple assignment statement

```
I := 4 + J - K
```

where I, J and K are integers, each stored in two bytes. A fairly optimal translation of this, making use of the HL register pair as a 16-bit accumulator, but not using a stack in any way, might be as follows:

```
LD    HL,4        ; HL := 4
LD    DE,(J)      ; DE := S[J]
ADD   HL,DE       ; HL := HL + DE          (4 + J)
LD    DE,(K)      ; DE := S[K]
OR    A           ; just to clear Carry
SBC   HL,DE       ; HL := HL - DE - Carry  (4 + J - K)
LD    (I),HL      ; S[I] := HL
```

Familiarity with the Z80 will show that this amounts to some 18 bytes of code. The only point worth noting is that, unlike addition, there is no 'simple' 16-bit subtraction operation, only one which involves the carry bit, which consequently must be unset before SBC is executed.

By contrast, the same statement coded for our hypothetical machine would have produced 17 bytes of code

```
LDA   I        ; push address of I
LDI   4        ; push constant 4
LDA   J        ; push address of J
LDV            ; replace with value of J
ADD            ; 4 + J
LDA   K        ; push address of K
LDV            ; replace with value of K
SUB            ; 4 + J - K
STO            ; store on I
```

How do we begin to map the one form of code to the other? One approach might be to consider the effect of these opcodes, as defined in the interpreter in Chapter 2, and to arrange that code generating routines like STACKADDRESS, STACKCONSTANT, ASSIGN and so on generate code equivalent to that which would be obeyed by the interpreter. For convenience we quote the relevant equivalences again:

```
LDA address :  T := T + 1; S[T] := address      (*push an address*)
LDI value   :  T := T + 1; S[T] := value        (*push a constant*)
LDV         :  S[T] := S[S[T]]                   (*dereference*)
ADD         :  T := T - 1; S[T] := S[T] + S[T+1] (*addition*)
SUB         :  T := T - 1; S[T] := S[T] - S[T+1] (*subtraction*)
STO         :  S[S[T-1]] := S[T]; T := T - 2     (*store top-of-stack*)
```

It does not take much imagination to see that this will produce a great deal more code than we should like. For example, the equivalent code for an LDI opcode, obtained from a translation of the sequence above, and generated by STACKCONSTANT(NUM) might be

```
T := T + 1   :  LD    HL,(T)    ; HL := T
                INC   HL        ; HL := HL + 1
                INC   HL        ; HL := HL + 1
                LD    (T),HL    ; T := HL
S[T] := NUM  :  LD    DE,NUM    ; DE := NUM
                LD    (HL),E    ; store low order byte
                INC   HL        ; HL := HL + 1
                LD    (HL),D    ; store high order byte
```

which amounts to some 14 bytes. We should comment that HL must be incremented twice to allow for the fact that memory is addressed in bytes, not words, and that we have to store the two halves of the register pair DE in two operations, 'bumping' the HL pair (used for register indirect addressing) between these.

If the machine for which we are generating code does not have some sort of hardware stack we might be forced or tempted into taking this approach, but fortunately most modern processors do incorporate a stack. Although the Z80 does not support operations like ADD and SUB on elements of its stack, the pushing implicit in LDI and LDA is easily handled, and the popping and pushing implied by

ADD and SUB are nearly as simple. Consequently, it would be quite simple to write code-generating routines which, for the same assignment statement as before, would have the effects shown below.

```
LDA  I   :   LD   HL,I     ;    HL := address of I
             PUSH HL       ; push address of I
LDI  4   :   LD   DE,4     ;    DE := 4
             PUSH DE       ; push value of 4
LDA  J   :   LD   HL,J     ;    HL := address of J
             PUSH HL       ; push address of J                    *
LDV      :   POP  HL       ;    HL := address of variable         *
             LD   E,(HL)   ;    E := S[HL]  low order byte
             INC  HL       ;    HL := HL + 1
             LD   D,(HL)   ;    D := S[HL]  high order byte
             PUSH DE       ; replace with value of J              *
ADD      :   POP  DE       ;    DE := second operand              *
             POP  HL       ;    HL := first operand
             ADD  HL,DE    ;    HL := HL + DE
             PUSH HL       ; 4 + J
LDA  K   :   LD   HL,K     ;    HL := address of K
             PUSH HL       ; push address of K                    *
LDV      :   POP  HL       ;    HL := address of variable         *
             LD   E,(HL)   ;    E := low order byte
             INC  HL       ;    HL := HL + 1
             LD   D,(HL)   ;    D := high order byte
             PUSH DE       ; replace with value of K              *
SUB      :   POP  DE       ;    DE := second operand              *
             POP  HL       ;    HL := first operand
             OR   A        ;    unset carry
             SBC  HL,DE    ;    HL := HL - DE - carry
             PUSH HL       ; 4 + J - K                           **
STO      :   POP  DE       ;    DE := value to be stored         **
             POP  HL       ;    HL := address to be stored at
             LD   (HL),E   ;    S[HL] := E  store low order byte
             INC  HL       ;    HL := HL + 1
             LD   (HL),D   ;    S[HL] := D  store high order byte
                           ; store on I
```

We shall not present the code generator routines in detail, but their intent should be fairly clear – the code generated by each follows distinct patterns, with obvious differences being handled by the parameters which have already been introduced. For example, procedure STACKCONSTANT would be on the lines of

```
procedure STACKCONSTANT (NUM : INTEGER);
  begin
    generate code for LD DE,NUM; generate code for PUSH DE
  end (*STACKCONSTANT*);
```

For the example under discussion we have generated 41 bytes, which is still quite a long way from the optimal 18 given before. However, little effort would be required to reduce this to 32 bytes; it is easy to see that 8 bytes could simply be removed (the ones marked with a single asterisk), since the operations of pushing a register pair at the end of one code-generating sequence and of popping the same pair at the start of the next are clearly redundant. Another byte could be removed by replacing the two marked with a double asterisk by a 1-byte opcode for exchanging the DE and HL pairs (the Z80 code EX DE,HL does this). These are examples of so-called 'peephole' optimization, and are quite easily included into the code-generating procedures we are contemplating. For example, the algorithm for ASSIGN could be

```
procedure ASSIGN;
(*generate code to store top-of-stack on address stored next-to-top*)
  begin
    if last code generated was PUSH HL
      then replace this PUSH HL with EX DE,HL
      else if last code generated was PUSH DE
              then delete PUSH DE
              else generate code for POP DE
    generate code for POP HL; generate code for LD (HL),E
    generate code for INC HL; generate code for LD (HL),D
  end (*ASSIGN*);
```

(The reader might like to reflect on the kinds of assignment statements that would give rise to the three possible paths through this procedure.)

Further possibilities exist for optimization. We have already commented that the sequence STACKADDRESS; DEREFERENCE occurs frequently, and a look at the code currently produced by this reveals that it is rather clumsy. The effect of LDA J ; LDV is far more directly achieved with Z80 code of the form

```
LD    HL,(J)     or     LD    DE,(J)
PUSH  HL                PUSH  DE
```

where the second form might seem to be preferable in view of the kind of sequences we seem to be generating (although in passing we might comment that this form would not be acceptable to the Intel 8080 processor, which is fairly similar to the Z80; furthermore, occasions arise where the use of HL would be preferable in any case). This optimization – derived from the form of the intermediate rather than the object code – might be effected by a DEREFERENCE procedure on the lines of

```
procedure DEREFERENCE;
  begin
    if last p-code handled was LDA J
      then
        delete both LD HL,J and PUSH HL
        generate code for LD DE,(J); generate code for PUSH DE
```

```
            else
              if last code generated was PUSH HL
                then delete PUSH HL
                else generate code for POP HL
              generate code for LD E,(HL); generate code for INC  HL
              generate code for LD D,(HL); generate code for PUSH DE
          end (*DEREFERENCE*);
```

This is a rather interesting case. A study of the code generation interface in Listing 10 will reveal that DEREFERENCE is called only from within FACTOR (line 102). Hence the optimization would seem to be better handled *ab initio* rather than *post facto*, by calling a special code-generating interface procedure as suggested in Exercise 7.57. The reader might wonder at the need for DEREFERENCE, or of the wisdom of introducing it. However, as we shall see in later chapters, access to some variables (for example, array elements) requires arithmetic to be performed on addresses before dereferencing can take place. The analyser can detect these cases and try to optimize accordingly, but we leave the point as one for the keen reader to consider. With the sorts of code-generation procedures we now have in mind we should be able to see that it would not be hard to generate rather more optimal code than before, on the lines of

```
LDA I     :   LD    HL,I      ;    HL := address of I
              PUSH  HL        ; push address of I
LDI 4     :   LD    DE,4      ;    DE := 4
              PUSH  DE        ; push value of 4
LDA J, LDV :  LD    DE,(J)    ;    DE := S[J]
              PUSH  DE        ; push value of J                    *
ADD       :   POP   DE        ;    DE := second operand            *
              POP   HL        ;    HL := first operand
              ADD   HL,DE     ;    HL := HL + DE
              PUSH  HL        ; 4 + J
LDA K, LDV :  LD    DE,(K)    ;    DE := S[K]
              PUSH  DE        ; push value of K                    *
SUB       :   POP   DE        ;    DE := second operand            *
              POP   HL        ;    HL := first operand
              OR    A         ;    unset carry
              SBC   HL,DE     ;    HL := HL - DE - carry
              PUSH  HL        ; 4 + J - K                         **
STO       :   POP   DE        ;    DE := value to be stored       **
              POP   HL        ;    HL := address to be stored at
              LD    (HL),E    ;    S[HL] := E  store low order byte
              INC   HL        ;    HL := HL + 1
              LD    (HL),D    ;    S[HL] := D  store high order byte
                              ; store on I
```

where, again, the operations marked with asterisks show room for obvious peephole optimization.

To do even better than this, we might reflect on the fact that, in translating the assignment statement, the interface procedures have seen fit to arrange for the target address to be stacked before the expression is evaluated. It is a relatively easy matter to arrange to generate hypothetical code of the form

```
LDI   4          ; push constant 4
LDA   J;  LDV    ; push value of J
ADD              ; 4 + J
LDA   K;  LDV    ; push value of K
SUB              ; 4 + J - K
STD   I          ; store directly on I
```

where STD is a new hypothetical code which could be interpreted as

STD address :   S[address] := S[T]; T := T - 1 (*store top-of-stack at address*)

and which could be handled by a code generation procedure of the form

```
procedure ASSIGNDIRECT (OFFSET : INTEGER);
  begin
    if last code generated was PUSH DE
      then replace this PUSH DE with EX DE,HL
      else if last code generated was PUSH HL
             then delete PUSH HL
             else generate code for POP HL
    generate code for LD (OFFSET),HL
  end (*ASSIGNDIRECT*);
```

With the peephole optimizations suggested earlier, code for the assignment statement would now come down to 22 bytes (we should, however, comment that if address arithmetic has to be done to yield the target address we shall not be able to do as well as this):

```
LDI 4      :   LD    DE,4      ;     DE := 4
               PUSH  DE        ; push value of 4
LDA J, LDV :   LD    DE,(J)    ;     DE := S[J]
ADD        :   POP   HL        ;     HL := first operand
               ADD   HL,DE     ;     HL := HL + DE
               PUSH  HL        ; 4 + J                        *
LDA K, LDV :   LD    DE,(K)    ;     DE := S[K]
SUB        :   POP   HL        ;     HL := first operand      *
               OR    A         ;     unset carry
               SBC   HL,DE     ; 4 + J - K
STD I      :   LD    (I),HL    ;     S[I] := HL
```

The astute reader will now be able to see that the codes marked with asterisks are redundant – although the PUSH and POP operations do not follow one another directly, nothing is done between the PUSH and the corresponding POP which disturbs the HL register pair. Rather more subtly, perhaps, had we chosen in this case to generate code for the LDI instruction of the form

```
LDI  4   :   LD   HL,4    ;   HL := 4
             PUSH HL       ; push value of 4
```

using the HL rather than the DE pair, we would be able to eliminate another PUSH and POP pair. We have so far been content to let the code generation use fixed register pairs. Given an architecture that supports multiple registers, a more sophisticated compiler could be programmed to generate code using the 'best' registers in each case, and will try to predict at compile time when their contents will need to be saved at run-time, or will be left undisturbed. For examples of the sort we have been considering it is quite easy to see that the first factor in an expression should be directed towards the HL pair, and remaining factors towards the DE pair, but in general the details of register selection are probably well beyond the scope of the present text.

By now, hopefully, it will have dawned on the reader that generation of native code is probably strongly influenced by the desire to make this compact and efficient, and that achieving this objective will require the compiler writer to be highly conversant with details of the target machine, and with the possibilities afforded by its instruction set. For best results we shall also have to consider tuning the analyser to the generator rather more finely than by simply choosing an arbitrary intermediate code, as we seem to have done. As another example of where this tuning would be needed, we can remark on the fact that on our hypothetical machine we postulated a stack which grew upwards in memory. On the Z80 and, indeed, on most microprocessors, the hardware stack grows downwards in memory. The effect of this might be to assign variable storage with decreasing OFFSET values, rather than increasing ones – a rather trivial modification to the parser so far developed, but one motivated by specific machine architecture rather than by the machine independence which we claimed to be a desirable property of parsing algorithms.

The examples we have used as illustrations have conveniently avoided one of the most awkward features of code generation – a really bad mismatch between what is required and what can be provided by very short object code sequences. For example, the operations the Z80 can perform on 16-bit data are very limited. It cannot even test a 16-bit quantity for zero directly, and tests for relative ordering are still more awkward. The closely related Intel 8080 cannot even perform 16-bit subtraction with a single opcode. To illustrate the effects of this it will suffice to consider how we might handle the EQL pseudocode. This is defined to have the effect:

```
EQL :  T := T - 1; if S[T] <> S[T+1] then S[T] := 0 else S[T] := 1
```

A translation suitable for either the Z80 or the 8080 processor might be

```
POP  DE     ; DE := second operand
POP  HL     ; HL := first operand
LD   A,L    ; A := low order byte
SUB  E      ; A := L - E
LD   L,A    ; store low order difference on L
```

```
        LD    A,H        ; A := high order byte
        SBC   A,D        ; A := H - D - carry
        OR    L          ; OR with low order byte
        LD    HL,0       ; HL := 0 (does not affect condition codes)
        JP    NZ,EXIT    ; if S[T] <> S[T+1] then prepare to push 0
        INC   HL         ;                    else prepare to push 1
EXIT:   PUSH  HL         ; push result
```

This amounts to some 16 bytes of code; what we have effectively done is to subtract DE from HL, followed by a logical OR of the two bytes of the result in the accumulator – if this yields zero it means that DE and HL were equal. Other relational operations like NEQ, LSS, LEQ, GTR and GEQ could be handled by variations on the same theme, albeit somewhat more complicated.

The code required for other operations can become dramatically longer. For example, 16-bit multiplication generates something of the order of 20 bytes of code, and 16-bit division of the order of 120 bytes. Code for operations involving conversion between internal and external representation of numbers (like that implied by INN and PRN) might run to the order of 100 bytes as well – and this assuming that reading or writing a single byte of data was a totally trivial operation. In practice it would not be, but would have to subscribe to conventions imposed by the operating system under which the program was to be executed. For this reason, one approach to code generation is to demand that a so-called **run-time package** (of commonly used but tedious routines) is always loaded into memory along with the user's code, which itself can be dramatically shortened by merely making appropriate subroutine calls. Of course, the run-time package may become rather large (even user programs that do nothing but halt may find themselves loading several thousand bytes of uncalled code), but this approach is typical of that taken by several commercial microcomputer compilers.

For example, rather than include the 16 bytes of code above every time an EQL is to be handled, we could introduce a 3-byte subroutine call JSR EQL, with the subroutine defined in the run-time package as the 26 bytes below:

```
EQL:    POP   HL          ; pop return address
        LD    (RADR),HL   ; save it
        POP   DE          ; DE := second operand
        POP   HL          ; HL := first operand
        LD    A,L         ; A := low order byte
        SUB   E           ; A := L - E
        LD    L,A         ; store low order difference on L
        LD    A,H         ; A := high order byte
        SBC   A,D         ; A := H - D - carry
        OR    L           ; OR with low order byte
        LD    HL,0        ; HL := 0 (does not affect condition codes)
        JP    NZ,EXIT     ; if S[T] <> S[T+1] then prepare to push 0
        INC   HL          ;                    else prepare to push 1
EXIT:   PUSH  HL          ; push result
```

```
        LD    HL,(RADR)
        JP    (HL)       ; return
RADR:   DS    2          ; reserve 2 bytes for saving return address
```

If there are n instances of the intermediate code to be handled, the direct expansion will generate $22n$ bytes of code, while the subroutine approach will generate $26 + 3n$ bytes. Obviously the saving in space becomes significant even with only a few instances of EQU. However, this must be offset against a marked deterioration in execution speed. Execution of the significant 22 bytes takes 75 or 81 clock cycles (depending on the outcome of the test) while execution of the subroutine code takes a further 63 clock cycles – almost as long again. In more complex situations – for example those where the significant code runs to hundreds, rather than tens of bytes – the overhead might well become almost insignificant, but, clearly, the decision of which approach to adopt will depend crucially on many machine-dependent factors, and cannot be undertaken without considerable familiarity with the target machine.

In passing, we might add that the run-time package approach might even be adopted for seemingly simple code like addition and subtraction, if one wished to monitor conditions of overflow and underflow.

We should also mention another approach often taken in providing native code compilers, especially on small machines. This is to generate intermediate code as we have done, write this to an intermediate file, and then process this in a second pass using a macro-assembler (alternatively, with a bit more work on the code-generator routines, one can produce standard assembly code rather than intermediate code). This approach has some strong points. It relieves the compiler writer of developing intensely machine-dependent bit-manipulating code (very tiresome in Pascal), handling awkward forward-referencing problems, dealing with operating system and linkage conventions, and so forth. Of course the second pass carries with it a rather serious overhead in terms of speed and inconvenience, but for development work this could be minimized by providing an interpreter to allow testing of the intermediate code form.

It is an almost trivial matter to modify the code generator to produce code that might be handled by a macro-assembler. We need only to be able to generate alphanumeric labels, and to insert these into the address fields of branch instructions, and into the label fields of the destinations for those branches. This can be done by extending the definition of INSTRUCTIONS to record which pseudo-instructions have to be labelled

```
type  INSTRUCTIONS = packed record
                LAB : BOOLEAN (*true if destination of branch*);
                F: OPCODES (*function code*);
                A: INTEGER (*address*)
            end (*INSTRUCTIONS*);
```

and introducing a further global variable LABELLED of Boolean type. This is initially set FALSE, but may temporarily be set TRUE by the STORELABEL and BACKPATCH code-generator interface routines.

```
procedure GEN (OP : OPCODES; ADDRESS : INTEGER);
(*Code generator for instruction with address field*)
  begin
    if NEXTCODE > CODEMAX then QUIT(2) (*program too long*);
    if CODEISTOBEGENERATED then
      begin
        with PCODE[NEXTCODE] do
          begin LAB := LABELLED; F := OP; A := ADDRESS end;
        NEXTCODE := NEXTCODE + 1; LABELLED := FALSE
      end
  end (*GEN*);

procedure STORELABEL (var LAB : INTEGER);
  begin LABELLED := TRUE; LAB := NEXTCODE end;

procedure BACKPATCH (LOCATION, ADDRESS : INTEGER);
  begin LABELLED := TRUE; PCODE[LOCATION].A := ADDRESS end;
```

Production of the assembler code is then easily handled by changes to DUMPCODE. The names given to the labels themselves are easily devised from the pseudo-machine addresses, as can be seen below.

```
procedure DUMPCODE;
(*List generated code for interest, debugging, or separate interpretation*)
  var
    I : INTEGER;
  begin
    (*open and REWRITE(CODEFILE) as appropriate*)
    for I := 0 to NEXTCODE - 1 do with PCODE[I] do
      begin
        if LAB
          then WRITE(CODEFILE, 'L', I + 1000:4) else WRITE(CODEFILE, ' ':5);
        if F in [BRN, BZE]
          then WRITELN(CODEFILE, MNEMONIC[F]:4, ' L', A + 1000:1)
          else
            if F in HASADDRESSFIELD
              then WRITELN(CODEFILE, MNEMONIC[F]:4, ' ', A:1)
              else WRITELN(CODEFILE, MNEMONIC[F]:4)
      end;
    (*close CODEFILE if necessary*)
  end (*DUMPCODE*);
```

Exercises

7.61 Inspection of the macro-assembler code generation routines suggested here will show that more labels are generated than are actually used. While this is not really serious, it could cause problems in large programs if the assembler's symbol table was limited. Can you find ways of generating only those labels that are really necessary?

7.62 How would you produce macro-assembler code for a source program that was too long all to be contained in the PCODE array? The main reason for containing it all in PCODE is surely to allow easy backpatching, but if this can be left to a subsequent assembler to handle, the need for PCODE diminishes somewhat. You might like to study the approach taken in the Pascal-P compiler (Pemberton and Daniels (1982) Chapter 4).

7.63 Investigate more fully the nuances of register allocation and optimization for evaluating CLANG expressions on Z80 and 8080 processors.

7.64 The worst example of mismatch between our hypothetical machine and a real microprocessor might be found in the way in which we treat the output of strings, by pushing them character by character onto the stack, merely to pop them character by character almost immediately. Suggest how this could be improved.

7.65 Try to implement a complete native code generator and run-time support package for CLANG as so far developed on one of the systems available for your use.

Further reading

As mentioned earlier, code generation tends to become highly machine dependent, and the literature reflects this. Although all of the standard texts cited earlier have a lot to say on the subject, those texts that do not confine themselves to generalities (and thus stop short of showing how it is actually done) inevitably relate their material to one or other real machine, which can become confusing for a beginner who has little if any experience of that machine. Discussion of code generation for Pascal on various machines can be found in Barron (1981). (In particular, Chapter 7 by Ammann gives a detailed description of the Zurich implementation for CDC machines.) Descriptions of code generation for a subset of Pascal on ICL 1900 machines can be found in Welsh and McKeag's book (1980); code generation for this series is also briefly discussed in the book by Hunter (1981). Readers who wish to experiment with writing code generators for CLANG for various microcomputers might find the descriptions of architecture in the book by Wakerly (1981) of interest, especially as much of his description is given in terms of interpreters such as we have discussed. Code generation for a CLANG compiler for the Intel 8080 microprocessor has been undertaken by Peter Clayton at the author's university, and his work can be made available on request; parts of it were used in the preparation of this section and his assistance is gratefully acknowledged. Collections of routines for handling operations such as multiplication and division and conversion between string and numeric representations of numbers on processors where this is awkward can be found in several good books on assembler programming; for example, Leventhal and Saville (1982, 1983a, b).

Chapter 8 **Block structure and storage management**

Our simple language has so far not provided for the procedure concept in any way; it is the aim of this chapter to show how the language and its compiler can be extended to allow procedures and functions to be added in the block-structured Pascal sense, including the use of local variables, local procedures and recursion. This involves a much deeper treatment of the concepts of storage allocation and management than we have seen previously; as a side issue we shall also see how this affects support for the fixed length *array*, which is present in almost all high-level languages.

8.1 Simple procedures

As in the previous chapter, we shall develop our arguments by a process of slow refinement. Initially we confine discussion to parameterless procedures, and discuss parameters and the closely related function concept later. We shall not give a complete compiler listing here, but save that until the discussions of the next chapters.

8.1.1 Syntax and semantics

Introduction of procedure declarations to our language is similar to the way it is done in Pascal, and may be described by an extension of the syntax diagram for BLOCK, as shown in Figure 8.1a.

The declaration of a procedure is most easily understood as a process whereby a compound statement is given a name. Quoting this name at later places in the program then implies execution of that compound statement; by analogy with Pascal we simply extend the language in Figure 8.1b, with the rest as before.

It might be thought that the same effect could be achieved with Figure 8.2, but the syntax in Figure 8.1 allows for nested procedures, and for named constants and variables to be declared local to procedures, in a manner familiar to all Pascal programmers.

Allowing nested procedures and local variables introduces the concept of **scope**, which is presumably familiar to readers used to block-structured languages, although it seems to cause tremendous problems to many beginners. In Algol-like languages, the 'accessibility' of an identifier *declared* in a block is limited to that block and to blocks themselves declared local to that block, with the exception that when an identifier is 'redeclared' in two or more

BLOCK

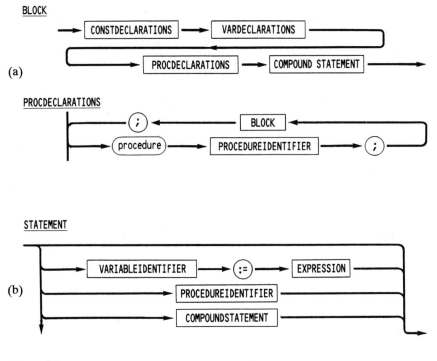

(a)

(b)

Figure 8.1

nested blocks, the innermost accessible declaration applies to each particular use of that identifier.

Perhaps the confusion that arises in beginners' minds is exacerbated by the fact that the fine distinction between compile-time and run-time aspects of scope is not always made clear. At compile-time, only those names that are currently 'in scope' may be used in statements and expressions. At run-time, the only variables that 'exist' (that is, have storage allocated to them) are those that were declared local to the blocks which are actively executing at that instant. One consequence of this, which many readers may have fallen foul of at some stage, is that variables declared local to a procedure cannot be

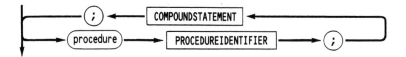

Figure 8.2

expected to retain their values between calls on the procedure. (In Pascal, as we have already had chance to remark when discussing our compiler, this means that many variables are declared 'globally' when they should, ideally, be 'out of scope' to many of the procedures in the program. We shall return to this theme in a later chapter.)

Another source of confusion arises from the fact that in implementations of languages like FORTRAN and BASIC the scope rules are very different – typically in FORTRAN all variables, whether explicitly or implicitly declared, exist for the entire duration of the program (but not always – FORTRAN 66 has peculiar rules stating under what conditions a variable might become 'undefined').

8.1.2 Lexical analysis

As with many of the extensions to be discussed in this chapter, the changes to the lexical analyser so as to handle procedures are trivial, and need not be detailed in full. All we have to do is to extend the list of reserved words, by making changes to KEYWORDS, WORD and WSYM and to INITIALIZE. Although we might add another value to type SYMBOLS, this is not really necessary. PROCSYM will do duty for both procedures and the main program; in a very real sense a program block is just a procedure block, which we can regard as being called by the operating system when the program is executed.

8.1.3 Syntactic and semantic analysis

The extensions needed to BLOCK are easy enough, as the basic changes (devoid of error recovery and code generation) reveal.

```
procedure PROCDECLARATION;
  begin
    GETSYM;
    ACCEPT(IDENT); ACCEPT(SEMICOLON); BLOCK; ACCEPT(SEMICOLON)
  end (*PROCDECLARATION*);
begin (*BLOCK*)
  if SYM = CONSTSYM then CONSTDECLARATION;
  if SYM = VARSYM then VARDECLARATION;
  while SYM = PROCSYM do PROCDECLARATION;
  COMPOUNDSTATEMENT
end (*BLOCK*);
```

The changes needed in STATEMENT are more interesting. We seem to have run into difficulty, for now we have two alternatives for STATEMENT (namely assignment statements and procedure calls) which begin with lexically indistinguishable symbols. There are various ways of avoiding the problem.

(a)   An obvious way would require the reserved word call before a procedure identifier, as in FORTRAN, but this rather detracts from readability of the source program (unless one is thoroughly enamoured of FORTRAN).

(b) A purely syntactic solution is possible if we refactor the grammar slightly as follows

<statement> ::= <assignment or procedure call> | <otherstatements>
<assignment or procedure call> ::= <identifier> <rest of statement>
<rest of statement> ::= := <expression> | ε

that is, a procedure call can be distinguished from an assignment by simply looking at the first symbol after the <identifier>.

(c) Probably because the semantics of procedure calls and of assignments are so different, the solution usually adopted is the semantic one. To the list of allowed CLASSES of identifier we add one for distinguishing procedure names from others; when the symbol starting STATEMENT is an identifier we can determine from its symbol table attributes whether an assignment or procedure call is to be parsed (assuming all identifiers to have been declared before use, as we have been doing).

The scope rules are quite easily handled as follows. To cater for accessibility aspects we treat the symbol table as a stack, adding to this each time an identifier is declared, but cutting it back whenever we complete parsing a block, thereby discarding the names declared local to that block. The stack structure also ensures that if two identifiers with the same names are declared in nested blocks the first to be found when searching the table will be the most recently declared. To handle the addressing aspects needed for code genera- tion, we shall need to associate with each identifier in our symbol table the 'level' at which it was declared. The outermost program block we can take as level 1 (some authors take it as level 0, others reserve this level for 'standard' identifiers – like MAXINT, READ, READLN, TRUE and FALSE in Pascal).

Our symbol table can be represented by

```
const
  LEVMAX = 5;
type
  LEVELS = 0 .. LEVMAX;
var
  TABLE : array [TABLEINDEX] of record
                          NAME    : ALFA;
                          CLASS   : CLASSES;
                          LEVEL   : LEVELS;
                          ADDRESS : INTEGER
                        end (*TABLE*);
```

and the procedure for adding to this table is simply

```
procedure ENTER (C : CLASSES);
(*Enter object of class C into symbol table*)
  begin
```

```
    if LASTENTRY = TABLEMAX then QUIT(4) (*symbol table overflow*);
    LASTENTRY := LASTENTRY + 1;
    with TABLE[LASTENTRY] do
       begin NAME := ID; CLASS := C; LEVEL := BLOCKLEVEL end
  end (*ENTER*);
```

where BLOCKLEVEL is the level of declaration. This level is conveniently passed by value as a parameter on calls to BLOCK, as is the initial value of LASTENTRY, the symbol table index for a block (the 'value' passing mechanism handles cutting back the symbol table stack very effectively).

Accordingly we declare our BLOCK parser as

```
procedure BLOCK (FOLLOWERS  : SYMSET     (*for error recovery*);
                 BLOCKLEVEL : LEVELS     (*level of static nesting*);
                 LASTENTRY  : TABLEINDEX (*index into symbol table*);
                 BLOCKCLASS : CLASSES    (*program or procedure*) );
```

and initiate parsing of the program by a call

```
BLOCK([PERIOD] + FIRSTBLOCK + FIRSTSTATEMENT, 1, 1, PROG);
```

Subsequent calls on BLOCK are made from within PROCDECLARATION which, when error recovery is added, takes the form

```
procedure PROCDECLARATION;
(*Handle declaration of parameterless procedures*)
  begin
    GETSYM;
    if SYM <> IDENT then ERROR(6) else begin ENTER(PROC); GETSYM end;
    ACCEPT(SEMICOLON, 2);
    if BLOCKLEVEL = LEVMAX then QUIT(1) (*too deeply nested*);
    BLOCK([SEMICOLON] + FOLLOWERS, BLOCKLEVEL + 1 , LASTENTRY, PROC);
    ACCEPT([SEMICOLON], 2)
  end (*PROCDECLARATION*);
```

Note that this ensures that the variables declared local to a block will be declared at a higher level than the block identifier itself.

8.1.4   Insecurities in scope rules

Although what we have done seems sensible enough, the reader should be aware that the scope rules in Pascal have come in for extensive criticism, as they were, in fact, incompletely formulated, and led to insecurities, especially when handled by one-pass systems. Most of the examples cited in the literature have to do with the problems associated with types, but we can give an example more in keeping with our own language to illustrate a typical difficulty. Suppose a compiler is presented with the following program:

```
program STUPID;
  procedure ONE (*first declared here*);
```

```
      begin
        . . .
      end (*ONE*);
   procedure TWO;
      procedure THREE;
        begin
          ONE
        end (*THREE*);
      procedure ONE (*then redeclared here*);
        begin
          . . .
        end (*ONE*);
      begin
        THREE; ONE
      end (*TWO*);
   begin
     TWO
   end (*STUPID*).
```

At the instant where procedure THREE is being parsed, and where the call to ONE is encountered, the first procedure ONE (in the symbol table at level 1) seems to be in scope, and code will be generated for a call to this. However, perhaps the second procedure ONE should be the one in scope for procedure THREE; one interpretation of the scope rules would require code to be generated for a call to this. In a one-pass system this would be a little tricky, as this second procedure ONE would not yet have been encountered by the compiler – but note that it would have been by the time the calls to THREE and ONE are made from procedure TWO.

This problem can be resolved to the satisfaction of a compiler writer if the scope rules are formulated so that the scope of an identifier extends from the point of its declaration to the end of the block in which it is declared, and not over the whole block in which it is declared. This makes for easy one-pass compilation, but it is doubtful whether this solution will please a programmer who writes code such as the above, and falls foul of the rules without the compiler reporting the fact.

8.1.5 Storage management and variable addressing

If we wish procedures to be able to call one another recursively, we shall have to think carefully about code generation and storage management. At run-time there may be several 'instances' of a procedure in existence, for each of which the 'instances' of the local variables must be distinct. This has a rather complicating effect at compile-time, for the compiler can no longer assign a simple address to each variable as it is declared (except, perhaps, for the variables in the program block). Other aspects of code generation are not quite such a problem – we must simply be on our guard always to generate so-called **re-entrant code**, which executes without ever modifying itself (code will, of course, inevitably modify 'data').

Just as the stack concept turns out to be useful for dealing with the compile-time accessibility aspects of scope in block-structured languages, so too does a stack structure provide a solution for dealing with the run-time aspects of existence. Every time a procedure is called, it needs to acquire a region of free store for its local variables, an area which can be later be freed again when control returns to the caller.

On a stack machine this is almost trivially easy, although it may be more obtuse on other architectures. Since procedure activations strictly obey a first-in-last-out scheme the areas needed for their local working store can be carved out of a single large stack. Such areas are usually called **activation records** or **stack frames**. In each of them is usually stored some standard information (such as the return address in the calling procedure, and information about how large the frame is, so that it can later be discarded – this section of the frame is often called the **mark stack**), as well as the values of local variables (and, possibly, parameters, as we shall see in a later section). A stack frame does not itself contain any code.

This may be made clearer by a simple example. Suppose we come up with the following variation for satisfying the irresistible urge to read a list and write it down backwards.

```
program BACKWARDS;
  var TERMINATOR;
  procedure START;
    var LOCAL1, LOCAL2;
    procedure REVERSE;
      var NUMBER;
      begin
        read(NUMBER);
        if TERMINATOR <> NUMBER then REVERSE;
        10: write(NUMBER)
      end;
    begin (*START*)
    REVERSE;
    20:
    end;
  begin (*BACKWARDS*)
  TERMINATOR := 9;
  START;
  30:
  end (*BACKWARDS*).
```

(Our language does not allow (*comments*) and labels; these have just been added to make the descriptions easier.)

A stack is the obvious structure to use in a non-recursive solution to the problem as well, so the example also highlights the connection between the implementation of recursion in 'non-recursive' languages and the use of stacks.

If the program were to be given exciting data like 56 65 5 9, then its dynamic execution would result in a stack frame history something like the following, where each line represents the relative layout of the stack frames as the procedures are entered and left.

	Stack grows	----→				
start main program	BACKWARDS					
call START	BACKWARDS	START				
call REVERSE	BACKWARDS	START	REVERSE			
read 56 and recurse	BACKWARDS	START	REVERSE	REVERSE		
read 65 and recurse	BACKWARDS	START	REVERSE	REVERSE	REVERSE	
read 5 and recurse	BACKWARDS	START	REVERSE	REVERSE	REVERSE	REVERSE
read 9, write 9, return	BACKWARDS	START	REVERSE	REVERSE	REVERSE	
write 5 and return	BACKWARDS	START	REVERSE	REVERSE		
write 65 and return	BACKWARDS	START	REVERSE			
write 56 and return	BACKWARDS	START				
return from START	BACKWARDS					
leave main program						

At **run-time** the actual address of a variable somewhere in memory will have to be found by adding an offset (which, fortunately, can be determined at **compile-time**) to the base address of the appropriate stack frame (which, naturally but unfortunately, cannot be predicted at compile-time). The code generated at compile-time must contain enough information for the run-time system to be able to find (or calculate) the base address of the appropriate stack frame as it then exists. This calls for considerable thought.

The run-time stack frames are conveniently maintained as a linked list. As a procedure is called, it can set up (in its mark stack area) a pointer to the base of the stack frame of the calling procedure. This pointer is usually called the **dynamic link**. The pointer to the start of this linked structure – that is, to the base of the most recently activated stack frame – is usually given special status, and is called the **base register** B. On procedure entry B is set to point to the next available location on the stack; on procedure exit it is reset by simply looking at the dynamic link emanating from the most recently activated frame.

If a variable is local to the procedure currently being executed, its run-time address is given by B + OFFSET, where OFFSET can be allocated at compile-time. The run-time addresses of non-local variables must be obtained by adding OFFSET to an address found by descending a chain of stack frame links. The problem is to know how far to traverse this chain, and at first seems easily solved. If at declaration time we associate a 'level' with each entry in the symbol table, as we have already arranged to do, then, when faced with the need to generate code to address an identifier, we can surely produce code (at compile-time) which uses this information to determine (at run-time) how far down the chain to go. This distance at first appears to be easily predictable – nothing other than the difference in levels between the level we have reached in compilation and the level at which the identifier (to which we want to refer) was declared.

This is nearly true, but in fact we cannot simply traverse the dynamic link chain by that number of steps. This chain, as its name suggests, describes the *dynamic* way in which procedures are called, while the level information in the symbol table is related to the *static* depth of nesting of procedures as they are declared. Consider the case when we have just read the second data number 65. At that stage the stack memory would appear as shown in Figure 8.3. The compiler would know (at compile-time) that TERMINATOR was declared at static level 1, and would have allocated it an offset address of 2. Similarly, when parsing the reference to TERMINATOR within REVERSE, it would know that it was currently compiling at a static level 3 – a level difference of 2. However, generation of code for descending two steps along the dynamic link chain would result (at run-time) in an access to the variable LOCAL1 in START, rather than to TERMINATOR (local to the main program).

8.1.6   The static link solution

One way of handling the problem raised above is to provide a second chain for linking data segments, one which must be maintained at run-time using only the information which could be embedded in the code generated at compile-time. This chain is called the **static link** chain, and is handled as follows.

When a procedure is entered at run-time, it stores in the first three elements of its activation record

(a)   the start of a chain which will link the bases of the stack frames for the most recent active instance of each procedure (forming the static link);

(b)   the base address of the stack frame of the calling routine (forming the dynamic link);

Address	Purpose	Contents	
0	DYNAMIC LINK	0	stack frame for main program (level 1)
1	RETURN ADDRESS	0	
2	TERMINATOR	9	
3	DYNAMIC LINK	0	stack frame for START (level 2)
4	RETURN ADDRESS	"30"	
5	LOCAL1	?	
6	LOCAL2	?	
7	DYNAMIC LINK	3	stack frame for REVERSE (level 3)
8	RETURN ADDRESS	"20"	
9	NUMBER	56	
10	DYNAMIC LINK	7	← B stack frame for REVERSE (level 3)
11	RETURN ADDRESS	"10"	
12	NUMBER	65	← T

Figure 8.3

(c)   the return address in the calling routine.

For accessing variables, the compiler embeds (into the generated code) address information as pairs of numbers indicating (a) the level difference between the static level from which the variable is being accessed and the static level where it was declared, and (b) the offset displacement to be added to the base of the run-time stack frame. At run-time the level difference information is used to chain down the static link chain for variable accesses; the dynamic link chain is used, as suggested earlier, to discard a stack frame at procedure exit.

When code for a procedure call is generated, this also provides (a) the (known) level difference between the static level at which the procedure was called and the static level at which it was declared and (b) the (known) starting address of the executable code. The static link is set up at entry to a procedure by following the static chain from the stack frame of the calling routine for as many steps as the level difference between calling and called routine dictates.

With this idea the stack would look as shown in Figure 8.4 (for the same program as before).

8.1.7   Code generation with the static link approach

Perhaps this will be made clearer if we examine the refinements to the compiler in more detail. The code generation interface alters but little, as the revised code for STATEMENT shows.

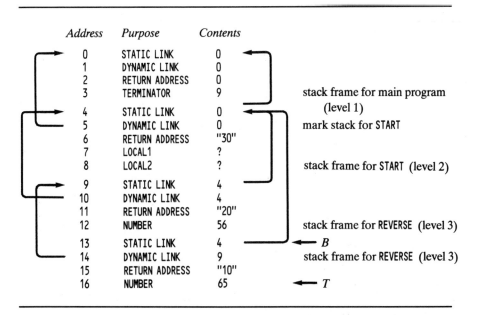

Figure 8.4

```
      begin (*STATEMENT*)
        if SYM in FIRSTSTATEMENT then
          case SYM of
            IDENT:
              begin
                SEARCHID(IDENTRY, [VARIABLE, PROC], 22);
                with TABLE[I] do
                  case CLASS of
                    CONSTANT, PROG, (*error - treat as assignment*)
                    VARIABLE:
                      begin
                        ADDRESSFOR(IDENTRY);
                        if SYM = BECOMES then GETSYM else
                          begin ERROR(21); if SYM = EQLSYM then GETSYM end;
                        EXPRESSION(FOLLOWERS);
                        ASSIGN
                      end;
**                  PROC : CALL(BLOCKLEVEL - LEVEL, ADDRESS);
                  end (*case CLASS*)
              end (*IDENT*);
            IFSYM     : IFSTATEMENT;
            BEGINSYM  : COMPOUNDSTATEMENT(FOLLOWERS);
            WHILESYM  : WHILESTATEMENT;
            WRITESYM  : OUTPUTSTATEMENT;
            READSYM   : INPUTSTATEMENT;
          end (*case SYM*)
        TEST(FOLLOWERS, [], 32)
      end (*STATEMENT*);
```

The procedure for generating addresses for variables also needs a simple change

```
      procedure ADDRESSFOR (I : TABLEINDEX);
        begin
          with TABLE[I] do STACKADDRESS(BLOCKLEVEL - LEVEL, ADDRESS)
        end (*ADDRESSFOR*);
```

The code for BLOCK changes little – offset addresses for variables in a stack frame now start at 3. However, there is one significant change. Since blocks can be nested, the compiler cannot predict, when a procedure name is *declared*, exactly when the code for that procedure will be *defined*, still less where it will be located in memory. To save a great deal of trouble which might arise from apparent forward references, we can arrange that the code for each procedure starts with an instruction which merely branches over the code for any nested blocks to the actual body of the procedure. When we come across the code for the block we then have to backpatch only this one instruction. The address of this instruction (just the value of NEXTCODE at the point where the procedure name is declared) can be entered in the symbol table in the ADDRESS field of the entry for the procedure name, and retrieved from there for use in calling the procedure.

This means that calls to a procedure will immediately result in a further branch instruction, but the decrease in efficiency will be very small.

```
begin (*BLOCK*)
   OFFSET := 3 (*Initialize offset addresses for variables*);
   ENTERBLOCK(STARTCODE);
   TABLE[LASTENTRY].ADDRESS := STARTCODE (*for future callers*);
   TEST(FIRSTBLOCK, FOLLOWERS, 3);
   repeat
     if SYM = CONSTSYM then CONSTDECLARATION;
     if SYM = VARSYM then VARDECLARATION;
     while SYM = PROCSYM do PROCDECLARATION;
     TEST([BEGINSYM], FOLLOWERS, 34)
   until SYM in FIRSTSTATEMENT + [PERIOD, SEMICOLON];
   BACKPATCH(STARTCODE, NEXTCODE) (*jump to code for this block*);
   OPENSTACKFRAME(OFFSET) (*reserve space for variables*);
   COMPOUNDSTATEMENT(FOLLOWERS);
   if TABLES then PRINTSYMBOLTABLE (*demonstration purposes*);
   LEAVEBLOCK(BLOCKCLASS);
   TEST(FOLLOWERS, [], 35)
end (*BLOCK*);
```

In terms of our stack computer, so that we can demonstrate actual code generation, we extend the form of an instruction to

```
INSTRUCTIONS = packed record
                   F : OPCODES    (*function code*);
                   L : LEVELS     (*level difference*);
                   A : INTEGER    (*address*)
                 end (*INSTRUCTIONS*);
```

and make simple changes to the code generator as follows:

```
procedure GEN (OP : OPCODES; LEV : LEVELS; ADDRESS : INTEGER);
(*Code generator for instructions with address field*)
  begin
    if NEXTCODE > CODEMAX then QUIT(2) (*program too long*);
    if CODEISTOBEGENERATED then
      begin
        with CODE[NEXTCODE] do begin F := OP; L := LEV; A := ADDRESS end;
        NEXTCODE := NEXTCODE + 1
      end
  end (*GEN*);
procedure EMIT (OP : OPCODES);
(*Code generator with no address field*)
  begin GEN(OP, 0, 0) end;
procedure STACKADDRESS (DIFFERENCE : LEVELS; OFFSET : INTEGER);
```

```
  begin GEN(LDA, DIFFERENCE, OFFSET) end;
procedure ENTERBLOCK (var LAB : INTEGER);
  begin STORELABEL(LAB); JUMP(0) end;
procedure LEAVEBLOCK (BLOCKCLASS : CLASSES);
  begin
    case BLOCKCLASS of
      PROG : EMIT(HLT);
      PROC : EMIT(RET)
    end
  end (*LEAVEBLOCK*);
procedure CALL (DIFFERENCE : LEVELS; ENTRYPOINT : INTEGER);
  begin GEN(CAL, DIFFERENCE, ENTRYPOINT) end;
```

Finally, the changes to the interpreter of Chapter 2 perhaps show most clearly
how the run-time system works.

```
procedure INTERPRET;
  var
    P,                          (*program counter*)
    B,                          (*base register*)
    T,                          (*stack pointer*)
    LOOP : INTEGER              (*for loops*);
    I  : INSTRUCTIONS           (*current*);
    S  : array [0 .. STACKMAX] of INTEGER (*stack memory*);
    PS : (RUNNING, FINISHED, STKCHK, DATCHK, EOFCHK, DIVCHK) (*status*);
  function BASE (L : LEVELS) : INTEGER;
  (*Find base L levels down*)
    var
      CURRENT : INTEGER;
    begin
      CURRENT := B;
      while L > 0 do begin CURRENT := S[CURRENT]; L := L - 1 end;
      BASE := CURRENT
    end (*BASE*);
  begin (*INTERPRET*)
    for LOOP := 0 to STACKMAX do S[LOOP] := 0 (*clear all memory*);
    T := -1; P := 0; B := 0 (*stack pointer, program count, base register*);
    PS := RUNNING;
    repeat
      I := CODE[P]; P := P + 1;
      with I do
        case F of
          (*most as before*)
          LDA :
            begin INCTBY(1); S[T] := BASE(L) + A end;
          CAL :
```

```
            begin
              S[T+1] := BASE(L)        (*set static link*);
              S[T+2] := B; S[T+3] := P (*save registers*);
              B := T + 1; P := A       (*update registers*)
            end;
          RET :
            begin
              T := B - 1               (*discard stack frame*);
              P := S[B+2]; B := S[B+1] (*restore registers*)
            end;
        end
    until PS <> RUNNING;
    if PS <> FINISHED then POSTMORTEM
    end (*INTERPRET*);
```

With this system the program above compiles as follows

```
0 program BACKWARDS;
0 var TERMINATOR;
1
1 procedure START;
1   var LOCAL1, LOCAL2;
2
2   procedure REVERSE;
2     var NUMBER;
3     begin
4       read(NUMBER);
6       if TERMINATOR <> NUMBER then REVERSE; write(NUMBER)
16      end;
18
18    begin
19      REVERSE
19    end;
21
21 begin
22   TERMINATOR := 9;
25   START
25 end.
```

with a symbol table

Identifier	Class	Level	Address
1 BACKWARD	PROGRAM	0	0 (irrelevant)
2 TERMINAT	VARIABLE	1	3 (offset from base)
3 START	PROCEDURE	1	1 (code address)
4 LOCAL1	VARIABLE	2	3
5 LOCAL2	VARIABLE	2	4
6 REVERSE	PROCEDURE	2	2 (code address)
7 NUMBER	VARIABLE	3	3

and produces the code

```
 0 BRN 0 21    jump to start of main program
 1 BRN 0 18    jump to start of START
 2 BRN 0 3     jump to start of REVERSE (next instruction in this case)
 3 INT 0 4     start of code for REVERSE (declared at level 3)
 4 LDA 0 3     address of NUMBER (declared at level 3)
 5 INN         read (NUMBER)
 6 LDA 2 3     address of TERMINATOR is two levels down
 7 LDV         dereference - value of TERMINATOR on stack
 8 LDA 0 3     address of NUMBER is on this level
 9 LDV         dereference - value of NUMBER now on stack
10 NEQ         compare for inequality
11 BZE 0 13
12 CAL 1 2     recursive call to REVERSE - note that REVERSE is declared
13 LDA 0 3     at a level below the variables local to it.
14 LDV
15 PRN         write(NUMBER)
16 NLN
17 RET         exit REVERSE
18 INT 0 5     start of code for START (declared at level 2)
19 CAL 0 2     call on REVERSE, which is declared at this level
20 RET         exit START
21 INT 0 4     start of code for main program (level now 1)
22 LDA 0 3     address of TERMINATOR on stack
23 LDI 0 9     push constant 9 onto stack
24 STO         TERMINATOR := 9
25 CAL 0 1     call START, which is declared at this level
26 HLT         stop execution
```

8.1.8   The use of the display

The other method widely used for handling variable addressing is the use of so-called **display** registers. Since at most one instance of a procedure can be active at one time, only the latest instance of each local variable can be accessible. This suggests that the tedious business of following a static chain for each variable access at execution time can be shortened by storing the base registers for the most recently invoked frames at each level (that is, the information which we would otherwise find after following the static chain) in a small array (which we shall, rather cleverly, call DISPLAY), and performing run-time addressing by adding the predicted stack frame offset to the appropriate dynamic entry in this array.

Variable address information is still passed to the code generator by the analyser as pairs of numbers, the first giving the (known) level at which the identifier was declared (an absolute level, not the difference between two levels), and the second giving the (known) offset from the run-time base of the stack frame. This involves only minor changes to the code generators so far developed.

When code for a procedure call is required, the interface takes into account the (known) absolute level at which the called procedure was declared and the (known) starting address of the executable code. The code generated is, however, rather different from that used by the static chain method. When a procedure is entered it still needs to store (in the mark stack) the dynamic link, and the return address. In place of setting up the start of the static link chain the system updates DISPLAY. This is quite easy, as the element in question can be predicted at compile-time to be that corresponding to a level one higher than that at which the name of the called procedure was declared. (Remember that the name of a procedure is given the level of the block in which it is declared, not the level of the block that defines its local variables and code.) However, a moment's thought will show that, when we leave a procedure, we must not only reset the program counter and base register, we may have to restore an element of DISPLAY. This is strictly only necessary if we have entered the procedure from one declared statically at a *higher* level, but it is simplest to update one element on all returns.

Consequently, when a procedure is entered, we arrange for it to store in the first three elements of its stack frame:

(a) a copy of the current value of the DISPLAY element for the level one higher than the level of the called routine (this will allow the display to be reset later if necessary);

(b) the base address of the stack frame of the calling routine, forming the dynamic link as before;

(c) the return address in the calling routine.

When the procedure is left, the base register is reset from the dynamic link, the program counter is reset from the return address, and one element of DISPLAY is restored from the 'display copy'. The element in question is that for a level one higher than the level at which the name of the called routine was declared – that is, the level at which the block for the routine was compiled – and this level information must be available to the code for procedure exit.

This may be clarified by tracing the sequence of procedure calls for the same program as before (see Figure 8.5).

After the recursive call the changes become rather more significant, as the display copy is now relevant for the first time (see Figure 8.6). When we unwind the recursion, on leaving REVERSE and losing the stack frame in 13–16 we must reset DISPLAY[3] to 9. When leaving REVERSE again and discarding the frame in 9–12, there is actually no need to alter DISPLAY[3], as it is no longer needed. Similarly after leaving START and discarding the frame 4–8 there is no need to alter DISPLAY[2].

The display method is clearly more efficient at run-time than the static chain method. In some systems special-purpose fast registers may be used to store the DISPLAY array, leading to even greater efficiency. It suffers from the drawback that an arbitrary limit must be placed on the depth to which pro-

When only the main program is active, the situation is

| STACK | | | | DISPLAY | |
Address	Purpose	Contents		Contents	Address
0	DISPLAY COPY	0	←	0	1
1	DYNAMIC LINK	0		?	2
2	RETURN ADDRESS	0		?	3
3	TERMINATOR	9			

After START is called and entered the situation changes to

| STACK | | | | DISPLAY | |
Address	Purpose	Contents		Contents	Address
0	DISPLAY COPY	0	←	0	1
1	DYNAMIC LINK	0		4	2
2	RETURN ADDRESS	0		?	3
3	TERMINATOR	9			
4	DISPLAY COPY	?			
5	DYNAMIC LINK	0			
6	RETURN ADDRESS	"30"			
7	LOCAL1	?			
8	LOCAL2	?			

After REVERSE is called for the first time it changes again to

| STACK | | | | DISPLAY | |
Address	Purpose	Contents		Contents	Address
0	DISPLAY COPY	0	←	0	1
1	DYNAMIC LINK	0		4	2
2	RETURN ADDRESS	0		9	3
3	TERMINATOR	9			
4	DISPLAY	?			
5	DYNAMIC LINK	0			
6	RETURN ADDRESS	"30"			
7	LOCAL1	?			
8	LOCAL2	?			
9	DISPLAY COPY	?			
10	DYNAMIC LINK	4			
11	RETURN ADDRESS	"20"			
12	NUMBER	56			

Figure 8.5

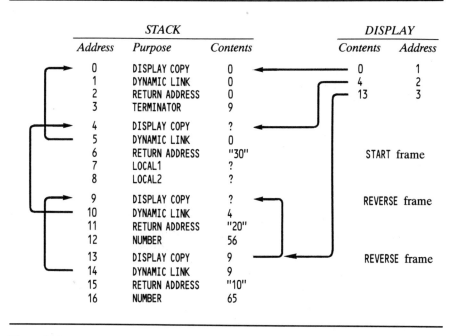

Figure 8.6

cedures may be statically nested. (The size of DISPLAY is the same as the maximum static depth of nesting allowed by the compiler at compile-time.) Murphy's Law will ensure that this depth will be inadequate for the program you were going to write to ensure you a niche in the Halls of Fame!

8.1.9 Code generation for the display method

The material of the last section will be made clearer if we highlight the changes needed to the compiler.

The procedure ADDRESSFOR changes to an equally simple one

```
procedure ADDRESSFOR (I : TABLEINDEX);
   begin with TABLE[I] do STACKADDRESS(LEVEL, ADDRESS) end;
```

The code for STATEMENT has to be changed very slightly

```
begin (*STATEMENT*)
   if SYM in FIRSTSTATEMENT then
     case SYM of
       IDENT :
         begin
           SEARCHID(ID, IDENTRY, [VARIABLE, PROC], 22);
           with TABLE[I] do
             case CLASS of
```

```
                  CONSTANT, PROG, (*error — treat as assignment*)
                  VARIABLE : (*as before*)
**             PROC    : CALL(LEVEL, ADDRESS)
              end (*case CLASS*)
          end (*IDENT*);
      IFSYM    : (*as before*)
      BEGINSYM : (*as before*)
      WHILESYM : (*as before*)
      WRITESYM : (*as before*)
      READSYM  : (*as before*)
    end (*case SYM*);
  TEST(FOLLOWERS, [], 32)
end (*STATEMENT*);
```

For our hypothetical stack machine the code-generation procedures are essentially as before, with a slight difference in meaning for the first parameter, which now represents a level, rather than a level difference:

```
procedure STACKADDRESS (LEVEL : LEVELS; OFFSET : INTEGER);
  begin GEN(LDA, LEVEL, OFFSET) end;

procedure CALL (LEVEL : LEVELS; ENTRYPOINT : INTEGER);
  begin GEN(CAL, LEVEL, ENTRYPOINT) end;
```

The code generator needs another slight modification – when we leave a block we must ensure that the appropriate level information is available at run-time for updating DISPLAY. This is easily done by calling on

```
LEAVEBLOCK(BLOCKCLASS, BLOCKLEVEL);
```

at the end of BLOCK. In terms of our stack computer, this has the effect

```
procedure LEAVEBLOCK (BLOCKCLASS : CLASSES; BLOCKLEVEL : LEVELS);
  begin
    case BLOCKCLASS of
      PROG : EMIT(HLT);
      PROC : GEN (RET, BLOCKLEVEL, 0)
    end
  end (*LEAVEBLOCK*);
```

Perhaps the modifications to the interpreter best demonstrate how the system actually works.

```
procedure INTERPRET;
  var
    P, B, T,                          (*counter, base, stack pointer*)
    LOOP : INTEGER                    (*for loops*);
    I  : INSTRUCTIONS                 (*current*);
    S  : array [0 .. STACKMAX] of INTEGER  (*stack memory*);
    DISPLAY : array [LEVELS] of INTEGER    (*display registers*);
    PS : (RUNNING, FINISHED, STKCHK, DATCHK, EOFCHK, DIVCHK) (*status*);
```

```
begin (*INTERPRET*)
  for LOOP := 0 to STACKMAX do S[LOOP] := 0 (*clear all memory*);
  T := -1; P := 0; B := 0 (*stack pointer, program count, base register*);
  DISPLAY[1] := 0 (*initialize main program display register*);
  PS := RUNNING;
  repeat
    I := CODE[P]; P := P + 1;
    with I do
      case F of
      (*most as before*)
      LDA :
        begin INCTBY(1); S[T] := DISPLAY[L] + A end;
      CAL :
        begin
          S[T+1] := DISPLAY[L+1]   (*save display register*);
          S[T+2] := B; S[T+3] := P (*save registers*);
          B := T + 1; P := A       (*update registers*);
          DISPLAY[L+1] := T + 1    (*set display register*)
        end;
      RET :
        begin
          T := B - 1               (*discard stack frame*);
          DISPLAY[L] := S[B]        (*restore display*);
          P := S[B+2]; B := S[B+1]  (*restore registers*)
        end;
      end
  until PS <> RUNNING;
  If PS <> FINISHED then POSTMORTEM
end (*INTERPRET*);
```

With this system the same source program produces the following object code
for our stack computer

```
 0 BRN 0 21     jump to start of main program
 1 BRN 0 18     jump to start of START
 2 BRN 0 3      jump to start of REVERSE
 3 INT 0 4      stack frame for REVERSE
 4 LDA 3 3      address of NUMBER (declared at level 3)
 5 INN          read(NUMBER)
 6 LDA 1 3      address of TERMINATOR (declared at level 1)
 7 LDV          dereference — value of TERMINATOR now on stack
 8 LDA 3 3      address of NUMBER
 9 LDV          dereference — value of NUMBER now on stack
10 NEQ          compare for inequality
11 BZE 0 13
12 CAL 2 2      recursive call to REVERSE (declared at level 2)
13 LDA 3 3
14 LDV
```

```
15 PRN        write (NUMBER)
16 NLN
17 RET 3 0    exit REVERSE
18 INT 0 5    start of START — get stack frame
19 CAL 2 2    call REVERSE (declared at level 2)
20 RET 2 0    exit START
21 INT 0 4    start of main program — get stack frame
22 LDA 1 3    address of TERMINATOR (declared at level 1)
23 LDI 0 9    push constant 9 onto stack
24 STO        TERMINATOR := 9
25 CAL 1 1    call START (declared at level 1)
26 HLT        stop execution
```

Exercises

8.1 When using nested procedures it is acceptable to use the same identifier name in several places in the source code, provided that the scope rules are obeyed. Modify the compiler to check that identifiers are not redeclared incorrectly.

8.2 Follow up the suggestion that a syntactic solution can be found to the problem of deciding whether an identifier heralds an assignment or a procedure call by examining the first terminal after it. Pay attention to the problems of error recovery.

8.3 On rather the same theme, in Exercise 7.32 we suggested that undeclared identifiers might be entered into the symbol table as variables at the point where they were first encountered. Can one perhaps do better than this by examining the symbol which appears after the offending identifier (which the SEARCHID procedure scans anyway)?

8.4 In calling BLOCK from within PROCDECLARATION the SEMICOLON symbol has had to be added to FOLLOWERS, as it becomes the legal follower of <block>. Is it a good idea to do this, since SEMICOLON (a widely used and abused terminal) will then be a member of all FOLLOWERS used in parsing parts of that block? If not, what does one do about it?

8.5 Follow up the suggestion that the DISPLAY does not have to be restored after every return from a procedure. When should the compiler generate code to handle this operation, and what form should the code take? Are the savings worth worrying about? (This is the way in which the Pascal-S system works. See Berry (1982) Chapter 11, for example.)

8.6 If one studies Pascal programs, one finds that many of the references to variables in a block are either to the local variables of that block or to the global variables of the main program block. Study the listings of the compiler given earlier and satisfy yourself of the truth of this. If this is indeed so, perhaps special forms of addressing should be used for these variables, to avoid the inefficient use of the static link search or display reference at run-time. (This is done, for example, in the UCSD p-System.) Explore this idea for the simple compiler–interpreter system we are developing.

8.7 Can you think of a way of avoiding the unconditional branch instructions with which every procedure starts, without using all the machinery of a separate branch ahead table?

8.8 How could one handle the forward declaration of procedures, as in Pascal, to allow mutually recursive procedures to work properly?

8.9 Our symbol table structure is rather crude. However, it effectively solves the problems of finding the most recent instance of a name in the event that it (legitimately) appears in the table more than once. Some compilers make use of the idea of the display at compile-time to cater for this; the elements of the display point to the roots of binary trees constructed for each level. For example, given source code like

```
program SILLY;
  var B, A, C;
  procedure ONE;
    var X, Y, Z;
    procedure TWO;
      var T, U;
```

the symbol table might look something like Figure 8.7 just after declaring D. Modify the compiler to make use of this approach. How do you discard the unwanted nodes after parsing a block?

8.10 The poor old goto statement is not only hated by protagonists of structured programming. It is also surprisingly awkward to compile. If you wish to add it to CLANG, why should you prevent users from jumping into procedure or function blocks, and if you let them jump out of them, what special action must be taken to maintain the integrity of the stack frame structures?

8.11 If we use the display method, is there any real need to use base register B as well?

8.12 If you have attempted to write a native code generator for the compiler (see Exercise 7.65), extend this to allow for procedure calls.

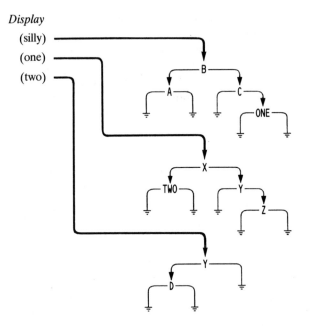

Figure 8.7

Further reading

Most texts on compiling block structured languages give a treatment of the material discussed here, but this will make more sense after the reader has studied the next section in this text.

The problems that arise in interpreting Pascal's scope rules are worth following up. The reader is directed to the classic paper by Welsh *et al.* (1977) (reprinted in Barron (1981) pages 5–19); to the discussion in the book by Brinch Hansen (1983) (pages 38–39); and to the articles by Cailliau (1982), Winkler (1984) and Sale (1979 a–c).

The problems with handling the goto statement are discussed in the books by Barrett and Couch (1979) (page 413) and by Bornat (1979) (page 227).

A more sophisticated approach to symbol table construction (see Exercise 8.9) is discussed in the book by Pemberton and Daniels (1982) (page 38).

8.2 Parameterized procedures and functions

It is the aim of this section to show how we can extend our language and its compiler to allow for function subprograms as well as procedures, and for parameter passing. Once again, the syntactic and semantic extensions we shall make to our language are simple, suggested by those familiar to the reader from a study of Pascal.

8.2.1 Syntax and semantics

In fact, the subject of parameter passing is more extensive than the reader may have realized, for in the design of programming languages several methods of parameter passing have been proposed, and the ones actually implemented vary semantically from language to language, while syntactically appearing deceptively similar. In most cases, declaration of a subprogram segment is accompanied by declaration of a list of **formal parameter** names, which have a status within the subprogram rather like that of local variable names. Invocation of the subprogram is accompanied by a corresponding list of **actual parameters**, and it is invariably the case that any relationship between formal and actual parameters is achieved by positional correspondence, rather than by lexical correspondence in the source text. Thus it would be quite legal, if a little confusing, to declare

    procedure ANYNAME (A,B)

and then to invoke it with a statement of the form

    ANYNAME (B,A)

when the A in the procedure would be associated with the B in the calling routine, and the B in the procedure would be associated with the A in the calling routine. It is the lack of 'name' correspondence that is at the root of a great deal of confusion in parameter handling for beginners.

The correspondence of formal and actual parameters goes deeper than just position in a parameter list. Of the various ways in which it is established, the two most used and most familiar parameter passing mechanisms are the so-called **call-by-value** and **call-by-reference**.

Implementation of these two methods is quite different.

(a)   In call-by-reference, an actual parameter must be supplied as a variable name, and it is the *address* of this that is handed over to the subprogram for processing. Within the subprogram, a reference to a formal parameter results, at run-time, in a direct reference to the actual parameter, and any changes to a formal parameter result in an immediate change to the corresponding actual parameter. In a very real sense, a formal parameter name may be regarded as an *alias* for the actual parameter name; an alias which lasts as long as the procedure is active, and which may be transmitted to other subprograms with parameters passed in the same way.

(b)   In call-by-value, an actual parameter may be an expression, and it is the run-time *value* of this expression that is handed over to the subprogram for processing. Formal parameters in a subprogram (when declared in this way) are effectively variables local to that subprogram, which start their lives initialized to the values of the corresponding actual parameter expressions. However, any changes made to the values of the formal parameter 'variables' are local to the subprogram, and cannot be transmitted back via the formal parameters to the calling routine.

Call-by-value is easily implemented, and is all we shall consider here. Call-by-reference is also easy, but may be left as an exercise for the reader.

Introduction of function and parameter declarations to our language is described by an extension of the syntax diagram for BLOCK, as shown in Figure 8.8.

We have to change the syntax for STATEMENT to allow procedures to be invoked with parameters. The changes can be seen from Figure 8.9.

PROCDECLARATIONS

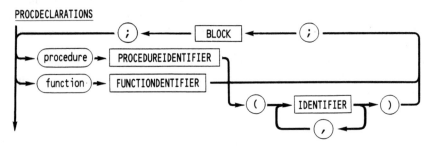

Figure 8.8

STATEMENT

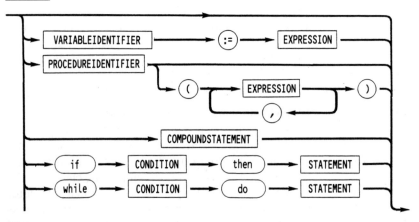

Figure 8.9

We also have to extend the definition of FACTOR to allow function references to be included with the appropriate precedence (Figure 8.10).

FACTOR

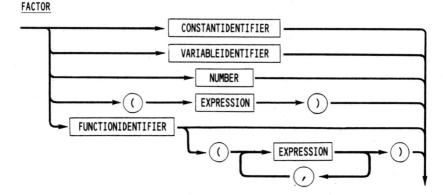

Figure 8.10

8.2.2 Syntactic and semantic analysis

Parsing the extensions to the declaration part is essentially simple. Devoid of error recovery, and ignoring the 'levels' issue, the changed algorithms would be

```
procedure PROCDECLARATION;
  begin
    GETSYM; ACCEPT(IDENT);
    if SYM = LPAREN then PARDECLARATION;
    ACCEPT(SEMICOLON);  BLOCK; ACCEPT(SEMICOLON)
  end (*PROCDECLARATION*);
```

and, in BLOCK itself

```
begin (*BLOCK*)
  if SYM = CONSTSYM then CONSTDECLARATION;
  if SYM = VARSYM then VARDECLARATION;
  while SYM in [PROCSYM, FUNCSYM] do PROCDECLARATION;
  COMPOUNDSTATEMENT
end (*BLOCK*);
```

However, there is rather more to it than that. To allow for checks that the number of formal and actual parameters agree it is convenient to extend the definition of our symbol table to

```
TABLE : array [TABLEINDEX] of record
                        NAME    : ALFA;
                        CLASS   : CLASSES;
                        LEVEL   : LEVELS;
                        SIZE,
                        ADDRESS : INTEGER
                      end (*TABLE*);
```

where SIZE is a field of no relevance other than for procedure and function identifiers, where it will be used to record the number of formal parameters. Entry
of identifiers in this table must be made with some care, as formal parameter
names for a subprogram must be entered at a higher level than the procedure or
function identifier, so as to reserve them local status. This suggests that the
simple modification to PROCDECLARATION is inadequate, and that PARDECLARATION might
be better called from within BLOCK. (Practical expediency is more important than
an aesthetically structured compiler; it could be done by appropriate
parameterization if the reader really wants to try!) As a result, the test for the
semicolon preceding the block is now better performed at the start of BLOCK as
well.

Accordingly we declare our BLOCK parser as

```
procedure BLOCK (FOLLOWERS  : SYMSET     (*for error recovery*);
                 BLOCKLEVEL : LEVELS     (*level of static nesting*);
                 LASTENTRY  : TABLEINDEX (*index into symbol table*);
                 BLOCKCLASS : CLASSES    (*program, proc or function*) );
```

and initiate parsing of the program by a call

```
BLOCK([PERIOD] + FIRSTBLOCK + FIRSTSTATEMENT, 1, 1, PROG);
```

Subsequent calls on BLOCK are made from within PROCDECLARATION which, when error
recovery is added, takes the form

```
procedure PROCDECLARATION;
(*Handle declaration of procedures and functions*)
  var
    BLOCKCLASS : CLASSES;
  begin
    if ID = 'FUNCTION' then BLOCKCLASS := FUNC else BLOCKCLASS := PROC;
    GETSYM;
    if SYM <> IDENT then ERROR(6) else begin ENTER(PROC); GETSYM end;
    BLOCK([SEMICOLON] + FOLLOWERS, BLOCKLEVEL + 1 , LASTENTRY, BLOCKCLASS);
    ACCEPT(SEMICOLON, 2)
  end (*PROCDECLARATION*);
```

We note that it is unnecessary to introduce both FUNCSYM and PROCSYM – the
distinction can be made in PROCDECLARATION on purely lexical grounds. The advantage of not using both symbols might become necessary with Pascal implementations which only allow very restricted set types.

8.2.3 Code generation

The code for BLOCK changes a little, for we shall not know, when a subprogram identifier is first declared, how many formal parameters will be associated with it.

```
procedure BLOCK (FOLLOWERS   : SYMSET      (*for error recovery*);
                 BLOCKLEVEL : LEVELS       (*level of static nesting*);
                 LASTENTRY  : TABLEINDEX   (*index into symbol table*);
                 BLOCKCLASS : CLASSES      (*program or proc or function*) );
  var
    BLOCKENTRY : TABLEINDEX (*initial symbol table entry*);
    STARTCODE,              (*code start address*);
    OFFSET,                 (*local variable address index*);
    PARAMS : INTEGER        (*number of parameters*);
  begin (*BLOCK*)
    PARAMS := 0; BLOCKENTRY := LASTENTRY (*save for later fixup*);
    OFFSET := 3 (*initialize offset addresses for variables*);
    ENTERBLOCK(STARTCODE);
    if BLOCKCLASS in [PROC, FUNC] then (*handle possible parameter list*)
      if SYM = LPAREN then PARDECLARATION;
    TABLE[BLOCKENTRY].SIZE := PARAMS;
    TABLE[BLOCKENTRY].ADDRESS := STARTCODE;
    ACCEPT(SEMICOLON, 2);
    TEST(FIRSTBLOCK, FOLLOWERS, 3);
    repeat
      if SYM = CONSTSYM then CONSTDECLARATION;
      if SYM = VARSYM then VARDECLARATION;
      while SYM = PROCSYM do PROCDECLARATION;
      TEST([BEGINSYM], FOLLOWERS, 34)
    until SYM in FIRSTSTATEMENT + [PERIOD, SEMICOLON];
    BACKPATCH(STARTCODE, NEXTCODE);
    OPENSTACKFRAME(OFFSET) (*reserve space for variables*);
    COMPOUNDSTATEMENT(FOLLOWERS);
    if TABLES then PRINTSYMBOLTABLE (*demonstration purposes*);
    LEAVEBLOCK(BLOCKCLASS, BLOCKLEVEL, PARAMS);
    TEST(FOLLOWERS, [], 35)
  end (*BLOCK*);
```

Here we call on procedure PARDECLARATION to process the formal parameter list. But before we do this we should consider what address offsets we must associate with parameters, for code generation for accessing formal parameters requires us to have entered these offsets into the symbol table when they were declared.

There are several ways in which the parameter passing could be effected. We could arrange for the actual values to be stored within the stack frame of the called subprogram, starting just above the standard mark stack locations used for storing the static link/display copy, dynamic link and return address. This is the way used in several Pascal compilers, such as the Pascal-P compiler (Pemberton and Daniels (1982) page 117), the derived UCSD Pascal compilers, and the Pascal-S compiler (Berry (1982) Chapter 11). Alternatively, and perhaps slightly more simply for our system, an easy way of passing value parameters at run-time will be to load their values onto the stack just before transferring control to the procedure or function which is to use them. The called subprogram will then set the base register to point just above the last actual parameter value, and so can access the actual parameters by adding a negative offset to this base (or to the appropriate element in the display). Similarly, to allow a function value to be returned, it is convenient to reserve a stack item for this just before the parameters are set up, and for the function subprogram to access this reserved location using a negative offset as well.

This may be made clearer by considering the following (traditional, but silly) example

```
program TESTFUNCTIONS;
  var N;
  function FACTORIAL (M);
    begin
      if M = 1 then FACTORIAL := 1;
      if M > 1 then FACTORIAL := M * FACTORIAL(M-1)
    end;
begin
  read(N);
  write(FACTORIAL(N))
end.
```

If this program were to be supplied with a data value of N=3, then just after the function was invoked for the first time the stack contents would be as shown in Figure 8.11.

FACTORIAL can now pick up its parameter M by adding an offset of -1 to B, and can assign the value to be returned to the stack element whose offset is -2 from B. (In practice the addressing might be done via DISPLAY[2], rather than via B.)

Note that this way of returning function values is entirely consistent with the use of the stack for expression evaluation.

Accordingly we develop PARDECLARATION as follows

```
procedure PARDECLARATION;
(*Handle declaration of formal parameters*)
  var
    I : TABLEINDEX;
  procedure ENTERPARAMETER;
    begin
      if SYM <> IDENT then ERROR(6) else
        begin ENTER(VARIABLE); PARAMS := PARAMS + 1; GETSYM end
    end (*ENTERPARAMETER*);
```

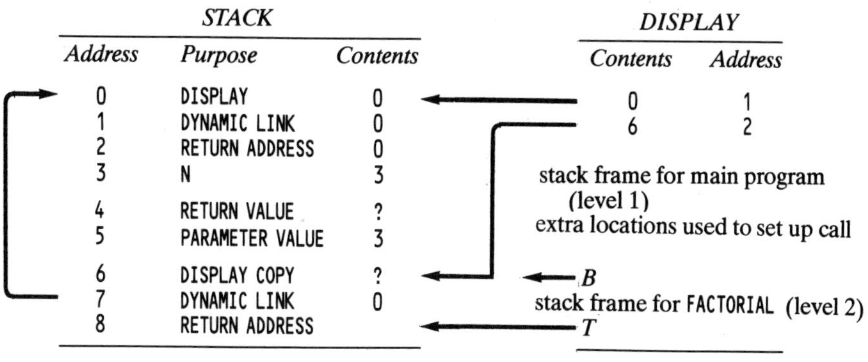

STACK				DISPLAY	
Address	Purpose	Contents		Contents	Address
0	DISPLAY	0	←	0	1
1	DYNAMIC LINK	0		6	2
2	RETURN ADDRESS	0			
3	N	3		stack frame for main program	
4	RETURN VALUE	?		(level 1)	
5	PARAMETER VALUE	3		extra locations used to set up call	
6	DISPLAY COPY	?	← B		
7	DYNAMIC LINK	0		stack frame for FACTORIAL (level 2)	
8	RETURN ADDRESS		← T		

Figure 8.11

```
begin
  GETSYM;
  TEST([IDENT], FOLLOWERS, 6);
  if SYM = IDENT then
    begin
      ENTERPARAMETER;
      while SYM = COMMA do begin GETSYM; ENTERPARAMETER end;
      ACCEPT(RPAREN, 13)
    end;
  for I := 1 to PARAMS do (*parameters have negative offsets*)
    TABLE[LASTENTRY - I + 1].ADDRESS := -I;
end (*PARDECLARATION*);
```

There are several modifications needed to the parser for STATEMENT and FACTOR. We must be able to parse parameter lists, and to allow function references as components of FACTOR. The appropriate code follows – note the necessity of declaring EXPRESSION 'forward'.

```
procedure STATEMENT (FOLLOWERS : SYMSET);
  var
    IDENTRY : TABLEINDEX;
    TESTLABEL, STARTLOOP : INTEGER;
  procedure EXPRESSION (FOLLOWERS : SYMSET); forward;
  procedure PARAMETERS (FORMAL : INTEGER; FOLLOWERS : SYMSET);
  (*Handle formation of actual parameter list*)
    var
      ACTUAL : INTEGER;
    begin
      ACTUAL := 0;
```

```
      if SYM = LPAREN then
        begin
          repeat
            GETSYM;
            if ACTUAL >= FORMAL then ERROR(12) else
              begin
                EXPRESSION([COMMA, RPAREN] + FOLLOWERS);
                ACTUAL := ACTUAL + 1
              end;
            TEST([COMMA, RPAREN], FOLLOWERS, 13)
          until SYM <> COMMA;
          ACCEPT(RPAREN, 13)
        end;
      if ACTUAL < FORMAL then ERROR(12)
    end (*PARAMETERS*);
  procedure FACTOR (FOLLOWERS : SYMSET);
    var
      IDENTRY : TABLEINDEX;
    begin
      TEST(FIRSTFACTOR, FOLLOWERS, 14);
      while SYM in FIRSTFACTOR do
        begin
          case SYM of
            IDENT:
              begin
                SEARCHID(IDENTRY, [CONSTANT, VARIABLE, FUNC], 14);
                with TABLE[IDENTRY] do
                  case CLASS of
                    CONSTANT : (*as before*)
                    VARIABLE : (*as before*)
                    FUNC    :
                      begin
                        OPENSTACKFRAME(1) (*for returned value*);
                        PARAMETERS(SIZE, FOLLOWERS);
                        CALL(LEVEL, ADDRESS);
                      end;
                    PROG, PROC: (*error already reported*)
                  end (*case CLASS*)
              end;
            NUMBER: (*as before*)
            LPAREN: (*as before*)
          end (*case SYM*);
          TEST(FOLLOWERS - FIRSTFACTOR, FIRSTFACTOR, 3)
        end (*while*)
    end (*FACTOR*);
```

The code for STATEMENT needs some care.

```
begin (*STATEMENT*)
  if SYM in FIRSTSTATEMENT then
    case SYM of
      IDENT:
        begin
          SEARCHID(IDENTRY, [VARIABLE, FUNC, PROC], 22);
          with TABLE[IDENTRY] do
            case CLASS of
              CONSTANT, PROG, (*error - treat as assignment*)
              FUNC, VARIABLE:
                begin
                  if CLASS in [VARIABLE, CONSTANT, PROG]
                    then ADDRESSFOR(IDENTRY)
                    else (*return of a function value*)
                      if BLOCKENTRY = IDENTRY
                        then STACKADDRESS(LEVEL+1, -SIZE-1)
                        else ERROR(20);
                  if SYM = BECOMES then GETSYM else
                    begin ERROR(21); if SYM = EQLSYM then GETSYM end;
                  EXPRESSION(FOLLOWERS);
                  ASSIGN
                end;
              PROC:
                begin
                  PARAMETERS(SIZE, FOLLOWERS); CALL(LEVEL, ADDRESS);
                end;
            end (*case CLASS*)
        end (*IDENT*);
      IFSYM    : (*as before*)
      BEGINSYM : (*as before*)
      WHILESYM : (*as before*)
      WRITESYM : (*as before*)
      READSYM  : (*as before*)
    end (*case SYM*);
  TEST(FOLLOWERS, [], 32)
end (*STATEMENT*);
```

The reader should note two subtleties here.

(a) The check that BLOCKENTRY = IDENTRY when assignment is contemplated to a function tries to ensure that we only try to make such assignments within the body of the function, and not at some later point where the function name is still in scope, but can only be used with the semantics of 'value', not 'address' (but see also Exercise 8.22). For example, the following source code should be outlawed

```
program SILLY;
  function F;
    begin
      F := F (*syntactically correct, although it causes
                an infinite loop*)
    end;
  begin
    write(F)  (*F is still in scope, and can be used like this*)
    F := 5    (*F is in scope, but cannot be used like this*)
  end.
```

(b) The call to STACKADDRESS for setting up the function return must use LEVEL+1 and
not LEVEL, since the function name is in the symbol table at a level one lower
than we are currently parsing, and it must use -SIZE-1 instead of ADDRESS for
the OFFSET, since for function entries ADDRESS gives the code address where the
function starts.

Leaving a BLOCK is slightly different, for the stack pointer must drop below the
space on the stack that contained the actual parameters when the call was
made. This is easily handled for our stack machine by altering the code
generator.

```
procedure LEAVEBLOCK (BLOCKCLASS : CLASSES; BLOCKLEVEL : LEVELS; PARAMS : INTEGER);
  begin
    case BLOCKCLASS of
      PROG      : EMIT(HLT);
      FUNC, PROC : GEN(RET, BLOCKLEVEL, PARAMS + 1);
    end
  end (*LEAVEBLOCK*);
```

with a corresponding trivial change in the interpreter

```
RET:
  begin
    T := B - A              (*discard stack frame and parameters*);
    DISPLAY[L] := S[B]      (*restore display*);
    P := S[B+2]; B := S[B+1] (*restore registers*)
  end;
```

As a final example we give the code for a complete program

```
0 program TEST;
0   var N;
0
1   function FACTORIAL(M);
2     begin
2       if M = 1 then FACTORIAL := 1;
11      if M > 1 then FACTORIAL := M * FACTORIAL(M-1)
24    end;
29
```

```
29 begin
30   read(N);
32   while N > 0 do begin write(FACTORIAL(N)); read(N) end
45 end.
```

The symbol table for this is as follows

	Identifier	Class	Level	Address	Size
1	TEST	PROGRAM	0	0	0
2	N	VARIABLE	1	3	0
3	FACTORIA	FUNCTION	1	1	1
4	M	VARIABLE	2	-1	0

and the code is

```
 0 BRN 0 28    jump to start of main program
 1 BRN 0 2     jump to start of FACTORIAL
 2 INT 0 3     stack frame for FACTORIAL
 3 LDA 2 -1    address of M (Level 2, parameter with negative offset)
 4 LDV         value of M
 5 LDI 0 1
 6 EQL         M = 1 ?
 7 BZE 0 11    if not, branch
 8 LDA 2 -2    address of FACTORIAL return value is offset by -2
 9 LDI 0 1
10 STO         FACTORIAL := 1
11 LDA 2 -1    address of M
12 LDV         value of M
13 LDI 0 1
14 GTR         M > 1 ?
15 BZE 0 27    if not, branch
16 LDA 2 -2    address of FACTORIAL return value
17 LDA 2 -1    address of M
18 LDV         dereference ready for multiplication
19 INT 0 1     reserve space for return of FACTORIAL(M-1)
20 LDA 2 -1    address of M
21 LDV         value of M
22 LDI 0 1
23 SUB         M-1 now on stack as value of parameter for
24 CAL 1 1     recursive call to FACTORIAL (level 1) from level 2
25 MUL         form M * FACTORIAL(M-1)
26 STO         store on return value space
27 RET 2 2     exit FACTORIAL (discard 1 parameter).
28 INT 0 4     start main program — reserve stack frame
29 LDA 1 3     address of N
30 INN         read (N)
31 LDA 1 3     address of N
32 LDV         value of N
33 LDI 0 0     while N > 0 do
```

```
34 GTR
35 BZE 0 45
36 INT 0 1      reserve space for return of FACTORIAL(N)
37 LDA 1 3      address of N
38 LDV          value of N now on stack as value of parameter
39 CAL 1 1      call of FACTORIAL (level 1) from level 1
40 PRN          write result
41 NLN
42 LDA 1 3
43 INN          read next N
44 BRN 0 31     to check while condition
45 HLT
```

Exercises

8.13   Implement call-by-reference parameter passing, or both call-by-value and call-by-reference, possibly using the Pascal convention of preceding formal parameters by the reserved word var if the call-by-reference mechanism is to be used.

8.14   How do you cater for forward declaration of functions and procedures when you have to take parameters into account?

8.15   If you add the extensions suggested in Chapter 7, how do you have to alter the material of the present section?

8.16   The code for PARAMETERS above is a bit messy. Has the error recovery been incorporated in the best possible way?

8.17   In the last section we suggested that a syntactic, rather than a semantic, solution could be found to deciding whether a <statement> commencing with an identifier was a procedure call or an assignment. Can this be done when we allow our procedures and functions to have parameters?

8.18   In previous exercises we have suggested that undeclared identifiers could be entered into the symbol table at the point of first declaration, so as to help with suppressing further spurious errors. What is the best way of doing this if we can have undeclared variables, functions or procedures?

8.19   In Pascal, the word var is used to denote call-by-reference, but no special word is used for the (default) call-by-value. Why does this come in for criticism? Is the word var a good choice?

8.20   Implement a different approach to parameter passing, where the actual parameters are placed above the mark stack in the called subprogram, and below the local variables, rather than below the mark stack, as we have done. This is actually the way found described in most texts, except for Barrett and Couch (1979). What are the advantages and disadvantages of the two systems?

8.21 The following silly program highlights a further problem with interpreting the scope rules of languages like Pascal.

```
program SILLY;
  function F;
    function F (*nested*);
      begin
        F := 1
      end (*inner F*);
    begin (*outer F*)
      F := 2
    end (*outer F*);
  begin
    write(F)
  end.
```

What would cause the problem in one-pass (or any) compilation, and what should the language designer and compiler writer do about solving it? You might like to see how this has been handled in languages like Modula-2 (see Wirth (1985) and Edison (Brinch Hansen (1983) page 35).

8.22 Is our check for ensuring that one can only assign to a function within the body of that function correct? If not, how should it be improved? How does this point relate to Exercise 8.21?

8.23 If your aesthetic senses are jarred by the way we have suggested that PARDECLARATION be called from within BLOCK rather than before calling BLOCK, suggest (and implement) a better way of doing it.

8.24 Several workers decry function subprograms for the reason that a compiler cannot readily prevent a programmer from writing functions that have 'side-effects'. Given that one really wishes to prevent these, to what extent *can* a compiler detect them and prevent them?

8.25 Several people have suggested that function subprograms are not really necessary; one can just use procedures instead. Examine the advantages and disadvantages of providing both in a language, from the compiler writer's and the user's viewpoints.

8.26 A Pascal function can only return a 'scalar' value, and not, for example, an array, record or set. Why do you suppose this should be? Is there any easy (legal) way around the problem?

8.27 The usual explanation of call-by-value leaves one with the impression that this mode of passing is very safe, in that changes within the subprogram are confined to that subprogram. However, if in Pascal the value of a pointer variable is passed by value this is not quite the whole story, as can be seen from the following example

```
procedure FUDGE (P : POINTER);
  begin
    READ(INPUT, P↑.FIELD)
  end (*FUDGE*);
```

Perhaps this suggests that one does not need the call-by-reference mechanism in a language. What do you feel about this? Do you know of any languages that take this approach?

8.28 Pascal, and a few other languages, also allow subprograms themselves to be passed as parameters, along the lines of the following silly example

```
program EXAMPLE;
  procedure SILLIER (I);
    begin
      write('goodbye', I);
    end (*SILLIER*);
  procedure UPALEVEL;
    procedure ONE (A, procedure B(L));
      begin
        B(A);
        SILLIER(2)
      end (*ONE*)
    procedure SILLY (I);
      begin
        write('hello', I);
      end (*SILLY*);
    begin (*UPALEVEL*)
      ONE (3 , SILLY);
      ONE (4 , SILLIER)
    end (*UPALEVEL*);
  begin
    UPALEVEL
  end (*EXAMPLE*).
```

which would

- call UPALEVEL,
- call ONE which then calls SILLY to write hello 3 and then calls SILLIER directly to write goodbye 2,
- return to UPALEVEL,
- call ONE which then calls SILLIER to write goodbye 4 and then call SILLIER directly to write goodbye 2 again,

- return to the main program.

Can you think of ways in which our system would need to be modified to handle this sort of program, and try to implement them? Be careful, for the problem might be more difficult than it looks, except for some special simple cases.

8.29 If you have attempted to write a native code generator for the compiler (see Exercise 7.65), extend this to allow for subprograms with parameter passing.

8.30 How do you handle the problem of compiling programs too large to co-reside with the compiler?

8.31 Explore the possibility of providing a fairly sophisticated post-mortem dump in the extended interpreter. For example, provide a trace of the subprogram calls up to the point where an error was detected, and give the values of the local variables in each stack frame. To be really user-friendly the run-time system will need to refer to the user names for such objects. How would this alter the whole strategy adopted in our symbol table?

8.32 Now that you have a better understanding of how recursion is implemented, study the compiler you are writing with new interest. It uses recursion a great deal. How deeply do you suppose this recursion goes when the compiler executes? Is recursive descent efficient for all aspects of the compiling process? Do you suppose a Pascal compiler would ever run out of space in which to allocate new stack frames for itself when it was compiling large programs?

Further reading

As mentioned earlier, most texts on recursive descent compilers for Pascal-like languages treat the material of the last few sections in some detail, discussing one or other approach. You might like to consult the texts by Welsh and McKeag (1980) (page 175); Berry (1982) (Chapter 11); Hunter (1981) (Chapter 9); Young (1982) (Chapter 4); Pemberton and Daniels (1982) (Chapter 9); and Brinch Hansen (1983) (pages 162–167 and 174–180).

The special problem of procedural parameters is discussed in the texts by Bornat (1979) (Chapter 13); Barrett and Couch (1979) (Chapter 9); Davie and Morrison (1981) (page 140); and in a paper by Morrison (1977). Parameter passing of various forms is also discussed by Kowaltowski (1981).

An article by Johnson (1979) makes some useful comments on what to expect from run-time debuggers.

8.3 Run-time storage management for simple fixed arrays

It is the aim of this section to show how we can extend our language and its compiler to allow for simple arrays. In fact, we shall make them very simple indeed, having only one dimension, a size fixed at compilation time, and a fixed lower subscript bound of zero. Arrays of this sort are easily handled, as they can be allocated N consecutive elements in memory. Addressing an individual element is done by computing the value of the subscripting expression, and adding this to the address of the first element in the array. If the size is fixed at compile-time it is a simple matter for a one-pass compiler to determine the offset addresses of all scalar variables relative to the base of a stack frame (as we have already been doing), and the offset addresses of the first elements of all arrays relative to the base of a stack frame – provided we insist, as we have been doing, that all variables are declared before use.

Some languages, notably Pascal, allow assignment of complete arrays one to another using the := operator. Others, such as FORTRAN, only allow assignment element by element (although FORTRAN does allow a complete array to be input or output, or transferred as a parameter). In what follows we shall restrict ourselves to access of individual elements only, and we shall not consider how to pass complete arrays as parameters. The interested reader can try the extensions to cover these cases as useful exercises.

The declaration of arrays can be handled easily by extending the syntax for VARDECLARATIONS as shown in Figure 8.12.

We shall also have to change the syntax for STATEMENT to allow assignment to be made to array elements, and for these to be read (see Figure 8.13).

We shall have to extend the definition of FACTOR to allow array elements to be accessed easily in expressions (see Figure 8.14).

Parsing these extensions is quite easy. To allow for checks on the bounds of arrays, and to allow space to be allocated for them conveniently on the stack, we can use the SIZE field in TABLE. The procedure for entering identifiers into the table can assume an initial SIZE of 1, and the procedure for processing VARDECLARA-TION can easily recognize the declaration of an array if a left square bracket follows the identifier, determine the SIZE and alter this in the table. The address associated with an array in the symbol table is, strictly, that to denote the offset

VARDECLARATIONS

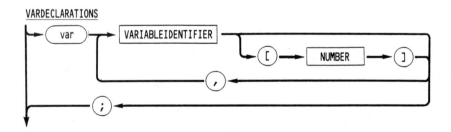

Figure 8.12

STATEMENT

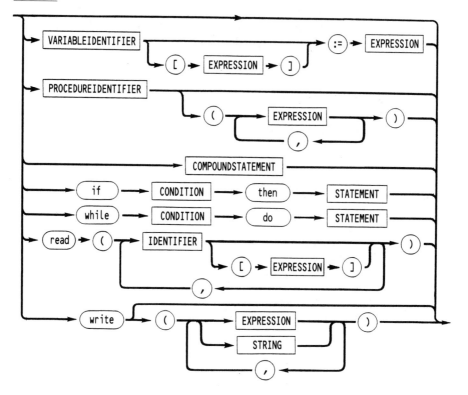

Figure 8.13

FACTOR

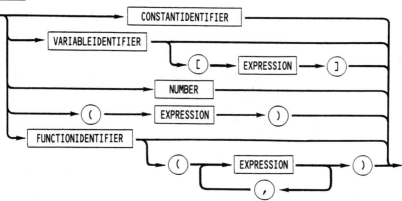

Figure 8.14

of the first element of the array (the zero-subscript one) from the base of the
stack frame at run-time. Since the length of the array is assumed known at
compile-time, the addresses of variables declared after an array declaration are
easily found too, as the following code shows

```
procedure ENTERVARIABLE;
  begin
    if SYM <> IDENT then ERROR(6) else
      begin
        ENTER(VARIABLE); GETSYM;
        if SYM = LBRACKET then (*array declaration*)
          begin
            GETSYM;
            if SYM <> NUMBER then ERROR(8) else
              begin
                if NUM < 1 then ERROR(31);
                TABLE[LASTENTRY].SIZE := NUM + 1; GETSYM
              end;
            ACCEPT(RBRACKET, 10)
          end;
        TABLE[LASTENTRY].ADDRESS := OFFSET;
        OFFSET := OFFSET + TABLE[LASTENTRY].SIZE (*arrays or scalars*)
      end
  end (*ENTERVARIABLE*);
```

In the rest of the parser we shall have to cater for the subscripts that may be
found after variable identifiers. The coding is all easily contained in procedure
ADDRESSFOR, which is extended to read

```
procedure ADDRESSFOR (I : TABLEINDEX);
(*load address for identifier at table entry I *)
  begin
    with TABLE[I] do
      begin
        STACKADDRESS(LEVEL, ADDRESS);
        if SYM = LBRACKET
          then (*subscript*)
            begin
              if SIZE = 1 then ERROR(11) (*unexpected subscript*);
              GETSYM;
              EXPRESSION([RBRACKET] + FOLLOWERS); ACCEPT(RBRACKET, 10);
              SUBSCRIPT(SIZE);
            end
          else if SIZE > 1 then ERROR(15) (*subscript expected*)
      end
  end (*ADDRESSFOR*);
```

Here we have also introduced an extra code-generating interface procedure,
SUBSCRIPT, whose purpose it will be to generate code that will add the value of

EXPRESSION to the value of the address of the first element of the array, so allowing access to be easily made to the required element. This code can also check that array bounds are not exceeded, hence the need for the parameter SIZE to SUBSCRIPT.

In terms of our simple stack computer, procedure SUBSCRIPT is trivial

```
procedure SUBSCRIPT (LIMIT : INTEGER);
    begin GEN(IND, 0, LIMIT - 1) end;
```

and the effect of the IND opcode is easily seen from the addition needed to the interpreter

```
IND: if (S[T] < 0) or (S[T] > A)
        then PS := INDCHK (*subscript out of range*)
        else begin DECTBY(1); S[T] := S[T] + S[T+1] end;
```

Finally, we present a complete program using these extensions, together with the generated code, from which the reader can see how everything fits together.

```
0 program TEST;
0 var
0   A[10], I;
1 begin
2   I := 0;
5   while I <= 10 do
10    begin
10      read(A[I]);
15      A[I] := A[I] + I;
28      write(A[I]);
35      I := I + 1
39    end
41 end.
```

Symbol table

Identifier	Class	Level	Address	Size
1 TEST	PROGRAM	0	0	0
2 A	VARIABLE	1	3	11
3 I	VARIABLE	1	14	1

Generated code

0 BRN 0 1			22 IND 0 10	subscript
1 INT 0 15	reserve space		23 LDV	value of A[I]
2 LDA 1 14	address of I		24 LDA 1 14	address of I
3 LDI 0 0			25 LDV	value of I
4 STO	I := 0		26 ADD	+ I
5 LDA 1 14	address of I		27 STO	assign to A[I]
6 LDV	value of I		28 LDA 1 3	address of A[0]
7 LDI 0 10	push 10		29 LDA 1 14	address of I
8 LEQ			30 LDV	value of I

```
 9 BZE 0 42   while I <= 10 do     31 IND 0 10    subscript
10 LDA 1 3     address of A[0]     32 LDV         value of A[I]
11 LDA 1 14    address of I        33 PRN         write (A[I])
12 LDV         value of I          34 NLN         next line
13 IND 0 10    subscript           35 LDA 1 14    address of I
14 INN         read (A[I])         36 LDA 1 14    address of I
15 LDA 1 3     address of A[0]     37 LDV         value of I
16 LDA 1 14    address of I        38 LDI 0 1     push 1
17 LDV         value of I          39 ADD
18 IND 0 10    A[I] := ...         40 STO         I := I + 1
19 LDA 1 3     address of A[0]     41 BRN 0 5     to start of loop
20 LDA 1 14    address of I        42 HLT
21 LDV         value of I
```

Exercises

8.33 Extend the parsing process to allow array dimensions to be set in terms of user-defined constants, for example

```
const
  MAX = 10;
var
  LIST[MAX];
```

8.34 Another relatively easy case is that of a one-dimensional array with fixed bounds, but with the lower bound chosen at the user's discretion. For example, an easy way to declare such arrays might be along the lines of

```
const
  BC = -44;
  AD = 300;
var
  WWII[1939 : 1945], ROMANBRITAIN[BC : AD];
```

Modify the parser and interpreter to cope with this case. (You will have to modify the analyser for CONSTDECLARATION to allow negative constants, for a start.) Note that it will not be possible to use the address field of the IND opcode to store both bounds for checking. However, addressing an element is quite easy. If we declare an array

```
var ARRAY[MIN : MAX]
```

then the address of the *I*th element in the array is computed as

```
I - MIN + address of first element of array
```

which may give ideas about the checking problem too, if you think of it as

```
(address of first element of array - MIN) + I
```

8.35 A little more ingenuity is called for if one is to allow two-dimensional arrays. Again, if these are of fixed size, addressing is quite easy. Suppose we declare a matrix

    var MATRIX[MINX : MAXX, MINY : MAXY]

Then we shall have to reserve (MAXX-MINX+1) * (MAXY-MINY+1) consecutive locations for the whole array. If we store the elements by rows (as in Pascal, but not as in FORTRAN), then the address of the *I,J*th element in the matrix will be found as

    (I - MINX) * (MAXY - MINY + 1) + (J - MINY) + address of first element

Checking array bounds and producing a new version of the IND opcode should keep you amused for a while.

8.36 Extend your system to allow whole arrays to be assigned one to another (providing they are of the same length).

8.37 Extend the system further to allow arrays to be passed as (value or reference) parameters to subprograms.

8.38 How would the material of this section be altered if all the extensions suggested earlier were to be incorporated into the compiler?

8.39 If you have attempted to generate native code for the compiler, make the necessary additions to handle arrays.

8.4 Storage allocation for other types

It will probably not have escaped the reader's attention, especially if he or she has attempted the exercises in the last section, that compilers for languages that handle a wide variety of types, both 'standard' and 'user defined', must surely take a far more sophisticated approach to constructing a symbol table and to storage allocation than the simple one we have used here. Although the nature of this text does not warrant a full discussion of this point, a few comments may be of interest, and in order.

In the first place, a compiler for a block-structured language will probably organize its symbol table as a collection of dynamically allocated trees, as was suggested in Exercise 8.9, with one root for each 'level' of nesting. Although using simple binary trees runs the risk of producing badly unbalanced trees, this is unlikely. Except for source programs which are produced by program generators, user programs tend to introduce identifiers with fairly random names; few compilers are likely to need really sophisticated tree-constructing algorithms.

Secondly, the nodes in the trees will be fairly complex record types. Besides the obvious links to other nodes in the tree, there will probably be pointers to other dynamically constructed nodes which contain descriptions of the types of the identifiers held in the main tree. For example, in the case of variables we might have, among other fields, something like

```
type
  KINDS = (ARRAYS, INTEGERS, BOOLEANS, CHARS, SETS, SUBRANGES);
  LINKS = ↑NODES;
  TYPES = ↑TYPEDESCRIPTORS;

  NODES = record
            NAME : ALFA;
            LLINK, RLINK : LINKS (*to other entries at this level*);
            TIPE : TYPES
          end (*NODES*);

  TYPEDESCRIPTORS = record
                      SIZE : INTEGER (*in storage units*);
                      case KIND : KINDS of
                        INTEGERS, BOOLEANS, CHARS : ( );
                        ARRAYS : (INDEX, BASETYPE : TYPES);
                        SETS   : (BASE : TYPES);
                        SUBRANGES : (LOWER, UPPER : INTEGER;
                                     RANGETYPE : TYPES);
                    end (*TYPEDESCRIPTORS*)
```

With this scheme, a Pascal declaration like

```
var
  MATRIX : array [1..10, 2..20] of set of CHAR;
```

might have entries which can be depicted something like Figure 8.15.

We may take this opportunity to comment on another rather poorly defined area in Pascal, one which has come in for much criticism. Suppose we were to declare

```
type
  LISTS = array [1 .. 10] of CHAR;
var
  X : LISTS;
  A : array [1 .. 10] of CHAR;
  B : array [1 .. 10] of CHAR;
  Z : LISTS
```

To most people it would seem obvious that A and B are of the same type, that an assignment of the form A := B would be quite legal, and, furthermore, that X and Z are of the same type as A and B. However, some compilers will be satisfied with mere **structural equivalence** of types before assignment may be permitted, while others may insist on so-called **name equivalence**. The original Pascal Report did not specify which was standard.

In this example A, B, X and Z all have structural equivalence. X and Z have name equivalence as well, as they have been specified in terms of a named type LISTS.

With the insight we now have we can see what this difference means from the compiler writer's viewpoint. Suppose A and B have entries in the symbol

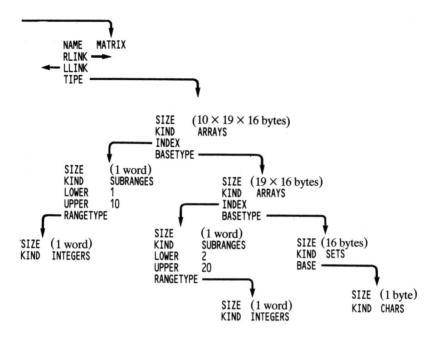

Figure 8.15

table pointed to by TOA and TOB respectively. Then for name equivalence we should insist on TOA↑.TIPE and TOB↑.TIPE being the same (that is, their TIPE pointers address the same descriptor), while for structural equivalence we should insist on TOA↑.TIPE↑ and TOA↑.TIPE↑ being the same (that is, their TIPE pointers address descriptors which have the same structure).

We have just touched on the tip of a large and difficult iceberg. If one adds the concept of type into a language, and insists on it being checked, the compilers become much larger and harder to follow than we have seen up till now. The energetic reader might like to follow up several of the ideas which now should come to mind. Try a selection of the following, which are deliberately rather vaguely phrased.

Exercises

8.40   As an exercise which is within your grasp, and which will give you a taste for what is involved, try adding the and and or operations to CLANG, with the same precedence rules as in Pascal, thus giving expressions which can be (anonymously) Boolean or integer (or, of course, incorrect. How does one cope with error recovery?) This could be described by the syntax diagrams in Figure 8.16.

CONDITION

EXPRESSION

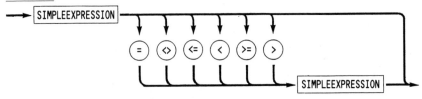

SIMPLEEXPRESSION

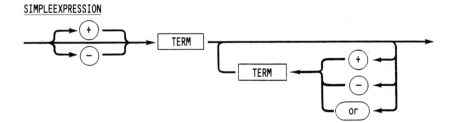

TERM

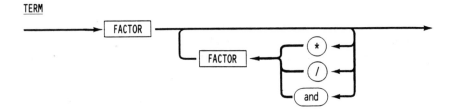

FACTOR

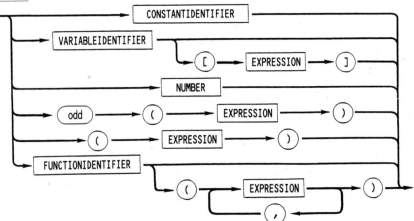

Figure 8.16

8.41 Generate code for these extensions using the 'short circuit' semantics, as well as the 'Boolean operator' approach. In the short circuit approach the operators and and or are defined to have semantic meanings such that

```
A and B    means   if A then B else FALSE
A or B     means   if A then TRUE else B
```

In Ada this has been made explicit: and and or alone have 'Boolean operator' semantics, but and then and or else have 'short circuit semantics'. Thus

```
A and then B    means   if A then B else FALSE
A or else B     means   if A then TRUE else B
```

Can you make your system accept both forms?

8.42 Just how do Pascal compilers deal with symbol tables?

8.43 Just how do real compilers keep track of type checking? Why should name equivalence be easier to handle than structural equivalence?

8.44 How do you suppose compilers keep track of storage allocation for structures like the Pascal record (with and without variants)?

8.45 How do you suppose the Pascal with statement might be handled?

8.46 Find out how storage is managed for dynamically allocated variables in a language like Pascal.

8.47 How does one cope with arrays of variable (dynamic) length in subprograms? You might like to read up on the concept of a **dope vector** in this regard.

8.48 In Pascal variable declarations a type specifier follows an identifier list, as for example in

```
var A, B, C : INTEGER;
```

Does this not make life more difficult for the compiler than if the type descriptor were to precede the identifier list? Why do you suppose Pascal uses the notation it does, what other alternatives are there, and what would be the advantages and disadvantages of each of them?

8.49 Why can we easily allow a Pascal pointer declaration to precede the definition of the type it points to? For example

```
type
  LINKS = ↑NODES (*NODES not declared yet*);
  NODES = record
             ETC : JUNK

             . . .
```

8.50 Brinch Hansen does not like the Pascal subrange type because it leads to ambiguities (for example, a value of 34 can be of type 0 .. 45, and also of type 30 .. 90 and so on), and so has omitted them from Edison. How should Pascal really have introduced the subrange concept, how could we overcome Brinch Hansen's objections, and what is the essential point he seems to have overlooked in discarding them?

8.51 In Edison, Brinch Hansen has changed the syntax popularized by Pascal for the declaration of types; for example Pascal's

```
type LISTS = array [1 .. 10] of RESULTS
```

becomes

```
array LISTS [1 .. 10] (RESULTS)
```

In what way is this an improvement over Pascal? Could something like this be done for function declarations, and if so how? Would it have any advantages or disadvantages?

8.52 One might accuse Pascal, Modula-2 and Edison of making a serious error of judgement – they do not introduce a string type as standard. Do you agree? Discuss whether what they offer in return is adequate and, if not, why not. Suggest why they might deliberately not have introduced a string type.

8.53 Brinch Hansen does not like variant records. (You may never have used them either.) What do they allow one to do in Pascal which is otherwise impossible, and why should it be necessary to provide the facility to do this? How is it provided in Edison and in Modula-2? Which is the better way, and why?

8.54 Many authors dislike Pascal's pointer types because they allow 'insecure programming'. What is meant by this? How could the security be improved? If you do not like pointer types, can you think of any alternative feature that would be more secure?

8.55 Some would claim that Pascal has at least two shortcomings that make it almost useless to the scientist – there are no COMPLEX types, one cannot pass 'variable length' arrays as parameters, and many implementations will not allow one to pass procedural parameters. Discuss this claim in some detail.

Further reading

There is quite a lot of material available on these subjects in many of the references cited previously. Rather than give explicit references, we leave the Joys of Discovery to the reader.

Chapter 9 **Concurrent programming**

It is the objective of this chapter to extend the CLANG language and its implementation to do what its name suggests – handle simple problems in concurrent programming. It is quite likely that this is a field which is new to the reader, and so we shall begin by discussing some rudimentary concepts in concurrent programming. Our treatment is necessarily brief, and the reader would be well advised to consult one of the recent excellent textbooks for more detail.

9.1 Fundamental concepts

A common way of introducing programming to novices is by the preparation of a 'recipe' or algorithm for some simple human activity, such as making a cup of tea, or running a bath. In such introductions the aim is usually to stress the idea of **sequential** algorithms, where 'one thing gets done at a time'. Although the process is probably familiar by now to most readers, on reflection it may be seen as a little perverse to try to twist all problem solving into this mould – indeed, that may be the very reason why some beginners find the sequential algorithm a difficult concept to grasp. Many human activities are better represented as a set of interacting processes, which are carried out in parallel. To take a simple example, a sequential algorithm for changing a flat tyre might be written

```
begin
  open boot
  take tool kit from boot
  remove hubcap
  loosen wheel nuts
  jack up car
  get spare from boot
  take off flat tyre
  put spare on
  lower jack
  tighten wheel nuts
  replace hubcap
  place flat tyre in boot
  place tool kit in boot
  close boot
end
```

but it might be difficult to convince a beginner that the order here was correct, especially if she was used to changing tyres with the aid of admirers. Based on such experience she might come up with something like

```
begin
                    open boot
    remove hubcap        and      take tool kit from boot
                    loosen wheel nuts
    jack up car          and      get spare from boot
                    take off flat tyre
                       put spare on
    lower jack           and      place flat tyre in boot
                    tighten wheel nuts
                 place tool kit in boot
    replace hubcap       and      closeboot
end
```

Here we have several examples of **concurrent processes**, which could in theory be undertaken by two or three almost autonomous processors – provided that they cooperate at crucial instants so as to keep in step (for example, taking off the flat tyre and getting the spare wheel from the boot are both processes which must be completed before the next process can start, but it does not matter which is completed first).

We shall define a **sequential process** as a sequence of operations carried out one at a time: the precise definition of an operation will depend on the level of detail at which the process is described. A **concurrent program** then contains a set or sets of such processes executing in parallel.

There are two motivations for the study of concurrency in programming languages. Firstly, concurrent facilities may be directly exploited in systems where one has genuine multiple processors, and such systems are becoming ever more common as technology improves. Secondly, concurrent programming facilities may allow some kinds of programs to be designed and structured more naturally in terms of autonomous (but almost invariably interacting) processes, even if they are eventually implemented on a single processing device, where their execution will, at best, be interleaved in **real-time**.

Concurrent multiprocessing of peripheral devices has been common for many years, as part of highly specialized operating system design. Because this usually has to be ultra-efficient, it has tended to be the domain of the highly skilled assembly-level programmer. It is only comparatively recently that high-level languages have approached the problem of providing reliable, easily understood constructs for concurrent programming; it is probably still true that few installations provide implementations of such high-level languages (perhaps because the demand for concurrency has been rather small). This is regrettable if one wishes to learn about concurrency, of course, but the situation is changing slowly, and the modern programmer should have at least some elementary knowledge of the constructs, and of the main problem areas that arise in concurrent programming.

9.2 Parallel processes, exclusion and synchronization

We shall introduce the notation

cobegin S_1; S_2; S_3 ; ... S_n coend

to denote that the statements S_k can be executed concurrently. Whether this execution takes place truly in parallel, or whether it is actually interleaved in time (as it would have to be if only one processor was available), is irrelevant here.

A convenient way to depict the effect of a concurrent statement, taking into account the statements S_0 and S_{n+1} which precede and follow it in a given program, is by the use of a **precedence graph**. The piece of code

S_0; cobegin S_1; S_2; S_3; ... S_n coend; S_{n+1}

can be represented by a precedence graph (Figure 9.1).

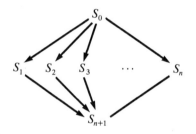

Figure 9.1

Only after all the statements S_1 ... S_n have been executed will S_{n+1} be executed. Similarly the construction

S_0
cobegin
  S_1
  begin
    S_2
    cobegin S_3; S_4 coend
    S_5
  end
coend
S_6

can be represented by the precedence graph in Figure 9.2.

Although it is easy enough to depict code using the cobegin...coend construct in this way, we should comment that precedence graphs can be constructed which cannot be translated into this highly structured notation. For example,

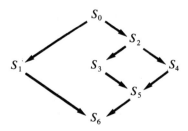

Figure 9.2

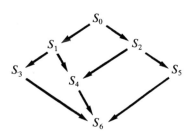

Figure 9.3

the graph in Figure 9.3 cannot be expressed entirely in terms of simple cobegin...coend statements.

As an example of the use of the construct, we give a Pascal-like excerpt from a program for file processing, using one procedure to UPDATE concurrently with GET and PUT operations.

```
UPDATE(BUFFER) (*for first record*);
while not EOF(INPUT) do
  begin
    OUTPUT ↑ := BUFFER;
    BUFFER := INPUT ↑;
    cobegin
      GET(INPUT); UPDATE(BUFFER); PUT(OUTPUT)
    coend
  end (*while not eof*)
```

We may use this example to introduce two problem areas in concurrent programming which simply do not arise in sequential programming (at least, not that the high-level user can ever perceive). We have already intimated that we build concurrent programs out of sequential processes that must be regarded as executing simultaneously. A sequential process must be thought of as a private data structure and a sequential algorithm that operates on it; the whole has the important property that it always gives the same result, regardless of how fast it is executed. When sequential processes start to execute in parallel their time independence remains invariant only if their data structures remain truly private. If a process uses variables which other processes may simultaneously be changing, it is easy to see that the behaviour of the program as a whole may depend crucially on the relative speeds of each of its parts, and may become totally unpredictable.

In our example the three processes access totally private variables, so their concurrent composition is equivalent to any of the six possible ways in which they could have been arranged sequentially. As concurrent processes, however, the total execution time might be reduced. However, if the program fragment were coded

```
UPDATE(BUFFER) (*for first record*);
while not EOF(INPUT) do
   cobegin
     begin (*write*) OUTPUT ↑ := BUFFER; PUT(OUTPUT) end;
     begin (*read*) BUFFER  := INPUT ↑; GET(INPUT)  end;
     UPDATE(BUFFER)
   coend (*while not eof*)
```

chaos might result, because we could never predict with certainty what was in any of INPUT ↑, OUTPUT ↑ or BUFFER. At the same time the reader should appreciate that it must be possible to allow processes to share data structures (such as the BUFFER above), otherwise concurrent processes could never exchange data and cooperate on tasks of mutual interest.

If one wishes to succeed in building large, reliable, concurrent programs, one will ideally want to use programming languages that cater specially for such problems, and are so well structured that time-dependent errors can be detected at compile-time, before they cause chaos – in effect the compiler must protect programmers from themselves. The simple cobegin…coend structure is inadequate as a reliable programming tool: it must be augmented with some restrictions on the forms of the statements which can be executed in parallel, and some method must be found of handling the problems of

(a) **Mutual exclusion** – where a process can be guaranteed that it can access a **critical region** of code and/or a data structure in real-time without simultaneous interference from competing processes.

(b) **Synchronization** – where two otherwise autonomous processes can be forced to wait in real-time for one another, or for some other event, and to signal one another when it is safe to proceed.

How best to handle these issues is a matter for current research; suffice it to say that various methods have been proposed and implemented in several modern languages, like Concurrent Pascal, Pascal-Plus, Modula, Edison, Concurrent Euclid and Ada. Alarums and excursions: we propose to study a simple one of these in CLANG in this chapter, and a more sophisticated one in the next chapter.

The exclusion and synchronization problems, although fundamentally distinct, have a lot in common. A simple way of handling them is to use the concept of the **semaphore**, introduced by Dijkstra in 1968. Although there is a simple integer value associated with a semaphore S, it must be thought of as a new type of variable, on which the only valid operations, beside the assignment of an initial associated integer value, are P(S) (from the Dutch *passeren*, meaning to pass) and V(S) (from the Dutch *vrijgeven*, meaning to release). In American or English these are often called 'wait' and 'signal'. The operations allow a process to cause itself to wait for a certain event, and then to be resumed when signalled by another process that the event has occurred. We define

- P(S) or wait(S)   Wait until the value associated with S is positive, then subtract 1 from S and continue execution
- V(S) or signal(S)   Add 1 to the value associated with S. This may allow a process that is waiting because it executed P(S) to continue.

Both wait(S) and signal(S) must be performed 'indivisibly' – there can be no partial completion of the operation while something else is going on.

As an example of the use of semaphores to protect a critical region, we give the following program, which also illustrates having two instances of a procedure active at once.

```
program CONCURRENT;
var
  SHARED, SEMAPHORE;
procedure PROCESS (LIMIT);
  var LOOP;
  begin
    LOOP := 1;
    while LOOP <= LIMIT do
      begin
        wait(SEMAPHORE); SHARED := SHARED + 1; signal(SEMAPHORE);
        LOOP := LOOP + 1
      end
  end;
begin
  SEMAPHORE := 1; SHARED := 0;
  cobegin
    PROCESS(4); PROCESS(5)
  coend;
  write(SHARED)
end.
```

Each of the processes has its own private local loop counter LOOP, but both increment the same global variable SHARED, access to which is controlled by the (shared) SEMAPHORE. Notice that we are assuming that we can use a simple assignment to set an initial value for a semaphore, even though we have implied that it is not really a simple integer variable.

As an example of the use of semaphores to effect synchronization, we present a solution to a simple producer–consumer problem. The idea here is that one process produces items, and another consumes them, asynchronously. The items are passed through a middleman, who can only hold one item in stock at one time. This means that the producer may have to wait until the middleman is ready to accept an item, and the consumer may have to wait for the middleman to receive a consignment before he can take an item. An algorithm for doing this follows.

```
program PRODUCERCONSUMER;
var
  CANSTORE, CANTAKE;
procedure PRODUCER;
  begin
    repeat
      PRODUCEITEM;
      wait(CANSTORE); GIVETOMIDDLEMAN; signal(CANTAKE)
    forever
  end;
procedure CONSUMER;
  begin
    repeat
      wait(CANTAKE); TAKEFROMMIDDLEMAN; signal(CANSTORE);
      CONSUMEITEM
    forever
  end;
begin
  CANSTORE := 1;  CANTAKE := 0;
  cobegin
    PRODUCER;  CONSUMER
  coend
end.
```

A problem that may not be immediately apparent is that communicating processes that have to synchronize, or ensure that they have exclusive access to a critical region, may become **deadlocked** when they all – perhaps erroneously – end up waiting on the same semaphore (or even different ones), with no process still active that can signal others. In the following variation on the above example this is quite obvious, but it is not always so simple to detect deadlock, even in quite simple programs.

```
program PRODUCERCONSUMER;
var
  CANSTORE, CANTAKE;
procedure PRODUCER (N);
  var I;
  begin
    I := 1;
    while I <= N do
```

```
      begin
        PRODUCEITEM; I := I + 1;
        wait(CANSTORE); GIVETOMIDDLEMAN; signal(CANTAKE)
      end
  end;
procedure CONSUMER (N);
  var I;
  begin
    I := 1;
    while I <= N do
      begin
        wait(CANTAKE); TAKEFROMMIDDLEMAN; signal(CANSTORE);
        CONSUMEITEM; I := I + 1
      end
  end;
begin
  CANSTORE := 1;  CANTAKE := 0;
  cobegin
    PRODUCER(12); CONSUMER(5)
  coend
end.
```

Here the obvious outcome is that only the first five of the objects produced can be consumed – when CONSUMER finishes, PRODUCER will find itself waiting forever for the middleman to dispose of the sixth item.

In the next section we shall show how we might implement concurrency using cobegin...coend, and the wait and signal primitives, by making additions to our simple language. In fact this is remarkably easy to do – so far as compilation is concerned. Concurrent execution of the programs so compiled is another matter, of course, but we shall suggest how an interpretive system can give the effect of simulating concurrent execution, using run-time support rather like that found in some real-time systems.

Exercises

9.1 One of the classic problems used to illustrate the use of semaphores is the so-called 'bounded buffer' problem. This is an enhancement of the example used before, where the middleman can store up to MAX items at one time. In computer terms these are usually stored in a circular buffer, stored in an array called, say, BUFFER and managed by using two indices, say HEAD and TAIL; in terms of our simple language we should have something like

```
const
  MAX = Size of BUFFER;
var
  BUFFER[MAX], HEAD, TAIL;
```

with HEAD and TAIL both initially set to 1. Adding to the buffer is always done at the tail, and removing from the buffer is done from the head, along the lines of

```
add to buffer:
    BUFFER[TAIL] := ITEM
    TAIL := (TAIL + 1) mod MAX
remove from buffer:
    ITEM := BUFFER[HEAD]
    HEAD := (HEAD + 1) mod MAX
```

How would one set up a system where one process continually added to the buffer, while a parallel process tried to empty it, with the restrictions that: (a) we cannot add to the buffer if it is full; (b) we cannot draw from the buffer if it is empty; (c) we cannot add to the buffer and draw from the buffer at exactly the same instant in real-time?

9.2 Another classic problem has become known as Conway's problem, after the man who first proposed it. Write a program to read the data from 10 column cards, and rewrite it in 15-column lines, with the following changes: after every card image an extra blank is added, and every adjacent pair of asterisks is replaced by an up-arrow (↑).

This is easily solved by a single sequential program, but may be solved (more naturally?) by three concurrent processes. One of these, INPUT, reads the cards and simply passes the characters (with the additional trailing blank) through a finite buffer, say INBUFFER to a process SQUASH which simply looks for double asterisks and passes a stream of modified characters through a second finite buffer, say OUTBUFFER, to a process OUTPUT, which extracts the characters from the second buffer and prints them in 15-column lines.

9.3 A semaphore based system – syntax, semantics and code generation

To provide a system with which the reader can experiment in concurrent programming, we shall add a few more permissible statements to our language, governed by the syntax diagrams in Figure 9.4.

There is no real restriction in limiting the statements that may be processed concurrently to procedure calls, as any other statement may be written into a trivial procedure.

For our simple implementation we shall limit the number of processes that may execute in parallel, and also the number of parameters that any procedure may have. We shall also restrict the cobegin...coend construction to

COBEGINSTATEMENT

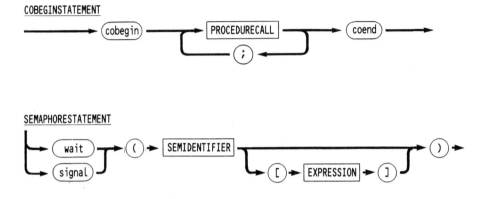

SEMAPHORESTATEMENT

Figure 9.4

appearing in the main program block. These restrictions are really imposed by our pseudo-machine, as we shall see. We therefore make the following changes to the constant and type declarations

```
const
  PARAMAX = 24 (*Max number of parameters*);
  PROCMAX = 10 (*Max concurrent processes*);
type
  SYMBOLS =
    (UNKNOWN, IDENT, NUMBER, STRINGSYM, PLUS, MINUS, TIMES, SLASH, ODDSYM,
     EQLSYM, NEQSYM, LSSSYM, LEQSYM, GTRSYM, GEQSYM, LPAREN, RPAREN,
     COMMA, SEMICOLON, PERIOD, LBRACKET, RBRACKET, BECOMES,
     BEGINSYM, ENDSYM, IFSYM, THENSYM, WHILESYM, DOSYM, READSYM, WRITESYM,
     STACKSYM, COBEGSYM, COENDSYM, WAITSYM, SIGNALSYM,
     CONSTSYM, VARSYM, PROCSYM);
```

and make some obvious additions to FIRSTSTATEMENT

```
FIRSTSTATEMENT := [IDENT, BEGINSYM, IFSYM, WHILESYM, WRITESYM, READSYM,
                   STACKSYM, COBEGSYM, WAITSYM, SIGNALSYM];
```

There are obvious minor additions to the list of reserved words, and we shall need some more error messages, but these need not be given in detail here. As implied above, the main difference comes about in parsing STATEMENTS. In implementing the restrictions on concurrency, it is expedient to introduce a global Boolean variable PROCCALL, which is set to FALSE for all statements except procedure calls. Setting PROCCALL within each of the subparsers like IFSTATEMENT and WHILESTATEMENT need not be shown in detail either; the changes to STATEMENT itself may be seen in the code below.

```
     begin (*STATEMENT*)
**     PROCCALL := TRUE;
       if SYM in FIRSTSTATEMENT then
```

```
          case SYM of
            IDENT:
              begin
                SEARCHID(IDENTRY, [VARIABLE, FUNC, PROC], 22);
                with TABLE[IDENTRY] do
                  case CLASS of
                    CONSTANT, PROG, (*error - treat as assignment*)
                    FUNC, VARIABLE:
                      begin
                        if CLASS in [VARIABLE, CONSTANT, PROG]
                          then ADDRESSFOR(IDENTRY)
                          else
                            if BLOCKENTRY = IDENTRY
                              then STACKADDRESS(LEVEL+1, -SIZE-1)
                              else ERROR(20);
                        if SYM = BECOMES then GETSYM else
                          begin ERROR(21); if SYM = EQLSYM then GETSYM end;
                        EXPRESSION(FOLLOWERS); ASSIGN;
**                      PROCCALL := FALSE
                      end;
                    MONI, (*error - treat as procedure call*)
                    PROC:
                      begin PARAMETERS(SIZE, FOLLOWERS); CALL(LEVEL, ADDRESS) end
                  end (*case CLASS*)
              end (*IDENT*);
            IFSYM    : IFSTATEMENT;
            BEGINSYM : COMPOUNDSTATEMENT(FOLLOWERS);
            WHILESYM : WHILESTATEMENT;
            WRITESYM : WRITESTATEMENT;
            READSYM  : READSTATEMENT;
**          WAITSYM,
**          SIGNALSYM : SEMASTATEMENT;
**          COBEGSYM  : COBEGINSTATEMENT;
**          STACKSYM  : begin CODEFORDUMP(BLOCKLEVEL); GETSYM; PROCCALL := FALSE end
          end (*case SYM*);
        TEST(FOLLOWERS, [], 32)
      end (*STATEMENT*);
```

The procedure for parsing COBEGINSTATEMENT is essentially just a variation on that for parsing COMPOUNDSTATEMENT, and follows as

```
procedure COBEGINSTATEMENT;
  var
    PROCESSES : INTEGER (*count number of processes*);
  begin
    if BLOCKLEVEL <> 1 then ERROR(44) (*only from global level*);
    PROCESSES := 0; STORELABEL(STARTLOOP); STARTPROCESSES; GETSYM;
    STATEMENT([SEMICOLON, COENDSYM] + FOLLOWERS);
```

```
  if PROCCALL
    then PROCESSES := PROCESSES + 1 else ERROR(42) (*only procedure calls*);
  while SYM in [SEMICOLON] + FIRSTSTATEMENT do
    begin
      ACCEPT(SEMICOLON, 2);
      STATEMENT([SEMICOLON, COENDSYM] + FOLLOWERS);
      if PROCCALL then PROCESSES := PROCESSES + 1 else ERROR(42)
    end;
  ACCEPT(COENDSYM, 43);
  BACKPATCH(STARTLOOP, PROCESSES); STOPPROCESSES;
  if PROCESSES > PROCMAX then ERROR(45) (*too many*);
  PROCCALL := FALSE
end (*COBEGINSTATEMENT*);
```

Notes

(a) We need to generate some extra code for cobegin and coend, so that the run-time system can prepare to initiate the correct number of processes; a count of the processes is maintained in PROCESSES, and later patched into the code generated by STARTPROCESSES for cobegin.

(b) The STARTPROCESSES procedure generates code such that the procedure calls which follow it are to be temporarily inhibited.

(c) The code generated by the STOPPROCESSES procedure signals to the run-time system that all the procedure calls so inhibited are to be performed concurrently, at the same time suspending operation of the main program. This will become clearer in the next section.

We also need to modify ENTERPARAMETER to check that the limit on the number of parameters is not exceeded

```
    procedure ENTERPARAMETER;
      begin
        if SYM <> IDENT then ERROR(6) else
          begin
            ENTER(VARIABLE); PARAMS := PARAMS + 1;
**          if PARAMS > PARAMAX then ERROR(41); GETSYM
          end
      end (*ENTERPARAMETER*);
```

Parsing the semaphore handlers is effected by a variation on the code for INPUTSTATEMENT, and presents no great problems either. Like the read statement, the wait and signal statements are really procedure calls with a var parameter, and the code for parsing them follows as

```
    procedure SEMASTATEMENT;
      var
        WAITSEM : BOOLEAN;
```

```
begin
  WAITSEM := SYM = WAITSYM; GETSYM;
  if SYM <> LPAREN then ERROR(18) else
    begin
      GETSYM;
      if SYM <> IDENT then ERROR(6) else
        begin
          SEARCHID(IDENTRY, [VARIABLE], 28);
          ADDRESSFOR(IDENTRY);
          if WAITSEM then CODEFORWAIT else CODEFORSIGNAL
        end;
      ACCEPT(RPAREN, 13)
    end;
  PROCCALL := FALSE
end (*SEMASTATEMENT*);
```

So far as actual code generation goes for our simple machine, we simply augment the instruction set to include four new opcodes, CBG, CND, WGT and SIG; the set of opcodes is now

```
OPCODES = (LDI, LDA, CAL, RET, STK, INT, IND, CBG, BRN, BZE,
           WGT, SIG, CND, NEG, ADD, SUB, MUL, DVD, OD,  EQL, NEQ,
           LSS, GEQ, GTR, LEQ, STO, HLT, INN, PRN, PRS, NLN, LDV);
```

and we have

```
procedure STARTPROCESSES;
  begin EMIT(CBG) end;
procedure STOPPROCESSES;
  begin EMIT(CND) end;
procedure CODEFORSIGNAL;
  begin EMIT(SIG) end;
procedure CODEFORWAIT;
  begin EMIT(WGT) end;
```

CBG actually takes an A parameter as well, to denote the number of processes to be launched; this is added by the BACKPATCH call in COBEGINSTATEMENT.

As before, this might be clarified by presenting a variation on an earlier example, which shows the use of semaphores to protect a critical region of code accessing a shared variable, the use of processes which use simple value parameters, and the invocation of more than one instance of the same process.

```
0 program CONCURRENT;
1 var
1   SHARED, SEMAPHORE;
1
1 procedure PROCESS (LIMIT);
2   var LOOP;
```

```
2  begin
3    LOOP := 1;
6    while LOOP <= LIMIT do
12     begin
12       write(LIMIT, SHARED);
19       wait(SEMAPHORE);  SHARED := SHARED + 1; signal(SEMAPHORE);
29       LOOP := LOOP + 1
33     end
35  end;
37
37 begin
38   SEMAPHORE := 1; SHARED := 0;
44   cobegin PROCESS(4); PROCESS(5 + 3) coend
51 end.
```

The code produced in the compilation of this program would read

```
0  BRN 0 37     jump to start of main code
1  BRN 0 2      start procedure PROCESS
2  INT 0 4      reserve stack space (1 local variable)
3  LDA 2 3
4  LDI 0 1
5  STO          LOOP := 1
6  LDA 2 3
7  LDV
8  LDA 2 -1
9  LDV
10 LEQ          LOOP <= LIMIT?
11 BZE 0 36
12 LDA 2 -1
13 LDV
14 PRN          write (LIMIT)
15 LDA 1 3
16 LDV
17 PRN          write (SHARED) - declared at main program level
18 NLN
19 LDA 1 4
20 WGT          wait (SEMAPHORE) - declared at main program level
21 LDA 1 3
22 LDA 1 3
23 LDV
24 LDI 0 1
25 ADD
26 STO          SHARED := SHARED + 1
27 LDA 1 4
28 SIG          signal (SEMAPHORE)
29 LDA 2 3
```

```
30 LDA 2 3
31 LDV
32 LDI 0 1
33 ADD
34 STO          LOOP := LOOP + 1 - declared at procedure level
35 BRN 0 6      jump to start of loop test
36 RET 2 2      leave process (looks like normal return)
37 INT 0 5      reserve main program stack space (2 variables)
38 LDA 1 4
39 LDI 0 1
40 STO          SEMAPHORE := 1
41 LDA 1 3
42 LDI 0 0
43 STO          SHARED := 0
44 CBG 0 2      prepare to initiate 2 processes
45 LDI 0 4      set parameter for first instance of PROCESS
46 CAL 1 1      prepare to launch first instance of PROCESS
                - looks like a normal procedure call, but
                it is delayed until all processes are ready
47 LDI 0 5
48 LDI 0 3
49 ADD          set parameter for second instance of PROCESS
50 CAL 1 1      prepare to launch second instance of PROCESS
51 CND          coend - actually start processes
52 HLT          end main program
```

Exercises

9.3 If you study the above code carefully you might come up with the idea that it could be optimized by adding 'level' and 'offset' components to the WGT and SIG opcodes. Is this a feasible proposition?

9.4 The reader might be struck with the apparently clumsy way in which the Boolean variable PROCCALL is first set true in STATEMENT and is then unset in almost all paths emanating from this. Why do we not set it false initially, and simply set it true when we detect a procedure call?

9.5 What possible outputs would you expect from the example program given here? What outputs could you expect if the semaphore was not used?

9.6 Is it not a better idea to introduce process as a reserved word, rather than just specifying a process as a procedure? Discuss arguments for and against this proposal, and try to implement it anyway.

9.4 Run-time support

We may now give some consideration to the problem of how one might interpret the stack machine code generated by this system. In essence, what we set out to do is to simulate one 'processor' which can share its time among several processes, executing each for a few steps, before moving on to the next. This is very close to what occurs in some time-sharing systems in real life, with one major difference. 'Real' systems are usually interrupt-driven by clock and peripheral controller devices, with hardware mechanisms controlling when some process switches occur, and software mechanisms controlling when others happen as a result of wait and signal operations on semaphores. On our toy system we shall simulate **time-slicing** by letting each active process execute for a small random number of steps before control is passed to another one.

The memory of the complete system must be divided up between the parallel processes while they are executing. This is not the place to enter into a study of sophisticated memory management techniques. Instead, what we shall do is to divide the memory (which remains after the allocation to the main program stack frame) equally among each of the processes which have been initiated.

The processes are started by the main program; while they are executing, the main program is effectively dormant. When all the processes have run to completion, the main program is activated once more. While they are running, one can think of each as a separate program, each requiring its own stack memory, and each managing it in the way discussed in Chapter 8. Each process must thus have its own set of registers, program counter, display and so on. To accomplish this, we shall introduce a linked ring structure of so-called **process descriptors**, defined as follows

```
type
  PROCINDEX = 0 .. PROCMAX;
var
  PROC : array [PROCINDEX] of (*process descriptors*)
            record
              DISPLAY  : array [LEVELS] of INTEGER;
              P, B, T,                (*program counter, base, stack pointer*);
              STACKEND : INTEGER   (*memory limit*);
              NEXT,                   (*ring pointer*)
              QUEUE    : PROCINDEX (*linked waiting on a semaphore*);
              READY    : BOOLEAN   (*process active flag*)
            end (*PROC*);
  CURPROC, CURRENT : PROCINDEX       (*point to currently executing process*);
```

The READY field indicates whether the process is still executing (READY = TRUE), or has run to completion or been suspended on a semaphore (READY = FALSE). The 0th entry is used for the main program – this is set READY = FALSE when the concurrent processes are started, and set back to READY = TRUE when the last of these has been completed.

As already mentioned, the process descriptors are linked to form a circular ring. As an example, consider the case where a main program has just launched three concurrent processes, as shown in Figure 9.5.

If a group of processes are all waiting on a semaphore, their READY fields will all be set to FALSE, and their QUEUE fields will be used to link them in a FIFO

Ring after main program launches three concurrent processes:

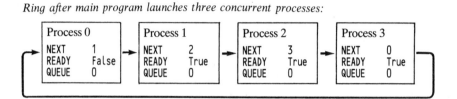

If process 2 is forced to wait on a semaphore:

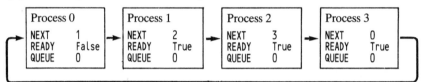

If process 3 runs to completion in the next 'time slice':

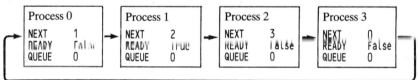

If process 1 then signals that process 2 may again proceed:

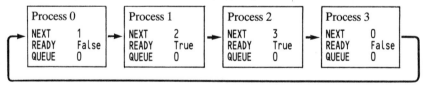

The ring when all processes have been completed:

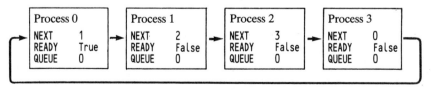

Figure 9.5

queue, set up in real-time as the wait operations were handled. We return to this point a little later on.

Initialization of the machine proceeds much as before; for the main program, for example, we set

```
for LOOP := 0 to STACKMAX do S[LOOP] := 0; PS := RUNNING;
with PROC[0] do (*start main program*)
  begin
    T := -1; P := 0; B := 0; DISPLAY[1] := 0;
    QUEUE := 0; READY := TRUE; STACKEND := STACKMAX; NEXT := 1
  end;
```

(Note that the limit on memory which the main program can use is now stored in STACKEND, rather than just being the constant STACKMAX.)

We go on to set all processes inactive

```
for CURPROC := 1 to PROCMAX do with PROC[CURPROC] do
  begin READY := FALSE; DISPLAY[1] := 0; QUEUE := 0 end
```

Note that DISPLAY[1] is set to zero, for all processes are able to access the global variables of the main program. Indeed, this is the only effective means we have of sharing data between them. Until we get on and do Exercise 8.13 we cannot even communicate using var parameters.

After this we can set CURPROC := 0 (to indicate that the main program is the one to be executed), and start the repetitive interpretation much as before. The essence of this can be expressed

```
INITIALIZE;
repeat
  NEXTSTEP; if PS = RUNNING then CHOOSEPROCESS
until PS <> RUNNING;
if PS <> FINISHED then POSTMORTEM
```

with NEXTSTEP as follows

```
procedure NEXTSTEP;
  var I : INSTRUCTIONS (*current*);
  begin
    CURRENT := CURPROC;
    with PROC[CURRENT] do
      begin
        I := CODE[P]; P := P + 1;
        with I do case F of (*most as before, but see later*)
      end (*with PROC*)
  end (*NEXTSTEP*);
```

that is, the use of the with PROC[CURRENT] construction (where CURRENT is the index into PROC for the currently executing process) makes for relatively little change in what has gone before, save that most secondary procedures called by the interpreter must make use of the same idea, for example

```
procedure DECTBY (I : INTEGER);
(*Decrement stack pointer*)
  begin with PROC[CURRENT] do T := T - I end;

procedure INCTBY (I : INTEGER);
(*Increment stack pointer*)
  begin
    with PROC[CURRENT] do
      begin T := T + I; if T > STACKEND - MARKSTKSIZE then PS := STKCHK end
  end (*INCTBY*);
```

The algorithm for CHOOSEPROCESS uses a variable STEPS which is set to a small random number at the start of concurrent processing, and is then decremented after each pseudo-machine instruction, or set to zero when a process is forced to wait, or terminates normally. When STEPS reaches zero, the process descriptor ring is searched cyclically (using the NEXT pointer), to find another process with which to continue for a further small (random) number of steps.

Of course this process must be READY to continue execution. There is a point of some little subtlety here. If the search is instigated by virtue of one process being forced to wait on a semaphore or terminating normally, it must find *another* process to execute. There may be no such process, in which case a state of **deadlock** has been detected. However, if the search is instigated by virtue of a process reaching the end of its selected number of STEPS, then control *can* return to the same process if no other ready process can be found. This necessitates the use of two pointers, CURRENT and CURPROC, as will be seen by a careful study of the code below. The search is easily programmed.

```
procedure CHOOSEPROCESS;
(*from current process traverse ring of descriptors to next ready process*)
  begin
    if CURPROC <> 0 then (*only need to switch if it is not the main program*)
      if STEPS <> 0 then STEPS := STEPS - 1 else (*time for a change*)
      begin
        repeat CURPROC := PROC[CURPROC].NEXT until PROC[CURPROC].READY;
        STEPS := RANDOM(STEPMAX) + 1
      end
  end (*CHOOSEPROCESS*);
```

We are here presuming that we have a suitable integer function RANDOM(LIMIT) for generating a sequence of random numbers, suitably scaled to lie in the range $0 \leqslant RANDOM < LIMIT$.

The mechanism of the cobegin...coend system is next to be discussed. As we have developed the system, processes are nothing other than procedures, and we have left the code generation between the cobegin and coend as a set of procedure calls. There is a fundamental difference, of course, in the way in which such procedure calls execute. After the cobegin, transfer of control must not pass immediately to the called procedures but must remain with the main program until all processes can be started together – the reason being that parameters may have to be set up, and this will have to be done in the environment of the main program.

Consequently, the code generated by the STARTPROCESSES procedure (in our simple machine, the CBG opcode) is used to set a flag (STARTINGPROCESSES), which can be inspected by the CAL opcode to see whether a direct, or delayed, transfer of control is wanted. At the point where CBG is obeyed the system can also decide on how to divide the remaining memory up among the imminent processes. This is done by examining the current top-of-stack pointer PROC[0].T. At first it might seem that the memory each process can acquire is given by

$$\frac{\text{STACKMAX} - \text{PROC[0].T}}{\text{NUMBERPROCESSES}}$$

and so it would be, except that one must allow for parameters which still have to be pushed onto the stack ready for the processes to pick them up. To make this simple, we limit the number of parameters which a procedure may have to some constant, say PARAMAX, and proceed as follows

```
CBG:
  begin
    STARTINGPROCESSES := TRUE; OLDT := T (*save current top of stack*);
    PARTITION := (STACKMAX - T) div A - PARAMAX (*divide up rest of memory*);
    if PARTITION <= 0 then PS := STKCHK
  end (*cobegin*);
```

The mechanics of coend are easy too, for we merely unset STARTINGPROCESSES, deactivate the main program, close the descriptor ring, and choose one of the processes (at random) to continue execution.

```
CND:
  begin
    STARTINGPROCESSES := FALSE;
    if NPROCS > 0 then
      begin
        PROC[0].READY := FALSE; PROC[NPROCS].NEXT := 0 (*close ring*);
        CURPROC := RANDOM(NPROCS) + 1 (*next process to execute*);
        STEPS := RANDOM(STEPMAX) + 1 (*initial simulated time slice*)
      end
  end (*coend*);
```

A procedure can now be either a *sequential procedure* or a *concurrent process*; this necessitates changes to the calling and returning action. The operation of a *call* can be understood with reference to the code below.

```
CAL:
  if not STARTINGPROCESSES
    then (*normal call*)
      begin
        S[T+1] := DISPLAY[L+1]; S[T+2] := B; S[T+3] := P;
```

```
      B := T + 1; P := A; DISPLAY[L+1] := B
    end
  else (*prepare for subsequent concurrent entry*)
    begin
      NPROCS := NPROCS + 1;
      with PROC[NPROCS] do
        begin
          B := PROC[CURRENT].T + 1; P := A; DISPLAY[L+1] := B;
          T := B - 1; S[T+1] := DISPLAY[L+1]; S[T+2] := B;
          S[T+3] := 0 (*fiddle return address*);
          STACKEND := T + PARTITION; READY := TRUE; NEXT := NPROCS + 1
        end;
      INCTBY(PARTITION) (*leave work area for process*)
    end;
```

Notes

(a)   If STARTINGPROCESSES is false, CAL behaves just as it did for the earlier interpreters.

(b)   If STARTINGPROCESSES is true we set up the mark stack portion of the stack frame for the procedure which will subsequently be activated by the CND code. This is done in the context of a new process descriptor, of course, which necessitates the with PROC[NPROCS] do statement.

(c)   When STARTINGPROCESSES is true we set the base B for the first intended process stack frame just above the stack top for the main program; the main program stack pointer is then moved PARTITION units higher, in preparation for setting up the next procedure call (which, as we have already remarked, may require the evaluation of parameters).

(d)   The return address for a process procedure is set to an artificial value of zero, which can later be detected by the *return* as an indication that the process is complete, and may be deactivated.

The operation of a *return* may be understood with reference to the code below:

```
RET:
  begin
    T := B - A; DISPLAY[L] := S[B]; P := S[B+2]; B := S[B+1];
    if P = 0 then (*we are completing a concurrent process*)
      begin
        NPROCS := NPROCS - 1;
        if NPROCS = 0
          then (*reactivate main program*)
            begin
              PROC[0].T := OLDT (*restore old stack pointer*);
              PROC[0].READY := TRUE; CURPROC := 0
            end
```

```
        else (*complete this process only*)
          begin
            STEPS := 0 (*force choice of new process*);
            CHOOSEPROCESS (*which may not be able to find another*);
            if CURRENT = CURPROC then PS := DEDCHK; READY := FALSE
          end
    end
end;
```

Notes

(a) Much of this is as before, except that we must check for the artificial return address mentioned above. If this is detected, we deactivate the process, and check for deadlock.

(b) When all processes have been completed, we restore the top-of-stack pointer to the value OLDT, saved at the start of process activation.

The last point to be considered is that of implementing semaphore operations. This is a little subtle. The simplest semantic meaning for the wait and signal operations is probably

```
wait(S)      while S ≤ 0 do (*nothing*)
             S := S - 1
signal(S)    S := S + 1
```

where, as we have remarked, the testing and incrementing must be be done as indivisible operations. The interpreter allows easy implementation of this otherwise rather awkward property, because the entire operation can be handled by one pseudo-operation (the WGT and SIG opcodes).

However, the simple semantic interpretation above is probably never implemented, for it implies what is known as a **busy–wait** operation, where a processor is tied up cycling around wasting effort doing nothing. Implementations of semaphores prefer to deactivate the waiting process completely, possibly adding it to a **queue** of such processes, which may later be examined efficiently when a signal operation gives the all-clear for a process to continue. Although the semantics of signal do not require a queue to be formed, we have chosen to employ one here.

Wait(SEMAPHORE) can be performed with an algorithm like

```
if SEMAPHORE > 0
  then SEMAPHORE ← SEMAPHORE - 1
  else set STEPS to 0 and CHOOSEPROCESS
       PROC[CURRENT].READY ← FALSE
       add PROC[CURRENT] to end of queue for SEMAPHORE
       PROC[CURRENT].QUEUE ← 0
```

Similarly, signal(SEMAPHORE) is readily implemented as

```
if SEMAPHORE >= 0
  then SEMAPHORE ← SEMAPHORE + 1
  else find which process should be WOKEN
       PROC[WOKEN].READY ← TRUE
       set start of queue for SEMAPHORE to point to PROC[WOKEN].QUEUE
```

The problem now arises of how to represent a semaphore variable. The first idea that might come to mind is to use something on the lines of

```
type
  SEMAPHORE = record
                COUNT : 0 .. MAXINT (*associated value*);
                QUEUE : PROCINDEX   (*pointer to first process waiting*)
              end (*SEMAPHORE*);
```

but this would be awkward, as we should have to introduce complications into the parser to treat variables of different kinds. We can retain simplicity by noting that we can use an integer to represent a semaphore if we take negative values to act as QUEUE values and non-negative values to act as COUNT values. With this idea we simply modify the interpreter to read

```
WGT: if CURRENT = 0 then PS := SEMCHK else begin WAIT(S[T]); DECTBY(1) end;
SIG: if CURRENT = 0 then PS := SEMCHK else begin SIGNAL(S[T]); DECTBY(1) end;
```

with WAIT and SIGNAL as procedures internal to the interpreter as follows:

```
procedure SIGNAL (SEMADDRESS : INTEGER);
  var
    WOKEN . PROCINDEX (*index into PROC of process to be woken*);
  begin
    with PROC[CURRENT] do
      if S[SEMADDRESS] >= 0
        then S[SEMADDRESS] := S[SEMADDRESS] + 1
        else
          begin
            WOKEN := -S[SEMADDRESS]; S[SEMADDRESS] := -PROC[WOKEN].QUEUE;
            PROC[WOKEN].QUEUE := 0; PROC[WOKEN].READY := TRUE;
          end
  end (*SIGNAL*);
procedure WAIT (SEMADDRESS : INTEGER);
  var
    LP, CP : PROCINDEX (*pointers*);
  begin
    with PROC[CURRENT] do
      if S[SEMADDRESS] > 0 (*nothing waiting*)
        then S[SEMADDRESS] := S[SEMADDRESS] - 1
        else (*suspend process*)
```

```
        begin
          STEPS := 0; CHOOSEPROCESS; READY := FALSE;
          if CURRENT = CURPROC then PS := DEDCHK else
            begin (*place at end of semaphore queue*)
              CP := -S[SEMADDRESS];
              while CP <> 0 do
                begin LP := CP; CP := PROC[CP].QUEUE end;
              if S[SEMADDRESS] = 0
                then S[SEMADDRESS] := -CURRENT (*first in queue*)
                else PROC[LP].QUEUE := CURRENT;
              PROC[CURRENT].QUEUE := 0
            end
        end
end (*WAIT*);
```

Notes

(a) A check should be made to see that wait and signal are only called from within a concurrent process. Because of the way in which we have extended the language, with processes being lexically indistinguishable from other procedures, this cannot readily be detected at compile-time, but has to be done at run-time. (See also Exercise 9.6.)

(b) Although the semantic definition above also seems to imply that the value of a semaphore is always increased by a signal operation, we have chosen not to do this if a process is found waiting on that semaphore. This process, when awoken from its implied busy–wait loop, would simply decrement the semaphore anyway; there is no need to alter it twice.

(c) The semantics of signal do not require that a process that is allowed to proceed actually gains control of the processor immediately.

Exercises

9.7 Add a facility for generating random numbers to your system if it does not already have one, and implement the system described here.

9.8 Allow a call to be made to a random number generator as part of the CLANG language (as a possibility for a FACTOR), which will allow you to write simple simulation programs.

9.9 Ben-Ari (1982) makes use of a repeat ... forever construct. How easy is it to add this to our language? How useful is it on its own?

9.10 A multi-tasking system can easily devote a considerable part of its resources to process switching and housekeeping. Try to identify potential sources of inefficiency in our system, and eradicate as many as possible.

9.11 One problem with running programs on this system is that in general the results of interleaving the processes are unpredictable. While this makes for a useful simulation in many cases, it can be awkward to debug programs that behave in this way, especially with respect to I/O (where individual elements in a read or write list may be separated by elements from another list in another process). It is easy to use a programmer-defined semaphore to prevent this; can you also find a way of ensuring that process switching is suspended during I/O, perhaps requested by a compiler directive, such as (*$S-*)?

9.12 Is it difficult to allow concurrent processes to be initiated from within procedures and/or other processes, rather than from the main program only? How does this relate to Exercise 9.6?

9.13 Do you suppose that when a process is signalled it should be given immediate access to the processor? What are the implications of allowing or disallowing this strategy? How could it be implemented in our system?

9.14 Our idea of simply letting a programmer treat a semaphore as though it were an integer is scarcely in the best traditions of strongly typed languages. How would you introduce a special semaphore type into CLANG source code (including arrays of semaphores) and how would you prevent programmers from tampering with them, while still allowing them to assign initial values to their COUNT fields?

9.15 In our system, if one process executes a read operation the whole system will wait for this to be completed. You may have an implementation of Pascal in which you can prevent this, for example by checking to see whether a key has been pressed, or by making use of real-time interrupts. As a rather challenging exercise, see if you can incorporate this into the interpreter to provide for so-called *asynchronous* input. (This is possible, for example, in UCSD Pascal, version IV, and in TurboPascal.)

9.16 The rather messy way in which parameters have to be limited in number can be avoided if they are stored above the mark stack area, rather than below it (see Exercise 8.20). Investigate and implement this idea.

Further reading

In several texts one can find descriptions of run-time mechanisms rather similar to the one discussed here for providing support for concurrent processing.

In Ben-Ari's book (1982) may be found an interpreter for a language based on Pascal-S, Wirth's subset Pascal. Although his code is unsatisfactory in some minor respects, our own interpreter was largely inspired by his approach. In passing we can comment that his implementation does not use 'queued' semaphores. When a signal occurs a cyclic search is performed around the descriptor ring, starting at a randomly chosen point, to find a process waiting for the signal. The QUEUE field is replaced by one that simply records the address of the semaphore on which the process is waiting.

A rather lower level system, programmed in Modula-2, may be found in Wirth (1985), in which, however, no mention is made of actual or simulated time-slicing.

Brinch Hansen's book (1983) discusses an interpretive system for Edison, which uses constructs rather different from those discussed here. Once again, no mention is made of actual or simulated time-slicing.

Young's book (1982) contains a useful discussion of several implementation aspects, including the one used in Modula-1 (this latter is also discussed by the author of Modula, in Wirth (1977)).

We should warn the reader that our treatment of concurrent programming, like that of so much else, has been rather dangerously superficial. He or she might do well to consult one or more of the excellent texts which have appeared on this subject in recent years. Besides those by Brinch Hansen (1983), Young (1982), Horwitz (1984), Ben-Ari (1982), and Welsh and McKeag (1980) mentioned earlier, we can recommend Holt (1983), Gehani (1984a) (the concurrent features of Ada are rather unlike anything discussed here), INMOS (1984), Peterson and Silberschatz (1985), and the very useful survey article by Andrews and Schneider (1983).

Chapter 10 Data abstraction

In this chapter we wish to extend our language and its implementation to cover some simple features of an increasingly important new development in Pascal-like languages, namely so-called **data abstraction**. This can be applied to purely sequential programming languages, as well as to concurrent programming languages, and we shall take the opportunity to discuss a system which applies to both of these. As in the previous two chapters, we shall not detail all of the changes needed to the compiler. As a fitting climax, however, we shall present a complete listing to show how the final system fits together.

10.1 The need for higher level abstraction mechanisms

The task of designing a computer program is greatly facilitated by the use of stepwise refinement techniques, which have as their essential ingredient the use of the **procedure** concept. As an abstraction mechanism the procedure has been found to be invaluable, especially in the sense of controlling the flow of execution, and almost all languages provide it in some form or another. However, as commonly implemented, it has some problem areas which are, perhaps, not immediately obvious. In languages like Pascal the block structure for a procedure is not merely a control mechanism, as objects like constants and variables needed in a particular block may be declared locally to that block, and remain invisible outside it. The area of source code in which an object is known at compile-time is called its **scope** – just as blocks can be nested, so too can scopes. However, traditional block structure controls not only an object's visibility but also its *existence* at run-time, and as a result is sometimes inadequate in providing the degree of protection needed across the modules of a large program. Scope rules may force a programmer to make objects accessible to procedures which should really not know about them, just to guarantee their existence between calls to those procedures that do need to know about them.

A standard (and rather overworked) example to illustrate this is involved with manipulating a *stack*. In our simple language, a stack and the operations on it might be realized as follows

```
var
  TOP, STACK[20];
procedure UNDERFLOW;
  begin
    halt('Stack empty')
  end;
```

```
procedure OVERFLOW;
  begin
    halt('Stack full')
  end;
procedure PUSH (ITEM);
  begin
    TOP := TOP + 1;
    if TOP > 20 then OVERFLOW;
    STACK[TOP] := ITEM
  end;
function POP;
  begin
    if TOP = 0 then UNDERFLOW;
    POP := STACK[TOP];
    TOP := TOP - 1
  end;
procedure INITIALIZE;
  begin
    TOP := 0
  end;
```

Before routines like PUSH and POP could be used to manipulate the elements of STACK, the globally accessible variable TOP would have to be initialized to 0. While the details of the legitimate stack operations are hidden within the procedures, there is no way that we can ensure that the user first calls on INITIALIZE, and no way that we can prevent him/her from inadvertently tampering with TOP, or with any of the values in the stack.

Ideally we should like to handle the abstract concept of a stack by a block structure which completely hides the data used to implement the stack, while at the same time guarantees its existence throughout the life of the program. This structure should also provide routines for manipulating the stack, and should see to any initialization needed, before allowing access to the legitimate operations (possibly it should clear the stack afterwards as well).

Various modern languages like Ada, Pascal-Plus, Edison and Modula-2 have extended the structuring mechanisms of languages like Pascal and Algol to give facilities for handling these problems, and the modern programmer should be aware of these, and have some practice in their use.

10.2 Syntax and semantics for a sequential abstraction mechanism

The basic ideas behind providing abstraction mechanisms are actually quite easy to introduce and to implement. We follow the conventions of Pascal-Plus, in a very much simplified way, and extend the syntax for BLOCK as in Figure 10.1 – note that we have elided some syntax diagrams used earlier just to save space,

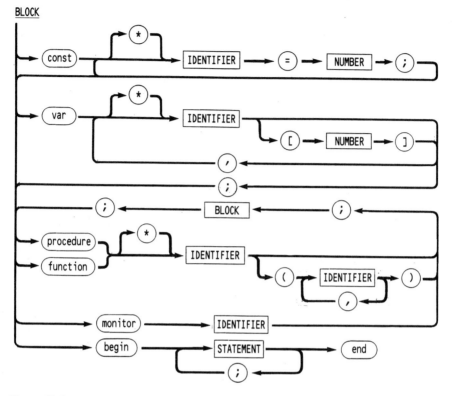

Figure 10.1

and reverted to the practice of using IDENTIFIER without attempting to draw the
semantic distinctions with which the reader should by now be familiar.

We have introduced a new class of block, which we have named the
monitor block, having the syntactic appearance of a parameterless procedure
block. However, for ease of implementation we shall impose further restrictions on the use of such blocks, not easily reflected in a single diagram:

(a) The declaration of monitors may take place in the program block only.

(b) Monitor blocks may not be nested within one another.

(c) The asterisk * may appear before the declaration of identifiers in monitor
blocks only.

The semantic features of a monitor may be summarized as follows:

(a) Objects declared 'locally' to it are to be regarded as global; they are
declared at the.same level as the objects in the program block, and have a
run-time existence for the entire duration of the program.

(b) From within, a monitor its locally declared constants, variables (monitor
variables), procedures and functions (monitor routines) may be used and
referenced like any other globally declared objects.

(c)   The scope of an object declared within a monitor, but with an asterisk preceding its name, is extended to be global to the program. However, variables declared in this way may only be examined – not changed – from outside the monitor. Variables declared without the preceding asterisk remain in existence throughout the life of the program, but are also totally invisible to code outside the monitor.

(d)   The starred identifier notation can only be used in 'defining occurrences' (declarations). Starred identifiers declared in a monitor are referenced outside of it by using a syntax similar to the record notation in Pascal, namely

QUALIFIED IDENTIFIER

(e)   We shall allow the appearance of a QUALIFIED IDENTIFIER everywhere that an IDENTIFIER could formerly appear in an 'applied occurrence' (such as in FACTOR and STATEMENT). This implies numerous small changes to all the other syntax diagrams for the language, which we shall not detail here.

(f)   Following the conventions in Pascal-Plus, we shall allow global variables declared in the main program before the first monitor to be examined (but, in the interests of even greater security, not changed) by routines in any monitor. The only way that code outside a monitor can alter monitor variables is by making deliberate calls on monitor routines; the only way that code inside a monitor can alter the global variables of the program is if they are passed as var parameters to monitor routines (see Exercise 8.13).

(g)   Finally, the compound statement of a monitor is to be regarded as part of the main program code, and is executed before the compound statement declared in the program itself. However, one cannot *call* a monitor (only the procedures and functions within it), and so one cannot execute this code more than once.

This may be made clearer by considering an example – based on the same one as before.

```
program REVERSE;
const
  TRUE  = 1;
  FALSE = 0;
var
  X;
monitor STACKHANDLER;
  var
    TOP, STACK[20];
  procedure UNDERFLOW;
    begin
```

```
      halt('Stack empty')
    end;
  procedure OVERFLOW;
    begin
      halt('Stack full')
    end;
  function *EMPTY;
    begin
      EMPTY := FALSE;
      if TOP = 0 then EMPTY := TRUE
    end;
  procedure *PUSH (ITEM);
    begin
      TOP := TOP + 1;
      if TOP > 20 then OVERFLOW;
      STACK[TOP] := ITEM
    end;
  function *POP;
    begin
      if TOP = 0 then UNDERFLOW;
      POP := STACK[TOP];
      TOP := TOP - 1
    end;
  begin
    TOP := 0
  end;
begin
  read(X);
  while X > 0 do
    begin STACKHANDLER.PUSH(X); read(X) end;
  while STACKHANDLER.EMPTY = FALSE do write(STACKHANDLER.POP)
end.
```

Here the main program (or, indeed, other procedures declared after STACKHANDLER) may refer to procedure PUSH and to the functions POP and EMPTY defined inside STACKHANDLER, but has no access to UNDERFLOW, OVERFLOW, TOP or STACK. Similarly the code in STACKHANDLER could have accessed global variable X, but only in a 'read-only' manner.

TOP is initialized before the main program commences – it is as though we had written

```
begin
  STACKHANDLER.TOP := 0;
  read(X);
  while X > 0 do
```

```
    begin STACKHANDLER.PUSH(X); read(X) end;
  while STACKHANDLER.EMPTY = FALSE do write(STACKHANDLER.POP)
end.
```

(except that we could not do it that way, even if we had declared TOP with a preceding asterisk, as TOP could never be altered outside STACKHANDLER).

Techniques for structuring program development based on mechanisms like this have become known as 'data abstraction', because, in a sense, the STACKHANDLER monitor has defined a rather abstract data type, together with the operations allowed on that type. If the programmer chooses to implement a stack in another way (for example, by using Pascal-like pointer types), he is free to do so – the only interface the user will have with the stack is via the procedure PUSH, and the functions POP and EMPTY; provided the calling conventions remain constant, the internal workings of STACKHANDLER may change considerably.

Further reading

We should add that the scheme we have suggested here is very simple. The schemes used in larger languages such as Modula, Modula-2, Pascal-Plus, Edison, Concurrent Pascal and Ada are more complex. Read up on the conventions used in these languages, and speculate on why they differ, both as regards syntactic simplicity and semantic subtlety. References that should be of interest include Welsh and McKeag (1980) (Chapter 1, on Pascal-Plus), Brinch Hansen (1983) (Section 2.5, on Edison), Young (1982) (Chapter 5), Gleaves (1985) (Chapter 1), Wirth (1977 – Modula; 1985 – Chapters 23–26), Chapter 5 of Welsh *et al.* (1984), and Chapter 3 of Gehani (1984b).

Not all authors share the current wave of enthusiasm for data abstraction mechanisms. For a contrary point of view the reader is referred to Chapter 16 of the book by Harland (1984).

Exercises

10.1 We should also comment on our choice of the reserved word monitor. This has become associated with concurrent programming, as we shall discuss shortly. Other languages use different reserved words to make the distinction clearer, but in the interests of maintaining a minimal language we have chosen not to do so. Do you suppose this is a good idea?

10.2 Describe the convention we are using in considerably tighter form, using BNF, EBNF and syntax diagram notations. How many of the subtle semantic overtones can be implied in the syntactic description?

10.3 The asterisk symbol is already used to denote multiplication. Is it a good idea to *overload* it with an extra meaning as we have done?

10.4 How many of the syntactic and semantic features we claim to be introducing for pragmatic reasons strike you as totally artificial and restrictive? How would you like to see them changed?

10.5 Chapter 5 mentioned that there is evidence that the language one has at one's command largely influences how one thinks. Do you suppose that you would think about programming very differently if you had first been taught it using a language that supported (or even encouraged) modularization using constructs such as those discussed here, and, if so, how? Do you suppose that your attention might have been focussed more on the data structures associated with a problem, rather than with the control structures, as is often the case in traditional Pascal courses?

10.6 Some authors suggest that many of the problems associated with scope rules like those found in Pascal could be overcome by denying subprograms access to any objects other than those declared locally, or passed to them as parameters. Criticize this suggestion from the point of view of compiler writer and programmer, and try to implement it.

10.3 Implementing data abstraction – syntactic and semantic considerations

Some of the ideas behind data abstraction are very easy to implement; some require considerably more thought. Most of the changes needed to our simple compiler will be concerned with symbol table entry and searching, and with the parsing of BLOCK. There are some fairly obvious minor alterations to the list of reserved words, and further error messages will be required, but these need not be given in detail here.

We extend the definition of the CLASSES type to read

```
type
  CLASSES = (CONSTANT, VARIABLE, PROG, PROC, FUNC, MONI);
```

The symbol table mechanism is beginning to creak, but we shall persist with it and add a further three BOOLEAN fields to each entry

```
TABLE : array [TABLEINDEX] of record
                          NAME  : ALFA;
                          CLASS : CLASSES;
                          LEVEL : LEVELS;
                          SIZE,
```

```
        ADDRESS : INTEGER;
        CANCHANGE, CANACCESS, INSIDE : BOOLEAN;
    end (*TABLE*);
```

The three new fields control the distortions of the scope rules, and are used as follows:

(a) CANACCESS is used to handle the extended scope rules. It will be set TRUE for starred identifiers declared within a monitor, and FALSE for all others.

(b) CANCHANGE is used to handle security aspects – it records whether code may be generated for altering the value of the corresponding identifier (by read or assignment operations) at the current level of parsing.

   While we are parsing a monitor block CANCHANGE must be set FALSE for truly global variables, but TRUE for variables declared in the monitor block itself. On the other hand, it must be set TRUE for global variables and FALSE for monitor variables when we are not parsing monitor blocks, and FALSE for monitor variables when we are parsing monitor blocks subsequent to the one in which they were declared.

(c) Since identifiers declared within a monitor block may have names that duplicate other global names, some distinction must be drawn for the purposes of symbol table scanning. INSIDE will be set TRUE for all identifiers declared inside monitor blocks.

The symbol table SIZE field has no intrinsic significance in the case of the PROG and MONI classes, but it turns out that it can be put to good use.

   We shall use the SIZE and ADDRESS fields as shown in Table 10.1. This may become clearer after considering the shell of a simple example, together with the state of the symbol table at various points in the parsing process.

Table 10.1

Class	Address	Size
PROG	offset address for last variable which will reside in main stack frame	symbol table index for the last global variable declared in program block
MONI	(see Section 10.6)	symbol table index for the last identifier in monitor
PROC, FUNC	address of first instruction	number of parameters
VARIABLE	offset address in run-time stack frame	number of elements taken on run-time stack frame
CONSTANT	numeric value of constant	—

```
 1   0 program TEST;
 2   1 var I, J;
 3   1
 4   1 monitor ONE;
 5   1   const
 6   1     Y = 50;
 7   1     *Z = 60;
 8   1   var
 9   1     A, *B[2], C;
10   1
11   1   procedure FIRST;
12   2     begin
13   3     end;
14   4
15   4   procedure *SECOND;
16   5     var P, Q;
17   5     begin
18   6     end;
19   7
20   7 begin
21   8 end;
22   9
23   9 begin
24   9 end.
```

At line 12, just after starting to parse FIRST, the state of the symbol table would be as shown in Table 10.2. Note how only B and Z are flagged CANACCESS = TRUE (TEST in a special case, which we need not worry about.) The SIZE field for TEST shows that table entry 3 is that for the last global identifier (J) in the main block. The ADDRESS field for TEST has not yet been updated, but note how the ADDRESS fields for ONE.A, ONE.B and ONE.C follow on from J, in being assigned values of 5, 6 and 9 respectively.

Table 10.2

	Name	Class	Level	Address	Size	Change	Access	Inside
1	TEST	PROGRAM	0	5	3	False	True	False
2	I	VARIABLE	1	3	1	False	False	False
3	J	VARIABLE	1	4	1	False	False	False
4	ONE	MONITOR	1	0	1	True	False	False
5	Y	CONSTANT	1	50	1	True	False	False
6	Z	CONSTANT	1	60	1	True	True	False
7	A	VARIABLE	1	5	1	True	False	False
8	B	VARIABLE	1	6	3	True	True	False
9	C	VARIABLE	1	9	1	True	False	False
10	FIRST	PROCEDURE	1	1	0	True	False	False

After parsing FIRST we proceed to parse SECOND. By the time we reach line 17 the state of the symbol table has changed to become Table 10.3. Note that we may not generate code to change I or J. SECOND, P and Q are now in the table as well, with SECOND flagged CANACCESS = TRUE, as it was starred in line 15.

Table 10.3

	Name	Class	Level	Address	Size	Change	Access	Inside
1	TEST	PROGRAM	0	5	3	False	True	False
2	I	VARIABLE	1	3	1	False	False	False
3	J	VARIABLE	1	4	1	False	False	False
4	ONE	MONITOR	1	0	1	True	False	False
5	Y	CONSTANT	1	50	1	True	False	False
6	Z	CONSTANT	1	60	1	True	True	False
7	A	VARIABLE	1	5	1	True	False	False
8	B	VARIABLE	1	6	3	True	True	False
9	C	VARIABLE	1	9	1	True	False	False
10	FIRST	PROCEDURE	1	1	0	True	False	False
11	SECOND	PROCEDURE	1	4	0	True	True	False
12	P	VARIABLE	2	3	1	True	False	False
13	Q	VARIABLE	2	4	1	True	False	False

After starting to parse the 'initialization' code for monitor ONE at line 20 the symbol table changes once more, to become Table 10.4. Note how the SIZE field for ONE is now 11, showing that future searches for monitor identifiers in ONE must be confined to table entries between 5 (for Y) and 11 (for SECOND). The ADDRESS field for TEST is now 10; variables in future monitors could be given offset addresses starting at this value, effectively adding them to the global variables which will reside in the stack frame for the main program.

Table 10.4

	Name	Class	Level	Address	Size	Change	Access	Inside
1	TEST	PROGRAM	0	10	3	False	True	False
2	I·	VARIABLE	1	3	1	False	False	False
3	J	VARIABLE	1	4	1	False	False	False
4	ONE	MONITOR	1	0	11	True	False	False
5	Y	CONSTANT	1	50	1	True	False	False
6	Z	CONSTANT	1	60	1	True	True	False
7	A	VARIABLE	1	5	1	True	False	False
8	B	VARIABLE	1	6	3	True	True	False
9	C	VARIABLE	1	9	1	True	False	False
10	FIRST	PROCEDURE	1	1	0	True	False	False
11	SECOND	PROCEDURE	1	4	0	True	True	False

After completing the parse of monitor ONE and starting the parse of the main program block in line 23 the symbol table reaches the state shown in Table 10.5. Note that I and J can again be changed, while other identifiers cannot, and that all the monitor identifiers are now flagged INSIDE = TRUE. The reason for not marking them INSIDE = TRUE earlier is that we can access them without using the qualified 'dot' notation for as long as we are parsing the monitor itself.

Table 10.5

	Name	Class	Level	Address	Size	Change	Access	Inside
1	TEST	PROGRAM	0	10	3	True	True	False
2	I	VARIABLE	1	3	1	True	False	False
3	J	VARIABLE	1	4	1	True	False	False
4	ONE	MONITOR	1	0	11	True	False	False
5	Y	CONSTANT	1	50	1	False	False	True
6	Z	CONSTANT	1	60	1	False	True	True
7	A	VARIABLE	1	5	1	False	False	True
8	B	VARIABLE	1	6	3	False	True	True
9	C	VARIABLE	1	9	1	False	False	True
10	FIRST	PROCEDURE	1	1	0	False	False	True
11	SECOND	PROCEDURE	1	4	0	False	True	True

As has already been mentioned, a monitor block looks very like a procedure block from the viewpoint of parsing, although there are a host of subtle differences internally, all to do with distorting the scope rules.

Let us start by considering the declaration of identifiers. The procedure for recognizing a starred identifier is very simple, and makes use of a Boolean variable STARRED, which can be declared local to BLOCK.

```
procedure GETSTARID;
(*Check for possible star preceding identifier*)
  begin
    GETSYM; STARRED := FALSE;
    if SYM = TIMES then
      begin
        if BLOCKCLASS = MONI
          then STARRED := TRUE
          else ERROR(47) (*starred only in monitor blocks*);
        GETSYM
      end
  end (*GETSTARID*);
```

This procedure is called upon in various places where previously a simple GETSYM sufficed. An example is in CONSTDECLARATION, as below; similar changes are needed in VARDECLARATION and PROCDECLARATION.

```
      procedure CONSTDECLARATION;
      (*Handle declaration of named constants*)
        begin
**        GETSTARID;
          TEST([IDENT], FOLLOWERS, 6);
          while SYM = IDENT do
            begin
              ENTER(CONSTANT); GETSYM;
              if SYM in [EQLSYM, BECOMES]
                then
                  begin
                    if SYM = BECOMES then ERROR(7); GETSYM;
                    if SYM <> NUMBER then ERROR(8) else
                      begin TABLE[LASTENTRY].ADDRESS := NUM; GETSYM end
                  end
                else ERROR(9);
**            if SYM = SEMICOLON then GETSTARID else ERROR(2)
            end (*while*)
        end (*CONSTDECLARATION*);
```

When we first enter identifiers into the symbol table we initialize the three new fields to standard default values, which will later be changed if necessary.

```
      procedure ENTER (C : CLASSES);
      (*Enter object of class C into table*)
        begin
          if LASTENTRY = TABLEMAX then QUIT(4) (*symbol table overflow*);
          LASTENTRY := LASTENTRY + 1;
          with TABLE[LASTENTRY] do
            begin
              NAME := ID; CLASS := C; LEVEL := BLOCKLEVEL; SIZE := 1;
              ADDRESS := 0;
**            CANCHANGE := TRUE; INSIDE := FALSE; CANACCESS := STARRED
            end
        end (*ENTER*);
```

We have already commented that the identifiers local to a monitor really have global status. This means that the level must not change as we start to parse a monitor. This requires a simple change to PROCDECLARATION. Other changes are needed in the same procedure to ensure that we do not nest monitor blocks other than in the program block; we now pass BLOCKCLASS as a value parameter to PROCDECLARATION.

```
      procedure PROCDECLARATION (BLOCKCLASS : CLASSES);
      (*Handle declaration of procedures, functions, monitors*)
        begin
          if ID = 'FUNCTION' then BLOCKCLASS := FUNC else
            if ID = 'PROCEDURE' then BLOCKCLASS := PROC else
```

```
                begin
 **                 if BLOCKCLASS <> PROG then ERROR(46) (*monitors only at global level*);
                    BLOCKCLASS := MONI
                end;
            GETSTARID;
            if SYM <> IDENT then ERROR(6) else begin ENTER(BLOCKCLASS); GETSYM end;
            if BLOCKLEVEL = LEVMAX then QUIT(1) (*too deeply nested*);
            if BLOCKCLASS = MONI
 **            then BLOCK([SEMICOLON] + FOLLOWERS, BLOCKLEVEL, LASTENTRY, MONI) (*same level*)
               else BLOCK([SEMICOLON] + FOLLOWERS, BLOCKLEVEL + 1, LASTENTRY, BLOCKCLASS);
            ACCEPT(SEMICOLON, 2)
          end (*PROCDECLARATION*);
```

After we leave off parsing a monitor, its identifiers must not be deleted from the symbol table, as we are able to do after leaving other blocks. Such a deletion is easily effected by passing LASTENTRY by value to BLOCK, but this will no longer suffice. We must pass it by reference, and arrange that for blocks other than monitors it should be reset to its entry value just before BLOCK is left. Parsing of the main program then starts by invoking a revised version of PROGRAMME.

```
          procedure PROGRAMME;
            var
 **           PROGENTRY : TABLEINDEX;
            begin
              ACCEPT(PROCSYM, 36);
              with TABLE[0] do
                begin
                  NAME := ID; CLASS := PROG; LEVEL := 0; SIZE := 1; ADDRESS := 0,
                  CANCHANGE := TRUE; INSIDE := FALSE; CANACCESS := TRUE
                end;
 **           TABLE[1] := TABLE[0] (*enter program name*); PROGENTRY := 1;
              if SYM <> IDENT then ERROR(6) else
                begin TABLES := ID = 'TEST    '; GETSYM end;
 **           BLOCK([PERIOD] + FIRSTBLOCK + FIRSTSTATEMENT, 1, PROGENTRY, PROG);
              if SYM <> PERIOD then ERROR(37)
            end (*PROGRAMME*);
```

Rather more complex are the changes needed to the routine SEARCHID for locating the position of an identifier in the symbol table. A little thought shows that when a 'qualified identifier' is detected, it is the name which appears after the period that is semantically the more important. The name of the monitor itself is only of use in deciding where the symbol table search for this second name must begin. However, it is convenient to return pointers to both entries in the symbol table. Suitable code appears below, with notes following.

```
 1    procedure SEARCHID (var MONENTRY, ENTRY : TABLEINDEX; ALLOWED : CLASSSET;
 2                         ERRORCODE : INTEGER);
 3    (*Find ID in table at location MONENTRY.ENTRY, check ALLOWED class*)
```

```
4     var
5       FOUND  : BOOLEAN;
6
7     procedure MONITORIDENTIFIERS;
8
9       procedure SEARCHFORWARD;
10      (*Search for identifiers in a referenced monitor*)
11        var
12          LAST : TABLEINDEX;
13        begin
14          LAST := TABLE[ENTRY].SIZE;
15          if LAST = 1 then LAST := LASTENTRY (*still in monitor*);
16          ENTRY := ENTRY + 1 (*to get past the monitor entry*);
17          while (ENTRY <= LAST) and (TABLE[ENTRY].NAME <> ID) do
18            ENTRY := ENTRY + 1;
19          if ENTRY > LAST then ENTRY := 0 (*not found*)
20        end (*SEARCHFORWARD*);
21
22      begin (*MONITORIDENTIFIERS*)
23        GETSYM;
24        if SYM <> PERIOD then ERROR(37) else
25          begin
26            GETSYM; MONENTRY := ENTRY;
27            if SYM <> IDENT then ERROR(6) else
28              begin
29                SEARCHFORWARD;
30                if TABLE[ENTRY].INSIDE and not TABLE[ENTRY].CANACCESS
31                  then ERROR(48);
32              end
33          end
34      end (*MONITORIDENTIFIERS*);
35
36    begin
37      TABLE[0].NAME := ID; ENTRY := LASTENTRY; MONENTRY := 0;
38      repeat
39        FOUND := TRUE;
40        while TABLE[ENTRY].NAME <> ID do ENTRY := ENTRY - 1;
41        if TABLE[ENTRY].INSIDE then (*should be "qualified"*)
42          begin FOUND := FALSE; ENTRY := ENTRY - 1 end
43      until FOUND;
44      if TABLE[ENTRY].CLASS = MONI then MONITORIDENTIFIERS;
45      if ENTRY = 0 (*not really there*)
46        then ERROR(5)
47        else if not (TABLE[ENTRY].CLASS in ALLOWED) then ERROR(ERRORCODE);
48      GETSYM (*side-effect*);
```

```
49      while SYM = PERIOD do (*confusing access methods*)
50         begin ERROR(3); GETSYM; if SYM = IDENT then GETSYM end
51      end (*SEARCHID*);
```

Notes

(a) The main section of this routine, as before, employs a simple linear search from the end of the table to locate an identifier, after first ensuring (line 37) that this will be successful.

(b) An identifier marked INSIDE = TRUE cannot be found directly, and if we match an identifier in this way we must skip over it (line 41). This allows monitors seemingly to duplicate global names with impunity.

(c) Identifiers declared inside a monitor are referenced outside the monitor using the dot notation. If a monitor identifier is found by SEARCHID, we must continue to search for the subsidiary identifier by calling on MONITORIDENTIFIERS (line 44).

(d) As we have already commented, a stack structure for the symbol table is ideal for coping with the elementary scope rules, but it needs distorting for the monitor concept, for the identifiers declared in a monitor will appear after the monitor identifier itself (that is, the subsidiary search must take place in the opposite direction). This is quite easily done once one grasps the usefulness of using TABLE[I].SIZE to act as a means of stopping the search if the identifier is not found (lines 14–19). While still parsing a monitor, this field may not yet have been set up, so some little care must be taken (line 15).

(e) MONITORIDENTIFIERS incorporates a check that access to the variable is allowed (line 30). Identifiers are only marked INSIDE = TRUE after we have completed parsing a monitor block, to allow this test to work correctly while we are still parsing within the monitor.

(f) A user may get confused about the dot notation, and attempt to apply it out of context. Hence, if periods are found after an identifier name which is not of the monitor class, we attempt to skip the period and the following identifier as often as necessary to allow parsing to get back into step (line 49).

All the calls to SEARCHID have to change as well, of course, to incorporate the extra parameter (which is not used at this stage).

At various places we must check, after calling SEARCHID, for possible assignment or other attempt to alter a starred variable from outside a monitor. The most obvious of these is in the code that parses an assignment statement; a similar test to the one shown below is also needed in READSTATEMENT.

```
begin (*STATEMENT*)
  PROCCALL := TRUE;
```

```
        if SYM in FIRSTSTATEMENT then
          case SYM of
            IDENT:
              begin
**                SEARCHID(MONENTRY, IDENTRY, [VARIABLE, FUNC, PROC], 22);
                with TABLE[IDENTRY] do
                  case CLASS of
                    CONSTANT, PROG, (*error - treat as assignment*)
                    FUNC, VARIABLE:
                      begin
                        if CLASS in [VARIABLE, CONSTANT, PROG]
                          then
                            begin
**                            if not CANCHANGE then ERROR(39);
                              ADDRESSFOR(IDENTRY)
                            end
                          else if BLOCKENTRY = IDENTRY
                            then STACKADDRESS(LEVEL+1, -SIZE-1) else ERROR(20);
                        if SYM = BECOMES then GETSYM else
                          begin ERROR(21); if SYM = EQLSYM then GETSYM end;
                        EXPRESSION(FOLLOWERS);
                        ASSIGN; PROCCALL := FALSE
                      end;
```

Exercises

10.7 A convention like that used in Modula-2 for handling the distortions of the scope rules can be illustrated by the following example:

```
program TEST;
var I, J;
monitor ONE;
  import I;
  export Z, B, SECOND;
  const
    Y = 50;
    Z = 60;
  var
    A, B[2], C;
  procedure FIRST;
    begin
    end;
  procedure SECOND;
    var P, Q;
```

```
      begin
      end;
      begin
      end;
   begin
      ONE.SECOND
   end.
```

Within the monitor we find explicit import and export lists, which specify which of the objects declared outside the monitor will be visible within it, and which objects declared within the monitor will be visible outside it. Discuss the advantages and disadvantages of this convention over the one we have proposed, and attempt to implement it.

10.8 Our use of the SIZE and ADDRESS fields for other purposes than their names suggest is surely poor practice. Suggest how we could have used a variant record declaration for TABLE, and implement this.

10.9 What would be the implications and complications if the symbol table were being stored in a tree, rather than in the simple array used here (see Exercise 8.9).

10.4 Implementing data abstraction – code generation considerations

We may now go on to consider the rather trickier changes that need to be made to BLOCK to cope with monitors. So far as code generation is concerned, these are related to the action as we enter and leave a block at run-time, where there is always some housekeeping to be done. The reader will recall that we defer the actual code generation to interface procedures like ENTERBLOCK, OPENSTACKFRAME and LEAVEBLOCK. Up until now we have arranged matters as follows.

(a)   At the start of parsing a block we have used ENTERBLOCK to generate an (incomplete) branch to the start of the code for that block, code which may become separated from this branch instruction because of the generation of code for intermediate blocks. This branch is backpatched when the start of the code is actually found.

(b)   After parsing the various nested declarations, we have used OPENSTACKFRAME to generate code which, when executed, will allocate a suitable stack frame for that block.

(c)   When we leave off parsing a block, we have called on LEAVEBLOCK to generate code for executing a RETURN from procedure and function blocks, and a HALT at the end of the main program.

When we add monitor blocks, things change a little. The first instruction generated as we start to parse the program block can still be an (incomplete) branch instruction, but this may have to branch to the start of monitor initialization code, rather than to the code for the program. If, while parsing, we come across a monitor, we need not generate another incomplete branch instruction at the start of this; once we are ready to generate the monitor initialization code we merely backpatch the branch instruction at the start of the program to branch to it. When we leave parsing a monitor we can generate an (incomplete) branch instruction, which we later complete to point to the initialization code for the next monitor, or to the code for the program itself.

This handles the flow of control; we have also to handle the storage management.

The initialization code for the first monitor must reserve stack frame storage for the global variables in the program and the global variables of the monitor as well. The initialization code for second and subsequent monitors may have to allocate further stack space for any further variables these may have declared. The initialization code for the program will not have to allocate any further stack space if any monitor initialization has already taken care of this, but will have to allocate stack space if no monitors were parsed.

Code for a heavily revised BLOCK parser to handle these features appears below, with notes following.

```
1    procedure BLOCK (FOLLOWERS    : SYMSET     (*for error recovery*);
2                     BLOCKLEVEL   : LEVELS     (*level of static nesting*);
3                     var LASTENTRY : TABLEINDEX (*index into symbol table*);
4                     BLOCKCLASS   : CLASSES    (*prog, proc, func, monitor*));
5     var
6       BLOCKENTRY : TABLEINDEX (*initial symbol table entry*);
7       STARTCODE,             (*start address*)
8       OFFSET,                (*variable address index*)
9       PARAMS,                (*number of parameters*)
10      I          : INTEGER   (*loop counter*);
11      STARRED    : BOOLEAN   (*whether identifier is exportable*);
12
13
14    begin (*BLOCK*)
15      PARAMS := 0; BLOCKENTRY := LASTENTRY;
16      case BLOCKCLASS of
17        PROC, FUNC:
18          begin
19            OFFSET := 3; ENTERBLOCK(STARTCODE);
20            if SYM = LPAREN then PARDECLARATION;
21            TABLE[BLOCKENTRY].SIZE := PARAMS;
22            TABLE[BLOCKENTRY].ADDRESS := STARTCODE;
23          end;
24        MONI:
25          begin (*make globals read only, and prepare to add to them*)
```

```
26        for I := 1 to TABLE[1].SIZE do TABLE[I].CANCHANGE := FALSE;
27        OFFSET := TABLE[1].ADDRESS (*resume addresses from global block*)
28      end;
29    PROG: begin OFFSET := 3; ENTERBLOCK(STARTMAINCODE) end;
30  end (*case*);
31  ACCEPT(SEMICOLON, 2);
32  TEST(FIRSTBLOCK, FOLLOWERS, 3);
33  repeat
34    if SYM = CONSTSYM then CONSTDECLARATION;
35    if SYM = VARSYM then VARDECLARATION;
36    if BLOCKCLASS = PROG then
37      begin TABLE[1].ADDRESS := OFFSET; TABLE[1].SIZE := LASTENTRY end;
38    while SYM = PROCSYM do PROCDECLARATION(BLOCKCLASS);
39    TEST([BEGINSYM], FOLLOWERS, 34)
40  until SYM in FIRSTSTATEMENT + [PERIOD, SEMICOLON];
41  case BLOCKCLASS of
42    PROG:
43      begin
44        BACKPATCH(STARTMAINCODE, NEXTCODE);
45        if not MONITORS then OPENSTACKFRAME(OFFSET)
46      end;
47    MONI:
48      begin
49        BACKPATCH(STARTMAINCODE, NEXTCODE);
50        TABLE[BLOCKENTRY].SIZE := LASTENTRY (*last ident for the monitor*);
51        if not MONITORS
52          then OPENSTACKFRAME(OFFSET) (*for globals so far*)
53          else OPENSTACKFRAME(OFFSET - TABLE[1].ADDRESS) (*extra globals*);
54        TABLE[1].ADDRESS := OFFSET; MONITORS := TRUE
55      end;
56    FUNC, PROC:
57      begin
58        BACKPATCH(STARTCODE, NEXTCODE) (*jump to code for this block*);
59        OPENSTACKFRAME(OFFSET) (*reserve space for variables*)
60      end
61  end (*case*);
62  COMPOUNDSTATEMENT(FOLLOWERS);
63  if TABLES then PRINTSYMBOLTABLE (*demonstration purposes*);
64  if BLOCKCLASS = MONI
65    then
66      begin
67        ENTERBLOCK(STARTMAINCODE);
68        for I := BLOCKENTRY + 1 to LASTENTRY do (*mon variables read only*)
69          begin TABLE[I].CANCHANGE := FALSE; TABLE[I].INSIDE := TRUE end;
70        for I := 1 to TABLE[1].SIZE do TABLE[I].CANCHANGE := TRUE (*reset*)
71      end
```

```
72      else
73        begin
74          LEAVEBLOCK(BLOCKCLASS, BLOCKLEVEL, PARAMS); LASTENTRY := BLOCKENTRY
75        end;
76      TEST(FOLLOWERS, [], 35);
77    end (*BLOCK*);
```

Notes

(a)   We declare BLOCK to have essentially the same parameters as before – the difference being, as we have already noted, that LASTENTRY, the symbol table index, must be passed by reference as well.

(b)   On entry to BLOCK things are much as before for function and procedure blocks (lines 17–23), but in the case of monitor blocks we need to ensure that the global variables declared in the main program block are marked read-only (line 26), and that the offset addresses of monitor variables are calculated as though they were global variables (line 27).

(c)   Processing internal declarations is done in essentially the same way as before (lines 33–40), save that after the program block variables have been entered in the symbol table, the ADDRESS and SIZE fields of TABLE[1] must be updated (lines 36–37), so that subsequent monitor parsing can use these as outlined previously.

(d)   After parsing the declarations we can complete the branch instruction generated as the block parsing began (in the case of program, function and procedure blocks), or generated as a previous monitor block was completed (lines 44, 49 and 58). We are using a new global variable STARTMAINCODE to keep track of the location of this branch instruction in the case of monitor and program blocks; the familiar STARTCODE is retained in the case of procedure and function blocks.

(e)   We also use OPENSTACKFRAME to generate code for reserving stack frames at execution time (lines 51–53). This is used in conjunction with the Boolean variable MONITORS, which records whether we have parsed monitor blocks at all, and which is initialized (to FALSE) before parsing begins.

(f)   Parsing of the statement part of the block follows as before (line 62).

(g)   At the exit from BLOCK, there is no change from earlier compilers in the case of program, procedure and function blocks, except to restore the value of LASTENTRY to its value on entry (line 74). In the case of monitor blocks we generate an incomplete branch instruction (line 67) to allow us to link onto the code for a subsequent monitor, or to the main program code itself. We also change the status of the global variables, and of the monitor variables, and mark the monitor identifiers with INSIDE = TRUE (lines 68–70).

Once again, this may be clarified by presenting a simple example, together with the code it should produce for our stack machine.

```
0  program TEST;
1  var
1    I, J;
1
1  monitor ONE;
1    var
1      *A, B;
1
1    procedure *SECOND;
2      begin
3        ONE.B := 56
5      end;
7
7    begin
8      A := 45
10   end;
12
12 monitor TWO;
12   var B;
12
12   begin
13     B := 34
15   end;
17
17 begin
17   write(ONE.A)
20 end.
```

```
 0 BRN 0 7   ──────┐      branch to initialization code for ONE
 1 BRN 0 2         │      start of ONE.SECOND
 2 INT 0 3         │      reserve stack space for ONE.SECOND
 3 LDA 1 6         │
 4 LDI 0 56        │
 5 STO             │      ONE.B := 56
 6 RET 2 1         │
 7 INT 0 7   ◄─────┘      initialization for ONE reserves space for
 8 LDA 1 5                all global variables so far
 9 LDI 0 45
10 STO                    ONE.A := 45
11 BRN 0 12  ──────┐      branch to initialization code for TWO after
                   │      completing initialization of ONE
12 INT 0 1   ◄─────┘      reserve stack space for global variable TWO.B
13 LDA 1 7
14 LDI 0 34
15 STO                    TWO.B := 34
```

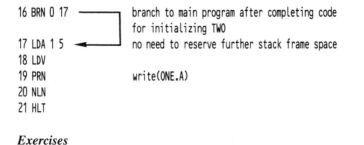

```
16 BRN 0 17  ─────┐   branch to main program after completing code
                  │   for initializing TWO
17 LDA 1 5  ◄─────┘   no need to reserve further stack frame space
18 LDV
19 PRN                write(ONE.A)
20 NLN
21 HLT
```

Exercises

10.10 Is it necessary to restrict the monitor concept to being used at the program level? Try to implement monitors nested within procedure or function blocks. Are there any advantages in being able to do this?

10.11 Pascal-Plus allows monitor code to perform both initialization and termination actions. A simple example might be along the lines of

```
program DEMO;
  monitor ONE;
    procedure *A;
      begin
      end;
    begin
      write('start ONE here');
      ***;
      write('end ONE here')
    end;
  begin
    write('continue here')
  end.
```

where the 'inner statement', written ***, separates the monitor initialization code from the main program code from the monitor termination code. How easy is it to add this to our language (and to implement it)?

10.12 Pascal-Plus is particularly appealing, as it extends the familiar syntax of Pascal in a very simple, yet powerful way. In particular, what we have termed a monitor becomes more like a Pascal type, and one can effectively declare instances of the type, to provide, for example, access to several stacks (which our simple language cannot do), along the lines of

```
program REVERSE;
const
  FALSE = 0;
var X;
```

```
monitor STACKHANDLER;
    . . . as before . . .
```
**   `instance STACK1, STACK2 : STACKHANDLER;`
```
begin
  read(X);
  while X > 0 do
    begin STACK1.PUSH(X); read(X) end;
  while STACK1.EMPTY = FALSE do
    begin STACK2.PUSH(STACK1.POP) . . .
    . . .
end.
```

How could you extend our system to allow instances (effectively copies) of monitors to be handled?

10.13 How would you develop a CLANG compiler if you could use a host language with abstraction mechanisms such as we have considered in this chapter?

Further reading

At present there is not a great deal to be found on case studies of compilers for languages that support data abstraction mechanisms. In Chapters 6 and 10 of his book, Brinch Hansen (1983) discusses his (interpretive) system for the language Edison. Chapter 1 of Bustard (1980) gives some of the thinking behind the Pascal Plus implementation.

Welsh and McKeag (1980) (Chapter 2) covers the development of a compiler for a subset of Pascal, using Pascal-Plus as the host language and making extensive use of its data abstraction features.

10.5 The monitor in concurrent programming

In the last chapter we introduced the reader to some elementary aspects of concurrent programming, including a brief discussion of the classical **semaphore** for handling some of the problems of mutual exclusion and synchronization which a system of cooperating processes may need to solve.

The semaphore is quite a versatile primitive, but a system built on semaphores alone is subject to disaster if even one occurrence of a semaphore operation is confused or omitted anywhere. For this reason, among others, considerable work has been undertaken in recent years to provide higher level and more reliable constructs in concurrent programs. One of these, which has had a measure of practical as well as theoretical success, was first put forward by Hoare and Brinch Hansen, and is very closely associated with the data abstraction mechanisms which we have just discussed.

In concurrent programming the semantics of the **monitor** demand that when concurrent processes simultaneously call monitor routines which, as we have implied, often operate on some hidden data structure, they are guaranteed mutual exclusion on the structure. That is to say, while in concurrent processing the primitive operations within one process can generally be interleaved in time with primitive operations taking place in other processes, primitive operations within a monitor routine can only be interleaved in time with operations taking place in processes that are not accessing the monitor. Where necessary, the underlying implementation undertakes to delay calling processes for short periods of time until it is their turn to execute a monitor routine. This relieves the programmer of the tedium of having to develop and test his own code for the purpose of providing exclusivity – instead he simply arranges to enclose the critical regions inside a suitable monitor.

A standard example used to illustrate this is the producer–consumer problem, which was mentioned in the last chapter. Here one or more processes (the producers) produce items and store them in a buffer, from which other processes (the consumers) draw items and use them. The buffer is a shared resource, and we should guard against the possibility that the competing processes attempt to change its state at exactly the same instant. A monitor may be used to protect it, along the lines of

```
program GETRICHQUICK;
  monitor MIDDLEMAN;
    var BUFFER (*some appropriate structure*)
    procedure *STORE (ITEM);
      begin
        add ITEM to BUFFER
      end (*STORE);
    procedure *DRAW (var ITEM);
      begin
        assign an item in BUFFER to ITEM
      end (*DRAW*);
    begin
      clear BUFFER (*initialization code for monitor*)
    end (*MIDDLEMAN*);
  procedure PRODUCER;
    begin
      repeat
        manufacture ITEM;
        MIDDLEMAN.STORE(ITEM)
      forever
    end (*PRODUCER*);
  procedure CONSUMER;
    begin
```

```
      repeat
        MIDDLEMAN.DRAW(ITEM);
        consume ITEM
      forever
    end (*CONSUMER*);
begin
  cobegin
    PRODUCER; CONSUMER; CONSUMER
  coend
end (*GETRICHQUICK*).
```

By itself the monitor concept provides only for exclusivity. Sometimes a programmer will need to be able to exercise further control on synchronization. A little thought should show that there is a potential problem with the above algorithm. Suppose that we wish to consume an item and gain entry to the procedure DRAW because the manufacturing process is not using the monitor at the time. As everyone knows, warehouses are not always well stocked; we have, however, incorporated nothing into the algorithm to specify what to do if the buffer is empty when we attempt to draw (or, for that matter, what the manufacturer should do if he tries to deposit items into a full buffer). What must happen, clearly, is that the process will have to wait.

The approach to process synchronization usually adopted with monitors is based on a queueing mechanism usually known as a **condition queue** or, simply, as a **condition**. For each condition that we require to be satisfied before a process using the monitor procedure can be allowed to continue we are allowed to define a queue on which a process may have to suspend itself and wait until it is later signalled by some other process. The idea is roughly as follows:

```
monitor MIDDLEMAN;
  var
    BUFFER (*some appropriate structure*),
    STATE  (*some means of recording the state of the BUFFER*);
  condition
    ITEMSAVAILABLE, STORAGEAVAILABLE;
  procedure *STORE (ITEM);
    begin
      if BUFFER is FULL then wait(STORAGEAVAILABLE);
      add ITEM to BUFFER; adjust STATE of BUFFER;
      signal(ITEMSAVAILABLE)
    end (*STORE);
  procedure *DRAW (var ITEM);
    begin
      if STATE is EMPTY then wait(ITEMSAVAILABLE);
      assign an item in BUFFER to ITEM; adjust STATE of BUFFER;
      signal(STORAGEAVAILABLE)
    end (*DRAW*);
```

```
begin
   clear BUFFER
end (*MIDDLEMAN*);
```

This is obviously very similar to the use of semaphores in the same context, at least at a first glance. However, as proposed by Hoare, there are distinct semantic differences, and further implications, which may not be immediately apparent from the code above (where the exclusivity on the data structure is no longer made explicitly visible to the reader).

The most striking differences are as follows. A procedure executing a wait on a condition always waits in a queue. Although the queueing mechanism is hidden it must be present – unlike a semaphore based system which does not demand a queueing mechanism, although one is often provided. If there is no process waiting on a specified condition, then the operation of a signal on a condition has a null effect – unlike the signal(SEMAPHORE) primitive, which increases the associated integer value of SEMAPHORE if no process is waiting on it.

What may not at first be obvious is that as soon as a process is delayed on a condition queue it must lose its exclusive access to the monitor until signalled to proceed. Since condition variables are invariably declared private to a monitor, the signalling will be effected by *another* process calling a procedure in the *same* monitor, and executing a signal operation on the appropriate condition. This raises further interesting consequences.

Suppose a process P enters a monitor and executes a signal operation on a condition on which a process Q is waiting. If the suspended process Q is to be allowed to resume execution immediately, the signalling process P must relinquish exclusive access, and wait (otherwise P and Q will be simultaneously active within the same monitor). Since, presumably, either P or Q *could* continue with their execution, some decision has to be made on which to delay. There are two possibilities:

(a) P waits politely, until Q leaves the monitor, or is suspended by waiting on another condition.

(b) Q waits politely, until P leaves the monitor, or is suspended by waiting on another condition.

We should comment that the problem of deciding between these falls away if we demand that there be at most one signal operation per monitor routine, and that it be the last statement in that routine. This is frequently what happens in simple examples (as in ours), but to demand this, as is sometimes proposed, would somewhat restrict the usefulness of monitors.

In any event, to make the distinction between condition and semaphore mechanisms still clearer, a different syntax is called for – the one often adopted (as we shall do) is to use one which resembles a Pascal record access. Rather than write wait(ACONDITION) and signal(ACONDITION) we shall write ACONDITION.cwait and ACON-DITION.csignal respectively. To illustrate this, we present a rather more complete version of the algorithm we have been discussing, in a notation consistent with that allowed by the implementation to be discussed shortly. The buffer is held in an array, but this is treated as a circular structure.

```
program GETRICHQUICK;
  const
    TRUE = 1;
  monitor MIDDLEMAN;
    const
      MAX = 5;
    var
      HEAD, TAIL, COUNT, BUFFER[5];
    condition
      ITEMSAVAILABLE, STORAGEAVAILABLE;
    procedure *STORE (I);
      begin
        if COUNT > MAX then STORAGEAVAILABLE.cwait;
        BUFFER[TAIL] := I; COUNT := COUNT + 1;
        TAIL := TAIL + 1; if TAIL > MAX then TAIL := 0;
        ITEMSAVAILABLE.csignal
      end;
    function *DRAW;
      begin
        if COUNT = 0 then ITEMSAVAILABLE.cwait;
        DRAW := BUFFER[HEAD]; COUNT := COUNT - 1;
        HEAD := HEAD + 1; if HEAD > MAX then HEAD := 0;
        STORAGEAVAILABLE.csignal
      end;
    begin
      HEAD := 0; TAIL := 0; COUNT := 0
    end;
  procedure PRODUCE;
    var ITEM;
    begin
      ITEM := 0;
      while TRUE = TRUE do
        begin
          write('Produce ', ITEM);
          MIDDLEMAN.STORE(ITEM);
          ITEM := ITEM + 1
        end
    end;
  procedure CONSUME;
    var I;
    begin
      while TRUE = TRUE do
        begin I := MIDDLEMAN.DRAW; write('Consume ', I) end
```

```
        end;
    begin
        cobegin PRODUCE; PRODUCE; CONSUME coend
    end.
```

It may help to give a graphical illustration of the semantics of a monitor. We can think of this as constituting a fenced area, with various 'gates' into it – there is a front gate (in front of which processes may have to wait on an 'entry' queue before they can gain access to the visible routines), a back gate associated with each condition (behind which suspended processes may have to queue), and a side gate (behind which processes may have to wait on a 'polite' queue while a signaller or signalled process continues its business).

Suppose we have a monitor with two visible procedures, and one condition, and that we have reached a stage where one process, P4, is inside the monitor, having come in via procedure ONE. Process P1 is blocked, in trying to enter via procedure ONE. A further two processes, P3 and P2 have already been into the monitor via procedure TWO, but have been forced to wait on condition A (Figure 10.2a). Were process P4 now to leave the monitor normally, by completing the code associated with ONE, P1 would be allowed to enter. If, instead, P4 executes A.csignal, then P3 should be allowed to enter. If we adopt strategy (a) above the situation would change immediately to that in Figure 10.2b. Were P3 next to execute A.csignal, then the situation would change to that in Figure 10.2c (assuming the queues were all maintained in a FIFO manner – one might argue for P3 to take preference over P4 in the existing polite queue). However, were P2 to execute A.csignal, P2 would remain active in the monitor, as there are no further processes waiting on A.

The reader will have noticed that in describing this scenario we have assumed that the action of A.csignal has been related only to manipulating the

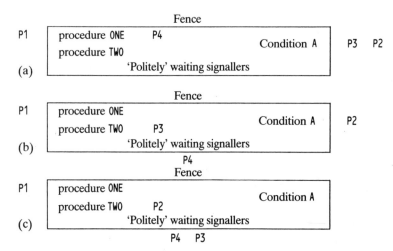

Figure 10.2

condition queues and the polite queue, and may wonder why we have neglected the entry queue on which P1 is so patiently waiting. But suppose when P4 executes A.csignal we were to give preference to P1, rather than to the processes P3 and P2 waiting for the signal. We then have the possibility that the action of the intruder could be such as to destroy the state for which P3 and P2 were longing, and this could have bizarre effects. For example, if P3 and P2 were consumers, A a condition that a buffer have something in it, and P4 was the producer who had just placed the (only) item into the buffer before executing A.csignal, then if P1 entered and consumed the item before P3 was allowed to do so, P3 would later be allowed to take from an empty buffer.

Similar arguments are usually put forward in favour of adopting strategy (a) over (b) for the action to be taken by a signal operation on a condition, namely that if a signalling process is given preference over the signalled process, the signaller might destroy the state of the structure for which the suspended process had been waiting. Of course, one can argue in exactly the opposite way, for if the signalled process is given preference there is every possibility that it might alter the state of the monitor variables; when the signaller is then later allowed to proceed it might do so unaware that this state had changed.

In general more than one process might be suspended on a condition, which, as we have implied, is usually maintained as a FIFO queue. In some applications it is desirable to extend the wait operation to specify relative priorities among the suspended processes. A very simple application of the use of prioritized queues is shown in the following job scheduler, which might form part of an operating system, a part which concurrent programs are required to invoke before they can gain access to the central processor, and again after they relinquish it. Many scheduling algorithms can be devised, of course; this one is the so-called *shortest-job-first* one. We assume that when each program requests the CPU, it has to specify the maximum time for which it plans to occupy it.

```
monitor CPUSCHEDULER;
  const FALSE = 0; TRUE = 1;
  var BUSY;
  condition CPUAVAILABLE;
  procedure *ACQUIRECPU (TIME);
    begin
      if BUSY = TRUE then CPUAVAILABLE.cwait(TIME);
      BUSY := TRUE
    end;
  procedure *RELEASECPU;
    begin
      BUSY := FALSE; CPUAVAILABLE.csignal
    end;
begin
  BUSY := FALSE
end;
```

While monitors raise the level of abstraction in concurrent programming, they take away some of the freedom of lower level constructs such as the semaphore. As we have seen, the implementation must incorporate some scheduling policy, which may not always be the most desirable. By the same token, the use of monitors probably lessens the degree of parallelism possible in a system, compared with that obtainable using lower-level primitives.

As the reader may have surmised, the semantics of monitors are fairly complex, and there is considerable scope for programmer confusion and error. Besides the dangers of not understanding the mechanism of what we have termed the 'polite' queue, there are two other areas of which the reader should be aware.

In the first place, deadlock is not necessarily avoided by the use of monitors, any more or less than it is by the use of semaphores. Consider, for example, a program fragment of the form:

```
monitor ONE;
  var RESOURCEA;
  procedure A1;
    begin
      . . .
      TWO.B1
monitor TWO;
  var RESOURCEB;
  procedure B1;
    begin
      . . .
      ONE.A1
procedure SILLY;
  begin
    ONE.A1
  end;
procedure SILLIER;
  begin
    TWO.B1
  end;
begin
  cobegin
    SILLY; SILLIER
  coend
end.
```

SILLY and SILLIER might simultaneously enter monitors ONE and TWO respectively; however, if they then simultaneously try to enter monitors TWO and ONE, they will each be queued indefinitely waiting for access.

The reader might argue that this program is illegal anyway, because monitor TWO is seemingly not in scope when compiling monitor ONE. However, that is really only true if one is limited to one-pass compilation (and then only without the possibility of using **forward** declared blocks, as one is allowed to do in Pascal).

More problematic still is the so-called **nested monitor** problem, which we can again illustrate with a simple fragment.

```
monitor ONE;
   condition A;
   procedure A1;
     begin
       . . .
       if something then A.cwait
       . . .
   procedure A2;
     begin
       . . .
       A.csignal
       . . .
monitor TWO;
   procedure B1;
     begin
       . . .
       ONE.A1
       . . .
   procedure B2;
     begin
       . . .
       ONE.A2
```

Suppose a process gains exclusive access to monitor TWO through calling TWO.B1, and then gains exclusive access to monitor ONE through calling ONE.A1, and then is forced to wait on condition A. It presumably has to relinquish exclusive access to monitor ONE. If it does not relinquish access to TWO as well, then no other process will be able to call on TWO.B2 and in turn call on ONE.A2 to signal when it can again proceed. If such chains of exclusive access rights are set up, it becomes difficult to maintain their integrities.

For these reasons, some implementations of monitors forbid a routine in one monitor to call on a routine in another monitor at all, which can rather restrict their usefulness, especially in designing large systems.

Exercises

10.14 Although it can be shown that the shortest-job-first algorithm is optimal in the sense that it keeps the average turnround time for jobs at a minimum, it is not suggested that this algorithm is anything like ones used in real operating systems which try to keep multi-access users happy, for example. A little thought shows that a steady stream of very short jobs would lead to indefinite postponement of much longer jobs, and this is usually unacceptable.

(a) Satisfy yourself that the shortest-job-first algorithm does in fact keep average turnround time to a minimum.

(b) One solution to the problem of indefinite postponement is to introduce the concept of **ageing**, whereby the priority of jobs that stay in the system for a long time is gradually increased – for example by increasing the priority of all jobs in the CPUAVAILABLE queue by one unit when the running job calls on RELEASECPU. Can you do this with only the features of monitors discussed here, or would you need further operations defined on condition queues?

10.15 In the MIDDLEMAN example given earlier, what would be the implications of coding the csignal operations in places other than those shown, for example

```
monitor MIDDLEMAN;
  const
    MAX = 5;
  var
    HEAD, TAIL, COUNT, BUFFER[5];
  condition
    ITEMSAVAILABLE, STORAGEAVAILABLE;
  procedure *STORE (I);
    begin
      if COUNT > MAX then STORAGEAVAILABLE.cwait;
      BUFFER[TAIL] := I; COUNT := COUNT + 1;
      ITEMSAVAILABLE.csignal;
      TAIL := TAIL + 1; if TAIL > MAX then TAIL := 0
    end;
  function *DRAW;
    begin
      if COUNT = 0 then ITEMSAVAILABLE.cwait;
      DRAW := BUFFER[HEAD]; STORAGEAVAILABLE.csignal;
      COUNT := COUNT - 1;
      HEAD := HEAD + 1; if HEAD > MAX then HEAD := 0
    end;
  begin
    HEAD := 0; TAIL := 0; COUNT := 0
  end;
```

Further reading

As with so much else, our treatment of monitors has been dangerously brief, and needs to be supplemented by consulting more specialized works. The seminal reference is probably the paper by Hoare (1974). Good treatments, together with many examples now regarded as standard, can be found in the books by Holt (1983) and Ben-Ari (1982).

Problems with monitors are discussed in papers by Haddon (1977). Lister (1977), Parnas (1978), Wettstein (1978), Silberschatz *et al.* (1977), Andrews and McGraw (1977) and Schneider and Bernstein (1978). Serious doubts as to whether the monitor is more than an academic toy are expressed by Keedy (1978).

10.6 Condition queue operations related to semaphore operations

The astute reader will probably have realized that, in spite of the semantic differences between them, there is a close relationship between the mechanics of the condition queue and that of the semaphore – especially when the semaphore mechanism involves a hidden queue, as is usually the case. The provision of exclusivity in a monitor can surely be enforced by an implementation simply by the automatic introduction of a hidden semaphore for that monitor, say MUTEX, accompanied by automatic generation of code to wait(MUTEX) whenever a routine in the monitor is called, and to signal(MUTEX) immediately after it is left, and this is very nearly correct.

The condition queue can be handled by the introduction of an associated semaphore, say CONDSEM; we shall, however, also introduce a further hidden semaphore, say POLITE, to handle the contention between signalling and signalled processes at a CONDITION.csignal operation.

The translation of CONDITION.cwait can then be accomplished with code of the form

```
if there is a process waiting on POLITE
   then signal(POLITE)     (*free a waiting signaller*)
   else signal(MUTEX)      (*release exclusivity on monitor*)
wait(CONDSEM)              (*and wait on the semaphore*);
```

The translation of CONDITION.csignal can be accomplished with code of the form

```
if there is a process waiting on CONDSEM
   then
     signal(CONDSEM) (*prefer waiting processes*);
     wait(POLITE)    (*wait politely*);
   else (*no action, as csignal has no effect in this case*)
```

Rather than a simple signal(MUTEX) at the end of each monitor routine, we must cater for the possibility that a process is waiting for re-entry, and this leads to code of the form

```
if there is a process waiting on POLITE
  then signal(POLITE)  (*let the polite one have a chance*)
  else signal(MUTEX)   (*monitor clear again*)
```

Only if there are no blocked processes is the monitor truly freed. The waiting processes inherit the exclusivity from the signallers and the polite waiters inherit it from the waiters – when the last polite one is cleared, it executes a signal(MUTEX), and lets the monitor be available to new callers.

For these equivalences to be successful, the initial integer values of the semaphores must be defined by the implementation as well. MUTEX is initially 1 – the first process executing wait(MUTEX) will, of course, be granted access to the monitor, but others attempting to enter before exclusivity is released must be forced to wait. CONDSEM is initially zero, as a wait(CONDSEM) always implies that the process is suspended. POLITE is initially zero for the same reason.

The reader should note carefully that these equivalences will not work properly if the semaphore mechanisms are not associated with the existence of queues. Nor, strictly, is one allowed to 'examine' a semaphore to determine whether there is already a process waiting on it. However, these points are of little moment if we are free to implement the semaphore mechanism as we choose, and do not have to rely on a preconceived underlying implementation. Similarly, simple modification allows one to handle prioritized condition queues, as we shall see.

10.7 Implementing monitors – syntactic and semantic considerations

By this stage the reader is probably able to follow developments without presenting complete specifications of syntax. (These can, in any event, be found in an appendix, which describes the whole of CLANG as we shall now develop it.)

To add monitor-based concurrent facilities to our system, we shall extend the language by the addition of the three new reserved words condition, cwait and csignal.

condition will be used to declare condition queues in a manner similar to var declarations; we shall demand that condition declarations follow var declarations, and may only appear at the outer level of a monitor.

Suppose that we have a condition queue TEDIUM. Then the action of the statement

```
TEDIUM.cwait(RANK)
```

is to suspend the calling process on the condition queue TEDIUM, in a position determined by the priority value RANK. A process is placed after processes with the same or smaller values of RANK (that is, a low RANK denotes a high priority, and the queue is FIFO if RANK remains constant in a program). RANK must be an expression which evaluates to a non-negative integer. The parameter is optional; the action of

TEDIUM.cwait

is the same as

TEDIUM.cwait(128)

When a process is suspended on a condition queue, exclusion on the monitor is released.

The action of

TEDIUM.csignal

is to activate the top process on the condition queue TEDIUM, and to delay the process that signals, in order to allow the signalled process to proceed. The delayed calling process is given priority when exclusion is again released on the monitor. If a condition queue is empty, calling csignal has no effect.

We shall not allow a monitor routine to invoke a routine in another monitor.

The code for the complete implementation is given in Listing 12, and we shall refer to this frequently by line number in the discussion which follows.

Several of the extensions needed, for example those to the list of reserved words and error messages, are trivial, and need not be detailed here. We introduce CONDSYM, CWAITSYM and CSIGNALSYM to our list defining the SYMBOLS type, with corresponding additions to the tables WORD and WSYM.

Handling the declaration of condition variables is a straightforward variation on declaring other variables, and is dealt with in lines 650–682, by appropriate parameterization of VARDECLARATION. We might have been tempted to declare conditions even more simply – just as variables – but this would give rise to severe semantic problems later, and also allow operations on them which we should wish to prevent (such as arithmetic). Some care must be taken to ensure that they are declared only at the outermost level of a monitor (line 1095).

As previously discussed, our implementation requires that two hidden semaphores are introduced as global variables in the main program as each monitor is parsed. These we shall call MUTEX and POLITE for the purposes of discussion. This necessitates some subtle changes to the code for BLOCK, which can be found in lines 1069–1139. The offset of MUTEX is recorded as the ADDRESS field for the monitor entry in the symbol table (line 1082); the offset of POLITE is readily computed from this. To leave space for these semaphores, OFFSET is incremented by 2 above the value of the ADDRESS field for the program entry which, it will be recalled, keeps track of the last offset allocated to a global variable, in case more of these are declared by subsequent monitors.

This may all be made clearer by considering the following code (for a useless program).

```
program SILLY;
var A , B;
  monitor ONE;
    var LOCAL1;
    condition FREE, EMPTY;
    procedure *X;
      begin
        FREE.cwait; EMPTY.cwait(10);
        FREE.csignal
      end;
  begin end;
  monitor TWO;
    var LOCAL2;
    condition FULL;
    procedure *XX;
      begin end;
  begin end;
  begin
    ONE.X; TWO.XX
  end.
```

The symbol table for this would appear as in Table 10.6 (not all attributes shown). We recall that the SIZE fields for program and monitor entries point to the last entry protected by the 'fences'.

Table 10.6

I	Name	Kind	Address	Size	I
1	SILLY	PROGRAM	14 (next level 1)	3	1
2	A	VARIABLE	3	1	2
3	B	VARIABLE	4	1	3
4	ONE	MONITOR	5 (5,6 implied) ONE.MUTEX = 5 ONE.POLITE = 6	8	4
5	LOCAL1	VARIABLE	7	1	5
6	FREE	CONDITION	8	1	6
7	EMPTY	CONDITION	9	1	7
8	X	PROCEDURE	(1) (entry point)	0	8
9	TWO	MONITOR	10 (10,11 implied) TWO.MUTEX = 10 TWO.POLITE = 11	12	9
10	LOCAL2	VARIABLE	12	1	10
11	FULL	CONDITION	13	1	11
12	XX	PROCEDURE	(32) (entry point)	0	12

Handling the syntactic and semantic aspects of the cwait and csignal operations is relatively easy, and is dealt with mainly by the code in lines 1018–1042
of procedure STATEMENT.

Notes

(a) These operations are not allowed except within a monitor. This is
     controlled by the global Boolean variable PARSEMON, which is initially
     set FALSE (line 330) and then set within BLOCK (lines 1084 and 1129).

(b) The operations are introduced by quoting the name of the condition
     variable, which will, of course imply a search of the symbol table
     through a call on SEARCHID. This, in turn, requires care to be taken that
     SEARCHID does not scan past the period, as it would normally do (lines
     625–627).

(c) The optional priority specification is handled in lines 1028–1034.
     Note that there is no attempt made at compile-time to ensure that a
     valid priority will be used.

10.8 Implementing monitors – code-generation considerations

As usual, there are a number of subtle points that have to be dealt with when
generating code to handle monitors using the semaphore based system
discussed in an earlier section. So far as monitor routines themselves are
concerned, the compiler has to be able to detect monitor routine calls, and to
generate the code for wait(MUTEX) before code generated to call the routine itself.
In these cases it has also to generate code for releasing exclusion, immediately
after generating code for the return operation. Lastly, it must arrange for MUTEX
to be given an associated value of 1 as part of the initialization code associated
with each monitor, and for the semaphores associated with condition queues and
with POLITE to be given initial values of zero.

In developing the code-generation interfaces we have further isolated the
procedures that deal with routine calling to a new procedure ROUTINECALL (lines
737–750). Calls to this may be made from STATEMENT (line 1016) or from within
FACTOR (line 823).

Notes

(a) Monitor routine calls are easily detected. The qualified identifier
     convention (as in MONITOR.ROUTINE) makes them syntactically dis-
     tinguishable from other calls, but in fact we make use of that fact
     rather indirectly. As we commented earlier, when catering for the
     qualified identifier notation, it is convenient to have the SEARCHID

procedure return the symbol table indices for both parts of the name – if there is no monitor name then the first of these will be zero (line 613).

(b)   We have to be careful to prevent calls from within one monitor to routines inside another monitor. This is handled by the test in line 743, code which makes use of THISMONITOR, a further parameter introduced into BLOCK (line 511). When BLOCK is called for the first time (line 1154) to parse the main program block, THISMONITOR is set to 1 (the symbol table index for the program name). When a monitor is being parsed, THISMONITOR is set to point to the symbol table entry for the monitor name (line 724), and retains this value while parsing all routines nested within it.

(c)   A user is free to use the qualified identifier notation in making calls to monitor routines from within the same monitor (although this is not necessary). Of course, in this case there is no need to request code for exclusive access – indeed, it would be wrong to do so, as the system would immediately deadlock – which accounts for the test in line 742.

(d)   THISMONITOR is also used when setting up the code-generation interface routines for the cwait and csignal operations (lines 1036 and 1040). In this case the motivation is to allow these routines to obtain the run-time addresses of the hidden semaphores POLITE and MUTEX.

(e)   The interface procedure for generating code to initialize MUTEX and POLITE is called from within BLOCK at line 1116. At the same point should appear calls to interface procedures to initialize all the semaphores associated with condition queues, but we have cheated a little, as we shall allow this to be done by the interpreter.

(f)   Incidentally, we have chosen to forbid calls to monitor procedures from within the cobegin...coend construct (Line 1014) (though procedures called within cobegin...coend may, of course, call monitor routines).

10.9   Run-time support for monitors

In common with the rest of this text, we shall deal only with the sort of code needed by our hypothetical stack based machine, and with how this might be interpreted. The full problem is far more difficult to follow, and is well beyond the scope of this text. Suffice it to say that it would require a rather sophisticated run-time support system, which would have to be closely bonded to whatever operating system was used to execute the program. However, these support systems would display some of the characteristics of the much simpler one we are about to describe.

We have already commented that our implementation will be semaphore based. In the system described in the last chapter we introduced opcodes WGT and SIG for operating on semaphores, which relied on the run-time address of the semaphore being pushed onto the stack. Code for csignal and cwait operations can, ultimately, make use of the same interpreter routines; because of the more involved semantics we shall introduce further opcodes, CSG and CWT respectively, and further opcodes INM and EXM to handle the acquisition and release of exclusion when calling a monitor routine, and arrange that before these are executed the stack will contain the addresses of various semaphores as shown in Table 10.7.

Table 10.7

COND.cwait (lines 470–474)	generates code to	push address of COND push address of POLITE push address of MUTEX CWT
COND.csignal (lines 467–468)	generates code to	push address of COND push address of POLITE CSG
enter a monitor procedure (lines 458–459)	generates code to	push address of MUTEX INM
returning from a monitor procedure (lines 461–465)	generates code to	push address of MUTEX push address of POLITE EXM

To allow prioritized queues in cwait operations the only extension needed is to ensure that the priority is also pushed onto the stack. This is conveniently done just after pushing the address of the condition itself (lines 1028–1035).

This may be made clearer by considering the code generated for the silly program given earlier.

```
 0 BRN 0 17    branch to initialization code for ONE
 1 BRN 0 2     branch to start ONE.X (redundant)
 2 INT 0 3     reserve stack space
 3 LDA 1 8     address of FREE
 4 LDI 0 128   default priority
 5 LDA 1 6     address of ONE.POLITE
 6 LDA 1 5     address of ONE.MUTEX
 7 CWT         cwait
 8 LDA 1 9     address of EMPTY
 9 LDI 0 10    priority = 10
10 LDA 1 6     address of ONE.POLITE
11 LDA 1 5     address of ONE.MUTEX
12 CWT         cwait(10)
13 LDA 1 8     address of FREE
```

```
14 LDA 1 6      address of ONE.POLITE
15 CSG          csignal
16 RET 2 1      return from ONE.X
17 INT 0 10     initialize ONE - reserve stack space
18 MON 0 5      initialize ONE.MUTEX
19 BRN 0 23     branch to initialization code for TWO
20 BRN 0 21     branch to code for TWO.XX (redundant)
21 INT 0 3      reserve stack space for TWO.XX
22 RET 2 1      return from TWO.XX
23 INT 0 4      initialize TWO - reserve stack space
24 MON 0 10     initialize TWO.MUTEX
25 BRN 0 26     branch to code for main program (redundant)
26 LDA 1 5      address of ONE.MUTEX
27 INM          seek exclusion
28 CAL 1 1      and then enter ONE.X
29 LDA 1 5      address of ONE.MUTEX
30 LDA 1 6      address of ONE.POLITE
31 EXM          release exclusion on ONE.X after return
32 LDA 1 10     address of TWO.MUTEX
33 INM          seek exclusion
34 CAL 1 20     and then enter TWO.XX
35 LDA 1 10     address of TWO.MUTEX
36 LDA 1 11     address of TWO.POLITE
37 EXM          release exclusion on TWO.XX after return
38 HLT
```

In handling prioritized queues we shall need to introduce a further field into our process descriptors, which are finally defined by

```
var
  PROC : array [PROCINDEX] of (*process descriptors*)
              record
                DISPLAY : array [LEVELS] of INTEGER;
                P, B, T,          (*program counter, base, stack pointer*);
                STACKEND,         (*memory limit*)
                PRIORITY : INTEGER (*condition queue ordering*);
                NEXT,             (*ring pointers*)
                QUEUE : PROCINDEX  (*linked waiting on a semaphore*);
                READY : BOOLEAN    (*process ready flag*)
              end (*PROC*);
```

The way in which some of these fields are used may be made clearer if we consider the case where a program has launched four processes – see Figure 10.3. (To save space the descriptor for the main program is not shown.)

The action taken by the interpreter for the opcodes CWT, CSG and EXM matches the discussion of Section 10.6, and can be found in lines 1366–1380.

As in Chapter 9, WAIT and SIGNAL are procedures in the interpreter. The action of SIGNAL is as before, but WAIT needs some modification to deal with the

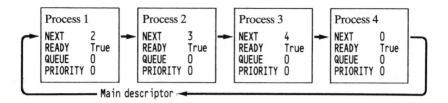

If process 4 is then forced to wait on a condition say FULL, with default priority:

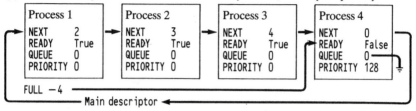

If process 2 then waits with the same priority on the same conditions:

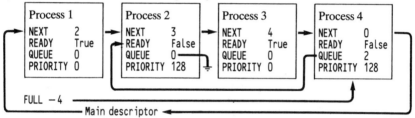

If process 1 then waits on the same condition with priority 100

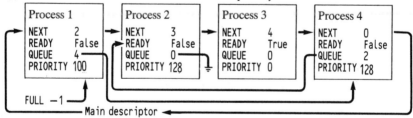

If a signal is now issued on this condition:

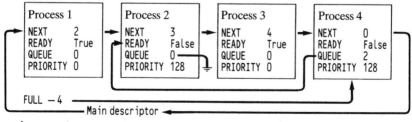

and so on

Figure 10.3

priority queueing mechanism, as can be seen from lines 1298–1308.

In our implementation the initialization of POLITE and of condition queue semaphores is achieved as part of an interpreter initialization which clears the stack frame of a monitor before interpretation commences (lines 1354–1358).

Exercises

10.16 Two other operations often allowed in implementations of condition queues are the ability to detect whether there are any processes waiting on the queue, and to determine the priority of the process at the head of the queue. Suggest ways in which these features might be added to CLANG, and then add them.

10.17 Another useful addition is for a process to be able to discover the number of processes that are ready to execute at a given time. This could be done by including, as a possible FACTOR, the reserved word ready, which allowed one to access an interpreter register in which this information was kept up to date. Try to implement this.

10.18 Suppose one wished to allow processes to have priorities, so that queueing on (ordinary) semaphores is done according to process priority. Add a statement

```
setpriority (PRIORITY)
```

to the language and modify the parser and interpreter to handle this conveniently. Would one have to add yet another field to the process descriptor record or not? (Be careful!)

10.19 Suppose one wanted high priority processes to receive preferential time-slicing in CLANG. How could this be achieved? What unforeseen complications might arise as a result?

10.20 We have stated that priorities used in the cwait operation should be non-negative, yet we have not checked for this. What might be the consequences of ignoring the check, and where could it be included?

10.21 What modifications would be needed to generate code explicitly to initialize the POLITE semaphore, and those associated with conditions?

10.22 We mentioned earlier that nested monitor calls are prone to cause problems. Detecting nested monitor calls is actually rather more difficult than our discussion may have brought out. Consider the following silly extract

```
monitor ONE;
  procedure *A;
    begin end;
  begin end (*ONE*);
```

```
procedure TWO;
  begin
    ONE.A (*monitor call*)
  end (*TWO*);
monitor THREE;
  procedure *B;
    begin
      ONE.A      (*this would be easy for a compiler to detect*);
      TWO        (*the nested call would be much more difficult*)
    end (*THREE.B*)
  begin end (*THREE*);
```

Can you think of a way in which this problem could be overcome, preferably at compile-time?

10.23 Can SEMIDENTIFIER in the diagram for SEMAPHORESTATEMENT be a 'qualified' identifier, referring to a monitor variable? How do our parsing algorithms treat this point, and do they need modification?

10.24 As the keen reader will discover, debugging concurrent programs is much more difficult than debugging sequential programs. What features do you suppose could be incorporated into the interpreter given here to allow, for example, process and statement tracing, the addition of breakpoints, partial dumps of memory, and so on? Try to implement some of these for yourself.

10.25 If you are taking a course in concurrent programming you will find the system developed here to be quite useful. Try implementing solutions to the various standard problems discussed in the textbooks mentioned earlier.

10.26 (Harder) In Pascal-Plus, data to be shared by several processes is only allowed to be modified by concurrent processes if they make appropriate monitor routine calls. The main program is deemed to be a monitor, and its global variables are all 'starred' from this viewpoint. What changes would have to be made to CLANG to provide this feature? Does this have any bearing on Exercise 10.22?

Listing 12   Compiler/interpreter system for CLANG level 5.0.

```
1 program CLANG5COMPILER(INPUT, OUTPUT, SOURCE, DATA, RESULTS, CODEFILE);
2 (*Simple compiler with stack machine code generation
3   includes procedures, functions, value parameters and simple arrays,
4   data abstraction, simple concurrency and monitors
5
6   P.D. Terry, February 1st, 1986  Standard Pascal version 5.1  *)
```

```
7
8 const
9   VERSION = '5.1'     (*level.release*);
10  LOWEST   = 0         (*ASCII ordinal value*);
11  HIGHEST  = 127       (*ASCII ordinal value*);
12  KEYWORDS = 23        (*number of reserved words*);
13  TABLEMAX = 100       (*length of identifier table*);
14  LINEMAX  = 120       (*max characters on source line*);
15  ALENG    = 8         (*length of identifiers*);
16  CODEMAX  = 2000      (*max size of code*);
17  LEVMAX   = 5         (*max static nesting*);
18  PARAMAX  = 24        (*max number of parameters*);
19  PROCMAX  = 10        (*max number of concurrent processes*);
20  STACKMAX = 3000      (*limit on pseudo-machine memory size*);
21  DEFAULTPRIORITY = 128 (*for wait queues*);
22 type
23  SYMBOLS =
24    (UNKNOWN, IDENT, NUMBER, STRINGSYM, PLUS, MINUS, TIMES, SLASH, ODDSYM,
25     EQLSYM, NEQSYM, LSSSYM, LEQSYM, GTRSYM, GEQSYM, LPAREN, RPAREN,
26     COMMA, SEMICOLON, PERIOD, LBRACKET, RBRACKET, BECOMES,
27     BEGINSYM, ENDSYM, IFSYM, THENSYM, WHILESYM, DOSYM, READSYM, WRITESYM,
28     STACKSYM, COBEGSYM, COENDSYM, WAITSYM, SIGNALSYM, CWAITSYM, CSIGNALSYM,
29     CONSTSYM, VARSYM, CONDSYM, PROCSYM);
30  CLASSES     = (CONSTANT, VARIABLE, COND, PROG, PROC, FUNC, MONI);
31  CLASSSET    = set of CLASSES;
32  SYMSET      = set of SYMBOLS;
33  SHORTSTRING = packed array [1 .. 3] of CHAR;
34  ALFA        = packed array [1 .. ALENG] of CHAR;
35  LINEINDEX   = 0 .. LINEMAX;
36  TABLEINDEX  = 0 .. TABLEMAX;
37  LEVELS      = 0 .. LEVMAX;
38  OPCODES     = (LDI, LDA, CAL, RET, STK, INT, IND, CBG, MON,
39                 BRN, BZE, WGT, SIG, CND, NEG, ADD, SUB, MUL,
40                 DVD, OD,  EQL, NEQ, LSS, GEQ, GTR, LEQ, STO, HLT,
41                 INN, PRN, PRS, NLN, LDV, INM, EXM, CWT, CSG);
42  INSTRUCTIONS = packed record
43                   F : OPCODES (*function code*);
44                   L : LEVELS  (*level*);
45                   A : INTEGER (*address*)
46                 end (*INSTRUCTIONS*);
47  TRANSFERS   = (NUMBERS, STRINGS, NEWLINE);
48
49 var
50  (*some implementations require INPUT, OUTPUT : TEXT*)
51  SOURCE, DATA, RESULTS, CODEFILE : TEXT;
52
```

```
53  (* +++++++++++ Used by the character and option handler +++++++++++ *)
54
55  CH     : CHAR                    (*latest character read*);
56  CC,                              (*character pointer*)
57  LL     : LINEINDEX               (*line length*);
58  ENDLINE,                         (*true when CC = LL*)
59  TABLES : BOOLEAN                 (*request tables*);
60  LINE   : array [LINEINDEX] of CHAR (*latest line read*);
61
62  (* +++++++++++ Used by the lexical analyser +++++++++++ *)
63
64  SYM  : SYMBOLS                   (*latest symbol read*);
65  ID   : ALFA                      (*latest identifier read*);
66  NUM  : INTEGER                   (*latest number read*);
67  STRINGTEXT : array [LINEINDEX] of CHAR  (*latest string read*);
68  WORD : array [1 .. KEYWORDS] of ALFA    (*reserved words*);
69  WSYM : array [1 .. KEYWORDS] of SYMBOLS (*matching symbols*);
70  CSYM : array [CHAR] of SYMBOLS          (*one character symbols*);
71
72  (* +++++++++++ Used by the syntax analyser +++++++++++ *)
73
74  ERRORS,                          (*whether we have any*)
75  PARSEMON,                        (*while we are parsing monitors*)
76  MONITORS,                        (*whether we have parsed any monitors*)
77  PROCCALL : BOOLEAN               (*type of latest statement*);
78  FIRSTBLOCK, FIRSTSTATEMENT, FIRSTFACTOR,
79  RELOPSYMS : SYMSET               (*for error recovery mostly*);
80  TABLE : array [TABLEINDEX] of record   (*symbol table entries*)
81                            NAME          : ALFA;
82                            CLASS         : CLASSES;
83                            LEVEL         : LEVELS;
84                            SIZE, ADDRESS : INTEGER;
85                            CANCHANGE, CANACCESS,
86                            INSIDE        : BOOLEAN;
87                        end (*TABLE*);
88
89  (* +++++++++++ Used by the code generator +++++++++++ *)
90
91  MNEMONIC : array [OPCODES] of SHORTSTRING     (*opcodes*);
92  STARTMAINCODE, NEXTCODE : INTEGER             (*code location counters*);
93  PCODE : array [0 .. CODEMAX] of INSTRUCTIONS  (*generated code*);
94  CODEISTOBEGENERATED : BOOLEAN                 (*not after errors*);
95  HASADDRESSFIELD : set of OPCODES;
96
97 procedure QUIT (N : INTEGER);
98 (* +++++ Implementation dependent for handling fatal errors +++++++++++ *)
```

```
 99   begin
100     WRITELN(OUTPUT);
101     case N of
102       1: WRITELN(OUTPUT, ' Procedures too deeply nested');
103       2: WRITELN(OUTPUT, ' Program too long');
104       3: WRITELN(OUTPUT, ' Program Incomplete - Unexpected EOF');
105       4: WRITELN(OUTPUT, ' Too many identifiers');
106     end (*case*);
107     (*close OUTPUT file if necessary and abort program*)
108   end (*QUIT*);
109
110 (* +++++++++++++++++++++++++++++++ Source handler +++++++++++++++++++++++ *)
111
112 procedure ERROR (ERRORCODE : INTEGER);
113 (*Handle error reporting for ERRORCODE
114   This procedure is split merely to allow it to be handled by compilers
115   that have a severe limit on the size of block they can handle*)
116
117   procedure ERROR2;
118     begin
119       case ERRORCODE of
120          0: WRITE(OUTPUT, 'NUMBER OUT OF RANGE');
121          1: WRITE(OUTPUT, 'STRING INCOMPLETE');
122          2: WRITE(OUTPUT, '; EXPECTED');
123          3: WRITE(OUTPUT, 'INVALID SEQUENCE');
124          5: WRITE(OUTPUT, 'UNDECLARED');
125          6: WRITE(OUTPUT, 'IDENTIFIER EXPECTED');
126          7: WRITE(OUTPUT, ':= IN WRONG CONTEXT');
127          8: WRITE(OUTPUT, 'NUMBER EXPECTED');
128          9: WRITE(OUTPUT, '= EXPECTED');
129         10: WRITE(OUTPUT, '] EXPECTED');
130         11: WRITE(OUTPUT, 'UNEXPECTED SUBSCRIPT');
131         12: WRITE(OUTPUT, 'WRONG NUMBER OF PARAMETERS');
132         13: WRITE(OUTPUT, ', OR ) EXPECTED');
133         14: WRITE(OUTPUT, 'INVALID START TO FACTOR');
134         15: WRITE(OUTPUT, '[ EXPECTED');
135         16: WRITE(OUTPUT, 'INVALID PROCEDURE REFERENCE');
136         17: WRITE(OUTPUT, ') EXPECTED');
137         18: WRITE(OUTPUT, '( EXPECTED');
138         19: WRITE(OUTPUT, 'RELATIONAL OPERATOR EXPECTED');
139         20: WRITE(OUTPUT, 'INVALID ASSIGNMENT');
140         21: WRITE(OUTPUT, ':= EXPECTED');
141         22: WRITE(OUTPUT, 'INVALID CLASS');
142       end (*case*);
143     end (*ERROR2*);
144
```

```
145  begin
146    ERRORS := TRUE; CODEISTOBEGENERATED := FALSE;
147    WRITE(OUTPUT,'**** ', ' ↑':CC);
148    if ERRORCODE < 23 then ERROR2 else
149      case ERRORCODE of
150        23: WRITE(OUTPUT, 'THEN EXPECTED');
151        24: WRITE(OUTPUT, 'END EXPECTED');
152        25: WRITE(OUTPUT, 'DO EXPECTED');
153        28: WRITE(OUTPUT, 'CANNOT BE READ');
154        31: WRITE(OUTPUT, 'INVALID ARRAY SIZE');
155        32: WRITE(OUTPUT, 'INVALID SYMBOL AFTER A STATEMENT');
156        34: WRITE(OUTPUT, 'BEGIN EXPECTED');
157        35: WRITE(OUTPUT, 'INVALID SYMBOL AFTER BLOCK');
158        36: WRITE(OUTPUT, 'PROGRAM EXPECTED');
159        37: WRITE(OUTPUT, '. EXPECTED');
160        39: WRITE(OUTPUT, 'CANNOT ALTER');
161        41: WRITE(OUTPUT, 'TOO MANY PARAMETERS');
162        42: WRITE(OUTPUT, 'ONLY GLOBAL PROCEDURE CALLS');
163        43: WRITE(OUTPUT, 'COEND EXPECTED');
164        44: WRITE(OUTPUT, 'CONCURRENCY ONLY IN MAIN PROGRAM');
165        45: WRITE(OUTPUT, 'TOO MANY CONCURRENT PROCESSES');
166        46: WRITE(OUTPUT, 'MONITORS ONLY IN MAIN BLOCK');
167        47: WRITE(OUTPUT, 'ONLY ALLOWED IN MONITORS');
168        48: WRITE(OUTPUT, 'ONLY STARRED IDENTIFIERS ACCESSIBLE');
169        49: WRITE(OUTPUT, 'CONDITIONS MUST BE PRIVATE');
170      end (*case*);
171    WRITELN(OUTPUT)
172  end (*ERROR*);
173
174 procedure GETCH;
175 (*Get next character from SOURCE, form source listing*)
176  begin
177    if CC = LL then
178      begin
179        if EOF(SOURCE) then QUIT(3);
180        LL := 0; CC := 0; WRITE(OUTPUT, NEXTCODE:5, ' ');
181        while not EOLN(SOURCE) do
182          begin
183            LL := LL + 1; READ(SOURCE, CH); WRITE(OUTPUT, CH);
184            LINE[LL] := CH
185          end;
186        WRITELN(OUTPUT); LL := LL + 1; READLN(SOURCE); LINE[LL] := ' '
187      end (*new line*);
188    CC := CC + 1; CH := LINE[CC]; ENDLINE := CC = LL
189  end (*GETCH*);
190
```

```
191 (* +++++++++++++++++++++++++ Lexical Analyser +++++++++++++++++++++++++ *)
192
193 procedure GETSYM;
194 (*Get next SYM from SOURCE, with its attributes*)
195   var
196     I, J, K  : INTEGER;
197     ENDSTRING : BOOLEAN;
198
199   function NOTLETTER : BOOLEAN;
200     begin NOTLETTER := not (CH in ['A' .. 'Z', 'a' .. 'z']) end (*NOTLETTER*);
201
202   function NOTDIGIT : BOOLEAN;
203     begin NOTDIGIT := not (CH in ['0' .. '9']) end (*NOTDIGIT*);
204
205   function DIGIT : INTEGER;
206     begin DIGIT := ORD(CH) - ORD('0') end (*DIGIT*);
207
208   begin (*GETSYM*)
209     while CH = ' ' do GETCH (*skip blanks*);
210     SYM := CSYM[CH] (*initial assumption*);
211     case CH of
212       'a', 'b', 'c', 'd', 'e', 'f', 'g', 'h', 'i', 'j', 'k', 'l', 'm',
213       'n', 'o', 'p', 'q', 'r', 's', 't', 'u', 'v', 'w', 'x', 'y', 'z',
214       'A', 'B', 'C', 'D', 'E', 'F', 'G', 'H', 'I', 'J', 'K', 'L', 'M',
215       'N', 'O', 'P', 'Q', 'R', 'S', 'T', 'U', 'V', 'W', 'X', 'Y', 'Z':
216         begin (*identifier or reserved word*)
217           K := 1; ID := '        ';
218           repeat
219             if CH in ['a'..'z'] then CH := CHR(ORD(CH) - ORD('a') + ORD('A'));
220             if K <= ALENG then begin ID[K] := CH; K := K + 1 end; GETCH
221           until NOTLETTER and NOTDIGIT;
222           I := 1; J := KEYWORDS;
223           repeat (*binary search*)
224             K := (I + J) div 2;
225             if ID <= WORD[K] then J := K - 1;
226             if ID >= WORD[K] then I := K + 1
227           until I > J;
228           if I - 1 > J then SYM := WSYM[K] else SYM := IDENT
229         end;
230       '0', '1', '2', '3', '4', '5', '6', '7', '8', '9':
231         begin
232           NUM := 0; SYM := NUMBER;
233           repeat
234             if NUM <= (MAXINT - DIGIT) div 10 (*check imminent overflow*)
235               then NUM := 10 * NUM + DIGIT else ERROR(0);
236             GETCH
```

```
237          until NOTDIGIT
238        end;
239      ':':
240        begin
241          GETCH;
242          if CH = '=' then begin SYM := BECOMES; GETCH end
243        end;
244      '<':
245        begin
246          GETCH;
247          if CH = '='
248            then begin SYM := LEQSYM; GETCH end
249            else
250              if CH = '>'
251                then begin SYM := NEQSYM; GETCH end
252                else SYM := LSSSYM
253        end;
254      '>':
255        begin
256          GETCH;
257          if CH = '='
258            then begin SYM := GEQSYM; GETCH end
259            else SYM := GTRSYM
260        end;
261      '''':
262        begin (*string*)
263          NUM := 0; GETCH; SYM := STRINGSYM; ENDSTRING := FALSE;
264          repeat
265            if CH = '''' then begin GETCH; ENDSTRING := CH <> '''' end;
266            if not ENDSTRING then
267              begin NUM := NUM + 1; STRINGTEXT[NUM] := CH; GETCH end
268          until ENDSTRING or ENDLINE;
269          if not ENDSTRING then begin NUM := 0; ERROR(1) end
270        end;
271      '*', '+', '-', '#', '=', '/', ')', '[', ']', ',', ';', '↑', 'τ', '@',
272      '{', '}', '(', '$', '.', '_', '%', '?', '"', '!', '¦', '¬':
273        begin SYM := CSYM[CH]; GETCH end (*implementation defined*);
274    end (*case*)
275  end (*GETSYM*);
276
277 (* ++++++++++++++++++++++++ Initialization ++++++++++++++++++++++++ *)
278
279 procedure INITIALIZE;
280   var
281     C : CHAR;
282
```

```
283  procedure RESERVEDWORDS;
284    begin
285      WORD[ 1] := 'BEGIN   '; WORD[ 2] := 'COBEGIN '; WORD[ 3] := 'COEND   ';
286      WORD[ 4] := 'CONDITIO'; WORD[ 5] := 'CONST   '; WORD[ 6] := 'CSIGNAL ';
287      WORD[ 7] := 'CWAIT   '; WORD[ 8] := 'DO      '; WORD[ 9] := 'END     ';
288      WORD[10] := 'FUNCTION'; WORD[11] := 'IF      '; WORD[12] := 'MONITOR ';
289      WORD[13] := 'ODD     '; WORD[14] := 'PROCEDUR'; WORD[15] := 'PROGRAM ';
290      WORD[16] := 'READ    '; WORD[17] := 'SIGNAL  '; WORD[18] := 'STACKDUM';
291      WORD[19] := 'THEN    '; WORD[20] := 'VAR     '; WORD[21] := 'WAIT    ';
292      WORD[22] := 'WHILE   '; WORD[23] := 'WRITE   ';
293      WSYM[ 1] := BEGINSYM  ; WSYM[ 2] := COBEGSYM  ; WSYM[ 3] := COENDSYM  ;
294      WSYM[ 4] := CONDSYM   ; WSYM[ 5] := CONSTSYM  ; WSYM[ 6] := CSIGNALSYM;
295      WSYM[ 7] := CWAITSYM  ; WSYM[ 8] := DOSYM     ; WSYM[ 9] := ENDSYM    ;
296      WSYM[10] := PROCSYM   ; WSYM[11] := IFSYM     ; WSYM[12] := PROCSYM   ;
297      WSYM[13] := ODDSYM    ; WSYM[14] := PROCSYM   ; WSYM[15] := PROCSYM   ;
298      WSYM[16] := READSYM   ; WSYM[17] := SIGNALSYM ; WSYM[18] := STACKSYM  ;
299      WSYM[19] := THENSYM   ; WSYM[20] := VARSYM    ; WSYM[21] := WAITSYM   ;
300      WSYM[22] := WHILESYM  ; WSYM[23] := WRITESYM;
301    end (*RESERVEDWORDS*);
302
303  begin
304    WRITELN(OUTPUT, 'CLANG Compiler Mark ', VERSION); WRITELN(OUTPUT);
305    RESERVEDWORDS;
306    MNEMONIC[LDI] := 'LDI'; MNEMONIC[LDA] := 'LDA'; MNEMONIC[CAL] := 'CAL';
307    MNEMONIC[INT] := 'INT'; MNEMONIC[BRN] := 'BRN'; MNEMONIC[BZE] := 'BZE';
308    MNEMONIC[IND] := 'IND'; MNEMONIC[RET] := 'RET'; MNEMONIC[NEG] := 'NEG';
309    MNEMONIC[ADD] := 'ADD'; MNEMONIC[SUB] := 'SUB'; MNEMONIC[MUL] := 'MUL';
310    MNEMONIC[DVD] := 'DVD'; MNEMONIC[OD]  := 'ODD'; MNEMONIC[EQL] := 'EQL';
311    MNEMONIC[NEQ] := 'NEQ'; MNEMONIC[LSS] := 'LSS'; MNEMONIC[GEQ] := 'GEQ';
312    MNEMONIC[GTR] := 'GTR'; MNEMONIC[LEQ] := 'LEQ'; MNEMONIC[STK] := 'STK';
313    MNEMONIC[STO] := 'STO'; MNEMONIC[HLT] := 'HLT'; MNEMONIC[INN] := 'INN';
314    MNEMONIC[PRN] := 'PRN'; MNEMONIC[PRS] := 'PRS'; MNEMONIC[NLN] := 'NLN';
315    MNEMONIC[LDV] := 'LDV'; MNEMONIC[CBG] := 'CBG'; MNEMONIC[CND] := 'CND';
316    MNEMONIC[WGT] := 'WGT'; MNEMONIC[SIG] := 'SIG'; MNEMONIC[EXM] := 'EXM';
317    MNEMONIC[INM] := 'INM'; MNEMONIC[CSG] := 'CSG'; MNEMONIC[CWT] := 'CWT';
318    MNEMONIC[MON] := 'MON';
319    for C := CHR(LOWEST) to CHR(HIGHEST) do CSYM[C] := UNKNOWN;
320    CSYM['+'] := PLUS    ; CSYM['-'] := MINUS   ; CSYM['*'] := TIMES;
321    CSYM['/'] := SLASH   ; CSYM['('] := LPAREN  ; CSYM[')'] := RPAREN;
322    CSYM['='] := EQLSYM  ; CSYM[','] := COMMA   ; CSYM['.'] := PERIOD;
323    CSYM['<'] := LSSSYM  ; CSYM['>'] := GTRSYM  ; CSYM[';'] := SEMICOLON;
324    CSYM['['] := LBRACKET; CSYM[']'] := RBRACKET;
325    RELOPSYMS      := [EQLSYM, NEQSYM, GTRSYM, GEQSYM, LSSSYM, LEQSYM];
326    FIRSTBLOCK     := [CONSTSYM, VARSYM, CONDSYM, PROCSYM, BEGINSYM];
327    FIRSTSTATEMENT := [IDENT, BEGINSYM, IFSYM, WHILESYM, WRITESYM, READSYM,
328                       STACKSYM, COBEGSYM, WAITSYM, SIGNALSYM];
```

```
329    FIRSTFACTOR   := [IDENT, NUMBER, LPAREN];
330    ERRORS := FALSE; PARSEMON := FALSE;
331    (*Initialize code generator*)
332    STARTMAINCODE := 0; NEXTCODE := 0; HASADDRESSFIELD := [LDI .. BZE];
333    CODEISTOBEGENERATED := TRUE; MONITORS := FALSE;
334    (*Initialize lexical analyser*)
335    CC := 0; LL := 0; CH := ' '; GETSYM
336  end (*INITIALIZE*);
337
338 (* ++++++++++++++++++++++++ Code Generator ++++++++++++++++++++++++ *)
339
340 procedure GEN (OP : OPCODES; LEV : LEVELS; ADDRESS : INTEGER);
341 (*Code generator for instruction with address field*)
342   begin
343    if NEXTCODE > CODEMAX then QUIT(2) (*program too long*);
344    if CODEISTOBEGENERATED then
345      begin
346        with PCODE[NEXTCODE] do begin F := OP; L := LEV; A := ADDRESS end;
347        NEXTCODE := NEXTCODE + 1
348      end
349   end (*GEN*);
350
351 procedure EMIT (OP : OPCODES);
352 (*Code generator with no address field*)
353   begin GEN(OP, 0, 0) end;
354
355 procedure NEGATEINTEGER;
356   begin EMIT(NEG) end;
357
358 procedure BINARYINTEGEROP (OP : SYMBOLS);
359   begin
360    case OP of
361      TIMES  : EMIT(MUL);
362      SLASH  : EMIT(DVD);
363      PLUS   : EMIT(ADD);
364      MINUS  : EMIT(SUB);
365    end
366   end (*BINARYINTEGEROP*);
367
368 procedure COMPARISON (OP : SYMBOLS);
369   begin
370    case OP of
371      EQLSYM : EMIT(EQL);
372      NEQSYM : EMIT(NEQ);
373      LSSSYM : EMIT(LSS);
374      LEQSYM : EMIT(LEQ);
```

```
375       GTRSYM : EMIT(GTR);
376       GEQSYM : EMIT(GEQ)
377     end
378   end (*COMPARISON*);
379
380 procedure INPUTOPERATION (OP : TRANSFERS);
381   begin
382     case OP of
383       NUMBERS         : EMIT(INN);
384       STRINGS, NEWLINE : (*not used*)
385     end
386   end (*INPUTOPERATION*);
387
388 procedure STACKSTRING;
389   var
390     I : INTEGER;
391   begin
392     for I := 1 to NUM do GEN(LDI, 0, ORD(STRINGTEXT[I])); GEN(LDI, 0, NUM)
393   end (*STACKSTRING*);
394
395 procedure OUTPUTOPERATION (OP : TRANSFERS);
396   begin
397     case OP of
398       STRINGS : begin STACKSTRING; EMIT(PRS) end;
399       NUMBERS : EMIT(PRN);
400       NEWLINE : EMIT(NLN);
401     end
402   end (*OUTPUTOPERATION*);
403
404 procedure STACKCONSTANT (NUM : INTEGER);
405   begin GEN(LDI, 0, NUM) end;
406
407 procedure STACKADDRESS (LEVEL : LEVELS; OFFSET : INTEGER);
408   begin GEN(LDA, LEVEL, OFFSET) end;
409
410 procedure DEREFERENCE;
411   begin EMIT(LDV) end;
412
413 procedure SUBSCRIPT (LIMIT : INTEGER);
414   begin GEN(IND, 0, LIMIT - 1) end;
415
416 procedure ASSIGN;
417   begin EMIT(STO) end;
418
419 procedure OPENSTACKFRAME (SIZE : INTEGER);
420   begin GEN(INT, 0, SIZE) end;
```

```
421
422 procedure STORELABEL (var LAB : INTEGER);
423   begin LAB := NEXTCODE end;
424
425 procedure JUMP(LAB : INTEGER);
426   begin GEN(BRN, 0, LAB) end;
427
428 procedure JUMPONFALSE (LAB : INTEGER);
429   begin GEN(BZE, 0, LAB) end;
430
431 procedure STARTPROCESSES;
432   begin EMIT(CBG) end;
433
434 procedure STOPPROCESSES;
435   begin EMIT(CND) end;
436
437 procedure CODEFORSIGNAL;
438   begin EMIT(SIG) end;
439
440 procedure CODEFORWAIT;
441   begin EMIT(WGT) end;
442
443 procedure ENTERBLOCK (var LAB : INTEGER);
444   begin STORELABEL(LAB); JUMP(0) end;
445
446 procedure INITMUTEX (I : TABLEINDEX);
447   begin GEN(MON, 0, TABLE[I].ADDRESS) end;
448
449 procedure LEAVEBLOCK (BLOCKCLASS : CLASSES; BLOCKLEVEL : LEVELS;
450                       PARAMS : INTEGER);
451   begin
452     case BLOCKCLASS of
453       PROG      : EMIT(HLT);
454       FUNC, PROC : GEN(RET, BLOCKLEVEL, PARAMS + 1);
455     end
456   end (*LEAVEBLOCK*);
457
458 procedure GAINEXCLUSION (I : TABLEINDEX);
459   begin STACKADDRESS(1, TABLE[I].ADDRESS); EMIT(INM) end;
460
461 procedure RELEASEEXCLUSION (I : TABLEINDEX);
462   begin
463     STACKADDRESS(1, TABLE[I].ADDRESS); STACKADDRESS(1, TABLE[I].ADDRESS + 1);
464     EMIT(EXM)
465   end (*RELEASEEXCLUSION*);
466
```

```
467 procedure CSIGNAL (I : TABLEINDEX);
468   begin STACKADDRESS(1, TABLE[I].ADDRESS + 1); EMIT(CSG) end;
469
470 procedure CWAIT (I : TABLEINDEX);
471   begin
472     STACKADDRESS(1, TABLE[I].ADDRESS + 1); STACKADDRESS(1, TABLE[I].ADDRESS);
473     EMIT(CWT)
474   end (*CWAIT*);
475
476 procedure CALL (LEVEL : LEVELS; ENTRYPOINT : INTEGER);
477   begin GEN(CAL, LEVEL, ENTRYPOINT) end;
478
479 procedure CODEFORODD;
480   begin EMIT(OD) end;
481
482 procedure CODEFORDUMP (LEVEL : LEVELS);
483   begin GEN(STK, LEVEL, 0) end;
484
485 procedure BACKPATCH (LOCATION, ADDRESS : INTEGER);
486   begin PCODE[LOCATION].A := ADDRESS end;
487
488 procedure DUMPCODE;
489 (*List generated code for interest, debugging, or separate interpretation*)
490   var
491     I : INTEGER;
492   begin
493     (*open and REWRITE(CODEFILE) as appropriate*)
494     for I := 0 to NEXTCODE - 1 do with PCODE[I] do
495       if F in HASADDRESSFIELD
496         then WRITELN(CODEFILE, I:10, MNEMONIC[F]:4, ' ', L:1, ' ', A:1)
497         else WRITELN(CODEFILE, I:10, MNEMONIC[F]:4);
498     (*close CODEFILE if necessary*)
499   end (*DUMPCODE*);
500
501 (* ++++++++++++++++++++++++++++ Analyser ++++++++++++++++++++++++++++ *)
502
503 procedure ACCEPT (EXPECTED : SYMBOLS; ERRORCODE : INTEGER);
504   begin
505     if SYM = EXPECTED then GETSYM else ERROR(ERRORCODE)
506   end (*ACCEPT*);
507
508 procedure BLOCK (FOLLOWERS    : SYMSET     (*for error recovery*);
509                  BLOCKLEVEL   : LEVELS     (*level of static nesting*);
510                  var LASTENTRY : TABLEINDEX (*index into symbol table*);
511                  THISMONITOR  : TABLEINDEX (*index for surrounding mon entry*);
512                  BLOCKCLASS   : CLASSES    (*prog, proc, func, monitor*));
```

```
513   var
514     BLOCKENTRY : TABLEINDEX (*initial symbol table entry*);
515     STARTCODE,              (*start address*)
516     OFFSET,                 (*variable address index*)
517     PARAMS,                 (*number of parameters*)
518     I         : INTEGER     (*loop counter*);
519     STARRED   : BOOLEAN     (*whether identifier is exportable*);
520
521   procedure PRINTSYMBOLTABLE;
522   (*List current entries in symbol table*)
523     var
524       I : TABLEINDEX;
525     begin
526       for I := 1 to LASTENTRY do with TABLE[I] do
527         begin
528           WRITE(OUTPUT, I:10, NAME:9);
529           case CLASS of
530             CONSTANT : WRITE(OUTPUT, ' CONSTANT  ');
531             VARIABLE : WRITE(OUTPUT, ' VARIABLE  ');
532             PROG     : WRITE(OUTPUT, ' PROGRAM   ');
533             MONI     : WRITE(OUTPUT, ' MONITOR   ');
534             FUNC     : WRITE(OUTPUT, ' FUNCTION  ');
535             COND     : WRITE(OUTPUT, ' CONDITION ');
536             PROC     : WRITE(OUTPUT, ' PROCEDURE ');
537           end (*case*);
538           WRITELN(OUTPUT, LEVEL:4, ADDRESS:4, SIZE:4,
539                   ORD(CANCHANGE):2, ORD(CANACCESS):2, ORD(INSIDE):2)
540         end
541     end (*PRINTSYMBOLTABLE*);
542
543   procedure TEST (ALLOWED, BEACONS : SYMSET; ERRORCODE : INTEGER);
544   (*Test whether current SYM is ALLOWED and recover if not*)
545     begin
546       if not (SYM in ALLOWED) then
547         begin
548           ERROR(ERRORCODE); while not (SYM in ALLOWED + BEACONS) do GETSYM
549         end
550     end (*TEST*);
551
552   (* +++++++++++++++++++++++++++++ Declarations part +++++++++++++++++++ *)
553
554   procedure GETSTARID;
555   (*Check for possible star preceding identifier*)
556     begin
557       GETSYM; STARRED := FALSE;
558       if SYM = TIMES then
```

```
559         begin
560           if BLOCKCLASS = MONI then STARRED := TRUE else ERROR(47); GETSYM
561         end
562     end (*GETSTARID*);
563
564   procedure ENTER (C : CLASSES);
565   (*Enter object of class C into symbol table*)
566     begin
567       if LASTENTRY = TABLEMAX then QUIT(4) (*symbol table overflow*);
568       LASTENTRY := LASTENTRY + 1;
569       with TABLE[LASTENTRY] do
570         begin
571           NAME := ID; CLASS := C; LEVEL := BLOCKLEVEL; SIZE := 1; ADDRESS := 0;
572           CANCHANGE := TRUE; INSIDE := FALSE; CANACCESS := STARRED
573         end
574     end (*ENTER*);
575
576   procedure SEARCHID (var MONENTRY, ENTRY : TABLEINDEX; ALLOWED : CLASSSET;
577                       ERRORCODE : INTEGER);
578
579   (*Find ID in symbol table at location MONENTRY.ENTRY, check ALLOWED class*)
580     var
581       FOUND  : BOOLEAN;
582
583     procedure MONITORIDENTIFIERS;
584
585       procedure SEARCHFORWARD;
586       (*Search for identifiers in a referenced monitor*)
587         var
588           LAST : TABLEINDEX;
589         begin
590           LAST := TABLE[ENTRY].SIZE;
591           if LAST = 1 then LAST := LASTENTRY (*still in monitor*);
592           ENTRY := ENTRY + 1 (*to get past the monitor entry*);
593           while (ENTRY <= LAST) and (TABLE[ENTRY].NAME <> ID) do
594             ENTRY := ENTRY + 1;
595           if ENTRY > LAST then ENTRY := 0 (*not found*)
596         end (*SEARCHFORWARD*);
597
598       begin (*MONITORIDENTIFIERS*)
599         GETSYM;
600         if SYM <> PERIOD then ERROR(37) else
601           begin
602             GETSYM; MONENTRY := ENTRY;
603             if SYM <> IDENT then ERROR(6) else
604               begin
```

```
605              SEARCHFORWARD;
606                if TABLE[ENTRY].INSIDE and not TABLE[ENTRY].CANACCESS
607                  then ERROR(48)
608              end
609          end
610      end (*MONITORIDENTIFIERS*);
611
612    begin (*SEARCHID*)
613      TABLE[0].NAME := ID; ENTRY := LASTENTRY; MONENTRY := 0;
614      repeat
615        FOUND := TRUE;
616        while TABLE[ENTRY].NAME <> ID do ENTRY := ENTRY - 1;
617        if TABLE[ENTRY].INSIDE then
618          begin FOUND := FALSE; ENTRY := ENTRY - 1 end;
619      until FOUND;
620      if TABLE[ENTRY].CLASS = MONI then MONITORIDENTIFIERS;
621      if ENTRY = 0 (*not really there*)
622        then ERROR(5)
623        else if not (TABLE[ENTRY].CLASS in ALLOWED) then ERROR(ERRORCODE);
624      GETSYM (*side-effect*);
625      if TABLE[ENTRY].CLASS <> COND then
626        while SYM = PERIOD do (*confusing access methods?*)
627          begin ERROR(3); GETSYM; if SYM = IDENT then GETSYM end;
628    end (*SEARCHID*);
629
630  procedure CONSTDECLARATION;
631  (*Handle declaration of named constants*)
632    begin
633      GETSTARID;
634      TEST([IDENT], FOLLOWERS, 6);
635      while SYM = IDENT do
636        begin
637          ENTER(CONSTANT); GETSYM;
638          if SYM in [EQLSYM, BECOMES]
639            then
640              begin
641                if SYM = BECOMES then ERROR(7); GETSYM;
642                if SYM <> NUMBER then ERROR(8) else
643                  begin TABLE[LASTENTRY].ADDRESS := NUM; GETSYM end
644              end
645            else ERROR(9);
646          if SYM = SEMICOLON then GETSTARID else ERROR(2)
647        end (*while*)
648    end (*CONSTDECLARATION*);
649
650  procedure VARDECLARATION (VARTYPE : CLASSES);
```

```
651    (*Handle declaration of variables and condition queues*)
652
653      procedure ENTERVARIABLE;
654        begin
655          if SYM <> IDENT then ERROR(6) else
656            begin
657              ENTER(VARTYPE); GETSYM;
658              if SYM = LBRACKET then (*array declaration*)
659                begin
660                  GETSYM;
661                  if SYM <> NUMBER then ERROR(8) else
662                    begin
663                      if NUM < 1 then ERROR(31);
664                      TABLE[LASTENTRY].SIZE := NUM + 1; GETSYM
665                    end;
666                  ACCEPT(RBRACKET, 10)
667                end;
668              TABLE[LASTENTRY].ADDRESS := OFFSET;
669              OFFSET := OFFSET + TABLE[LASTENTRY].SIZE;
670            end
671        end (*ENTERVARIABLE *);
672
673      begin (*VARDECLARATION*)
674        GETSTARID;
675        TEST([IDENT], FOLLOWERS, 6);
676        if SYM = IDENT then
677          begin
678            ENTERVARIABLE;
679            while SYM = COMMA do begin GETSTARID; ENTERVARIABLE end;
680            ACCEPT(SEMICOLON, 2)
681          end
682      end (*VARDECLARATION*);
683
684    procedure PARDECLARATION;
685    (*Handle declaration of formal parameters*)
686      var
687        I : TABLEINDEX;
688
689      procedure ENTERPARAMETER;
690        begin
691          if SYM <> IDENT then ERROR(6) else
692            begin
693              ENTER(VARIABLE); PARAMS := PARAMS + 1;
694              if PARAMS > PARAMAX then ERROR(41); GETSYM
695            end
696        end (*ENTERPARAMETER*);
```

```
697
698      begin (*PARDECLARATION*)
699        GETSYM; STARRED := FALSE;
700        TEST([IDENT], FOLLOWERS, 6);
701        if SYM = IDENT then
702          begin
703            ENTERPARAMETER;
704            while SYM = COMMA do begin GETSYM; ENTERPARAMETER end;
705            ACCEPT(RPAREN, 13);
706          end;
707        for I := 1 to PARAMS do (*parameters have negative offsets*)
708          TABLE[LASTENTRY - I + 1].ADDRESS := -I;
709      end (*PARDECLARATION*);
710
711    procedure PROCDECLARATION (BLOCKCLASS : CLASSES);
712    (*Handle declarations of procedures, functions, monitors*)
713      begin
714        if ID = 'FUNCTION' then BLOCKCLASS := FUNC
715          else if ID = 'PROCEDUR' then BLOCKCLASS := PROC else
716            begin if BLOCKCLASS <> PROG then ERROR(46); BLOCKCLASS := MONI end;
717        GETSTARID;
718        if SYM <> IDENT then ERROR(6) else begin ENTER(BLOCKCLASS); GETSYM end;
719        if BLOCKLEVEL = LEVMAX then QUIT(1) (*too deeply nested*);
720        if BLOCKCLASS = MONI
721          then BLOCK([SEMICOLON] + FOLLOWERS, BLOCKLEVEL,
722                     LASTENTRY, LASTENTRY, MONI)
723          else BLOCK([SEMICOLON] + FOLLOWERS, BLOCKLEVEL + 1,
724                     LASTENTRY, THISMONITOR, BLOCKCLASS);
725        ACCEPT(SEMICOLON, 2)
726      end (*PROCDECLARATION*);
727
728 (* +++++++++++++++++++++++ Statement Part +++++++++++++++++++++++++ *)
729
730    procedure COMPOUNDSTATEMENT (FOLLOWERS : SYMSET);
731
732      procedure STATEMENT (FOLLOWERS : SYMSET);
733        var
734          MONENTRY, IDENTRY : TABLEINDEX;
735          TESTLABEL, STARTLOOP : INTEGER;
736
737        procedure ROUTINECALL (MONENTRY, IDENTRY : TABLEINDEX);
738        (*Call routine, with possible request for exclusion*)
739          begin
740            with TABLE[IDENTRY] do
741              if (MONENTRY <> 0) (*monitor procedure call*)
742                  and (MONENTRY <> THISMONITOR) (*to another monitor*)
```

```
743                  then if (THISMONITOR <> 1) then ERROR(16) else
744                    begin
745                      GAINEXCLUSION(MONENTRY);
746                      CALL(LEVEL, ADDRESS);
747                      RELEASEEXCLUSION(MONENTRY)
748                    end
749                  else CALL(LEVEL, ADDRESS)
750        end (*ROUTINECALL*);
751
752    procedure EXPRESSION (FOLLOWERS : SYMSET); forward;
753
754    procedure ADDRESSFOR (I : TABLEINDEX);
755    (*Load address for identifier at table entry I*)
756      begin
757        with TABLE[I] do
758          begin
759            STACKADDRESS(LEVEL, ADDRESS);
760            if SYM = LBRACKET
761              then (*subscript*)
762                begin
763                  if SIZE = 1 then ERROR(11); GETSYM;
764                  EXPRESSION([RBRACKET] + FOLLOWERS); ACCEPT(RBRACKET, 10);
765                  SUBSCRIPT(SIZE)
766                end
767              else if SIZE > 1 then ERROR(15)
768          end
769      end (*ADDRESSFOR*);
770
771    procedure PARAMETERS (FORMAL : INTEGER; FOLLOWERS : SYMSET);
772    (*Handle formation of actual parameter list*)
773      var
774        ACTUAL : INTEGER;
775      begin
776        ACTUAL := 0;
777        if SYM = LPAREN then
778          begin
779            repeat
780              GETSYM;
781              if ACTUAL >= FORMAL then ERROR(12) else
782                begin
783                  EXPRESSION([COMMA, RPAREN] + FOLLOWERS);
784                  ACTUAL := ACTUAL + 1
785                end;
786              TEST ([COMMA, RPAREN], FOLLOWERS, 13)
787            until SYM <> COMMA;
788            ACCEPT(RPAREN, 13)
```

```
789              end;
790           if ACTUAL < FORMAL then ERROR(12)
791        end (*PARAMETERS*);
792
793      procedure EXPRESSION;
794        var
795          ADDOP : SYMBOLS;
796
797        procedure TERM (FOLLOWERS : SYMSET);
798          var
799            MULOP : SYMBOLS;
800
801          procedure FACTOR (FOLLOWERS : SYMSET);
802            var
803              MONENTRY, IDENTRY : TABLEINDEX;
804            begin
805              TEST(FIRSTFACTOR, FOLLOWERS, 14);
806              while SYM in FIRSTFACTOR do
807                begin
808                  case SYM of
809                    IDENT:
810                      begin
811                        SEARCHID(MONENTRY, IDENTRY,
812                              [CONSTANT, VARIABLE, FUNC], 14);
813                        with TABLE[IDENTRY] do
814                          case CLASS of
815                            CONSTANT :
816                              STACKCONSTANT(ADDRESS);
817                            VARIABLE :
818                              begin ADDRESSFOR(IDENTRY); DEREFERENCE end;
819                            FUNC :
820                              begin
821                                OPENSTACKFRAME(1) (*for returned value*);
822                                PARAMETERS(SIZE, FOLLOWERS);
823                                ROUTINECALL(MONENTRY, IDENTRY)
824                              end;
825                            MONI, PROG, PROC, COND : (*error already reported*)
826                          end (*case CLASS*)
827                      end (*IDENT*);
828                    NUMBER:
829                      begin STACKCONSTANT(NUM); GETSYM end;
830                    LPAREN:
831                      begin
832                        GETSYM; EXPRESSION([RPAREN] + FOLLOWERS);
833                        ACCEPT(RPAREN, 17)
834                      end;
```

```
835                    end (*case SYM*);
836                      TEST(FOLLOWERS - FIRSTFACTOR, FIRSTFACTOR, 3)
837                  end (*while*)
838              end (*FACTOR*);
839
840          begin (*TERM*)
841            FACTOR([TIMES, SLASH] + FOLLOWERS);
842            while SYM in [TIMES, SLASH] do
843              begin
844                MULOP := SYM; GETSYM; FACTOR([TIMES, SLASH] + FOLLOWERS);
845                BINARYINTEGEROP(MULOP)
846              end
847          end (*TERM*);
848
849        begin (*EXPRESSION*)
850          if SYM in [PLUS, MINUS]
851            then
852              begin
853                ADDOP := SYM; GETSYM; TERM([PLUS, MINUS] + FOLLOWERS);
854                if ADDOP = MINUS then NEGATEINTEGER
855              end
856            else TERM([PLUS, MINUS] + FOLLOWERS);
857          while SYM in [PLUS, MINUS] do
858            begin
859              ADDOP := SYM; GETSYM; TERM([PLUS, MINUS] + FOLLOWERS);
860              BINARYINTEGEROP(ADDOP)
861            end
862        end (*EXPRESSION*);
863
864      procedure CONDITION (FOLLOWERS : SYMSET);
865        var
866          RELOP : SYMBOLS;
867        begin
868          if SYM = ODDSYM
869            then
870              begin
871                GETSYM; ACCEPT(LPAREN, 18);
872                EXPRESSION([RPAREN] + FOLLOWERS); ACCEPT(RPAREN, 17);
873                CODEFORODD
874              end
875            else
876              begin
877                EXPRESSION(RELOPSYMS + FOLLOWERS);
878                if not (SYM in RELOPSYMS) then ERROR(19) else
879                  begin
880                    RELOP := SYM; GETSYM; EXPRESSION(FOLLOWERS);
```

```
881                  COMPARISON(RELOP)
882               end
883            end;
884        TEST(FOLLOWERS, [], 3)
885      end (*CONDITION*);
886
887    procedure IFSTATEMENT;
888      begin
889        GETSYM; CONDITION([THENSYM, DOSYM] + FOLLOWERS);
890        if SYM = THENSYM then GETSYM else
891          begin ERROR(23); if SYM = DOSYM then GETSYM end;
892        STORELABEL(TESTLABEL); JUMPONFALSE(0) (*Incomplete*);
893        STATEMENT(FOLLOWERS); BACKPATCH(TESTLABEL, NEXTCODE);
894        PROCCALL := FALSE
895      end (*IFSTATEMENT*);
896
897    procedure WHILESTATEMENT;
898      begin
899        STORELABEL(STARTLOOP);
900        GETSYM; CONDITION([DOSYM] + FOLLOWERS); ACCEPT(DOSYM, 25);
901        STORELABEL(TESTLABEL); JUMPONFALSE(0) (*Incomplete*);
902        STATEMENT(FOLLOWERS); JUMP(STARTLOOP);
903        BACKPATCH(TESTLABEL, NEXTCODE); PROCCALL := FALSE
904      end (*WHILESTATEMENT*);
905
906    procedure WRITESTATEMENT;
907      begin
908        GETSYM;
909        if SYM = LPAREN then
910          begin
911            repeat
912              GETSYM;
913              if SYM <> STRINGSYM
914                then
915                  begin
916                    EXPRESSION([COMMA, RPAREN] + FOLLOWERS);
917                    OUTPUTOPERATION(NUMBERS)
918                  end
919                else
920                  begin OUTPUTOPERATION(STRINGS); GETSYM end (*string*)
921            until SYM <> COMMA;
922            ACCEPT(RPAREN, 13)
923          end;
924        OUTPUTOPERATION(NEWLINE); PROCCALL := FALSE
925      end (*WRITESTATEMENT*);
926
```

```
927     procedure READSTATEMENT;
928       begin
929         GETSYM;
930         if SYM <> LPAREN then ERROR(18) else
931           begin
932             repeat
933               GETSYM;
934               if SYM <> IDENT then ERROR(6) else
935                 begin
936                   SEARCHID(MONENTRY, IDENTRY, [VARIABLE], 28);
937                   if not TABLE[IDENTRY].CANCHANGE then ERROR(39);
938                   ADDRESSFOR(IDENTRY); INPUTOPERATION(NUMBERS)
939                 end
940             until SYM <> COMMA;
941             ACCEPT(RPAREN, 13)
942           end;
943         PROCCALL := FALSE
944       end (*READSTATEMENT*);
945
946     procedure SEMASTATEMENT;
947       var
948         WAITSEM : BOOLEAN;
949       begin
950         WAITSEM := SYM = WAITSYM; GETSYM;
951         if SYM <> LPAREN then ERROR(18) else
952           begin
953             GETSYM;
954             if SYM <> IDENT then ERROR(6) else
955               begin
956                 SEARCHID(MONENTRY, IDENTRY, [VARIABLE], 28);
957                 if not TABLE[IDENTRY].CANCHANGE then ERROR(39);
958                 ADDRESSFOR(IDENTRY);
959                 if WAITSEM then CODEFORWAIT else CODEFORSIGNAL
960               end;
961             ACCEPT(RPAREN, 13)
962           end;
963         PROCCALL := FALSE
964       end (*SEMASTATEMENT*);
965
966     procedure COBEGINSTATEMENT;
967       var
968         PROCESSES : INTEGER (*count number of processes*);
969       begin
970         if BLOCKLEVEL <> 1 then ERROR(44);
971         PROCESSES := 0; STORELABEL(STARTLOOP); GETSYM; STARTPROCESSES;
972         STATEMENT([SEMICOLON, COENDSYM] + FOLLOWERS);
```

```
973         if PROCCALL then PROCESSES := PROCESSES + 1 else ERROR(42);
974         while SYM in [SEMICOLON] + FIRSTSTATEMENT do
975           begin
976             ACCEPT(SEMICOLON, 2);
977             STATEMENT([SEMICOLON, COENDSYM] + FOLLOWERS);
978             if PROCCALL then PROCESSES := PROCESSES + 1 else ERROR(42)
979           end;
980         ACCEPT(COENDSYM, 43);
981         BACKPATCH(STARTLOOP, PROCESSES); STOPPROCESSES;
982         if PROCESSES > PROCMAX then ERROR(45) (*too many*);
983         PROCCALL := FALSE
984       end (*COBEGINSTATEMENT*);
985
986   begin (*STATEMENT*)
987     PROCCALL := TRUE;
988     if SYM in FIRSTSTATEMENT then
989       case SYM of
990         IDENT:
991           begin
992             SEARCHID(MONENTRY, IDENTRY, [VARIABLE, FUNC, PROC, COND], 22);
993             with TABLE[IDENTRY] do
994               case CLASS of
995                 CONSTANT, PROG, (*error - treat as assignment*)
996                 FUNC, VARIABLE:
997                   begin
998                     if CLASS in [VARIABLE, CONSTANT, PROG]
999                       then
1000                        begin
1001                          if not CANCHANGE then ERROR(39);
1002                          ADDRESSFOR(IDENTRY)
1003                        end
1004                      else if BLOCKENTRY = IDENTRY
1005                        then STACKADDRESS(LEVEL+1, -SIZE-1) else ERROR(20);
1006                    if SYM = BECOMES then GETSYM else
1007                      begin ERROR(21); if SYM = EQLSYM then GETSYM end;
1008                    EXPRESSION(FOLLOWERS);
1009                    ASSIGN; PROCCALL := FALSE
1010                  end;
1011                MONI, (*error - treat as procedure call*)
1012                PROC:
1013                  begin
1014                    PROCCALL := not INSIDE;
1015                    PARAMETERS(SIZE, FOLLOWERS);
1016                    ROUTINECALL(MONENTRY, IDENTRY)
1017                  end;
1018                COND:
```

```
1019                     begin
1020                       ADDRESSFOR(IDENTRY); PROCCALL := FALSE;
1021                       if not PARSEMON then ERROR(47);
1022                       if SYM <> PERIOD then ERROR(37) else
1023                         begin
1024                           GETSYM;
1025                           if SYM = CWAITSYM then
1026                             begin
1027                               GETSYM;
1028                               if SYM = LPAREN
1029                                 then
1030                                   begin
1031                                     GETSYM;
1032                                     EXPRESSION([RPAREN] + FOLLOWERS);
1033                                     ACCEPT(RPAREN, 17)
1034                                   end
1035                                 else STACKCONSTANT(DEFAULTPRIORITY);
1036                               CWAIT(THISMONITOR);
1037                             end
1038                           else
1039                             if SYM <> CSIGNALSYM then ERROR(3) else
1040                               begin GETSYM; CSIGNAL(THISMONITOR) end
1041                         end
1042                   end
1043                 end (*case CLASS*)
1044           end (*IDENT*);
1045       IFSYM     : IFSTATEMENT;
1046       BEGINSYM  : COMPOUNDSTATEMENT(FOLLOWERS);
1047       WHILESYM  : WHILESTATEMENT;
1048       WRITESYM  : WRITESTATEMENT;
1049       READSYM   : READSTATEMENT;
1050       WAITSYM,
1051       SIGNALSYM : SEMASTATEMENT;
1052       COBEGSYM  : COBEGINSTATEMENT;
1053       STACKSYM  :
1054         begin CODEFORDUMP(BLOCKLEVEL); GETSYM; PROCCALL := FALSE end
1055       end (*case SYM*);
1056     TEST(FOLLOWERS, [], 32)
1057   end (*STATEMENT*);
1058
1059 begin (*COMPOUNDSTATEMENT*)
1060   ACCEPT(BEGINSYM, 34);
1061   STATEMENT([SEMICOLON, ENDSYM] + FOLLOWERS);
1062   while SYM in [SEMICOLON] + FIRSTSTATEMENT do
1063     begin
1064       ACCEPT(SEMICOLON, 2); STATEMENT([SEMICOLON, ENDSYM] + FOLLOWERS)
```

```
1065       end;
1066     ACCEPT(ENDSYM, 24); PROCCALL := FALSE
1067   end (*COMPOUNDSTATEMENT*);
1068
1069 begin (*BLOCK*)
1070   PARAMS := 0; BLOCKENTRY := LASTENTRY;
1071   case BLOCKCLASS of
1072     PROC, FUNC:
1073       begin
1074         OFFSET := 3; ENTERBLOCK(STARTCODE);
1075         if SYM = LPAREN then PARDECLARATION;
1076         TABLE[BLOCKENTRY].SIZE := PARAMS;
1077         TABLE[BLOCKENTRY].ADDRESS := STARTCODE;
1078       end;
1079     MONI:
1080       begin (*make globals read only, and prepare to add to them*)
1081         for I := 1 to TABLE[1].SIZE do TABLE[I].CANCHANGE := FALSE;
1082         TABLE[BLOCKENTRY].ADDRESS := TABLE[1].ADDRESS (*mutex sem address*);
1083         OFFSET := TABLE[1].ADDRESS + 2 (*resume from last global block*);
1084         PARSEMON := TRUE
1085       end;
1086     PROG: begin OFFSET := 3; ENTERBLOCK(STARTMAINCODE) end;
1087   end (*case*);
1088   ACCEPT(SEMICOLON, 2);
1089   TEST(FIRSTBLOCK, FOLLOWERS, 3);
1090   repeat
1091     if SYM = CONSTSYM then CONSTDECLARATION;
1092     if SYM = VARSYM then VARDECLARATION(VARIABLE);
1093     if SYM = CONDSYM then
1094       begin
1095         if BLOCKCLASS <> MONI then ERROR(47); VARDECLARATION(COND)
1096       end;
1097     if BLOCKCLASS = PROG then
1098       begin TABLE[1].ADDRESS := OFFSET; TABLE[1].SIZE := LASTENTRY end;
1099     while SYM = PROCSYM do PROCDECLARATION(BLOCKCLASS);
1100     TEST([BEGINSYM], FOLLOWERS, 34)
1101   until SYM in FIRSTSTATEMENT + [PERIOD, SEMICOLON];
1102   case BLOCKCLASS of
1103     PROG:
1104       begin
1105         BACKPATCH(STARTMAINCODE, NEXTCODE);
1106         if not MONITORS then OPENSTACKFRAME(OFFSET)
1107       end;
1108     MONI:
1109       begin
1110         BACKPATCH(STARTMAINCODE, NEXTCODE);
```

```
1111          TABLE[BLOCKENTRY].SIZE := LASTENTRY (*last ident for the monitor*);
1112          if not MONITORS
1113            then OPENSTACKFRAME(OFFSET) (*for globals so far*)
1114            else OPENSTACKFRAME(OFFSET - TABLE[1].ADDRESS) (*extra globals*);
1115          TABLE[1].ADDRESS := OFFSET; MONITORS := TRUE;
1116          INITMUTEX(BLOCKENTRY)
1117        end;
1118      FUNC, PROC:
1119        begin
1120          BACKPATCH(STARTCODE, NEXTCODE) (*jump to code for this block*);
1121          OPENSTACKFRAME(OFFSET) (*reserve space for variables*)
1122        end
1123    end (*case*);
1124    COMPOUNDSTATEMENT(FOLLOWERS);
1125    if TABLES then PRINTSYMBOLTABLE (*demonstration purposes*);
1126    if BLOCKCLASS = MONI
1127      then
1128        begin
1129          ENTERBLOCK(STARTMAINCODE); PARSEMON := FALSE;
1130          for I := BLOCKENTRY + 1 to LASTENTRY do (*mon variables read only*)
1131            begin TABLE[I].CANCHANGE := FALSE; TABLE[I].INSIDE := TRUE end;
1132          for I := 1 to TABLE[1].SIZE do TABLE[I].CANCHANGE := TRUE (*reset*)
1133        end
1134      else
1135        begin
1136          LEAVEBLOCK(BLOCKCLASS, BLOCKLEVEL, PARAMS); LASTENTRY := BLOCKENTRY
1137        end;
1138    TEST(FOLLOWERS, [], 35)
1139  end (*BLOCK*);
1140
1141 procedure PROGRAMME;
1142   var
1143     PROGENTRY : TABLEINDEX;
1144   begin
1145     ACCEPT(PROCSYM, 36);
1146     with TABLE[0] do
1147       begin
1148         NAME := ID; CLASS := PROG; LEVEL := 0; SIZE := 1; ADDRESS := 0;
1149         CANCHANGE := TRUE; INSIDE := FALSE; CANACCESS := TRUE
1150       end;
1151     TABLE[1] := TABLE[0] (*enter program name*); PROGENTRY := 1;
1152     if SYM <> IDENT then ERROR(6) else
1153       begin TABLES := ID = 'TEST    '; GETSYM end;
1154     BLOCK([PERIOD] + FIRSTBLOCK + FIRSTSTATEMENT, 1, PROGENTRY, 1, PROG);
1155     if SYM <> PERIOD then ERROR(37)
1156   end (*PROGRAMME*);
```

```
1157
1158 (*+++++++++++++++++++++++++++++++ Interpreter +++++++++++++++++++*)
1159
1160 procedure INTERPRET;
1161   const
1162     STEPMAX = 8        (*max before switch*);
1163     MARKSTKSIZE = 3    (*mark stack reserved area*);
1164   type
1165     PROCINDEX = 0 .. PROCMAX;
1166   var
1167     PS : (RUNNING, FINISHED, STKCHK, DATCHK, EOFCHK, DIVCHK, INDCHK,
1168          DEDCHK, SEMCHK)              (*status*);
1169     S : array [0 .. STACKMAX] of INTEGER (*stack memory*);
1170     LOOP,                            (*work variable*)
1171     PARTITION,                       (*stack increment as procs launched*)
1172     STEPS,                           (*number of operations in time slice*)
1173     OLDT : INTEGER                   (*preserve top-of-stack pointer*);
1174     NPROCS,                          (*number of concurrent processes*)
1175     CURRENT, CURPROC : PROCINDEX     (*process pointers*);
1176     STARTINGPROCESSES : BOOLEAN      (*concurrent call flag*);
1177     PROC : array [PROCINDEX] of      (*process descriptors*)
1178                 record
1179                   DISPLAY : array [LEVELS] of INTEGER;
1180                   P, B, T,            (*program counter, base, stack pointer*)
1181                   STACKEND,           (*memory limit*)
1182                   PRIORITY : INTEGER  (*condition queue ordering*);
1183                   NEXT,               (*ring pointers*)
1184                   QUEUE : PROCINDEX   (*linked waiting on a semaphore*);
1185                   READY : BOOLEAN     (*process ready flag*);
1186                 end (*PROC*);
1187
1188   (* ++++++++++++++++++++++++++++++++ we assume the existence of a standard
1189           function RANDOM (LIMIT : INTEGER) : INTEGER;
1190     which generates a random integer in the range 0 <= RANDOM < LIMIT
1191     If your system does not provide such a function, one should be
1192     added here +++++++++++++++++++++++++++++++++++++++++++++++++++++++++ *)
1193
1194   procedure CHOOSEPROCESS;
1195   (*From current process traverse ring of descriptors for next ready process*)
1196     begin
1197       if (CURPROC <> 0) then
1198         if STEPS <> 0 then STEPS := STEPS - 1 else (*time for a change*)
1199           begin
1200             repeat CURPROC := PROC[CURPROC].NEXT until PROC[CURPROC].READY;
1201             STEPS := RANDOM(STEPMAX) + 1
1202           end
```

```
1203    end (*CHOOSEPROCESS*);
1204
1205  procedure DECTBY (I : INTEGER);
1206  (*Decrement stack pointer*)
1207    begin with PROC[CURRENT] do T := T - I end;
1208
1209  procedure INCTBY (I : INTEGER);
1210  (*Increment stack pointer*)
1211    begin
1212      with PROC[CURRENT] do
1213        begin T := T + I; if T > STACKEND - MARKSTKSIZE then PS := STKCHK end
1214    end (*INCTBY*);
1215
1216  procedure CHECKDATA;
1217  (*Check 'numeric' data for validity*)
1218    begin
1219      while not EOF(DATA) and (DATA↑ = ' ') do GET(DATA);
1220      if EOF(DATA) then PS := EOFCHK
1221        else if not (DATA↑ in ['0' .. '9', '+', '-']) then PS := DATCHK
1222    end (*CHECKDATA*);
1223
1224  procedure STACKDUMP (LEV : LEVELS);
1225  (*Dump stack and display - useful for debugging*)
1226    var
1227      LOOP : INTEGER;
1228    begin
1229      with PROC[CURRENT] do
1230        begin
1231          WRITELN(RESULTS);
1232          WRITELN(RESULTS, 'Stack dump at ', P-1:1, ' T= ', T:1, ' B= ', B:1,
1233                  ' Return address= ', S[B+2]:1, ' Process= ', CURRENT:1);
1234          WRITE(RESULTS, 'Display ');
1235          for LOOP := 1 to LEV do WRITE(RESULTS, DISPLAY[LOOP], ' ');
1236          WRITELN(RESULTS);
1237          for LOOP := 0 to T do
1238            begin
1239              WRITE(RESULTS, LOOP:4, ':', S[LOOP]:5);
1240              if (LOOP+1) mod 8 = 0 then WRITELN(RESULTS)
1241            end;
1242          WRITELN(RESULTS)
1243        end (*with*)
1244    end (*STACKDUMP*);
1245
1246  procedure POSTMORTEM;
1247  (*Report run-time error and position*)
1248    begin
```

```
1249      WRITELN(RESULTS); WRITE(RESULTS, '**** ');
1250      case PS of
1251        DIVCHK : WRITE(RESULTS, 'Division by zero');
1252        EOFCHK : WRITE(RESULTS, 'No more data');
1253        DATCHK : WRITE(RESULTS, 'Invalid data');
1254        STKCHK : WRITE(RESULTS, 'Stack overflow');
1255        INDCHK : WRITE(RESULTS, 'Range error');
1256        DEDCHK : WRITE(RESULTS, 'Deadlock');
1257        SEMCHK : WRITE(RESULTS, 'Semaphore with no concurrent processes');
1258      end (*case*);
1259      WRITELN(RESULTS, ' at ', PROC[CURPROC].P-1:1, ' in process ', CURPROC:1);
1260    end (*POSTMORTEM*);
1261
1262  procedure NEXTSTEP;
1263    var
1264      LOOP : INTEGER      (*for loop control*);
1265      I    : INSTRUCTIONS (*current*);
1266
1267    procedure SIGNAL (SEMADDRESS : INTEGER);
1268    (*signal operation on semaphore at SEMADDRESS*)
1269      var
1270        WOKEN : PROCINDEX (*index into PROC of process to be woken*);
1271      begin
1272        with PROC[CURRENT] do
1273          begin
1274            if S[SEMADDRESS] >= 0 (*nothing waiting*)
1275              then S[SEMADDRESS] := S[SEMADDRESS] + 1
1276              else (*waken process and update queue*)
1277                begin
1278                  WOKEN := -S[SEMADDRESS]; S[SEMADDRESS] := -PROC[WOKEN].QUEUE;
1279                  PROC[WOKEN].QUEUE := 0; PROC[WOKEN].READY := TRUE;
1280                  PROC[WOKEN].PRIORITY := 0
1281                end
1282          end (*with*)
1283      end (*SIGNAL*);
1284
1285    procedure WAIT (SEMADDRESS, WAITPRIORITY : INTEGER);
1286    (*wait on semaphore at SEMADDRESS, queued according to WAITPRIORITY*)
1287      var
1288        LP, CP   : PROCINDEX (*last and current pointers*);
1289        SEARCHING : BOOLEAN;
1290      begin
1291        with PROC[CURRENT] do
1292          if S[SEMADDRESS] > 0 (*nothing waiting*)
1293            then S[SEMADDRESS] := S[SEMADDRESS] - 1
1294            else (*suspend process*)
```

```
1295                 begin
1296                   STEPS := 0; CHOOSEPROCESS; READY := FALSE;
1297                   if CURRENT = CURPROC then PS := DEDCHK;
1298                   (*now queue according to priority requested*)
1299                   CP := -S[SEMADDRESS]; SEARCHING := TRUE;
1300                   while (CP <> 0) and SEARCHING do
1301                     if WAITPRIORITY < PROC[CP].PRIORITY
1302                       then SEARCHING := FALSE
1303                       else begin LP := CP; CP := PROC[CP].QUEUE end;
1304                   if CP = -S[SEMADDRESS]
1305                     then S[SEMADDRESS] := -CURRENT
1306                     else PROC[LP].QUEUE := CURRENT;
1307                   PROC[CURRENT].QUEUE := CP;
1308                   PROC[CURRENT].PRIORITY := WAITPRIORITY
1309                 end
1310       end (*WAIT*);
1311
1312   begin (*NEXTSTEP*)
1313     CURRENT := CURPROC;
1314     with PROC[CURRENT] do
1315       begin
1316         I := PCODE[P]; P := P + 1 (*fetch*);
1317         with I do case F of
1318         NEG: S[T] := -S[T];
1319         ADD: begin DECTBY(1); S[T] := S[T] + S[T+1] end;
1320         SUB: begin DECTBY(1); S[T] := S[T] - S[T+1] end;
1321         MUL: begin DECTBY(1); S[T] := S[T] * S[T+1] end;
1322         DVD:
1323          begin
1324            DECTBY(1);
1325            if S[T+1]=0 then PS := DIVCHK else S[T] := S[T] div S[T+1]
1326          end;
1327         OD : if ODD(S[T]) then S[T] := 1 else S[T] := 0;
1328         EQL: begin DECTBY(1); S[T] := ORD(S[T] = S[T+1]) end;
1329         NEQ: begin DECTBY(1); S[T] := ORD(S[T] <> S[T+1]) end;
1330         LSS: begin DECTBY(1); S[T] := ORD(S[T] < S[T+1]) end;
1331         GEQ: begin DECTBY(1); S[T] := ORD(S[T] >= S[T+1]) end;
1332         GTR: begin DECTBY(1); S[T] := ORD(S[T] > S[T+1]) end;
1333         LEQ: begin DECTBY(1); S[T] := ORD(S[T] <= S[T+1]) end;
1334         STK: STACKDUMP(L);
1335         PRN: begin WRITE(RESULTS, S[T]); DECTBY(1) end;
1336         PRS:
1337          begin
1338            for LOOP := T - S[T] to T - 1 do WRITE(RESULTS, CHR(S[LOOP]));
1339            DECTBY(S[T] + 1)
1340          end;
```

```
1341        NLN: WRITELN(RESULTS);
1342        INN:
1343         begin
1344           CHECKDATA; if PS = RUNNING then READ(DATA, S[S[T]]); DECTBY(1)
1345         end;
1346        LDI: begin INCTBY(1); S[T] := A end;
1347        LDA: begin INCTBY(1); S[T] := DISPLAY[L] + A end;
1348        LDV: S[T] := S[S[T]];
1349        IND: if (S[T] < 0) or (S[T] > A)
1350              then PS := INDCHK
1351              else begin DECTBY(1); S[T] := S[T] + S[T+1] end;
1352        STO: begin S[S[T-1]] := S[T]; DECTBY(2) end;
1353        INT: INCTBY(A);
1354        MON:
1355         begin
1356           for LOOP := T downto A + 1 do S[LOOP] := 0;
1357           S[A] := 1 (*initialize MUTEX*)
1358         end;
1359        HLT: PS := FINISHED;
1360        BRN: P := A;
1361        BZE: begin if S[T] = 0 then P := A; DECTBY(1) end;
1362        WGT: if CURRENT = 0 then PS := SEMCHK else
1363              begin WAIT(S[T], DEFAULTPRIORITY); DECTBY(1) end;
1364        SIG: if CURRENT = 0 then PS := SEMCHK else
1365              begin SIGNAL(S[T]); DECTBY(1) end;
1366        CWI: if CURRENT = 0 then PS := SEMCHK else
1367         begin
1368           if S[S[T-1]] <> 0 then SIGNAL(S[T-1]) else SIGNAL(S[T]);
1369           WAIT(S[T-3], S[T-2]); DECTBY(4)
1370         end;
1371        CSG: if CURRENT = 0 then PS := SEMCHK else
1372         begin
1373           if S[S[T-1]] <> 0 then begin SIGNAL(S[T-1]); WAIT(S[T], 1) end;
1374           DECTBY(2)
1375         end;
1376        INM: begin WAIT(S[T], DEFAULTPRIORITY); DECTBY(1) end;
1377        EXM:
1378         begin
1379           if S[S[T]] <> 0 then SIGNAL(S[T]) else SIGNAL(S[T-1]); DECTBY(2)
1380         end;
1381        CBG:
1382         begin
1383           STARTINGPROCESSES := TRUE;
1384           OLDT := T (*save current top-of-stack pointer*);
1385           PARTITION := (STACKMAX - T) div A - PARAMAX (*divide up memory*);
1386           if PARTITION <= 0 then PS := STKCHK
```

```
1387               end;
1388            CND:
1389            begin
1390              STARTINGPROCESSES := FALSE;
1391              if NPROCS > 0 then
1392                begin
1393                  PROC[0].READY := FALSE (*deactivate main program*);
1394                  PROC[NPROCS].NEXT := 0 (*close ring*);
1395                  CURPROC := RANDOM(NPROCS) + 1 (*next to activate*);
1396                  STEPS := RANDOM(STEPMAX) + 1 (*initial time slice*)
1397                end
1398            end;
1399            CAL:
1400            begin
1401              if not STARTINGPROCESSES
1402                then (*normal call*)
1403                  begin
1404                    S[T+1] := DISPLAY[L+1]; S[T+2] := B; S[T+3] := P;
1405                    B := T + 1; P := A; DISPLAY[L+1] := B
1406                  end
1407                else (*prepare for subsequent concurrent entry*)
1408                  begin
1409                    NPROCS := NPROCS + 1;
1410                    with PROC[NPROCS] do
1411                      begin
1412                        B := PROC[CURRENT].T + 1; P := A; DISPLAY[L+1] := B;
1413                        T := B - 1; S[T+1] := DISPLAY[L+1]; S[T+2] := B;
1414                        S[T+3] := 0 (*fiddle return address*);
1415                        STACKEND := T + PARTITION; READY := TRUE; NEXT := NPROCS + 1
1416                      end;
1417                    INCTBY(PARTITION) (*leave work area for process*)
1418                  end
1419            end (*CALL*);
1420            RET:
1421            begin
1422              T := B - A; DISPLAY[L] := S[B]; P := S[B+2]; B := S[B+1];
1423              if P = 0 then (*we are completing a concurrent process*)
1424                begin
1425                  NPROCS := NPROCS - 1;
1426                  if NPROCS = 0
1427                    then (*reactivate main program*)
1428                      begin
1429                        PROC[0].T := OLDT (*restore old top-of-stack pointer*);
1430                        PROC[0].READY := TRUE; CURPROC := 0
1431                      end
1432                    else (*complete this process only*)
```

```
1433                       begin
1434                          STEPS := 0 (*force choice of new process*);
1435                          CHOOSEPROCESS (*may not be able to find another*);
1436                          if CURRENT = CURPROC then PS := DEDCHK; READY := FALSE
1437                       end
1438                    end
1439                 end (*RETURN*);
1440              end (*case*)
1441           end (*with PROC*)
1442        end (*NEXTSTEP*);
1443
1444    begin (*INTERPRET*)
1445       for LOOP := 0 to STACKMAX do S[LOOP] := 0 (*entire stack*); PS := RUNNING;
1446       (* open and RESET(DATA), REWRITE(RESULTS) as appropriate *)
1447       with PROC[0] do (*start main program*)
1448         begin
1449           (*initialize main stack frame*)
1450           T := -1; P := 0; B := 0; DISPLAY[1] := 0;
1451           QUEUE := 0; READY := TRUE; STACKEND := STACKMAX; NEXT := 1;
1452           PRIORITY := 0
1453         end;
1454       for CURPROC := 1 to PROCMAX do (*processes inactive*) with PROC[CURPROC] do
1455         begin READY := FALSE; DISPLAY[1] := 0; QUEUE := 0; PRIORITY := 0 end;
1456       CURPROC := 0; STARTINGPROCESSES := FALSE; NPROCS := 0; STEPS := 0;
1457       repeat
1458         NEXTSTEP;
1459         (*+++++++ useful to be able to add  if BREAKIN then PS := FINISHED; *)
1460         if PS = RUNNING then CHOOSEPROCESS
1461       until PS <> RUNNING;
1462       if PS <> FINISHED then POSTMORTEM;
1463       WRITELN(RESULTS);
1464       (*close RESULTS and DATA files if necessary*)
1465    end (*INTERPRET*);
1466
1467
1468 begin (*CLANG5COMPILER*)
1469    (*open and RESET(SOURCE), RESET(INPUT), REWRITE(OUTPUT)  as appropriate*)
1470    INITIALIZE;
1471    PROGRAMME;
1472    if ERRORS then WRITELN('Compilation errors') else
1473      begin
1474        WRITELN('Compiled Correctly');
1475        DUMPCODE;
1476        INTERPRET
1477      end;
1478    (*close OUTPUT file if necessary*)
1479 end (*CLANG5COMPILER*).
```

Appendix 1
Implementing the programs in this book

Machine-readable source code

Although three assemblers, two interpreters, four parsers, and compiler--interpreters for five distinct levels of the CLANG language have been defined in the course of this text, listings of only six of these have been provided in full. The author is prepared to distribute machine-readable versions of all the programs, in a variety of media, and for various systems, essentially for the cost of distribution, on the understanding that they will not be used for commercial gain.

Specifically, the following programs are available:

(a) Simple interpreter for stack based language (Chapter 2, as in Listing 1)

(b) Complete interpreter for 8-bit machine (Chapter 3)

(c) Two-pass assembler for 8-bit machine (Chapter 2)

(d) One-pass assembler for 8-bit machine (Chapter 3)

(e) Macro-assembler for 8-bit machine (Chapter 4, as in Listing 5)

(f) Simple table driven LR parser (Chapter 6, as in Listing 7)

(g) Simple parser for CLANG (Chapter 7, as in Listing 8)

(h) Parser with error recovery (Chapter 7)

(i) Compiler for CLANG level 1 (Chapter 7)

(j) Compiler for CLANG level 2 (Chapter 8)

(k) Compiler for CLANG level 3 (Chapter 9)

(l) Compiler for CLANG level 4 (Chapter 10, without concurrent monitors)

(m) Compiler for CLANG level 5 (Chapter 10, as in Listing 12)

They are available in the following versions:

(a) *Suitable for compilation under UCSD Pascal*   As supplied, these do not use 'units', although on slow systems it is worth taking the trouble to rearrange them slightly to do so.

(b) *Suitable for compilation under Turbo Pascal*   For CLANG these systems 'chain' the interpreter after the compiler to allow larger source programs to be handled.

(c) Essentially as in the text, with file opening routines omitted.

Currently they can be supplied on floppy diskette in formats suitable for Apple II, IBM PC, Sage II/IV, Stride, North Star, Sirius.

Special arrangements can be made to distribute them on magnetic tape, but the floppy diskette formats should make them available to a wide range of users.

Extended system

As mentioned in the preface, an extended version of CLANG has been developed, and can be made available in the same way to interested parties. At present the extensions allow repeat and for loops, mod, and and or operators, random number generation, character I/O, forward declarations, arrays with both bounds specified, parameter passing for integers and arrays by reference as well as by value, further operations on condition queues, screen addressing primitives, and several compiler directives. This system is supplied with several example programs, as well as its own set of syntax diagrams and manual.

Specific portability issues

The programs in this book were originally developed in UCSD Pascal; they have also been moved to various other systems, including ICL and CDC mainframes. Considerable care has been taken to conform as closely as possible to standard (as opposed to UCSD) Pascal, and it is to be hoped that they can be implemented on whatever system the reader has available with the minimum of trouble. However, it is well known that portability problems exist with Pascal, and the following notes are intended to provide some assistance in this regard.

Limited character sets
The programs have been written under the assumption that the host system uses a character set, typically ASCII, which incorporates both upper and lower case, and a wide range of other characters. These dependencies are mostly confined to the lexical analysers, and should be easily isolated. For example, in Listing 12, the places that may require attention are

- Lines 10–11   which define the range of ordinal values in the host set,
- Line 200   which defines function NOTLETTER,
- Line 219   which converts lower case letters to upper case equivalents,
- Lines 212–215 which define the first characters of an identifier,
- Lines 271–272 which define the other printable characters explicitly.

Similarly, in the macro-assembler, Listing 5, the places that may require attention are

- Line 269   which defines function ALETTER,
- Line 282   which converts lower case letters to upper case equivalents,
- Lines 309–312   which define the first characters of an identifier.

Limited set size

The programs have been written under the assumption that the host system can support sets of 'moderate' size, in particular supporting set of CHAR.

The set of CHAR problem can be overcome quite easily. The code that makes use of it is found, in Listing 12, in

- Line 200   which defines the set of allowed letters,
- Line 203   which defines the allowed digits,
- Line 1221   which defines the characters that could start a signed number.

Code like

```
NOTLETTER := (CH < 'A') or (CH > 'Z')
```

could be used instead; for example, for a system supporting only upper case.

Sets are also used in other places, typically for error recovery. In CLANG 5.0 the type SYMSET requires that the host system be able to support sets of at least 42 elements; the extended system takes this to about 59 elements. In the macro-assembler the sets ONEBYTEOPS and TWOBYTEOPS require sets of at least 48 elements. If smaller sets have to be used this will require considerable recoding; for example, by using a single element in SYMBOLS to represent all operators and having a subsidiary smaller enumerated scalar declaration to distinguish these.

The buffer or window variable in a text file

The code in lines 1216–1222 of Listing 12 makes use of the buffer variable DATA ↑ to check for valid data at interpretation time. Turbo Pascal does not allow access to this variable. The quick solution is to turn the procedure into one that does nothing. The best solution is to write to Borland International and complain about a non-standard feature in their otherwise excellent product.

Premature termination

The systems assume that some method is available for terminating a program when it is found impossible to continue. This is used in procedure QUIT. If a specific primitive like HALT or EXIT is not available on your system you may be able to define a label right at the end of the main program and then goto this explicitly. Remember that files may need to be closed before premature termination is attempted.

Random number generation

The CLANG system requires the ability to generate random numbers. The USCD and Turbo Pascal versions come with suitable routines; on other systems local documentation will need to be consulted. The quality of the random sequence need not be particularly high (provided that all numbers can be generated – one attempt to install the system was found very lacking because the generator used only yielded even numbers). If the host system can provide access to a real-time clock this will often form a useful seed.

Break-in function

The interpreters have no way of detecting infinite loops, or of aborting prematurely. Several Pascal systems allow one to respond to special 'break' keys, and if this can be done the addition is worth installing. The place where this can be done is shown, for example, in line 1459 of Listing 12.

Limited memory

The constants TABLEMAX, LINEMAX, CODEMAX, PARAMAX, PROCMAX and STACKMAX defined in lines 12–20 of Listing 12 may be altered, if necessary, to allow the system to be tuned for various machine sizes. Alternatively, in Turbo Pascal one may make use of chaining the compiler and interpreter together – the system which is supplied in this format already does this.

File opening

Many Pascal implementations extend the RESET and REWRITE operations in some way so as to specify the external file name as well as the internal file name. Some go further to demand that files be explicitly closed before the program terminates. The systems which can be supplied for UCSD Pascal and for Turbo Pascal already incorporate routines for doing this in a 'friendly' manner. The places where files are opened are clearly marked in the listings.

A suitable procedure, which is coded for UCSD Pascal (but which is easily modified for Turbo Pascal) for opening an input file is as follows:

```
procedure TEXTINPUT (var INPUT : TEXT; PROMPT : STRING);
(*Open INPUT from console or named file*)
  const
    ESCAPE = 27 (*ASCII <ESC>*);
  var
    FINISHED : BOOLEAN;
    FILENAME : STRING;
  begin
    FINISHED := FALSE;
    repeat
      WRITE
```

```
                         ('What ', PROMPT, ' file (<RET> for CONSOLE:, </-RET> to abandon)? ');
                       READLN(FILENAME);
                       if LENGTH(FILENAME) = 0
                         then begin FINISHED := TRUE; RESET(INPUT, 'CONSOLE:') end
                         else
                           begin
                             if FILENAME[1] in [CHR(ESCAPE), '/', '?'] then EXIT(program);
                             (*$I- turn off IO checks *) RESET(INPUT, FILENAME);
                             if IORESULT = 0
                               then FINISHED := TRUE
                               else if POS('.text', FILENAME) + POS('.TEXT', FILENAME) = 0 then
                                 begin
                                   FILENAME := CONCAT(FILENAME, '.TEXT');
                                   RESET(INPUT, FILENAME); FINISHED := IORESULT = 0
                                 end
                           end;
                       if not FINISHED then
                         begin WRITELN; WRITELN('No such file. Try again') end
                     until FINISHED (*$I+ turn IO checks back on*);
                 end (*TEXTINPUT*);
```

A similar procedure is easily devised for opening an output file.

The ORD function

Since in Pascal

```
        type BOOLEAN = (FALSE, TRUE)
```

it follows that ORD(Boolean) should return 0 or 1. Some systems do not do this,
which can have funny effects in the interpreters, especially if the exercises
involving and and or operators are attempted. If this is the case on your system,
simply define your own ORD function within the interpreter:

```
        function ORD (B : BOOLEAN) : INTEGER;
          begin
            if B then ORD := 1 else ORD := 0
          end (*ORD*);
```

Appendix 2
Cross-reference of identifiers in Listing 5 (macro-assembler)

ACTUAL 625, 637, 652, 654, 657
ADD 6, 827
ADDRESS 80, 226, 227, 422, 428, 440, 476, 546
ADDRESSES 52, 62, 444
ADDRESSFIELD 62, 180, 341, 366, 444, 502, 566, 633, 649, 675, 709, 710, 725, 726, 732, 733, 743, 749, 750, 765
ADDRESSSYMS 336, 339, 343, 355
ADDTOMACROTABLE 559, 586
ADDTOSYMBOLTABLE 433, 663, 717, 723, 732, 741, 758
ADI 6, 827
ADIGIT 271, 272, 280, 293, 306
ADR 433, 439, 440
ADX 6, 828
ALENG 24, 35, 283, 296
ALETTER 268, 269, 280, 306
ALFA 35, 46, 60, 76, 92, 114, 126, 404, 433, 519, 609, 817
ALLOWED 336, 338, 339, 345, 355
ALPHAMERIC 42, 367, 462, 468
ASSEMBLELINE 603, 668, 785
ASSEMBLER 1
ASTERISK 37, 327, 338, 463
ASTRING 116, 318, 321, 375, 381, 385
BADADR 44, 208, 345
BAENTRY 456, 479, 480, 485
BALINK 72, 429, 482, 492
BALINKS 68, 72, 79, 422, 456
BAREFERENCES 68, 69
BASIGN 71, 428, 483, 493
BEG 15, 677, 684, 703, 705, 828
BLANK 26, 304, 365, 662, 677, 679, 716, 722, 740, 757
BLANKS 174, 182

BLANKSTRING 27, 318, 365
BLINK 79, 416, 439, 440, 482, 485, 489, 490, 547
BNG 6, 829
BNZ 6, 829
BOOLEAN 57, 78, 109, 268, 271, 401, 449, 609, 612
BPZ 6, 830
BRN 7, 830
BYTE 70, 428, 483, 492
BYTES 30, 70, 80, 135, 136, 154, 422, 433
BZE 7, 831
C1 335, 340, 350, 353, 356
C2 335, 352, 353
CC 105, 163, 166, 171, 305, 350, 851
CH 104, 168, 171, 269, 272, 275, 282, 284, 297, 305, 306, 308, 321, 369
CHAR 35, 36, 104, 107, 108
CHECKSEMANTICS 672, 698
CHR 282
CLA 7, 831
CLX 7, 832
CMP 7, 832
CODEFILE 1, 103, 802, 805
COMMA 37, 328, 339, 577, 639
COMMENT 63, 189, 365, 375, 381, 385
COMSYM 37, 318, 375, 381, 385
CPI 7, 833
CPX 8, 833
CS 105, 305, 340, 356
DC 15, 681, 703, 738, 834
DEC 8, 834
DEFINED 78, 416, 440, 472, 475, 544, 548
DEFINEMACRO 554, 590, 785
DEX 8, 835

Appendix 3
Cross-reference of identifiers in Listing 12 (CLANG 5.0 compiler)

A 45, 346, 486, 496, 1346, 1347,
1349, 1353, 1356, 1357, 1360,
1361, 1385, 1405, 1412, 1422
ACCEPT 503, 666, 680, 705, 725, 764,
788, 833, 871, 872, 900, 922, 941,
961, 976, 980, 1033, 1060, 1064,
1066, 1088, 1145
ACTUAL 774, 776, 781, 784, 790
ADD 39, 309, 363, 1319
ADDOP 795, 853, 854, 859, 860
ADDRESS 84, 340, 346, 447, 459, 463,
468, 472, 485, 486, 538, 571, 643,
668, 708, 746, 749, 759, 816,
1077, 1082, 1083, 1098, 1114,
1115, 1148
ADDRESSFOR 754, 818, 938, 958, 1002,
1020
ALENG 15, 34, 220
ALFA 34, 65, 68, 81
ALLOWED 543, 546, 548, 576, 623
ASSIGN 416, 1009
B 1180, 1232, 1233, 1404, 1405,
1412, 1413, 1422, 1450
BACKPATCH 485, 893, 903, 981, 1105,
1110, 1120
BEACONS 543, 548
BECOMES 26, 242, 638, 641, 1006
BEGINSYM 27, 293, 326, 327, 1046,
1060, 1100
BINARYINTEGEROP 358, 845, 860
BLOCK 508, 721, 723, 1154
BLOCKCLASS 449, 452, 512, 560, 711,
714, 715, 716, 718, 720, 724,
1071, 1095, 1097, 1099, 1102,
1126, 1136
BLOCKENTRY 514, 1004, 1070, 1076,
1077, 1082, 1111, 1116, 1130,

1136
BLOCKLEVEL 449, 454, 509, 571, 719,
721, 723, 970, 1054, 1136
BOOLEAN 59, 77, 86, 94, 197, 199, 202,
519, 581, 948, 1176, 1185, 1289
BRN 39, 307, 426, 1360
BZE 39, 307, 332, 429, 1361
C 281, 319, 564, 571
CAL 38, 306, 477, 1399
CALL 476, 746, 749
CANACCESS 85, 539, 572, 606, 1149
CANCHANGE 85, 539, 572, 937, 957,
1001, 1081, 1131, 1132, 1149
CBG 38, 315, 432, 1381
CC 56, 147, 177, 180, 188, 335
CH 55, 183, 184, 188, 200, 203, 206,
209, 210, 211, 219, 220, 242, 247,
250, 257, 265, 267, 273, 335
CHAR 33, 34, 55, 60, 67, 70, 281
CHECKDATA 1216, 1344
CHOOSEPROCESS 1194, 1296, 1435, 1460
CHR 219, 319, 1338
CLANG5COMPILER 1
CLASS 82, 529, 571, 620, 623, 625,
814, 994, 998, 1148
CLASSES 30, 31, 82, 449, 512, 564, 650,
711
CLASSSET 31, 576
CND 39, 315, 435, 1388
COBEGINSTATEMENT 966, 1052
COBEGSYM 28, 293, 328, 1052
CODEFILE 1, 51, 496, 497
CODEFORDUMP 482, 1054
CODEFORODD 479, 873
CODEFORSIGNAL 437, 959
CODEFORWAIT 440, 959
CODEISTOBEGENERATED 94, 146, 333, 344

Appendix 4
Specification of CLANG 5.0

Figures A4.1–A4.8 give syntax diagrams for the CLANG language as finally developed. These are rather simpler than they might be, and notes have been added to cover some features that otherwise would require considerable repetition – for example, monitors may not be nested, but to specify this accurately would require two very similar diagrams for BLOCK. The reader is invited to attempt a more satisfactory specification, both in diagram and EBNF form as a worthwhile exercise.

1. The program identifier (Figure A4.1) has no significance (except as a comment).

2. The only data type supported in var and const declarations (Figure A4.2) is INTEGER.

3. Semaphores are declared (and initialized) as though they were integers. There is nothing to distinguish them from integers, and it is the programmer's responsibility not to abuse them.

4. Arrays are declared by specifying the fixed upper bound for the subscript in square brackets. The lower bound is taken to be zero.

5. The 'star' notation (denoting that an object is visible outside a monitor block) may only be used in declarations inside monitor blocks.

6. Monitor blocks may only be declared in the main program. It follows that they may not be nested, or contain instances of one another, contrary to what the syntax diagrams might suggest.

7. Within monitor blocks the global variables of the main program block may be examined, but not altered.

8. LETTER (Figure A4.3) is taken to mean any upper or lower case letter of the Roman alphabet.

9. Starred objects in monitor blocks are referenced outside the monitor using this 'dot' notation (Figure A4.4). Other objects in monitor blocks are totally inaccessible outside it.

10. Starred variables declared in a monitor may be examined, but may not be altered, outside of the monitor.

PROGRAM

Figure A4.1

BLOCK

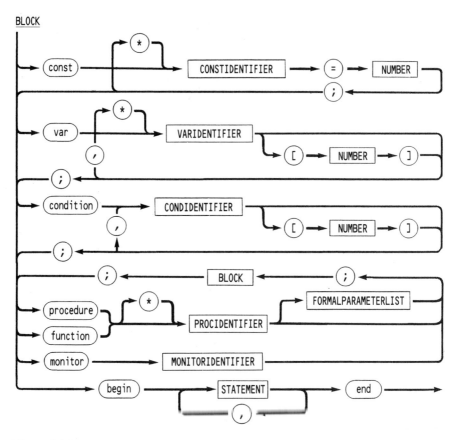

Figure A4.2

IDENTIFIER (including all semantic variations)

Figure A4.3

QUALIFIEDIDENTIFIER

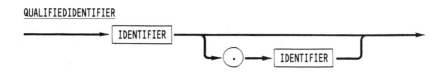

Figure A4.4

11. DIGIT (Figure A4.5) is taken to mean a decimal digit, and the diagram has been omitted.

12. CHARACTER (Figure A4.6) here means any printable character.

13. The quote character itself is specified within a string using a repeated quote, as in How''s that for an original idea?

14. Parameters are passed by value only. (Figure A4.7.)

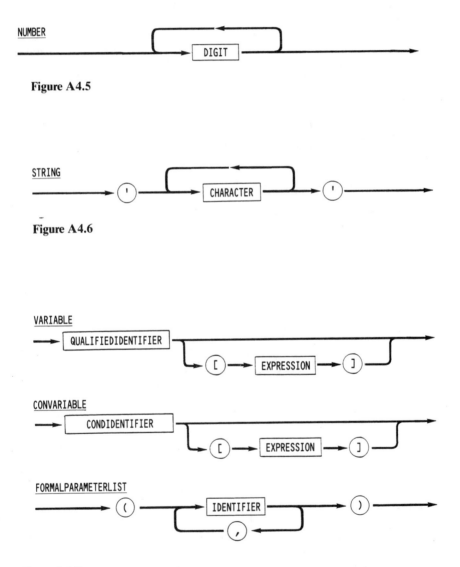

NUMBER

Figure A4.5

STRING

Figure A4.6

VARIABLE

CONVARIABLE

FORMALPARAMETERLIST

Figure A4.7

CONDITION

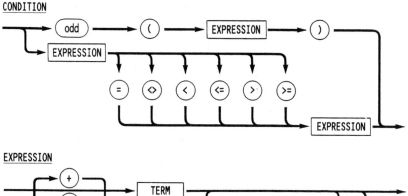

EXPRESSION

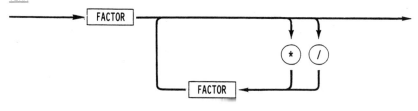

TERM

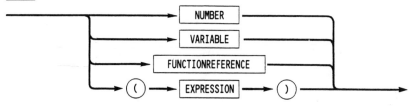

FACTOR

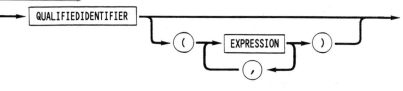

FUNCTIONREFERENCE

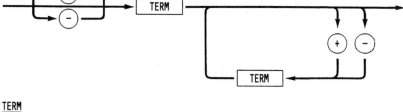

PROCEDURECALL

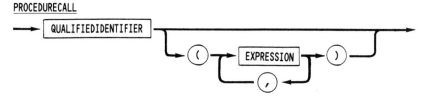

15. It is not possible to pass complete arrays as parameters.

16. Nested monitor calls are not allowed (a function or procedure in one monitor may not call on a routine in another monitor).

17. stackdump (Figure A4.8) allows one to examine the run-time stack. It is used for run-time debugging, but requires a knowledge of the underlying architecture.

18. Concurrency is introduced by the cobegin...coend construct. At present concurrent processes may only be launched from the main program, although they may call upon other procedures thereafter. A concurrent process is defined as a procedure and may have parameters.

19. Assignment may only be made to a function within the body of that function itself, and not at other points where its name is in scope.

20. Write always terminates by issuing a carriage-return-line-feed to the output device. The effect of write with no parameter list is simply to issue this sequence (and thus to leave a blank line).

21. Recursion is fully supported.

22. In monitors, synchronization is achieved by means of *condition queues*. COND.cwait, COND.csignal operate on these queues. These operations may only be used within monitor blocks.

23. COND.cwait may take an optional parameter denoting priority (low numbers denote high priority; default priority is 128).

24. Monitor procedures may not be treated as processes.

Reserved words

The list of reserved words is as follows. Those given in (brackets) are not currently used in a reserved sense, but are reserved for use in exercises and extensions, and should probably not be used as identifiers.

(and)	(else)	odd	(seminit)
begin	end	(or)	(setpriority)
(boolean)	(false)	procedure	signal
(char)	(for)	(process)	stackdump
cobegin	(forever)	program	then
coend	(forward)	(queue)	(to)
condition	function	(random)	(true)
const	(halt)	read	(until)
csignal	if	(readln)	var
cwait	(integer)	(ready)	wait
do	(mod)	(repeat)	while
(downto)	monitor	(semaphore)	write
			(writeln)

STATEMENT

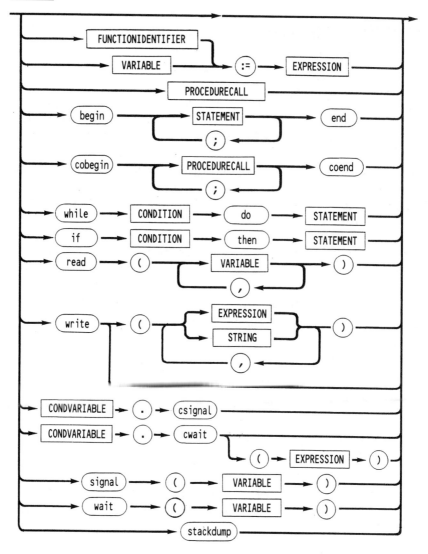

Figure A4.8

Bibliography

Addyman, A. M., Brewer, R., Burnett-Hall, D. G., De Morgan, R. M., Findlay, W., Jackson, M. I., Joslin, D. A., Rees, M. J., Watt, D. A., Welsh, J. and Wickman, B. A., 1979, A draft description of Pascal. *Software – Practice and Experience*, **9(5)**, 381–424.

Aho, A. V. and Ullman, J. D., 1977. *Principles of Compiler Design*, Addison-Wesley, Reading, Mass.

Andrews, G. R. and McGraw, J. R., 1977. Language features for process interaction. *ACM SIGPLAN Notices*, **12(3)**, 114–127.

Andrews, G. R. and Schneider, F. B., 1983. Concepts and notation for concurrent programming. *ACM Computing Surveys*, **15**, 3–43.

Backhouse, R. C., 1979. *Syntax of Programming Languages: Theory and Practice*, Prentice-Hall, Englewood Cliffs, NJ.

Bailes, P. A., 1984. A rational Pascal. *Australian Computer Journal* **16(4)**, 155–176.

Barrett, W. A. and Couch, J. D., 1979. *Compiler Construction: Theory and Practice*, Science Research Associates, Chicago.

Barron, D. W., 1977. *An Introduction to the Study of Programming Languages*, Cambridge University Press, Cambridge.

Barron, D. W. (ed.) 1981. *Pascal – the Language and its Implementation*, Wiley, New York.

Bauer, F. L. and Eickel, J., 1976. *Compiler Construction: an Advanced Course*, Springer, Berlin.

Ben-Ari, M., 1982. *Principles of Concurrent Programming*, Prentice-Hall, Englewood Cliffs, NJ.

Berry, R. E., 1982. *Programming Language Translation*, Ellis Horwood, Chichester.

Bornat, R., 1979. *Understanding and Writing Compilers*, Macmillan, London.

Brinch Hansen, P., 1983. *Programming a Personal Computer*, Prentice-Hall, Englewood Cliffs, NJ.

Brinch Hansen, P., 1985. *On Pascal Compilers*, Prentice-Hall, Englewood Cliffs, NJ.

Brown, P. J., 1974. *Macro Processors, and Techniques for Portable Software*, Wiley, New York.

Brown, P. J., 1979. *Writing Interactive Compilers and Interpreters*, Wiley, New York.

Bustard, D. W., 1980. An introduction to Pascal-Plus. In: *On the Construction of Programs*, edited by R. M. McKeag and A. M. Mcnaughten. Cambridge University Press, Cambridge.

Caillian, R., 1982. How to avoid getting SCHLONKED by Pascal. *SIGPLAN Notices*, **17(12)**, 31–40.

Calingaert, P., 1979. *Assemblers, Compilers, and Program Translation*, Computer Science Press, Rockville, Md.

Chomsky, N., 1959. On certain formal properties of grammars. *Information and Control*, **2(2)**, 137–167.

Davie, F. J. T. and Morrison, R., 1981. *Recursive Descent Compiling*, Ellis Horwood, Chichester.

Earley, J. and Sturgis, H., 1970. A formalism for translator interactions. *Communications of the ACM*, **13**, 607–617.

Gehani, N., 1984a. *ADA: Concurrent Programming*, Prentice-Hall, Englewood Cliffs, NJ.

Gehani, N., 1984b. *ADA, an Advanced Introduction*, Prentice-Hall, Englewood Cliffs, NJ.

Gleaves, R., 1985. *Modula-2 for Pascal Programmers*, Springer, Berlin.

Gries, D., 1971. *Computer Construction for Digital Computers*, Wiley, New York.

Haddon, B. K., 1977. Nested monitor calls. *ACM Operating Systems Review*, **11(4)**, 18–23.

Harland, D. M., 1984. *Polymorphic Programming Languages – Design and Implementation*, Ellis Horwood, Chichester.

Hartmann, A. C., 1977. *A Concurrent Pascal Compiler*, Springer, Berlin.

Hoare, C. A. R., 1974. Monitors: an operating system structuring concept. *Communications of the ACM*, **17(10)**, 549–557.

Hoare, C. A. R. and Wirth, N., 1973. An axiomatic definition of the programming language Pascal. *Acta Informatica*, **2**, 335–355.

Hennessy, J. L. and Mendelsohn, N., 1982. Compilation of the Pascal case statement. *Software – Practice and Experience*, **12(9)**, 879–882.

Holt, R. C., 1983. *Concurrent Euclid, the Unix System, and Tunis*, Addison-Wesley, Reading, Mass.

Horowitz, E., 1984. *Fundamentals of Programming Languages*, Springer, Berlin.

Hunter, R. B., 1981. *The Design and Construction of Compilers*, Wiley, New York.

Hunter, R. B., 1985. *The Design and Construction of Compilers with Pascal*, Wiley, New York.

INMOS, 1984. *Occam Programming Manual*, Prentice-Hall, Englewood Cliffs, NJ.

Johnson, M. S., 1979. Translation design to support debugging. *Software – Practice and Experience*, **9(12)**, 1035–1041.

Keedy, J. L., 1978. On structuring operating systems with monitors. *Australian Computer Journal*, **10**, 23–27.

Kowaltowski, T., 1981. Parameter passing mechanisms and run time data structures. *Software – Practice and Experience*, **11(7)**, 757–765.

Lecarme, O. and Peyrolle-Thomas, M. C., 1973. Self-compiling compilers: an appraisal of their implementation and portability. *Software – Practice and Experience*, **8(2)**, 149–170.

Ledgard, H. F. and Marcotty, M., 1981. *The Programming Language Landscape*, Science Research Associates, Chicago.

Lee, J. A. N., 1972. The formal definition of the BASIC language. *Computer Journal*, **15**, 37–41.

Leventhal, L. A., 1978. *Introduction to Microprocessors – Software, Hardware, Programming*, Prentice-Hall, Englewood Cliffs, NJ.

Leventhal, L. A. and Saville, W., 1982. 6502 *Assembly Language Subroutines*, Osborn/McGraw-Hill, Berkeley, Calif.

Leventhal, L. A. and Saville, W., 1983a. 8080/8085 *Assembly Language Subroutines*, Osborn/McGraw-Hill, Berkeley, Calif.

Leventhal, L. A. and Saville, W., 1983b. Z-80 *Assembly Language Subroutines*, Osborn/McGraw-Hill, Berkeley, Calif.

Lister, A. M., 1977. The problem of nested monitor calls. *ACM Operating Systems Review*, **11(3)**, 5–7.

McGettrick, A. D., 1980. *The Definition of Programming Languages*, Cambridge University Press, Cambridge.

Miller, A. R., 1981. 8080/Z80 *Assembly Language – Techniques for Improved Programming*, Wiley, New York.

Morrison, R., 1977. A method of implementing procedure entry and exit in block structural high-level language. *Software – Practice and Experience*, **7(4)**, 537–539.

Nori, K. V., Ammann, U., Jensen, K., Nageli, H. H. and Jacobi, Ch., 1981. *Pascal – the Language and its Implementation*, Wiley, New York.

Parnas, D. L., 1978. The non-problem of nested monitor calls. *ACM Operating Systems Review*, **12(1)**, 12–18.

Pemberton, S., 1980. Comments on an error-recovery scheme by Hartmann. *Software – Practice and Experience*, **10(3)**, 231–240.

Pemberton, S. and Daniels, M., 1982. *Pascal Implementation – the P4 Compiler*, Ellis Horwood, Chichester.

Peterson, J. L. and Silberschatz, A., 1985. *Operating System Concepts*, 2nd edn, Addison-Wesley, Reading, Mass.

Sale, A. H. J., 1979a. Scope and Pascal. *ACM SIGPLAN Notices*, **14(9)**, 61–63.

Sale, A. H. J., 1979b. A note on Scope, one-pass compilers, and Pascal. *Pascal News*, **15**, 61–63.

Sale, A. H. J., 1979c. A note on Scope, one-pass compilers, and Pascal. *Australian Computer Science Communications*, **1(1)**, 80–82.

Sale, A. H. J., 1981. The implementation of case statements in Pascal. *Software – Practice and Experience*, **11(9)**, 929–942.

Schneider, F. B. and Bernstein, A. J., 1978. Scheduling in Concurrent Pascal. *Operating Systems Review*, **12(2)**, 15–20.

Silberschatz, A., Kieburtz, R. B. and Bernstein, A. J., 1977. Extending Concurrent Pascal to allow dynamic resource management. *IEEE Transactions on Software Engineering*, **SE-3(3)**, 210–217.

Tennent, R. D., 1981. *Principles of Programming Languages*, Prentice-Hall, Englewood Cliffs, NJ.

Topor, R. W., 1982. A note on error recovery in recursive descent parsers. *ACM SIGPLAN Notices*, **17(2)**, 37–40.

Tremblay, J. P. and Sorenson, P. G., 1982. *An Implementation Guide to Compiler Writing*, McGraw-Hill, New York.

Tremblay, J. P. and Sorenson, P. G., 1985. *Theory and Practice of Compiler Writing*, McGraw-Hill, New York.

Ullman, J. D., 1976. *Fundamental Concepts of Computer Systems*, Addison-Wesley, Reading, Mass.

Wakerly, J. F., 1981. *Microcomputer Architecture and Programming*, Wiley, New York.

Welsh, J. and McKeag, M., 1980. *Structured System Programming*, Prentice-Hall, Englewood Cliffs, NJ.

Welsh, J. and Quinn, C., 1972. A Pascal compiler for ICL 1900 series computers. *Software – Practice and Experience*, **2(1)**, 73–78.

Welsh, J., Sneeringer, W. J. and Hoare, C. A. R., 1977. Ambiguities and insecurities in Pascal. *Software – Practice and Experience*, **7**, 685–696.

Welsh, J., Elder, J. and Bustard, D., 1984. *Sequential Program Structures*, Prentice-Hall, Englewood Cliffs, NJ.

Wettstein, H., 1978. The problem of nested monitor calls revisited. *ACM Operating Systems Review*, **12(1)**, 19–23.

Winkler, J. F. M., 1984. Some improvements of 150-Pascal. *ACM SIGPLAN Notices*, **19(7)**, 65–78.

Wirth, N., 1976. *Algorithms + Data Structures = Programs*, Prentice-Hall, Englewood Cliffs, NJ.

Wirth, N., 1977. Modula: a language for modular multiprogramming. *Software – Practice and Experience*, **7(1)**, 3–36.

Wirth, N., 1985. *Programming in Modula-2*, Springer, Berlin.

Young, S. J., 1982. *Real Time Languages – Design and Implementation*, Ellis Horwood, Chichester.

Index